THE RISE OF
AMERICAN RESEARCH
UNIVERSITIES

■ THE RISE OF ■

AMERICAN RESEARCH UNIVERSITIES

Elites and Challengers in the Postwar Era

HUGH DAVIS GRAHAM
NANCY DIAMOND

■

THE JOHNS HOPKINS UNIVERSITY PRESS
BALTIMORE AND LONDON

The Johns Hopkins University Press
2715 North Charles Street
Baltimore, Maryland 21218-4319
The Johns Hopkins Press Ltd., London

ISBN 0-8018-5425-3

Library of Congress Cataloging-in-Publication
Data will be found at the end of this book.

A catalog record for this book is available
from the British Library.

CONTENTS

■

ACKNOWLEDGMENTS

■

Many colleagues have generously given their time and attention to our project, but a few deserve special mention. Stephen R. Max, acting dean of the University of Maryland Graduate School, Baltimore, helped us to obtain a research grant, and the University of Maryland Baltimore County (UMBC) College of Arts and Sciences also financed the early stages of research. Miles Goosens, at Vanderbilt University, provided invaluable computer support. Howard Curnoles, of UMBC's Albin O. Kuhn Library, provided library and computer support, especially with the Institute for Scientific Information databases. Elliott Brownlee and John Douglass, of the University of California, Santa Barbara, offered encouragement as well as data, as did Special Collections librarian Deborah Kennedy. At the Johns Hopkins University Press, Robert J. Brugger's thoughtful comments clearly enhanced the final product. Theresa Reifsnider typed the book's many tables with care and precision.

Christopher Haffer and Ching and Wenke Wang contributed considerable computer support and analysis, and Dean Yates and Jennifer Beaumont collected data in the early stages of the project. Thanks go to Robert Spinney, Robert Scot Kraeuter, and Brian Hall for research assistance, and to Craig Kaplowitz for indexing. Necessary data was obtained from Patricia Q. Brown, of the Office of Educational Research and Improvement, U.S. Department of Education; Tina Buck, of the U.S. Department of Agriculture; Richard Silverman, of the National Science Foundation; Karen Fuglie Miles, of the National Endowment for the Humanities; Martha Levin, of the Association of Schools of Public Health; Susan Meyer, of the American Association of Colleges of Pharmacy; Tom Berger, of the American Dental Association; Sarah Haux, of the American Association of Colleges of

Nursing; and Brooke E. Whiting and Donna Williams, of the Association of American Medical Colleges.

Gottlieb C. Friesinger, of the Vanderbilt University School of Medicine; Richard S. Ross, dean emeritus of the Johns Hopkins School of Medicine; and John H. Hash and William Schaffner, of the Vanderbilt University School of Medicine, read and commented on the discussion of medical schools. For their critical judgment and reading of other portions of the manuscript, we are also indebted to Richard W. Lyman, James C. Mohr, John K. Folger, John Braxton, and David Webster. George LaNoue made helpful suggestions. Special thanks go to John W. Jeffries for sustained support and judicious advice.

The present work has been substantially enhanced by the studies that preceded it. Most of these are mentioned in the text, but we particularly relied on Roger Geiger's work, especially his two-volume history of the American research university. The generosity of Clark Kerr, who shared unpublished materials and contributed to our understanding of the University of California's development, also deserves mention. Finally, we acknowledge the value and fun of collaboration, and the importance of the support offered by our family members Janet Graham, Marc Diamond, and Daniel Diamond during this process.

■

INTRODUCTION

This is a book about the rise of American research universities since World War II.[1] Here the term *rise* has a dual meaning. The first meaning refers to success in the international competition for recognition and prestige. American universities, not widely respected in the international community of scholars and scientists prior to World War II, subsequently won preeminence among the world's leading research institutions. This claim, controversial for a generation after the war, has been widely acknowledged outside the United States since the 1960s. Robert M. Rosenzweig, president of the Association of American Universities during 1983–93, wrote in 1982 that most informed observers throughout the world would agree that the American research university must be judged a success by virtually any imaginable standard of measurement. "A form of social organization barely known elsewhere in the world," Rosenzweig continued, "has so clearly demonstrated its value in the United States that the wisdom of sustaining it is almost beyond serious debate."[2] "We chose to combine basic research, a fair mixture of applied research, training for research, and undergraduate education in the same place, done by the same people, frequently at the same time. For all the problems that arise from such a volatile mixture, the evidence from elsewhere in the world provides no basis for regret at the direction taken here."[3] Whether measured by the distribution of Nobel prizes, by international applications for student admissions and faculty appointments, or by reputational surveys, the prestige of America's universities has soared since World War II.

The second meaning of the research universities' "rise" concerns the relative postwar success of American institutions competing with one another in the research enterprise. In the uniquely competitive

1

marketplace of postwar American higher education, strong new research institutions rose to challenge and in some instances to displace old elites. Traditional hierarchies of achievement and recognition were upset, much as they were in the international rise of American universities, and for some of the same reasons. The distinctive attributes of the higher education environment that helped postwar American institutions dominate the Nobel prizes — a decentralized, pluralistic, and intensely competitive academic marketplace fueled by federal research dollars — encouraged innovative, risk-taking behavior by ambitious universities. Because this competition produced winners and losers, rising new research campuses emerged, and the best among them displaced traditional elites.

This perhaps controversial claim — that there have been rising new stars and declining elites among postwar American universities — finds ready confirmation in the world of intercollegiate sports but not in the world of research. Reputational surveys of American universities conducted in the 1950s, 1960s, and 1970s revealed an academic pecking order of remarkable stability.[4] In the competition for top-twenty rankings, rarely was there a new institutional face. The American universities most frequently acknowledged as international leaders — the Ivy League elite schools, and the great state flagships of the Midwest and the West Coast — were the same institutions found at the top of the reputational surveys of faculty and graduate education. The rising tide of the postwar American economy and demography had raised all boats but apparently had not much changed the order of convoy.

But tension between a dynamic competitive order and a static hierarchy of perceived achievement was puzzling. The rise of American research universities to international prominence was grounded in the development of a decentralized, pluralistic, academic market in which competitive pressures drove institutions to change far more quickly than did the sheltered public universities in other parts of the world. After 1945 these forces were accelerated in the United States by economic growth, defense needs, the baby boom, unprecedented institutional expansion, and a comprehensive array of new federal support programs. Yet the reordered hierarchy of international prestige among universities was not accompanied within the United States by a new hierarchy of domestic leadership in university research prowess. Why not?

Several plausible explanations help account for the stability of institutional prowess even in the face of unprecedented postwar change.[5] Research universities, rooted in systems of academic

2

tenure, are complex institutions resistant to rapid change. For the elite private universities, large endowments permit unmatched investments in research capacity, and institutional autonomy provides freedom from programmatic constraints that bind public sector competitors. For the great state universities, generations of public service and political networking provide protection for the interests of the flagship campuses against populistic incursions. For leading scholars in the professions and the academic disciplines, university prestige becomes a self-fulfilling prophecy, attracting top talent that maintains the advantage of established leaders. For government, business, and the major foundations, the best criterion for research investment is the proven performance of blue-chip institutions.

Yet there are reasons to question the reliability of established institutional hierarchies. Studies of reputational rankings have found systematic bias toward large institutions.[6] By magnifying the authority of academic "stars" such rankings create a "halo effect" that elevates the status of other individuals and programs within an institution.[7] Moreover, they suffer from temporal lag, permitting past institutional prestige to mask subsequent decline. Because reputational surveys are often weak in information content, they may convey a false precision. As university researchers and academic fields have grown increasingly specialized and fragmented, faculty have been asked to rate entire departments and their instructional effectiveness in more than one hundred institutions. These disaggregated program ratings, designed by such sponsoring organizations as the American Council on Education and the National Research Council, are intended to assess specific disciplines. Yet unfailingly the graduate program rankings are reaggregated by other scholars into grand institutional rankings that include only a small number of top-ranked institutions, usually twenty or twenty-five. Objective rankings, by contrast, have typically included more institutions and avoided time-lag distortions. But in their attention to numerical accumulations they tend to conflate quantity and quality. Academic institutions, not immune to a *Guinness Book of Records* approach, compete for high ranking in quantitative superlatives — the largest dollar value of research grants received, the greatest number of doctoral degrees annually awarded, the most library volumes held, and so forth. This tradition favors institutional size, discounting or ignoring the importance of pound-for-pound ratios of productive achievement.

Despite the evidence from reputational rankings and objective indicators, it seems plausible that the unprecedented changes in American higher education during the half-century following World War II might have produced greater changes in institutional research quality and achievement than was apparent from the periodic studies and reputational surveys of faculty and graduate education. To test the hypothesis that such changes have occurred but have been obscured by standard methods of assessing institutional performance, we needed to devise a new method, one that could accomplish the daunting task of measuring changes in a large number of doctorate-granting institutions since 1945 while controlling for institutional size. The study that follows thus builds on the strong shoulders of previous comparative studies of American higher education. But it differs from most of them in seven respects.

First, this book concentrates on one role of universities: the creation of new knowledge. This is only one, and arguably not the most important, of the university's several major roles. Fortunately, a robust literature addresses the role of the campuses in undergraduate teaching, graduate education, professional training, and the quality of institutional life. An especially vigorous genre of this literature, written from both conservative and radical perspectives, attacks modern universities and especially the professoriate for selling out to the false god of sponsored research.[8] We concede the artificiality of singling out research in such a uniquely multipurpose institution. Yet few would question the centrality of knowledge creation to the university's mission, or challenge the importance of research in the knowledge-based economy of the future, or quarrel with the claim that leadership in knowledge creation is crucial to academic and national prosperity.

Second, the analysis is historical. It tells an important story—broadly covering 1945–95, and intensively covering 1965–90—about the development of federal research policy and the rapid growth of research among public and private universities. It is based upon a body of scholarship that emphasizes both the historical distinctiveness of American state-building and the uniquely decentralized, pluralistic, and competitive development of higher education in the United States. To structure a narrative involving so many institutions, we emphasize the benchmarks of federal science policy and stress the common circumstances that lend a retrospective character to the decades—the expansionist "golden years" of the 1960s, the belt-tightening adjustments of the 1970s, the entrepreneurial ethos of the 1980s, and the darkening horizon of the 1990s.

Third, we compare the research performance of faculty at more than two hundred institutions. While the major studies of graduate programs have included most doctorate-granting institutions, they have avoided institutional generalizations. On the other hand, most individual studies of research universities have concentrated on a small number of prestigious institutions. One leading work that has greatly eased our burden, Roger Geiger's two-volume history of twentieth-century American research universities, concentrates on sixteen elite institutions.[9] As Stephen Graubard has noted, only by going beyond the handful of prestigious institutions to include the full range of institutional types and sizes that exist within the much larger galaxy of doctorate-granting universities can we understand what happened to American higher education following World War II.[10]

Fourth, our basic unit of measure is the entire institution, not just selected components, such as departmental graduate programs or professional schools. The major comparative studies of the postwar era, the American Council on Education (ACE)–sponsored Cartter and Roose-Andersen assessments (published in 1966 and 1970, respectively), and the National Research Council (NRC) studies of 1982 and 1995, compared the performance of institutions by aggregating a combination of subjective data (chiefly reputational surveys) and objective data for graduate programs in selected fields.[11] By limiting their assessments to program-specific rankings, they attempted to avoid the reductionist "ratings game" that identifies the "top" twenty or twenty-five universities.[12] For traditional, discipline-based graduate programs in the arts and sciences and engineering, these major studies have periodically provided benchmarks of national comparison that commanded wide respect. They have nonetheless shared the limitations imposed by subjective survey evidence and by objective data limited to selected programs. In no case did they measure the aggregate performance of all instructional or research units on the campuses.[13]

Fifth, to avoid conflating quantity with quality and to compensate for what we call the "horsepower" problem of comparing institutions on the basis of total output scores — for instance, ranking the leading universities according to the number of federal research and development (R&D) dollars awarded — we interpret measures of research activity in terms of institutional size. To do this we divide various indicators of aggregate faculty performance by the number of full-time instructional faculty on a given campus. This produces a *per capita* measure that allows us to compare universities of different size and type as their performance changes over time.[14]

Sixth, this study includes quantifiable measures of research achievement across the academic spectrum. Such measures are commonplace in the sciences and engineering, where R&D dollar awards and journal publications are routinely counted and compared. In the social sciences, however, they are more difficult to find, and in the arts and humanities they are scarce indeed. This study relies on a core set of data, covering the years 1965–90, that measures research performance in five categories. Together they reflect scientific research and scholarly creativity across the academic spectrum of science, the social and behavioral sciences, and the arts and humanities (see the Note on Method and Sources).

Finally, our comparisons of institutional, campuswide research required a fresh effort to break down the walls separating the world of academic medicine from the rest of the university. The 1960s are remembered as the golden age of American universities, but by historical standards academic medicine has enjoyed a golden age reaching back to 1946, when the Hill-Burton Hospital Survey and Construction Act began a massive federal program of hospital and medical school subsidies. Although the National Institutes of Health (NIH) has long been the largest sponsor of academic research in American universities, and biomedical science has dominated the global traffic in scientific and scholarly journals, the community of campus researchers in this gigantic enterprise has been split by its own Berlin Wall. Historically, academic medical schools have enjoyed unmatched autonomy within universities, their independence won through a unique combination of financial resources, clinical responsibilities, professional traditions and prestige, and standards of remuneration that set them apart from the rest of the university community.

The literature on higher education and academic research is vast but similarly divided. Library shelves groan with the weight of books about universities that scarcely mention the colossus of academic medicine, and with volumes about medical education and clinical research entirely confined to the insular world of the teaching hospitals and the biomedical researchers they have subsidized. We wish to impose no artificial unity on these profound and enduring divisions. But in the pages that follow we try to reconnect these two worlds, describing and comparing their performance in a common frame of reference, acknowledging their differences and their institutional commonalities. If the twenty-first century brings to academic medicine a widely anticipated financial crisis, the entire university community will feel the shock and share in the long-term consequences.

The central argument of this book is that new research universities *did* emerge from the competitive scramble after 1945 to challenge, more successfully than has been recognized, the hegemony of traditional elites. To some extent, this success has been obscured over the years by the strong tradition of the ratings game. We reserve such discoveries, many of them surprising, until the concluding chapters. In the process of applying our research method to data from the years 1965–90, we found several patterns of research performance that were also surprising. One is the magnitude of the advantage that private universities derived during the postwar era from their affluence, their traditions, and especially their entrepreneurial freedom from the growing constraints imposed by legislatures and public bureaucracies. In the post-1960s era of stiffening competition accompanied by tightening state regulation, private institutions have exploited their relative freedom from government control.

A second source of advantage to universities competing for research scholars and dollars is the presence of a medical school on campus. In the world of academic health centers, the golden age of American higher education did not begin with *Sputnik* and end with the 1960s. Instead it began with the Hill-Burton Act of 1946 and continued with the growth of the NIH budget and the Great Society commitment to Medicare and Medicaid. In the postwar era, federal support levels for biomedical research soared, like a rocket, into the 1990s, where, for the first time, they collided with fiscal realities of ominous portent.

The third source of advantage to universities in the postwar era is confined to the public sector and is strongly associated with the central query of our book—the search for emerging new elites. This is the advantage enjoyed by public campuses whose designated status as research-oriented institutions is especially protected and nurtured by the state university system. Most notable in this regard have been the University of California (UC) and the State University of New York (SUNY). Readers with patience should wait until the concluding chapters to observe the stunning difference this designated status has made in the meteoric ascent of such institutions as UC Santa Barbara, which was founded as a State Normal School and joined the University of California system in 1944 as a teacher-training school for industrial arts.[15]

Critics of market-driven entrepreneurialism have argued that in the postwar era too many four-year institutions, claiming the mantle of "research university" but lacking the substance associated with that name, have penalized their students while rewarding trivial research. We agree. But we offer no formula for determining at what point, for example, the establishment of "second flagship" campuses builds healthy intrastate competition and better serves regional interests, or at what point a proliferation of campuses with research-intensive ambitions only "levels down" the flagship or established research campuses through a kind of academic Gresham's Law. Because this is a work primarily of history and comparison, not of theory or prescription, readers may draw their own conclusions about the relative success of different governing systems. Formulas that work in one state may fail in others—much as California's tripartite system, emulated by other states in the 1960s, seems to have failed when exported from California. Fortunately for the United States, there are fifty state systems, and by 1990 there were more than 130 public and 70 private doctorate-granting institutions. It is one argument of this book that America's decentralized and pluralistic system of higher education, long an object of condescension among world critics, provided an academic marketplace in which competition for research achievement could thrive in the postwar era.

Fifty years after the conclusion of the Manhattan Project, there is evidence that the golden era of American higher education may be nearing an end. Most federal budget scenarios of the 1990s project into the twenty-first century severe reductions in federal support for research and student aid. Changes in the nation's health care industry, together with deep projected cuts in Medicare and Medicaid funding, may turn university hospitals, long the chief sources of medical center income, into financial liabilities. Retrenchment by a deficit-ridden federal government may cripple the engines that powered the university research economy.

But maybe not. We have heard the cries of Jeremiah in the halls of the American academy before. Our historical analysis of the half-century following World War II emphasizes the unusual resilience of the American system of higher education. Our postwar history demonstrates the system's capacity to adjust to rapidly changing market conditions in a decentralized, pluralistic, competitive environment. We do not deny that the price of institutional adjustment and survival, especially for marginal and vulnerable colleges and universities, has often been steep. It has been paid in the coin of lowered standards, academic fad-chasing, the decline of teaching, marketing fraud, and for some institutions, ultimate collapse. But in a global economy increasingly dependent on advanced training and knowledge-creation, the dual rise of American research universities has given the nation a double success story. This book attempts to describe its contours.

1

■

Origins of the American
Research University

The rise of American universities to a position of world preeminence was not achieved until after World War II, when federal policy makers turned to the top universities for scientific expertise. The conditions that made this ascent probable, however, were shaped not by planning but by two centuries of haphazard evolution. A peculiar combination of historical circumstances shaped the American system of higher education, like a benevolent Providence, turning its negative features—fragmentation, incoherence, qualitative unevenness, and economic vulnerability—almost into assets.

From the perspective of the 1990s, the global leadership of America's research universities was an accepted source of national pride and international discourse. For more than a generation, international students had voted with their feet by flocking to the American campuses and had contributed to making English the international language of science, technology, and trade in the postwar world. The flow of foreign students to U.S. campuses in the 1950s and 1960s, accelerated by the cold war, grew to a flood in the 1970s and 1980s, filling the empty seats that an academic recession had left in American graduate schools and technical faculties. As the Soviet empire began to disintegrate in the late 1980s, the cold war competition for brains and loyalties lost its bipolarity, and American hegemony was virtually unchallenged. The Institute of International Education reported in 1984: "The United States is currently overwhelmingly the primary national destination for students going abroad; only African students went in substantial numbers to a host (France) other than the United States."[1]

By the 1990s the United States had lost its postwar dominance in the production of steel, automobiles, home appliances, electronics, and machine tools. At the same time, American preeminence in higher education was universally acknowledged. The most visible barometer was the Nobel prize. Prior to World War II, even the best universities in the United States provided weak competition for venerable institutions such as the University of Berlin, L'Ecole Polytechnique, and the Universities of Cambridge, Göttingen, and Oxford. During the first three decades of Nobel prize competition, beginning in 1901, only four of ninety-two prizes were won by Americans. Then came the turning point, World War II and the Manhattan Project. During the 1950s American scientists not only won more Nobel prizes than any other nation, they won more than all other nations combined. By the mid-1970s the United States had more Nobel laureates than any other country, having won ninety-one prizes between 1943 and 1976. The American "men of science" bestrode the scientific world like a colossus.[2]

In 1990 Henry Rosovsky, dean of the Harvard faculty during 1973–84, concluded in his decanal memoir that "fully two thirds to three quarters of the best universities in the world are located in the United States."[3] Rosovsky cited a mid-1980s survey of Asian scholars that ranked eight American universities among the world's top dozen. Even if the list was extended to the world's top thirty or fifty universities, Rosovsky claimed, that rough margin of U.S. dominance would hold. The Asians had listed Harvard first, with Oxford and Cambridge tied for second. Stanford was third, Berkeley fourth, the Massachusetts Institute of Technology (MIT) fifth, Yale sixth, Tokyo seventh, Paris-Sorbonne eighth, Cornell ninth, and Michigan and Princeton tied for tenth. Such reputational rankings were crude, Rosovsky added, but "Columbia, Chicago, UCLA, Caltech, Wisconsin, and many others would find little competition abroad."[4] When the Yale historian Jaroslav Pelikan published his "re-examination" of "the idea of the university" in 1992, Lord Noel Annan, former vice chancellor of the University of London, began his *New York Times* review by observing the commonplace: "America has the greatest university system in the world."[5]

Such a claim was unimaginable prior to World War II. When the Japanese attacked Pearl Harbor, American scientists had won only 11 percent of the 126 Nobel awards. American achievements in the world of higher education had historically been quantitative rather than qualitative. In 1888 Lord Bryce, in *The American Commonwealth,* his affectionate portrait of the United States, observed that England had four degree-granting bodies and the United States had 415, very few of which "answer to the modern conception of a university." Ohio, with 3 million inhabitants and thirty-seven institutions, "scarce any one of which deserves to be called a University," typified the distinctive American pattern.[6] England could serve a population of 23 million in the 1880s with four universities because higher education in the European tradition was reserved for a tiny social and intellectual elite. To European critics, even to as sympathetic an observer as Bryce, the U.S. proliferation of hundreds of state schools and small private sectarian colleges, most of them teaching undergraduate general education, was no pathway to advanced scholarship and scientific excellence.

The European criticism was echoed by American critics of the early twentieth century, most notably Thorstein Veblen and Abraham Flexner, who admired the European tradition and its American exemplar, the Johns Hopkins University.[7] Seen from this perspective, great universities were inherently elitist; their meritocratic standards were eroded by the downward pull of broad market forces. In modern society, it appeared, institutions of higher learning could not have it both ways, seeking intellectual distinction through rigorous selection while serving democratic markets through mass education.

Events since 1945 would prove this assertion false. The growth in the postwar United States of a mass market in higher education was not only compatible with the rise to world dominance of the American research university, it was essential to the efficient functioning of the American academic marketplace. During the postwar era three new forces drove American higher education to unprecedented levels of growth and achievement: the rising tide of economic prosperity, the baby boom, and the revolution in federal science policy. Because this book concentrates on research rather than on teaching or other important roles of higher education, it emphasizes the last of the new forces—the postwar flood of federal research dollars and its impact on the research economy of American universities and colleges. The development of federal science policy, a new and crucial ingredient in the postwar rise of American research universities, is the theme of chapter 2.

We must acknowledge at the outset, however, that most of the elements that were essential to catapulting the top American universities into positions of global leadership after 1945 were present well prior to the Manhattan Project. The most important of these were decentralization; pluralism, which enabled a prominent role for private institutions; a large, nationalized academic market united by common organizational forms and professional standards; and consequently, competition between the campuses for students and faculty and sources of funding. None of this was planned. Taken together, these four attributes are mirror-image opposites of the European university system. Through colonial conquest and widespread emulation during the eighteenth and nineteenth centuries, the prestigious European model became the university standard for most nations of the world. To appreciate the distinctive qualities of the American higher education system, we must recognize how sharply it differed from the European standard against which it was historically measured.

The European Model of Higher Education: Centralization and State Control

By the late nineteenth and early twentieth centuries, higher education systems in Europe were typically centralized under a national ministry of education.[8] As a consequence, higher education policy was essentially government policy. Like most public bureaucracies, Europe's state-dominated systems of higher education were organized hierarchically by function. Competition was minimized by bureaucratic boundaries, much as it was in ministries of justice, war, or public health. Teaching faculty were typically civil servants. The European university was the training ground for the middle and professional classes, and for this reason, attendance was confined to a small, closely screened cadre of academically talented students who sought advanced professional and vocational training rather than general education in the liberal arts, the goal of American college students.[9]

The European model of elite higher education was spread throughout the globe by colonial expansion and imperial conquest. Its chief attributes were state funding and control, centralized planning and policy making, and institutional specialization with an emphasis on advanced study, professional training, and research. Competition was rigorous both for student admissions and for faculty appointments. Competition between institutions, however, was minimal. The European system's greatest strengths lay in its ability to establish and maintain high academic and scholarly standards, to clarify institutional missions and apportion resources with minimal redundancy, and to coordinate efficiently with the secondary-school system in a coherent national screening plan for student selection and training. In such a system, university students were a proven elite, already well versed in the liberal arts and sciences through their study of the demanding secondary school curricula.

By contrast, American colleges recruited students from notoriously weak secondary schools, in which the democratic commitment to provide a high-school education for all citizens pulled standards toward their lowest common denominator. As a consequence, American colleges concentrated on liberal arts education largely by default. As Bryce pointed out in *The American Commonwealth*, the curriculum at most American colleges at the turn of the century resembled the curriculum not of Europe's universities but rather of its secondary schools—the gymnasia of Germany, the lycées of France, the grammar schools of England, and the high schools of Scotland.[10] Graduating seniors at American colleges thus often performed at levels comparable to those of entering students at European universities.[11]

The crowning achievement of this institutional tradition, the great German research universities, was based on continental Europe's "chair" system. Unlike the more fluid and loosely organized system of academic departments that developed in the United States (and partially in the United Kingdom), this system centered around a distinguished professor who customarily directed his own research institute. A legacy of medieval guilds and master professors, the chair system became a traditional form of organization and control in continental and Latin American universities. The roster of distinguished chair professors of the nineteenth-century and early-twentieth-century European universities reads like an honor role of Nobel laureates. But the chair system also symbolized the chief liabilities of the European model. Although chair professors dominated their institutes and periodically elected a rector from among their number, basic decisions about university budgets, student admissions, and academic programs and degrees were made not by campus academic officers but by central ministry officials. On the whole, the system proved too rigid to accommodate the accelerating pace of scientific change.

Much as the chair system institutionalized individual achievement at the expense of flexibility and interdisciplinary creativity, the centralized nature of European higher education purchased organizational rationality and bureaucratic efficiency at the expense of competition and innovation. Such state-controlled systems conferred quasi-monopolies and often reinforced patterns of institutional inbreeding. Chair professors were too powerful for too long, typically dominating a structure that was resistant to innovation and isolated from disciplinary cross-fertilization.[12] This arrangement could provide extraordinary advantages to favored institutions, such as the Universities of Tokyo and Kyoto, as well as Cambridge, Oxford, and the *grandes écoles* of France.

Like the chair system, however, the vertical organization of specialized institutions was poorly designed to respond to the brisk pace of competition that characterized modern scientific development.[13] Typically, in the European model, funds for research were allocated to universities, laboratories, and research institutes by central government bodies—the University Grants Committee in the United Kingdom, the Centre Nationale de Recherche Scientifique in France, and the Max Planck Gesellschaft in Germany. Burton Clark, a pioneering scholar of comparative higher education, concluded that the British government's University Grants Committee, established in 1919, led to control by oligarchs who were "inhospitable to applied science and technology" and who resisted innovative research programs. "Nationalized procedures for approving courses and assigning staff, as in France and Italy," Clark continued, "institutionalize the power of old fields over new ones, as members of traditional fields sitting on government councils veto changes sought by newer fields that seem suspect educationally or that threaten to dilute one's own powers and resources."[14]

By the 1960s, when American university researchers were sweeping the honors in international competition, there was a consensus among comparative specialists in higher education such as Joseph Ben-David, Burton Clark, and Martin Trow that in the international research competition, countries with national ministries of education, centralized higher education systems, and national degree structures have tended to suffer from institutional immobility.[15] The accelerating pace of scientific change thus had transformed the nineteenth-century virtues of Europe's centralized state university systems into a growing liability. By the same token, the anarchical American system, historically weak and parochial in the quality of its teaching and research, was marvelously resilient in the face of change.

The Unplanned Evolution of American Higher Education

It is a great irony that in the global competition for world leadership in creating new knowledge, the fragmentation of American higher education should emerge as an unintended asset. As Martin Trow and others have observed, the United States by 1900 had developed a system of higher education that, unlike any other in the world, possessed an enormous capacity for expansion without fundamental structural change. Trow called this a "preternaturally precocious" system.[16]

14

The product of no coherent scheme, it could scarcely have been better designed to accommodate a vast future expansion. Only 4 percent of Americans of college age were attending college in 1900. By 1910, when a third of a million students in the United States were studying at almost one thousand colleges and universities, the sixteen universities in France enrolled about fourteen thousand students — a number almost equalled by the number of faculty members in American colleges and universities. In most European countries, including Britain, college enrollments did not exceed 5 percent of the traditional college-age group until after World War II.

What is most striking about the pre-1945 American system of higher education is its inadvertent, unplanned quality, its sharp departures from the centralized and state-dominated European pattern, and its uncanny instinct for survival and growth in a shifting market environment. Decentralization was accelerated by a colonial and revolutionary environment in America that combined community isolation, entrepreneurial incentives for upward mobility, fractious Protestant denominationalism, republican faith in education, and, by the late eighteenth century, revolutionary egalitarianism. The U.S. Constitution, shaped by classical liberalism's respect for contract and fear of centralized state power, created a federal system that limited and fragmented national authority and reserved education policy for state and local governments. The early Congress, by rejecting the appeals of President Washington and five of his successors that a national university be established, thereby removed the threat that more stringent national standards might pose to proliferating local colleges. In the nineteenth century the land-grant policy channeled national resources into the expanding state systems with remarkably few strings attached. As a result, there was no national university or U.S. ministry of education; rather, by 1945 there were forty-eight state systems containing 641 public institutions of widely varying purpose, size, and quality, teaching a total of 1.6 million American college students.

By the standards of most nations in the mid–twentieth century, 641 was an extraordinary number of colleges. Even more striking, these public institutions were outnumbered by twice as many private colleges and universities. Decentralization in American higher education was accompanied by pluralism. The historic strength of the private sector in American higher education has been unequaled in any other nation. In 1950, two-thirds of America's colleges and universities were private. By 1988, despite the rapid growth of public sector institutions and enrollments in the 1960s and 1970s, private institutions still were in the majority (54%). The number of public institutions in the United States, however, more than doubled between 1950 and 1988, increasing from 641 to 1,548. During the same period, enrollments in public institutions soared. By 1990, 77 percent of college students in the United States were attending public institutions, 45 percent of them in the strongest growth sector, the two-year community colleges.

The private sector has thus been of great importance in enriching higher education in the United States. But more important has been the role of the great private universities in forcing upward the nation's traditionally low standards of quality. In a sense, the role of a standard-setting national university was served by the elite colonial colleges that developed into prestigious "Ivy League" universities. As the sociologist Edward Shils observed of America's glittering array of private elite universities: "No other national higher education system possesses anything like them."[17] Historically, these campuses have competed vigorously with each other and with the leading public universities for students, faculty, and research funding—a form of competition that has been rare in European, Latin American, and Asian universities.

Many excellent private universities have developed elsewhere, such as the Ecole Libre des Sciences Politiques, the Stockholm School of Economics, and Keio and Waseda Universities in Japan. But these superior private institutions, while serving special constituencies well, have been too few in number to affect significantly the priorities of state-dominated systems of higher education. Other nations, for example Belgium and the Netherlands, have private universities that parallel their public systems. But their primary role has been to serve separate cultural and ethnic or religious constituencies. In several other countries—Japan, the Philippines, and Brazil, for example—a large private sector may serve between two-thirds and three-quarters of the college student population. But the role of mass private higher education in these countries has been to provide more, not better, education. Private institutions offer more open access to higher education in societies in which qualitatively superior state institutions offer limited admissions on a competitive basis. Only in the United States have private colleges and universities developed in sufficient number and quality to set the competitive tone at the top.[18]

American higher education derived its original character from private colleges that developed in a haphazard fashion during the colonial era. From the founding of Harvard College in 1636 to the opening of Dartmouth in 1769, the nine colonial colleges, seven of them

Protestant-sectarian in origin, taught young men a classical curriculum in preparation for civic leadership and the ministry.[19] To govern the new American colleges, the colonial fathers turned not to the small and transient teaching staff, most of the tutors being scarcely older than the students themselves, but rather to lay boards of trustees — "gentlemen of property and standing." There being neither medieval traditions nor an academic profession in colonial America, European patterns of faculty control and professional specialization were irrelevant. By the mid–eighteenth century, early experiments in dual control by internal professional bodies (presidents and residential teaching fellows) and external lay boards (visitors and overseers), proving unstable at Harvard and the College of William and Mary, had evolved at Yale and Princeton into the characteristic pattern of American private college government: control through a unitary board of nonresident, nonacademic trustees; institutional dominance by a strong president; and independence from either control or support by the state.[20] As a consequence, the American college, forming the institutional core of the new universities of the nineteenth century, enjoyed an institutional coherence and unity that centered on a baccalaureate education in the liberal arts and sciences. Professional specialization and advanced or "postgraduate" training were postponed for subsequent degrees.[21]

The American university was thus rooted in the distinctive history of the prestigious private colleges of the colonial era. But private founding was also characteristic of the great state universities of Europe, which evolved from ecclesiastical origins as largely autonomous, self-governing institutions. The modern distinction between the public and private spheres is a problematic one when discussing medieval institutions, but the development of nation-states in Europe brought government control over the budgets, admissions, program curricula, and academic degrees of almost all of Europe's universities. In the new United States, however, the Constitution's first amendment protected religious institutions from government interference. In 1819 a crucial Supreme Court decision in the *Dartmouth College* case strengthened the sanctity of private contracts and shielded private institutions from the kind of state takeover that had nationalized universities in Europe and elsewhere.[22]

These developments accelerated the founding of colleges affiliated with Protestant denominations throughout the United States and encouraged the creation of a second wave of private universities. The latter commonly took their name from the patrons who had endowed them from large personal fortunes: Tulane, founded in 1834; Emory,

1836; Duke, 1838; Cornell, 1865; Vanderbilt, 1873; Johns Hopkins, 1876; Stanford, 1885; Chicago (founded by the Rockefellers), 1890; and Carnegie, 1900.[23] At the same time, the state governments constructed a parallel system of public universities. The University of Georgia was chartered in 1785, North Carolina in 1789, Vermont in 1800, South Carolina in 1801, and Virginia in 1819. The University of Michigan, opening in 1841, set the early pace for the great Midwestern universities, and after the Civil War, land-grant universities were established in every state in response to the Morrill Act of 1862.[24] Unlike most private universities, the state universities and colleges undertook public service obligations in agricultural experimentation and extension services, industrial training, teacher education, home economics, public health, and veterinary medicine.

Despite these differences in function, the American public and private universities developed a remarkably similar structure that differed significantly from the European model. By 1925, when the first national study of American graduate education was published, the leading American universities had a remarkable resemblance.[25] The top-ranked private sector universities (Chicago, Harvard, Columbia, Yale, and Princeton) and their public sector counterparts (Wisconsin, Michigan, California, Illinois, Minnesota) shared a common academic structure and set of professional norms. Historical forces in the United States had produced, through no conscious design, a combination of structural arrangements and professional incentives that encouraged competition in the academic market.

University Organization and a National Academic Market

Decentralization and pluralism, as distinguishing characteristics of American higher education, are easier to describe than a third characteristic, the large, nationalized academic market. Structural factors were primary in shaping a common academic culture. Almost without exception, American universities were built around a large, core college of arts and sciences, organized into discipline-based departments in which faculty appointments and tenure were based. This common organizational form traced its origin to the colonial colleges and, by the nineteenth century, to the peculiar need for American undergraduate education to fill the void left by a democratic system of public secondary schools that valued high graduation rates over demanding standards. The raison d'être of "the college" was thus to provide baccalaureate education in the liberal arts and sciences for residential undergraduates, while the graduate school offered masters and doctoral degrees, and separate schools offered professional degrees. During the nineteenth century the private and public universities added to the undergraduate core college professional schools in medicine, law, architecture, engineering, business, education, and various applied, or practitioner, fields, and graduate degree programs in the scientific and scholarly disciplines. Medical schools were opened in the late eighteenth century at the College of Philadelphia (forerunner of the University of Pennsylvania), King's College (Columbia), and Dartmouth; by 1850 law schools operated at Harvard and the University of Michigan and thirteen other campuses. In 1861 Yale awarded the first American Ph.D. degree (in chemistry). Graduate programs in the academic disciplines proliferated after the Civil War, enhancing the stature and prestige of the universities and offering their faculties the option of advanced instruction and research. However, from the viewpoint of student numbers, instructional effort, university finance, and alumni loyalty, the professional schools and graduate programs were ancillary to the heart of the university, its undergraduate liberal arts curriculum and baccalaureate degree.[26]

When the German model of the research university was imported to the United States by way of Johns Hopkins late in the nineteenth century, it was admired and emulated. But it was also quickly Americanized. The research and graduate orientation of the German model took a prominent and permanent place in the hierarchy of American academic prestige. But the American graduate school was superimposed on the colleges of arts and sciences, with their undergraduate-centered departmental organization. By the early twentieth century even Johns Hopkins looked more like Yale, or like the University of North Carolina, than like von Humboldt's model in Berlin.

In such American universities, the faculty who taught the graduate students literature, government, and biology held appointments and pursued tenure in undergraduate academic departments. And unlike most university students in Europe, Asia, and Latin America, who were selectively screened and who studied at relatively advanced levels of specialization, the typical American undergraduate students were weakly prepared and pursued a four-year curriculum of general education. Faculty eager to teach advanced courses and conduct research sought university rather than college appointments. Young faculty who demonstrated research prowess through scholarly publications won increased upward mobility as the American academic market matured. Department heads and university administrators valued faculty who could win research funding from private philanthropy, business firms, or government agencies seeking specialized expertise in agriculture, public health, civil engineering, and other practical fields.

Unlike European universities, which often appointed their own star graduates to faculty posts and rarely recruited faculty from other universities, American universities competed in a diverse academic market. European universities featured great institutional loyalty and continuity of professional personnel. Senior faculty at the leading American universities, however, typically won their posts through participation in a competitive academic marketplace. Their entries in *Who's Who in American Colleges and Universities* reflected appointments in a half-dozen or more institutions. Upward mobility was won through lateral movement. Faculty escaped heavy teaching responsibilities and weaker students through research and publication. One's value in the academic market was in large part a function of the length of one's curriculum vitae.

It would be misleading to suggest that this now-familiar profile of faculty incentives was widespread in American higher education prior to World War II. Before the war, most faculty spent their careers bound by local or regional horizons, teaching heavy course loads in undergraduate colleges and engaging in academic research only marginally if at all. But early in the twentieth century—roughly between 1900, when the Association of American Universities was established, and 1925, when Raymond Hughes conducted his first assessment of American graduate education—a national academic marketplace linked the twenty-six institutional members of the AAU and perhaps a dozen other aspirants.[27] These American elite universities, still no match for Cambridge or Berlin, nonetheless set the bidding standard for an increasingly competitive environment that was building toward the first mass-based higher education market in the world.

The undergraduate college at the heart of the American university thus linked the three principal campus constituencies—students, faculty, and administration—in symbiotic patterns of growth. Thus, all three constituencies enjoyed incentives and freedom for initiative not generally available at non-American universities. Decades before World War II and the subsequent baby boom, college-bound students shopped for admission at campuses that shared an increasingly standardized list of academic practices. These included the elective system, with its general education requirements and a menu of discipline-based majors, and the modular course and its attached academic credits. Because degree requirements in American colleges were defined in terms of the accumulation of course credits rather than success on a national examination or presentation of a thesis as in the European model, the unit credit became the common currency of American higher education. Credits accumulated over time were "banked," allowing students to "stop out" and later to return or transfer to another institution.[28]

Such a system enabled American campuses to adapt from elite to mass patterns of student traffic without major disruption in academic routines or prohibitive costs in faculty resources. In 1900 only 4 percent of the American population aged eighteen to twenty-four attended college. This represented a total of 232,000 undergraduate students and 5,700 graduate students and resulted in the award of twenty-nine thousand degrees. By 1950 the figure stood at 16.5 percent, representing 2.7 million students and a total of almost half a million degrees.[29] Academic departments at the larger universities could handle the increase in enrollments through low-cost graduate teaching assistantships, which in turn provided tuition and stipends to support students in expanding graduate programs. The system relied on large lecture courses, supplemented by discussion and laboratory sections taught by junior faculty and graduate students.

The elective system, by allowing students to shop for majors and to declare or change their choice, gave American undergraduates a consumer voice that helped shape patterns of institutional growth. Given a large measure of choice and control over their course of study, their weekly class schedule, and their progress toward a degree, students could devote more time and energy to noncurricular activities: the social exchanges of residential living, including fraternities and sororities; intramural and intercollegiate sports; and the cultural offerings of an intellectual and artistic community. At larger universities the faculty, obliged to teach both undergraduates and graduate students and to create new knowledge through research, were freed from the kind of close engagement with undergraduates that was expected in liberal arts colleges. At the best research universities, faculty members' classroom "contact" with undergraduate students might average six or fewer hours a week. This arrangement was especially important for the largest public universities—the great "flagship" institutions such as Michigan, Wisconsin, and UC Berkeley[30]—which had to compete for faculty talent with Harvard, Yale, and Chicago. Public institutions could offer faculty members salaries and teaching loads that were competitive with private university standards only by achieving economies of scale—that is, by sharply increasing student admissions, enlarging class size, and shifting instructional costs downward by employing lower-cost instructors and graduate students supported through teaching assistantships.[31]

These changes explain much of the dramatic shift in the relative size of American private and public universities in the mid–twentieth century. In the 1920s, Columbia and Chicago had larger student bodies than Michigan or Wisconsin.[32] In the years before Pearl Harbor, private universities with substantial endowments also tended to have undergraduate enrollments that were large by the standards of the day; and football teams from Brown, Columbia, Harvard, and Pennsylvania played in the Rose Bowl. Since the 1960s the leading state flagship campuses have typically employed twice as many faculty and taught three times as many students as the elite private universities.

Like their students, faculty at American universities benefited from the system's more egalitarian standards and expanding market norms, especially in comparison with university faculty in other countries. Historically, in the European-model universities, faculty ranks were steeply stratified; most teachers were instructors, lecturers, tutors, and preceptors; and professorial rank was achieved only by perhaps 10 percent of the teaching faculty. Prior to World War II, chair professors commonly dominated the academic governance system of continental universities. In the postwar era, campus governance in universities in continental Europe often became politicized by elections to various boards and committees in which representatives of the university's various "estates" (professors, junior faculty, students, and administrative staff) campaigned along the lines of the national political parties. In American colleges and universities, by contrast, most faculty have followed a common career path from the rank of assistant professor, to associate professor, and then to full professor, a process that has increased faculty cohesion across ranks and allowed junior faculty considerable professional authority.

In addition to the common rank structure, another force for nationalization of the American faculty marketplace has been the disciplinary basis of departmental organization. This has pulled faculty members' loyalties outward, toward their colleagues in the same fields of study at other institutions. The process of academic professionalization, which resembled the nineteenth-century changes in the "learned professions," medicine and law, was accelerated by the growth of national scholarly associations that functioned as horizontal peer colleges. The annual meetings, scientific and scholarly journals, and job placement services of the discipline-based associations

increased the cohesion of the academic marketplace. But these na-
tionalizing and professionalizing forces extracted a high price — weakened institutional loyalty.[33]

For the third major campus constituency, the academic administration, the expanding market offered broader opportunities for recruiting students and faculty and soliciting outside support but
added to the complexity of patterns of authority and control. Much
has been written about the development in America of lay boards of
trustees and strong college presidents.[34] In the European tradition,
ministry officials have paid the costs and set the agenda for the university. As Trow observed of the European-model university: "Apart
from the freedom to teach and to learn, the university rarely has much
authority to manage its own size and shape, its entry or exit requirements, or its broad character and function."[35] Weak campus rectors
were elected from the professorial ranks and served short-term appointments, while permanent civil service officials on campus — the
Kurator in Germany, for example — answered to the central ministry
for finances and major policies on academic programs. In exchange
for full funding, the universities served the government's definition of
the public interest. Until as recently as the 1970s, two-thirds to three-
quarters of university graduates in Denmark, France, Sweden, and
West Germany took jobs in the public sector.

In the United States, by contrast, even for public institutions lay
boards of trustees acted as a buffer between the campus and the
state. The historic proliferation of underfinanced American colleges
led to a competitive scramble for survival that diversified sources of
support. American state governments, following the private practice
of charging tuition, never fully funded their public institutions in the
meritocratic European fashion. Because most colleges were private
and many had religious affiliations, they received little or no state
support and hence relied on tuition, endowments, and philanthropic donations. As a consequence, schools courted organized interest
groups, seeking financial support and offering institutional services.
To support the often-struggling colleges, lay trustees, regents, overseers, visitors, and alumni tapped their own pocketbooks and those
of their colleagues in business and the professions. In response,
American campuses developed academic and service programs tailored to meet the community needs of donors and patrons rather than
the national standards and public service needs established by central ministry officials. Correspondingly, presidents increasingly became fund raisers, delegating their duties of academic leadership to
provosts, academic vice chancellors, and deans.

Strengths and Weaknesses of Decentralized
Market Competition

On the eve of World War II, the unplanned evolution of higher education in the United States had produced a loose, sprawling, largely un-
regulated system that was decentralized, pluralistic, competitive, and
vast. The system's manifest deficiencies, long noted by foreign visitors who were puzzled by the large number and uneven quality of
American colleges, flowed from the tension between the democratic
impulse to maximize access to education and higher education's inherent elitist tendencies. Every year more students attended more
college campuses in the expanding U.S. system than in the higher education system of any other country, both in absolute numbers and
as a percentage of the population. By 1940, the percentage of college-
age Americans attending institutions of higher education was three
times higher than the European average (roughly 12% versus 4%).
Yet, on average, American college students were less well prepared by
secondary schooling than were their European counterparts, less
able intellectually as measured by traditional standards of ability,
and more heavily burdened financially. Most American college students were still predominantly white, Protestant, and upper middle
class. In 1940, when the U.S. population stood at 132 million, 1.5 million American college students were being taught by 146,930 faculty
at 1,708 institutions—a majority of which were too small, financially
marginal, poorly equipped with library books and laboratory equipment, and academically weak to be regarded as providing "higher" education by contemporary European standards.

However, America's decentralized academic marketplace produced brisk competition at the top, where an array of about three
dozen private and public universities benefited from economies of
scale. Roger Geiger summarized this American advantage: "The sheer
size of American higher education created huge communities of scientists in every discipline and field. Although much of the instruction
given at American colleges and universities took place at less than an
advanced level, teaching itself created secure professional employment for thousands of scientists and scholars; and training these
cadres gave work of a higher order to the graduate schools."[36] Although American campuses remained in the shadow of the prestigious European universities during the first third of the twentieth
century, evidence was accumulating that the American research universities were reducing the lead of Europe's premier institutions in
the creation of new knowledge, and in some scientific quarters were

outperforming them. By World War I the United States led all other nations in the number of medical discoveries, and by 1930 U.S. scientists claimed the world's largest share of chemistry and physics abstracts. America's great leap forward in knowledge creation and university prestige following World War II was thus not solely dependent on the destruction of European institutions and infrastructures or the importation of refugee scientists.[37]

World War II convinced American society, however, that in one respect the United States needed to emulate the European model. The link between research universities and a nation's economic strength and national security was too vital for the national government to leave unattended. A postwar policy of national investment was essential. During World War II and the postwar reconversion, a brisk debate over federal science policy showed deep disagreements among American leaders that mirrored partisan and ideological divisions. In the dispute over a new federal science policy, hopes for a new river of research funding for American universities were tempered by fears that centralized research priorities and funding would favor established elites, especially those in the private sector.

2

■

The Revolution
in Federal Science Policy

The postwar debate over the nature of federal science policy exposed a fault line in American political life, a rift between advocates of meritocratic competition and populist critics of privileged elites. These tensions, inherent in a capitalist democracy, were heightened by the prospect that federal officials in Washington would now set priorities in a national research agenda that previously had been shaped in a decentralized, pluralist environment by local and regional forces. In the new era of federal research funding, fueled by a surging economy and justified politically by national defense and health needs, would federal bureaucrats designate favored recipient institutions (a practice followed by most other nations and familiar to American policy makers in the land-grant program)? The question was answered, in characteristic American fashion, by a Madisonian government in which interest-group bargaining and congressional compromises produced pluralist policy solutions. In the postwar era, federal science policy would be shaped not by a new ministry of higher education or a federal science agency but rather by a whole array of new agencies, subagencies, and programs in established mission departments. Their expanding, overlapping, often duplicative menu of sponsored research programs invited individual researchers to shop for funding.[1]

In reaching this compromise, however, those who spoke for American academic science, armed with the prestige of brilliant wartime achievements, were strong enough to stipulate the criteria for selecting winners in the competition for research funding. Unable to create and dominate a new federal science agency, they insisted successfully that research grants and contracts awarded by the major support programs be determined by peer-review panels on the basis of merit. This practice, followed through the 1950s as cold war pressures and the *Sputnik* challenge expanded federal research expenditures, by 1960 had produced high concentrations of research funding in a small number of elite universities, the majority of them private. This concentration of taxpayer support was challenged in the 1960s.

As egalitarian, populist pressures grew in the 1960s, the Kennedy and Johnson administrations responded by retaining the core formula of agency funding through peer-review competition, but added new policies and programs in three areas. First, agencies were directed to widen the geographic distribution of federal research support, emphasizing physical facilities and attempting to double the number of strong research universities. Second, federal research support was extended to include the social sciences, the humanities, and the visual and performing arts. Third, federal support was significantly expanded, extending beyond the roughly one hundred doctorate-granting universities, to provide funding for construction and nonscientific programs, including student financial aid, to more than three thousand institutions. These included community colleges, private liberal arts colleges, state colleges and regional universities, historically black institutions, and vocational and proprietary schools. Thus, in the Great Society agenda, federal science policy expanded and blurred into higher education and social policy.

By 1968, when Congress amended the National Science Foundation Act to require annual statistical reports on the distribution of federal funds to institutions, federal aid to higher education had expanded to include almost every campus in the country. Yet the nation's established elite campuses still dominated the competition for federal research support. The top-ranked American universities, claiming more Nobel laureates than the universities of all other nations combined, had risen to the pinnacle of world prestige. What was not yet clear was whether, in the enriched funding environment of the 1960s, new research universities could rise to challenge the hegemony of traditional elites.

Origins of a Federal Science Policy

In 1945 the prospect of a coherent, statute-based federal policy to aid knowledge-creation in the nation's universities was novel. Roger Geiger, in his history of American research universities prior to World War II, describes the development, between the two world wars, of a research economy in which the role of the federal government was relatively insignificant.[2] The academic research base was funded primarily by philanthropic foundations (such as the Rockefeller and Carnegie Foundations) and large corporations (such as du Pont, General Electric, Borden, and Lilly). The nation's academic research was dominated by the efforts of sixteen preeminent universities: UC Berkeley, Chicago, the California Institute of Technology (Caltech), Columbia, Cornell, Harvard, Illinois, Johns Hopkins, MIT, Michigan, Minnesota, Pennsylvania, Princeton, Stanford, Wisconsin, and Yale. Eleven of the sixteen were private institutions.

During World War II the U.S. government harnessed the talent of the top scientists and engineers at these universities, not—as had been done in World War I—by inducting them into uniformed service in war-related bureaucracies but by developing a new contract and grant system under the leadership of civilian scientific elites. The success story of the wartime Office of Scientific Research and Development (OSRD) is well known.[3] To lead the mobilization of scientific manpower, President Roosevelt in 1940 summoned Vannevar Bush, former dean of engineering at MIT and, since 1938, president of the Carnegie Institution of Washington. Bush in turn brought in a powerful trio of senior associates: Karl T. Compton, president of MIT; James B. Conant, president of Harvard; and Frank B. Jewett, board chairman of Bell Telephone Laboratories and president of the National Academy of Sciences. A formidable group, they represented the major sectors of science and technology outside of government. The OSRD developed an intense and intimate model of collaboration between Washington and the nation's leading universities. The wartime development of radar, the proximity fuse, penicillin, DDT, the computer, jet propulsion, and the climactic trump card, the atomic bomb, brought enormous prestige to the scientific community. From the development of radar at MIT, through the control of nuclear fission at the University of Chicago, to the University of California's secret operations at Los Alamos, scientific brilliance in the national interest was associated with the great universities. When demobilization after the war closed down the OSRD, national political leaders agreed that the government-university collaboration should continue. A deep split developed, however, over its structure and control.

One pole in the debate was represented by New Deal Democrats and populists in Congress, who criticized the domination of war mobilization and university research by big business. Led by Senator Harley M. Kilgore of West Virginia, they championed small business, organized labor, consumer interests, and applied research, and proposed a strong new science agency controlled by nonscientists. Kilgore valued the land-grant model and the agricultural extension system, in which government officials were accountable to elected political leaders and program funds were distributed through formulas that guaranteed wide geographic distribution. In this populist–New Deal vision, the proposed National Science Foundation (NSF) would be governed by a broadly representative, presidentially appointed lay board and administered by a director appointed by and responsible to the president. The NSF board would thus be accountable to elected officials and would represent a broad coalition of interest groups, including consumers and small business as well as scientists. The new agency would fund pure research at universities but would emphasize applied research and government laboratories.[4]

Vannevar Bush and his colleagues in the scientific establishment, however, feared that political control by elected officials and government bureaucrats would stifle scientific creativity and impose agency agendas. They shared an ideology favoring disinterested, pure research and wanted a system in which scientists of proven achievement would review proposals and make funding decisions based on competitive merit. They wanted funding priorities to be determined by scientists who were largely shielded from political constraints such as formulas for geographic distribution, and from the short-term pressures of applied research.[5] The politically astute Bush, taking advantage of his strategic position in government and of the wartime prestige of scientists, prepared for President Roosevelt a report on how the nation should support scientific research after the war. The result was *Science—the Endless Frontier*, a classic of modern public agenda-setting, submitted by Bush to President Truman in July 1945.[6]

In his report, Bush recommended that Congress establish a National Research Foundation to set policies in science and technology under the independent direction of a part-time board, appointed by the president but dominated by scientists outside of government. The board would appoint the foundation's director and would establish separate divisions to preside over research in national defense and medicine as well as the physical and natural sciences. In short, government would fund the research, but nongovernment scientists would determine its contours.[7] Bush's vision of a national foundation for science was embodied in a Senate bill introduced in the fall of 1945, and for the next five years the two sides of the NSF debate jousted without resolution. Congress struggled with fundamental disputes over the foundation's structure and control, including disagreements over patent policy (whether ownership rights were to go to government or to discoverers), the geographic distribution of research grants (whether grants were to be allocated to states and institutions according to a formula or on the basis of merit competition), and whether to include funding for the social sciences (most scientists would have excluded it).

In 1950, a compromise National Science Foundation Act was signed by President Truman. The modest NSF of 1950 was, however, a faint shadow of the muscular agency envisioned by both Bush and Kilgore in 1945. Even the enormous prestige of wartime science could not propel the Bush vision past the multiple barriers of American pluralist politics. The core trade-off produced a traditional agency structure, politically accountable to elected officials, while the science establishment and the university community won a commitment to basic science research funded through merit competition. The costs of the five-year delay were substantial, however. The NSF was given a budget that was small by comparison with the budgets of the research programs of established agencies, and its research jurisdiction was narrowed to concentrate on the physical sciences and engineering.[8]

The Pluralist Nature of Federal Science Policy

The delayed creation of the NSF underlined the pluralist nature of postwar federal science policy. There would be no science czar or dominant science agency. Congress has traditionally resisted the statutory creation of new agencies. Rather, the congressional committee structure has paralleled the departmental organization of the executive branch, and the politics of Congress and the agency bureaucracies has produced "iron triangles" of mutual accommodation that link congressional committees, agency programs, and beneficiary groups.[9] The land-grant universities themselves had long participated in a classic example of such mutual back-scratching with the Department of Agriculture, the agricultural committees of Congress, and the American Farm Bureau Federation. In the Hill-Burton Act of 1946, which provided federal aid for hospital and medical school construction, Congress launched its popular postwar programs assisting urban development and the construction of airports, highways, and water and sewer systems.[10] But research programs, like education programs, were too general in nature to be claimed as privileged turf by specific constituencies such as veterans or farmers, or monopolized by constituency-based agencies such as the Veterans Administration, the Department of Agriculture, or the Army Corps of Engineers. Like education programs, research programs were too important to the mission agencies to permit their concentration in a superagency of any kind.[11]

During the five-year debate over the NSF, the established agencies and their congressional allies moved quickly to take advantage of the new consensus behind federal contract funding for scientific research. The navy, anxious to crack the wartime atomic monopoly of the army and the Army Air Corps, won congressional approval for a permanent research operation in August 1946 with the creation by statute of the Office of Naval Research (ONR).[12] The creation of the Atomic Energy Commission (AEC) in 1946 represented a lobbying victory by prestigious scientists who opposed military control of atomic technology. Like the wartime OSRD, the AEC undertook much of its research via contractual agreements with universities and industry, and it used the contract model to shift from government to university management most of the Manhattan Project's secret government-owned laboratories, including those at Los Alamos, Lawrence, Argonne, Ames, and Brookhaven, and parts of Oak Ridge.[13] In biomedical research, the demise of the OSRD, whose effective Committee on Medical Research had nurtured the development of penicillin, left a vacuum that was filled with entrepreneurial energy by the National Institute of Health (NIH), the research branch of the Public Health Service. (In 1948, when Congress added a separate heart institute to the cancer institute it had created in 1937, the NIH became plural — the National Institutes of Health.) The NIH, which had operated its own in-house or intramural research laboratories since 1930, seized the moment of opportunity in 1945. Taking over fifty wartime research grant projects from the expiring OSRD, the NIH became the chief supporter of extramural research in the nation's expanding network of medical schools. Congress, which in 1946 had passed the Hill-Burton program to aid hospital construction, encouraged the NIH initiative and between 1945 and 1950 expanded its budget from $3 million to $52 million.[14]

By 1950 the pluralistic nature of the federal research system was well established, and the new NSF, despite its distinctive primary research mission, was disadvantaged by its tardy entry. The NSF's research funds would modestly enlarge the federal aid pot, but the foundation would not significantly reshape or coordinate national science policy. During the 1950s, federal mission agencies expanded their programs of R&D support under the broad rubric of "mission-related basic research." Under this umbrella, agencies stretched their traditionally applied R&D programs to include basic research, thereby offering universities a growing cafeteria of funding opportunities. In 1954 President Eisenhower affirmed this arrangement, which permitted many mission agencies to sponsor basic research projects, by signing an executive order that recognized the unique, "general-purpose basic research" role of the NSF but also authorized the "conduct and support of other Federal agencies of basic research in areas which are closely related to their missions."[15] That same year, federal agencies accounted for 69 percent of total university research budgets, while the universities' own funds contributed only 8.5 percent. By comparison, private foundations provided only 11 percent of university research budgets and industry provided only 9 percent—both shares having declined sharply from the peaks they had reached in the interwar years.[16]

The new, federally subsidized research economy of the postwar years by no means provided a blank check to subsidize the research agenda of university scientists and scholars. Federal R&D expenditures primarily were allocated to development, not to research. And most of this money would be spent by industry, particularly defense contractors, not universities. During the 1950s roughly 80 percent of all federal R&D funding went to profit-seeking organizations, with almost 60 percent provided by the Department of Defense (DOD). Most federal research funds, moreover, were provided to support applied, programmatic research, not basic, "pure," or "disinterested" research. Even the federally funded basic research program was dominated by "big science" projects with military applications. In 1956 the budget for basic science research was $72 million at the Department of Defense and $45 million at the AEC. At the NIH, the major supporter of "little science" projects in fundamental research, the basic research budget was only $26 million. By 1960 the NSF, after a decade of growth, still provided only 7 percent of federal R&D funding.[17]

Moreover, the federal funding offered by the mission agencies was uneven. Support was generous for the physical sciences (funded by the Defense Department, the AEC, the National Aeronautics and Space Administration [NASA], and the NSF), the life sciences (funded by the NIH), and engineering (funded by the NSF and the federal contract research laboratories, such as the Jet Propulsion Laboratory at Caltech, and the Applied Physics Laboratory at Johns Hopkins). Federal funding remained tiny for the social sciences, which depended primarily on private sources such as the new Ford Foundation and the Social Science Research Council. The social sciences were in effect held hostage by the natural science directorates at the NSF, which only spent approximately 3 percent of the agency's R&D budget on social science research. Finally, prior to 1965, federal research funding in the arts and humanities was virtually nonexistent.

Sputnik and the Ascent of Basic Research

Nonetheless, the pluralist structure of federal science support offered university scientists and scholars a widening array of funding sources, and federal science policy took both a quantitative jump and a qualitative turn after the Soviets launched the world's first artificial satellite, *Sputnik,* in 1957. Following the shock of *Sputnik,* Congress hurriedly passed the stopgap National Defense Education Act (NDEA) of 1958, which began regular federal support for graduate students and for foreign language and area studies. Eisenhower brought MIT president James R. Killian to the White House as his special assistant for science and technology, and Killian chaired the newly formed President's Science Advisory Committee (PSAC). Representing the nation's scientific and academic elite — the National Academy of Sciences (NAS), the American Association for the Advancement of Science (AAAS), and the Association of American Universities (AAU) — PSAC members exploited their strategic forum and the *Sputnik* crisis to press for federal support of basic rather than programmatic research.

Roger Geiger calls the vision shared by the PSAC leaders an ideology of basic research, a scientific faith based in the final analysis "upon neither analysis nor empirical evidence."[18] Its credo emerged in the Seaborg Report of 1960, a set of recommendations made by a PSAC panel chaired by UC Berkeley's chancellor, Glenn Seaborg.[19] Strengthening academic science, especially basic research and graduate studies, was an essential federal responsibility, the Seaborg Report argued. This meant that federal funding was required not just for contract research projects but for the entire infrastructure of academic science — scientific buildings and equipment, teaching and research laboratories, and graduate fellowships and training programs.[20]

The *Sputnik* crisis provided the leaders of academic science with a window of opportunity during the Eisenhower and Kennedy presidencies, and the PSAC enjoyed a half-decade of high visibility and effective policy advocacy. During these years, 1958–63, federal policy makers made two historic decisions. First, the federal government assumed primary responsibility for supporting basic research in the United States. Second, the research enterprise was to be carried out primarily by the nation's universities as an integral component of graduate education. The Seaborg Report explained the rationale for a partnership between the national government and the universities based on the symbiosis of graduate education and research: "Whether the quantity and quality of basic research and graduate education in the United States will be adequate depends primarily upon the government of the United States. From this responsibility the Federal Government has no escape." "Either it will find the policies — and the resources which permit our universities to flourish and their duties to be adequately discharged," the report warned, "or no one will."[21]

Increasing support from Washington for basic science drove the "pure science" component of university research expenditures on American campuses from 52 percent in 1953 to 76 percent in 1963.[22] The share of campus R&D budgets devoted to "development," never large outside the federal contract centers, was only 2.9 percent in 1963. Between 1953 and 1963 the total federal budget for R&D grew by 250 percent in constant dollars, and the proportion obligated to universities grew by 455 percent. During the same period, and largely as a consequence, sponsored research expenditures at American universities grew from $255 million to $1.1 billion, and the federal share of the funding grew from 54 percent in 1953 to 70 percent in 1963.

During the half-decade following *Sputnik*, three separate studies of the university–federal government relationship agreed on two conclusions. First, the ideology of basic research had generally (and somewhat surprisingly) prevailed over the narrow programmatic emphasis of the first postwar decade. Second, by 1963 the research universities no longer feared that large increases in federal funding would distort the university's mission and dominate its research agenda.[23] The post-*Sputnik* surge of federal research funding had indisputably inaugurated a golden age for academic science. In fiscal year 1963, federal R&D funds flowed to universities primarily from six agencies, all of them heavily science-oriented (table 2.1). Only 492 institutions of higher education (of a total of 2,139) were awarded federal R&D funds in fiscal 1963. Of the $830 million total, the top hundred recipients won 90 percent. By 1963 the flood of R&D funds to university campuses, most of it awarded competitively by peer review panels at the NIH, the NSF, and other agencies, was distributed to a growing number of institutions. But it remained concentrated in the hands of a familiar few.[24]

The "Matthew Effect" and the Academic Ratings Game

In 1963, University of California president Clark Kerr, in his famous Godkin lectures at Harvard, applauded the success of the nation's top

"From the cyclotron of Berkeley to the labs of M.I.T.,
We're the lads that you can trust to keep our country strong and free."

twenty research campuses. Kerr called these institutions the "federal grant university." When the U.S. government increased its research support for higher education almost a hundredfold between 1940 and 1960, Kerr observed, "Washington did not waste its money on the sec-

TABLE 2.1

Federal R&D Funding to Academic Institutions, by Funding Agency
(Percentage Distribution), Fiscal 1963

Funding Agency	% of Federal Academic R&D Funding
NIH	36.6
DOD	26.4
NSF	12.9
AEC	8.4
NASA	5.8
USDA	5.0
Other	4.9

Source: National Science Foundation, *Federal Support for Academic Science and Other Educational Activities in Universities and Colleges, Fiscal Years 1963–1966* (Washington, D.C.: U.S. Government Printing Office, 1967).

Abbreviations: AEC, Atomic Energy Commission; DOD, Department of Defense; NASA, National Aeronautics and Space Administration; NIH, National Institutes of Health; NSF, National Science Foundation; USDA, U.S. Department of Agriculture.

ond-rate."[25] With becoming candor, Kerr echoed the meritocratic sentiments of James Conant, the former Harvard president appointed by Truman in 1951 as the first chairman of the National Science Board, the policy-advisory body for the National Science Foundation. In the NSF's first annual report Conant wrote (with a gender bias that was then commonplace): "In the advance of science and its application to many practical problems, there is no substitute for first-class men. Ten second-rate scientists or engineers cannot do the work of one who is in the first rank."[26]

The consequence of applying the competitive principles of meritocratic science in the national interest, Kerr agreed, was that federal research expenditures had been heavily focused on a relatively few institutions. "If both project research and large research centers are included," Kerr said, "six universities received 57 percent of the funds in a recent fiscal year, and twenty universities received 79 percent." "These twenty universities are only about one tenth of all universities in the United States," Kerr concluded. "They constitute the primary federal grant universities."[27]

Kerr did not identify the top twenty universities by name. Specific information about which universities received how many tax dollars from the federal government in any given year was difficult to obtain from government sources until the late 1960s, when the NSF began to publish the annual distribution of federal obligations to specific universities and colleges. When institutional-level data for 1963 was made public in 1966, Kerr's assessment of the concentration of research support was confirmed.[28] In a felicitous phrase, Kerr referred to the postwar partnership between the national government and the federal grant universities as "a common-law marriage unblessed by predetermined policies" but bound by a mutual self-interest.[29] The leading research universities, having attracted the top talent, were increasingly supported by a system of institutional funding that in effect required the part-time leasing of the research faculty. The system was mutually beneficial to the main buyers (government agencies) and sellers (top research universities), but it posed a political problem: tax dollars were concentrated on a small number of prestigious universities, at least half of them private institutions associated with high tuitions, selective admissions, and affluent alumni.

In 1967 the sociologist of science Robert K. Merton of Columbia University, seeking a metaphor to capture the phenomenon of the rich getting richer in the competitive world of science, turned to the Gospel according to St. Matthew, a favorite text of Protestant Calvinists. In his parable of the "talents" on the Mount of Olives, Jesus praised the stewardship of "good and faithful servants" whose profitable industry demonstrated signs of election into the Kingdom of Heaven: "For unto every one that hath shall be given, and he shall have abundance: but from him that hath not shall be taken away even that which he hath" (Matt. 25:29). Merton was examining the impact of prestige on the scientific reward system. In particular, he focused on the halo effect of Nobel laureates on their institutions, the tendency of the world's most prestigious prize to distort the field of scientific recognition. Merton called this the "Matthew effect."[30] At the level of individual competition, the attention showered on the work of Nobel laureates crowded out the work of non-Nobel scientists, despite their considerable achievement and distinction. Drawing on interviews with Nobel science laureates conducted by his student, Harriet Zuckerman, Merton emphasized the large number of eminent scientists who labored all their days in the shadow of giants.

Zuckerman's research on Nobel laureates demonstrated a parallel Matthew effect for elite institutions. Like the scientific celebrities they recruited, the elite research universities were sharply graded in achievement and recognition. "The two stratification hierarchies—of individuals and organizations—are in fact tightly interconnected through exchanges of prestige and through self-selection and selective recruitment," Zuckerman wrote.[31] The American Nobel laureates had been educated as undergraduates at a small number of prestigious private institutions dominated by the Ivy League, and at the leading public research universities. Columbia had conferred the baccalaureate on seven Nobel laureates, Harvard on five, Yale and MIT on four each, and Chicago and Caltech on three each. Among the public institutions, the University of California at Berkeley led with four, and three each had graduated from Illinois, Wisconsin, and the City College of New York (CCNY), the "people's Harvard" of the American immigrant success story.

The success of CCNY notwithstanding, Zuckerman found that America's Nobel science laureates had been educated not in the classrooms of the people's colleges and universities but rather in the laboratories of Nobel prize-winning faculty, most of them at private elite universities. Of the 77 laureates in Zuckerman's sample, Harvard had awarded the doctorate to 16.2 percent, followed by Columbia with 14.9 percent.[32] Berkeley, Johns Hopkins, and Princeton were tied with 8.1 percent each. These five universities, four of them private, had provided the doctoral training for more than *half* (55.4%) of America's Nobel laureates. Ten institutions—including the five just mentioned, as well as Chicago (6.8%), Caltech (5.4%), and Illinois, MIT, and Yale (4% each) — accounted for almost four-fifths of all American Nobel winners' doctorates. The preeminence of these institutions, moreover, was not limited to Nobel science laureates. The same ten schools had provided the doctoral training for 71.4 percent of American scientists elected to membership in the prestigious National Academy of Sciences from 1900 through 1967.

By 1963, a generation of merit competition had left most federal research support still concentrated in the hands of a small group of elite institutions. In fiscal year 1963, federal agencies obligated a total of $1.4 billion ($6 billion in 1990 dollars) to American universities and colleges. Of the 1,487 four-year and 584 two-year campuses in the United States in 1963, 840 received federal funds. Support for R&D was by far the largest category of federal aid to the campuses. The twenty top-ranked universities received approximately half the federal R&D allocation of $813 million ($3.5 billion in 1990 dollars). The top-ranked ten universities in terms of federal support claimed approximately one-third of the project R&D total, and more than half (53%) of the federal contract center funds. Moreover, a majority of the top ten, and of the top twenty as well, were private universities. Support for science and technology so dominated federal funding for American universities and colleges that in 1963 only 6 percent of the $1.4 billion that campuses received was awarded for nonscientific purposes.[33] Funds for R&D — competitive awards from federal agencies to support campus research proposals, as distinct from the highly specialized contract centers, such as Los Alamos or the Kitt Peak National Observatory — constituted 62 percent of the federal budget for academic science in 1963. The top twenty recipient universities, ranked in order of their R&D totals in 1963, were as follows:

1.	MIT	11.	Minnesota
2.	Columbia	12.	Cornell
3.	Michigan	13.	Pennsylvania
4.	Berkeley	14.	Johns Hopkins
5.	Harvard	15.	Wisconsin
6.	Chicago	16.	Yale
7.	Stanford	17.	Washington (Seattle)
8.	UCLA	18.	Ohio State
9.	Illinois	19.	Texas
10.	New York University	20.	Pittsburgh

The list, reported for the first time by the NSF in 1966, was familiar. The NSF's top twenty in federal R&D looked remarkably like the customary pecking order of university prestige that had been appearing in periodic rankings since early in the century.

In chapter 1 we referred to a pioneering study of twenty-four graduate programs in thirty-eight doctorate-granting universities conducted in 1925 by Raymond M. Hughes, then president of Iowa State College. Hughes ranked only individual departments in the various disciplines, but others converted his departmental scores into institutional rankings.[34] The ten top-ranked universities according to data from the Hughes study were Chicago, Harvard, Columbia, Yale, Wisconsin, Princeton, Johns Hopkins, Michigan, Berkeley, and Cornell.[35] In 1957, Hayward Keniston of the University of Pennsylvania surveyed department chairmen in twenty-five "leading" American universities. From their rankings of the quality of graduate departments in the arts and sciences, Keniston constructed the following overall institutional ranking:[36]

1.	Harvard	11.	Pennsylvania
2.	Berkeley	12.	Michigan
3.	Columbia	13.	Stanford
4.	Yale	14.	UCLA
5.	Michigan	15.	Indiana
6.	Chicago	16.	Johns Hopkins
7.	Princeton	17.	Northwestern
8.	Wisconsin	18.	Ohio State
9.	Cornell	19.	New York University
10.	Illinois	20.	Washington

Keniston's top-twenty ranking included campuses with strong reputations in graduate education, such as Princeton and Indiana, that in 1963 were not among the top twenty recipients of R&D funding, in part because they lacked NIH-funded medical schools.[37] In 1963 the NIH provided $567 million, or approximately one-third, of all federal R&D funding given to the campuses. This made the NIH the largest distributor of R&D funds among the mission agencies, and in the competition for research dollars gave a strong advantage to campuses with medical schools.

In 1966 the ACE sponsored another reputational survey of graduate education, directed by Allan Cartter. The Cartter study, based on reputational rankings by outside experts, expanded both the number of departments surveyed and the institutional and respondent base.[38] Cartter was careful to avoid compiling a controversial grand ranking, with the invidious comparisons that might result among the

ACE's constituent universities. Consequently, the Cartter study of 1966—and its successor, the ACE-sponsored Roose-Andersen study published in 1970—concentrated on graduate program assessments in specific disciplines.[39] Other scholars, however, converted these disaggregated comparisons into grand rankings.[40] For the Cartter study, this produced once again a familiar array of institutional leaders:

1.	Berkeley	11.	Cornell
2.	Harvard	12.	Minnesota
3.	Wisconsin	13.	Johns Hopkins
4.	Michigan	14.	UCLA
5.	Stanford	15.	Pennsylvania
6.	Yale	16.	Washington
7.	Columbia	17.	Northwestern
8.	Illinois	18.	Caltech
9.	Chicago	19.	Indiana
10.	Princeton	20.	Texas

The academic community, fascinated by the ratings game, concentrated its attention on the rising stars such as Stanford and UCLA, and on the ostensibly declining ones, such as Pittsburgh and Ohio State. Most striking however, was the continuity of leadership among America's elite universities.

Science and Higher Education Policy during the Kennedy and Johnson Presidencies

Populist and geographic resentment of the elite institutions had given a sharp edge to the postwar debate over American science policy. As a consequence, the research establishment in the universities, foundations, and federal funding agencies was reluctant to publicize the institutional distribution of tax dollars. The populist complaints of the 1940s led by West Virginia's James Kilgore had represented the fading fires of New Deal liberalism, with its confidence in government and its suspicion of business motives. These complaints quieted after 1945, however, as the economy boomed, the cold war intensified, federal funding expanded, especially during the Eisenhower years, and a more conservative atmosphere prevailed.[41] The Seaborg Report of 1960, following close on the heels of *Sputnik*, called for doubling the number of "first-rate centers of academic science."[42] But this was a distributionist, not a redistributionist, proposal, advanced by confident scientific elites whose prestige was still unchallenged.

On the eve of the Free Speech Movement at Berkeley in 1964, however, resentment of favored elites was rekindled. There was a resumption of populist complaints about the disproportionate flow of funds to prestigious universities, especially to heavily endowed private institutions. Congressional critics attacked the geographic concentration of funding in the Ivy League, the Big Ten universities, and the Pacific Coast campuses. Between 1954 and 1964, total federal expenditures for R&D had grown from $3 billion to $14.7 billion, and appropriations of this magnitude drew the attention of congressional hearings. In 1963 the House Committee on Science held hearings on the distribution of federal R&D support, and in 1964 the committee issued a report criticizing federal agencies for concentrating research support in a handful of favored states, most of them in the Northeast and the West.[43] Most commonly at the top in receipt of federal research support were California, Illinois, Maryland and the District of Columbia, Massachusetts, Nevada, New Mexico, and New York. Most commonly at the bottom were southern and Great Plains states, such as Arkansas, Kentucky, Mississippi, Nebraska, North and South Dakota, South Carolina, and West Virginia. Federal R&D investments were concentrated in a few prestigious university communities, the committee found, at the expense of economically distressed areas, small business, and small colleges. Elite universities seemed to be clustered together, pulling talented young people toward developed centers of science, technology, and research. This created a brain drain, the committee report concluded, that widened the gap between the nation's prosperous and depressed areas.[44]

Government officials testifying before the House science committee generally recommended a proven, positive-sum strategy: Congress should continue to fund the established R&D programs while encouraging the agencies to develop new programs to address the problems of geographic maldistribution. Leland J. Haworth, head of the NSF, defended the geographic distribution of his agency's research funds, explaining that the government must "not go to the institutions which would first have to build up a capability," but rather should turn to "our great centers of scientific and technological activity" even though they were "quite concentrated geographically."[45] Donald F. Hornig, director of the Office of Science and Technology and the chief scientific advisor for presidents Kennedy and Johnson, agreed: the "first criterion for funding an R&D program by Government agencies is the excellence of the institution. The capability of this country for accomplishing development efficiently and effectively is commendable and must not be changed."[46]

Spokesmen for the leading research universities concurred: "The use of funds solely for the purpose of expanding geographical scientific base could be dangerous," argued Caltech president Lee A. DuBridge. "Money might be contributed to small universities which do not have the potential to carry out their scientific and technological objectives. This would result in a waste of money." "To disperse scientific know-how across the Nation on some political basis," warned Yale president Kingman Brewster, "would slow down, if not destroy, the American scientific effort." "Although the number of first-rate teaching and research centers should be increased geographically," acknowledged ACE president Logan Wilson, "it does not seem sensible to take funds away from scientifically excellent institutes and to spread these funds thinly among aspiring institutions."

In 1964, however, the tide of liberal-populist politics was resurgent. Lyndon Johnson's electoral triumph carried a mandate for a Great Society agenda that emphasized redistributive programs for social equality as well as distributive programs to stimulate economic growth. The House science report recommended giving the building of new research centers priority over strengthening old ones. To avoid "undue dependence on the customary technological centers," the report concluded, "priority should be given to support for new facilities in the less favored areas."[47]

The following year, President Johnson, a graduate of Southwest Texas State Teachers College, signed an executive order directing all agencies to administer their research support programs "not only with a view to producing specific results, but also with a view to strengthening academic institutions and increasing the number of institutions capable of performing research of high quality." Explaining his order to the Cabinet, Johnson complained that research funds were "still concentrated in too few institutions in too few areas of the country." "At present," Johnson said, "one-half of the federal expenditures for research go to 20 major institutions, most of which were strong before the advent of Federal research funds."[48]

Johnson's executive order came at the legislative apex of his presidency and fell in the middle of the longest unbroken period of peacetime prosperity in American history. During the boom years 1962–69 the country's economic growth rate doubled, its gross national product grew by $500 billion, more than 10 million new jobs were created, and real per capita income increased by one-fifth.[49] The rising economic tide enabled Democratic leaders in the White House and

Congress to practice the incremental, coalition-building politics of interest-group liberalism. Unlike the 1930s, when lack of economic growth created a zero-sum environment that helped to limit and foreshorten the New Deal's redistributionist reforms, the 1960s enjoyed a period of economic growth that eased the tensions between the distributive politics of the scientific and university establishment and the redistributive politics of the congressional populists and the land-grant institutions.

Johnson built on a program base of federal aid launched in the wake of *Sputnik,* when as Senate majority leader and later as vice president he had worked to expand the federal investment in defense-related science and also to extend its benefits to a wider range of institutions and regions. When Congress passed the NDEA in 1958, it created a new program of graduate fellowships, most of them in science and engineering, and directed the Office of Education to correct for the maldistribution of Ph.D.'s and doctoral programs by concentrating new resources in areas of the country, such as the Southeast, where "doctoral programs were weakest."[50] In 1963 President Kennedy, though unable to persuade Congress to aid elementary and secondary education, signed into law the Higher Education Facilities Act. This statute launched an expansive program of grants and loans to universities and colleges for building and equipping classrooms, laboratories, and libraries. By 1968 the program was distributing more than $1 billion annually to both private and public institutions, many of which had never before received federal aid. Between 1963 and 1966 the number of institutions receiving federal support of some kind increased more than two and a half times, from 840 to 2,174.[51] By the end of Johnson's presidency, new statutes and executive orders in higher education and federal research policy had expanded the budgets of existing programs while also allowing elected policy makers to extend federal aid to underserved regions, previously neglected institutions, and new constituencies.

In 1965, the Great Society's peak year of legislative productivity, Johnson signed the two most significant laws of his presidency for higher education. These were the Higher Education Act and the National Foundation for the Arts and Humanities Act. Like most legislation of the 1960s, both laws were primarily distributive, adding programs to serve new beneficiaries while increasing benefits for existing client groups. The Higher Education Act (HEA) of 1965 was a companion to the Johnson administration's breakthrough Elementary and Secondary Education Act (ESEA) of 1965, but the higher education statute lacked the ESEA's accompanying robust budget. Johnson preferred to provide "off-budget" aid for college costs by subsidizing tuition loans from private lending institutions. (Congress later would provide major funding for tuition aid during Nixon's presidency.) Nevertheless, the HEA authorized for the first time a program of federal scholarships to undergraduate students. The act also included, in Title III, a program of grants for "developing institutions," which were small, isolated, impoverished colleges. Because the Johnson administration's education legislation was politically driven by the momentum of the civil rights movement and the war on poverty, the intended beneficiaries of Title III were the approximately one hundred historically black colleges. But because the administration insisted on nondiscriminatory social programs, the most numerous potential beneficiaries of Title III were historically white, rural, sectarian colleges whose institutional resources were similarly depressed.[52]

The second higher education law in Johnson's Great Society legislation of 1965 established public foundations for the arts and humanities. By creating separate national "endowments" for the arts and the humanities, it provided a sponsoring agency for two groups not previously funded to any significant extent by the federal government. One beneficiary was the large and varied community of cultural institutions—community theater and dance groups, orchestras and opera companies, and nonaffiliated artists and sculptors—that previously had relied for support on private philanthropy and state and local governments. The National Endowment for the Arts (NEA), as the new federal funding agency for this constituency, thus dealt primarily with noncampus organizations and individuals.

The second new constituency given federal support consisted of scholars in the humanities and professionals serving related cultural institutions—museums, libraries, special collections, and archives. The National Endowment for the Humanities (NEH) provided fellowships for scholars in the humanities disciplines (chiefly classics, literature, history, and philosophy), and program grants for cultural resources (the acquisition and processing of collections, the preservation of documents, and the expansion of access to collections). Thus, unlike the NEA, the NEH developed a large, campus-based constituency: the forty thousand teaching faculty in the humanities disciplines on college and university campuses. The annual budgets for the two endowments remained quite small by comparison with the support budgets of the major funding agencies, and support from the endowments often required matching contributions from recipient institutions. In fiscal 1968 the NEA program budget was $7 million and the NEH budget was $6 million. Nonetheless, the nation's artists and humanists had finally gotten their camel's nose under the large tent of federal aid, joining farmers, veterans, scientists, engineers, and, since 1958, specialists in education, international relations, foreign languages, and area studies. By the end of 1965 all of the major academic blocs except social scientists had a formally designated agency sponsor for their research. Social scientists continued to rely on private foundations, most notably the Carnegie, Rockefeller, and Ford foundations, and on token support from the NSF. By the mid-1960s, however, the NIH (including the National Institute of Mental Health) was providing more than 40 percent of federal support for sociology and psychology.[53]

In 1965 President Johnson, a Texas populist who shared Harley Kilgore's resentment of northeastern elites, directed all agencies to develop research capacities outside the customary favored circle of established universities. Johnson warned agency heads that he would closely monitor their response, and the agencies heeded the message. The NSF in 1965 established a new program of awards to departments, colleges, and universities to develop their capability for science teaching and research. The following year the NIH began a similar program of awards to develop new institutional strengths in the health sciences. In 1967 the Department of Defense announced Project THEMIS, which would widen the distribution of defense-related grants to institutions not previously so engaged. By 1967, growing academic opposition to the Vietnam War produced campus-based opposition to THEMIS. But the criticism came primarily from the established research universities, where opposition to the Vietnam War was strongest, not from campuses where Defense support might be extended.[54] By 1968, agency justifications for federal aid to institutions ranged the spectrum from the traditional merit competition — the vintage Bush and Conant approach, which excluded the second-rate — through program assistance to accelerate the maturing of promising new centers of excellence, to remedial aid programs such as Title III, in which the chief criterion for receiving federal grants was institutional weakness.

Congress in 1968 rounded out the liberal policy revisions of the Great Society by amending the 1950 law establishing the National Science Foundation. One provision of the 1968 amendments formally added support for the social sciences to NSF responsibilities. The orphaned social sciences had at last won official agency sponsorship. But whereas the arts and the humanities had in 1965 won their own agency, the research interests of social scientists remained ancillary to the main agenda of their sponsoring agency. The NSF accepted the inclusion of social scientists within the fraternity of scientists only partially and grudgingly. Both the agency's leadership and its scientific constituency had traditionally regarded social science research, however competent in design and execution, as inherently applied rather than basic, and therefore not appropriate for NSF support.[55] Nonetheless, as of 1968, support for the nation's cadre of 253,500 campus-based scientists and engineers would include assistance for 52,900 social scientists. Second in number only to the country's 102,800 academic life scientists, the campus social science constituency in 1968 outnumbered the physical scientists (34,300), engineers (25,800), and mathematicians (22,800).[56] The 1968 amendments also broadened the NSF's jurisdiction to include applied as well as basic research, and imposed new requirements of accountability on the agency.[57]

Finally, the 1968 amendments required the NSF to report annually to Congress on the state of academic science and research. This began the foundation's important statistical series *Federal Support to Universities, Colleges, and Selected Nonprofit Institutions*, which annually provided detailed information on the distribution of federal support according to funding agency and recipient organization.[58] Reporting on fiscal year 1968, the NSF for the first time published the amount and purpose of the support awarded by federal agencies to each university and college in the nation. The NSF's first comprehensive statistical report, published in 1969, told a story of extraordinary expansion of federal assistance to the nation's campuses, accompanied by continued, though reduced, concentration of research funding in the familiar citadels of top-ranked universities.

In the key congressional compromise of the 1960s, R&D funds for the science-dominated university research establishment were doubled, and support for areas outside of science research were quadrupled. Robust economic growth during most of the 1960s enabled political leaders in Washington not only to support the post-*Sputnik* agenda of generously increased funding for the existing programs in higher education and beneficiary groups (medical professionals, physical scientists, engineers, and mathematicians) but also to start new programs to serve additional professional constituencies (the arts, humanities, and social sciences) and institutions (state colleges, developing institutions, community colleges, and private liberal arts colleges). At the heart of the political negotiation that kept the peace among competing constituent groups was a basic accommodation between the interests of, on the one hand, roughly one hundred doctorate-granting, research-oriented universities, and, on the other hand, the more than two thousand institutions whose primary concern was undergraduate teaching. In pluralist bargaining under conditions of prosperity, the haves received more, and the have-nots were included.

The golden age in federal funding of academic research was the post-*Sputnik* decade, 1958–68. In that span, federal R&D funding for universities jumped from $254 million to $1.57 billion, an increase of 618 percent in nominal dollars and 523 percent when controlled for inflation. Between 1958 and 1968, the nation's total academic research expenditures more than tripled. Federal funds for basic university research rose from $178 million to $1,251 million — a sevenfold increase.[59] The number of academic research personnel in doctorate-granting universities grew from thirteen thousand to twenty-three thousand in public institutions and from twelve thousand to twenty-three thousand in private institutions. With increased funding, average combined operational and capital expenditures for these researchers rose on a per capita basis from $94,000 to $188,000 (in 1990 dollars).[60]

The first constituency to benefit from the growing federal largesse was the best organized and most respected: the two-score research universities whose interests were represented by the AAU.[61] When the funding surge initiated by the Kennedy and Johnson administrations began in 1963, federal support for universities already stood at levels unprecedented in history, especially for the top-ranked research campuses. That year, the federal project R&D funding provided to universities and colleges totaled $829 million, an amount that had increased five and a half times since 1953. By 1963 even the great public universities, such as UC Berkeley and Michigan, received more money for annual operations from the federal government than from their own state legislatures. Between 1963 and 1968, federal R&D support to universities doubled again. And the budgets of the two federal agencies whose missions concentrated on basic university research, the NIH and the NSF, almost doubled as well. The extramural research budget of the NIH, the largest single agency budget for university research, increased from $298 million in 1963 to $560 million in 1968.[62] The NSF's R&D obligations grew during the same period from $105 million to $213 million.[63]

Despite the explosion of federal R&D funding during the 1960s, the most dramatic growth in programs and budgets for higher education lay elsewhere. The federal bonanza for higher education during 1963–68 was so great that the R&D component, which increased by 70 percent, nonetheless *decreased* (from 60% to 42%) as a share of total federal outlays to the campuses. Total federal support for universities and colleges in the five years following 1963 increased by 140 percent, from $1.41 billion to $3.37 billion. Most of the new funds went to two areas. One was "other science," meaning primarily science education programs. Department of Health, Education, and Welfare (HEW) and NSF expenditures for science education grew rapidly during the 1960s, although they remained modest at the Department of Defense, NASA, and the AEC, agencies where R&D funds primarily supported development contracts with industry and university-administered contract centers.

More striking was the growth in federal support for "nonscience" activities, most of which was confined to HEW. In 1963 the Higher Education Facilities Act triggered a budgetary explosion at HEW, most of it in construction grants and loans for college classrooms, laboratories, and libraries. The HEW budget of $84 million in 1963 zoomed to $983 million in 1968, an increase of 1,166 percent. By 1968 HEW, including the NIH, was by far the largest funding agency for the nation's campuses. A conglomerate "superagency," HEW presided over two fairly independent subempires: the NIH, the research arm of the Public Health Service and since World War II the aggressive entrepreneur of biomedical research; and the Office of Education (USOE), long the runt in HEW, now a prime mover of social reconstruction.[64] By 1968 HEW, with its expenditure of $2.21 billion to universities and colleges, provided two-thirds of all federal support to the campuses. Roughly half of the HEW obligations ($943 million in 1968) came from the NIH and supported research in medical schools and life science departments. A similar amount, $932 million in 1968, came from the USOE to support nonscience programs and campus construction, including the Title III program of aid for developing institutions.

By 1968 federal assistance in some direct form reached 92 percent of the nation's 2,734 colleges and universities. Only about 200 institutions failed to receive some form of direct federal assistance in 1968 under the new dispensation of the Great Society, and only a small minority of these had refused on principle to ask for it. Most of the nonapplicants were church-affiliated colleges fearful of secular controls from government agencies.[65] Yet most institutions in most states received no research funding. Federal R&D support was won in 1968 by fewer than a third of the 135 colleges and universities in California, where the University of California had research priority, and by only 28 of the 98 campuses in Illinois. Indeed, in California the 9 campuses of the University of California system, plus the state's 3 major private institutions — Caltech, Stanford, and the University of

Southern California (USC)—accounted for 97 percent of the federal R&D funding for universities in the state. In Illinois, only 2 universities, the flagship campus at Urbana and the private University of Chicago, accounted for three-fourths of the state's federal R&D total. By 1968 there was little doubt that Berkeley and Stanford, and Illinois and Chicago, were world leaders. What remained unclear was whether the postwar explosion of federal funding for research and institutional development, when combined with investments by state and local governments and private institutions, was building a new group of first-class universities to enliven the competition so long dominated by traditional elites.[66]

The evidence pointed to continued concentration. But it was skewed in two respects. First, reputational rankings drew attention to established leaders and obscured the efforts of challengers. The top twenty included UC Berkeley and Michigan but not UC Santa Barbara and SUNY–Stony Brook; Harvard and Stanford, but not Brandeis and Rochester. Second, the tradition of judging "horsepower" by amassing institutional totals, as in the annual rankings of the top hundred federal R&D winners, conflated quantity and quality. It was difficult to compare the research quality of faculty at universities both large and small, with established and newly developed reputations. How could the research quality of universities be compared, using objective measures and controlling for institutional size?

In the next chapter we describe a method of per capita comparison of research achievement that controls for institutional size. We use per capita measures to level the playing field on which research universities are evaluated in terms of resources, achievement, and prestige. When we first applied per capita measures to institutional data from the late 1960s in order to compare campus performance in federal R&D awards, scientific publications, and fellowships in the arts and humanities, we found evidence of challenges to the expected academic pecking order. When measured by per capita standards some of the top-ranked elite schools slipped, while other campuses rose. Some universities not included among the top-ranked twenty or twenty-five in the reputational surveys outperformed traditional leaders.

What most surprised us, however, were pronounced differences in performance among *types* of institutions. By controlling both for the size advantage that skewed the horsepower rankings and for the Matthew effect that skewed the reputational ratings, per capita comparisons of institutional research performance revealed important structural variables that contributed to research success. Most striking by far was the powerful advantage in research productivity that private universities enjoyed over their public competitors, and the advantage that campuses with medical schools enjoyed over campuses without them.

3

■

COMPARING UNIVERSITIES IN THE GOLDEN DECADE OF THE 1960S

In this chapter we pause in the historical narrative to describe our per capita method and use it to compare faculty research performance at the end of the "golden" 1960s. The method has three components: a defined universe of institutions, a set of objective indicators for measuring research performance, and a way of controlling for institutional size. The first was provided by the Carnegie Commission on Higher Education, which in 1970 devised a classification system that was subsequently revised in 1976, 1987, and 1994. To measure research performance we selected indicators that provide objective evidence of scholarly activity across the academic spectrum. For the 1960s we measured federal R&D awards, publications in scientific journals, and fellowships in the arts and humanities. Finally, to control for institutional size we divided the results in each category by the number of full-time instructional faculty on each campus.

We describe the method more fully in the Note on Method and Sources. In the book's concluding chapters we compare university performance during 1980–90, using more abundant data (for example, five indicators of research performance rather than three). As a consequence, in later chapters we emphasize the relative achievements of individual campuses and stress the book's central theme, the rise of research universities not traditionally considered among the top-ranked.

In discussing the 1960s, however, we emphasize not individual universities but rather groups or types of institutions that show similar patterns of performance.[1] Per capita comparisons using the 1960s data show wide variations in performance by certain types of institutions and provide strong support for generalizations about why certain types of universities outperform others. Such comparisons reveal surprisingly large differences in the performance of faculty at universities otherwise thought to be similar. For example, universities found in close proximity in the top-twenty rankings of 1966 or 1970 might reasonably be expected to show similar levels of research performance irrespective of whether they are publicly or privately controlled. Yet among top-rated universities, per capita comparisons show a persistent and large margin of superiority in private institutions. Per capita comparisons also highlight the positive effect of medical schools on scientific research, and underline the diverse responsibilities of public sector institutions.

Identifying Research Universities: The Carnegie Classification System

Historically, the tradition of rank-ordering the elite campuses has served several purposes. The studies that identified the top twenty or thirty institutions were conducted and read by academics, whose fascination with the ratings game was rooted partly in their competitive instincts and partly in alumni loyalty to old-school affiliations. Paradoxically, hunger for confirmation of academic prestige also reflected the ambiguity of status inherent in America's decentralized, pluralistic, competitive system of higher education. (Status anxiety, as Tocqueville observed, was a concomitant of social fluidity in democratic societies.) Moreover, the method of ranking according to reputation inherently limited the number of institutions compared. The major comparative studies of the "golden age"—the Cartter study of 1966 and its 1970 follow-up, the Roose-Andersen study—were careful to avoid grand rankings.[2] Instead, they hoped to focus attention on the graduate programs being assessed. However, their efforts to balance subjective, reputational rankings with objective measures— such as the number of library volumes or doctoral degrees, or the amount of federal research funding awarded—were frustrated by the university community's fixation on the academic pecking order.[3]

This perennial jockeying for institutional status narrowed the analytic vision of policy makers. To officials in federal funding agencies, in which peer-review panels annually awarded the lion's share of federal research dollars to a small group of elite institutions, comparative studies of the leading graduate programs were of modest utility.[4] To leaders of the liberal-populist coalition in Congress, such studies confirmed the problem of geographic concentration and private privilege. To governors and state legislative leaders attempting to build more comprehensive higher education systems, national rankings such as the list of the top twenty-five institutions drawn from the ACE-sponsored Cartter study, which included private universities in only sixteen states and public universities in only nine, were not helpful. In the traditional academic ratings game, perception of institutional achievement faded rapidly with decreasing rank; somewhere not very far beyond the number twenty-five, the country's more than seventeen hundred four-year campuses blurred into a vast collage. It was partly for this reason that in 1970 the Carnegie Commission on Higher Education, convinced of the need for a new classification scheme that would identify the different functional types of institutions and legitimize their differences, designed a more varied taxonomy for the country's more than twenty-eight hundred institutions of higher education.

From the research-oriented perspective of this study, the provenance of the Carnegie system for classifying research universities is ironic. Accepted after 1970 as the standard taxonomy for American higher education, the Carnegie system was designed to pull the attention of policy makers away from the nation's research institutions, and to emphasize instead the variety and social importance of the vast majority of institutions that were not research oriented. The Carnegie Commission, established in 1967 by the Carnegie Foundation for the Advancement of Teaching, supported the broad shift toward goals of social justice and equal opportunity which complemented the government, foundation, and academic emphasis during the 1960s. Policy makers shifted their focus from strengthening academic research capacity to expanding educational access for previously excluded groups — blacks, Hispanics, working women, and the children of parents who themselves had not attended college.[5]

The goal of the Carnegie Commission, headed by Clark Kerr, was to use Carnegie prestige as leverage to change the way in which money was invested in American higher education. This required expanding the traditionally elitist definition of "higher education" to encompass the full spectrum of "postsecondary" education. It meant emphasizing the neglected role of two-year community colleges, vocational and proprietary institutions, technical and specialized schools, and "comprehensive universities" — the Carnegie Commission's term for four-year, masters-level institutions. To facilitate statistical projections and policy planning, the Carnegie staff developed a taxonomy of five institutional categories and eighteen subcategories. In the first report based on the new classification system, the commission concluded, "We find no need whatsoever in the foresee-

TABLE 3.1

Carnegie Classification of Institutions of Higher Education, and Enrollment, by Type and Public/Private Status, 1970

Type of Institution	Enrollment (thousands)			Percentage		Number of Institutions			Percentage	
	Total	Public	Private	Public	of Total	Total	Public	Private	Public	of Total
Total	8,520	6,372	2,148	74.8	100.0	2,837	1,322	1,515	46.6	100.0
Doctorate-granting institutions	2,674	2,028	646	75.8	31.4	173	109	64	63.0	6.1
Research universities I	1,097	843	254	76.8	12.9	52	30	22	57.7	1.8
Research universities II	611	499	112	81.7	7.2	40	27	13	67.5	1.4
Doctorate-granting universities I	641	421	220	65.6	7.5	53	34	19	64.2	1.9
Doctorate-granting universities II	325	265	60	81.7	3.8	28	18	10	64.3	1.0
Comprehensive universities and colleges	2,519	1,981	538	78.6	29.6	456	309	147	67.8	16.1
Liberal arts colleges	690	43	647	6.3	8.1	721	32	689	4.4	25.4
Two-year institutions	2,347	2,214	133	94.3	27.5	1,063	808	255	76.0	37.5
Specialized institutions	290	106	184	36.5	3.4	424	64	360	15.1	14.9

Source: Reprinted from Carnegie Commission on Higher Education, A Classification of Institutions of Higher Education (Berkeley, Calif.: Carnegie Commission on Higher Education, 1973).

able future for any more research-type universities granting the PhD."[6]

The Carnegie classification of 1970, first used in-house for the commission's planning and published in 1973, included 2,837 institutions. Only 173 of these were classified as doctorate-granting institutions. The remaining 94 percent of the campuses, enrolling 68.5 percent of the country's 8.5 million students, were classified as comprehensive universities and colleges, liberal arts colleges, two-year institutions, or specialized institutions. The Carnegie system divided the 173 doctorate-granting universities into four categories, classifying each by type of control (public or private), as summarized in table 3.1.

The Carnegie taxonomy was simple. Only two threshold variables were used to assign institutions to the four categories: annual totals of federal financial support, and annual awards of doctoral degrees.[7] The Carnegie system, revised in 1976, 1987, and 1994 to reflect institutional change, has provided an important common standard of classification and reference in higher education research. Its simple, functional definitions classifying the doctorate-granting universities have produced, with a few exceptions, sensible and useful group assignments. By listing institutions alphabetically by state within categories, it avoided many of the abuses of ordinal rankings. And by dividing all categories into public sector and private sector subgroups, the Carnegie system recognized the centrality of pluralist control in the American system—a recognition largely avoided or minimized in other analytical or reporting systems, including those produced by federal government agencies and by the American Association of University Professors (AAUP).[8]

Horsepower Rankings and University Size

For all its utility and convenience, however, the Carnegie system provided only a taxonomy, not a system of measurement and comparison. It was never intended to be such a system. Coming at the end of the 1960s, the Carnegie classification helped expand the narrow universe of research universities identified by the periodic top-twenty-five ratings. (By 1994, Carnegie's Research and Doctoral categories would include 236 institutions.) By the late 1960s, the National Science Foundation's annual statistical reports provided a convenient new source of ordinal data, especially with regard to federal R&D obligations. This expanded the rank-ordered comparisons to include as many as one hundred institutions. But it provided no relief from the tendency of horsepower contests to conflate quantity and quality.

The need to control for institutional size when comparing the research achievement of universities is illustrated by an examination of the flow of federal R&D dollars to the campuses. When the NSF in 1968 began publishing a list of the leading one hundred institutions in federal R&D support for each fiscal year, the top-hundred ranking in federal R&D became the most frequently cited barometer of university research prowess. The *Chronicle of Higher Education,* which was founded in 1967 and quickly captured the exploding campus market, made the NSF's R&D rankings an annual feature story. The *Chronicle* routinely published lists of academic "horsepower," ranking institutions according to the size of such desirable assets as their endowments, their student enrollments, the number of volumes in their libraries, and the numbers of National Merit semifinalists enrolled, patents received, doctoral degrees awarded, and so forth. The national NSF rankings provided official, objective data showing relative campus success in competing for a crucial component of the research enterprise. But like the other horsepower rankings, the NSF rankings of R&D support ignore institutional size. Comparisons using the 1968 NSF rankings illustrate the problem.

In 1968 virtually all of the institutions listed in the NSF's top-hundred ranking (table 3.2) were respected research universities. But several institutions with top-twenty rankings in the contemporary reputational surveys, the Cartter and Roose-Andersen studies, did not receive enough funding to qualify for the NSF's top third in R&D funding.[9] These included, among private universities, Princeton and Northwestern (ranked 37th and 46th, respectively, in R&D totals), and among public universities, Texas-Austin (40th) and UNC–Chapel Hill (49th). By contrast, several large universities listed among the NSF's top third in R&D totals, such as Ohio State (ranked 19th), Michigan State (25th), Miami (29th), and Pittsburgh (30th), were not ranked in the top twenty by the reputational surveys. Rockefeller University, a smaller institution but one that was unmatched on a pound-for-pound basis in the number of Nobel laureates among the faculty and alumni, and in the award of federal R&D dollars as well, ranked 88th in the amount of federal R&D received.

Beyond such problems as how to compare the quality of Princeton with that of Ohio State—a rather improbable comparison of two powerful but sharply different institutions—was a more intriguing problem. At the elite level of nationally ranked universities, per capita comparisons between public and private institutions can produce

TABLE 3.2

Federal R&D Funding Obligations to the One Hundred Universities and Colleges Receiving the Largest Amounts, Ranked by Amount of Obligation, Fiscal 1968

Institution	Amount (thousands)	Institution	Amount (thousands)
1 MIT	$79,776	51 Pennsylvania State	8,554
2 Stanford	41,407	52 Oregon	8,352
3 Harvard	39,177	53 Kentucky	7,816
4 Michigan	37,754	54 Carnegie Mellon	7,575
5 UC Los Angeles	36,534	55 Tulane	7,557
6 Columbia	34,693	56 Iowa State	7,260
7 UC Berkeley	34,031	57 Vanderbilt	7,190
8 Wisconsin-Madison	30,993	58 Texas A&M	7,186
9 Illinois-Urbana	29,804	59 North Carolina State	7,067
10 Washington (Seattle)	27,940	60 George Washington	6,985
11 Chicago	26,956	61 SUNY-Buffalo	6,961
12 Minnesota	26,378	62 Kansas	6,953
13 New York University	24,318	63 Missouri-Columbia	6,824
14 UC San Diego	23,996	64 Georgia	6,755
15 Cornell	23,306	65 Virginia	6,679
16 Johns Hopkins	22,201	66 Rice	6,674
17 Yale	19,637	67 Alabama-Tuscaloosa	6,594
18 Pennsylvania	18,414	68 Arizona	6,166
19 Ohio State	16,398	69 Texas–M. S. Anderson Hospital	6,147
20 Duke	16,226	70 Alaska	6,101
21 Washington (St. Louis)	14,928	71 Emory	5,783
22 Case Western Reserve	14,690	72 Brown	5,628
23 Maryland	14,253	73 CUNY–Mt. Sinai School of Medicine	5,586
24 Rochester	14,128	74 Cincinnati	5,352
25 Michigan State	13,435	75 New Mexico	5,137
26 Yeshiva	13,418	76 Temple	5,041
27 Caltech	13,211	77 Louisiana State–Baton Rouge	4,892
28 Colorado	13,067	78 Massachusetts	4,876
29 Miami	13,037	79 Denver	4,783
30 Pittsburgh	13,022	80 Boston University	4,760
31 Southern California	12,875	81 Nebraska	4,641
32 UC San Francisco	12,648	82 New Mexico State	4,603
33 Utah	12,429	83 Wayne State	4,602
34 Purdue	11,617	84 Georgia Tech	4,575
35 Indiana	11,531	85 Notre Dame	4,557
36 Baylor (Houston)	11,222	86 Oklahoma	4,276
37 Princeton	10,756	87 Rensselaer	4,085
38 Florida	10,460	88 Rockefeller	4,014
39 Iowa	10,325	89 Texas–Southwestern Medical	3,948
40 Texas-Austin	10,309	90 Dayton	3,924
41 Florida State	10,209	91 Oklahoma State	3,906
42 UC Davis	9,927	92 SUNY Downstate Medical Center	3,864
43 Oregon State	9,814	93 Dartmouth	3,843
44 Tennessee	9,646	94 Kansas State	3,841
45 Hawaii	9,168	95 Washington State	3,839
46 Northwestern	9,001	96 Georgetown	3,793
47 Rutgers–New Brunswick	8,900	97 Arkansas-Fayetteville	3,622
48 Colorado State	8,779	98 New York Medical College	3,599
49 North Carolina–Chapel Hill	8,720	99 Brandeis	3,514
50 Syracuse	8,666	100 West Virginia	3,453

Source: Data from National Science Foundation, *Federal Support of Research and Development at Universities and Colleges and Selected Nonprofit Institutions, Fiscal Year 1968.*

counterintuitive results. The problem may be illustrated, for example, by comparing Stanford and the University of Michigan. Indisputably two of the world's greatest universities, Stanford and Michigan were ranked in the top five according to both the 1966 Cartter study (which ranked Michigan fourth and Stanford fifth) and the 1970 Roose-Andersen study (which ranked Michigan fourth and Stanford third). In the NSF rankings of R&D awards in 1968, both universities were ranked among the top five (Stanford was second and Michigan fourth).[10] Yet Stanford, with a faculty only 40 percent the size of Michigan's, won $41.4 million in federal R&D grants in 1968, as compared with Michigan's total of $37.8 million, suggesting that faculty members at Stanford were on average more than twice as successful as their counterparts at Michigan in winning federal research awards. The national rankings compiled from the Cartter and Roose-Andersen studies, rating the two universities as virtually in a dead heat, seemed intuitively more correct. Yet something important needed explaining, some fundamental difference that appeared to be rooted in the differences between public and private systems of control.

The Value of Per Capita Comparison

In measuring engine performance, automotive engineers calculate ratios of efficiency, such as miles per gallon. Similarly, production of new knowledge by university faculty, if it is to be compared usefully, could be measured in terms of output per researcher. Such comparisons, documented in a substantial literature, have been made with some precision in specific academic disciplines and professions. In such ratings analysts can be precise about the number of researchers (often citing them by name) as well as the output of specific scientific papers, scholarly books and articles, fellowships and prizes, patents, grants, or artistic performances being measured and compared.[11]

For example, in 1989 the *Chicago-Kent Law Review* began publishing an annual ranking of the top fifty law schools based on the frequency of faculty publication in the leading fifty law reviews.[12] The Chicago-Kent rankings demonstrate the advantage of single-discipline comparisons: they offer specificity of field (law), of numerator (number of books, book chapters, law review articles), and of denominator (number of law faculty members). This level of precision brings authority to ordinal rankings, which are inherently controversial, especially among academics and the learned professions. Such comparisons of single fields across institutions, aided by the computerized bibliometrics of citation analysis, avoid the danger of comparing apples and oranges, physicists and poets.[13]

The chief disadvantage of single-field comparisons is compartmentalization. Such comparisons are useful to academics interested in a particular research specialization or in rankings based on disciplines or professions. But they are less useful to campus academic officials, trustees, and business and political leaders who wish to improve their communities and regions by building powerful engines of economic development. The value of research universities as sources of scientific advances, technical training, and economic stimulus has increased in importance to policy makers since the national economic slowdown of the 1970s. Impressed by the success of Silicon Valley, Boston's Route 128, and the Research Triangle in North Carolina during the 1970s and 1980s, political and business leaders have viewed universities through the lens of investment strategy. Commercial exploitation of the campuses posed dangers, but in the new environment of global economic competition, universities were seen as a key to success in the knowledge-based economy of the future. These trends placed a premium on measuring and increasing research productivity across a broad spectrum of scientific and scholarly endeavor.[14]

For American universities, the heart of knowledge-creation lies in the full-time faculty. Modern universities are complex institutions, however, and many productive campus researchers do not hold regular faculty appointments. At research-intensive institutions, sponsored research grants provide direct or indirect support for a variety of researchers who are not tenure-track or tenure-ladder faculty. Clark Kerr called this cadre of ambiguous, soft-money personnel the "unfaculty."[15] They include research and visiting faculty, postdoctoral fellows, research associates, administrative staff, technicians, and graduate students. Studies of individual institutions offer evidence, however, that the universities' tenure-ladder faculty and the sponsored research projects they bring to their institutions account for the vast majority of campus research.[16]

If faculty size is not factored into assessments of institutional productivity, comparisons between campuses may suggest similarities that are misleading or that disguise important differences. For example, when the NSF in 1968 published a list ranking the hundred universities and colleges that received the largest federal R&D awards, Michigan State, with $13.4 million, was ranked twenty-fifth, and Caltech, with $13.2 million, was ranked twenty-seventh. Michigan State, however, had 41,500 students in 1968 and a full-time instructional faculty of 2,049.[17] Caltech had 1,500 students and a full-time faculty of 241. Taking the number of faculty into account, Michigan State had an average of $6,540 in per capita federal R&D support, while Caltech's per capita average was $54,770—more than eight times the Michigan State figure. Both institutions were powerful engines of research in 1968, and were respected members of the Association of American Universities (AAU). Both were rated among the nation's top twenty-five graduate schools in the aggregations based on the Roose-Andersen study of 1970.[18] But the sharp differences in the per capita R&D support levels at Caltech and Michigan State call attention to profound institutional dissimilarities. Many of these are self-evident. Michigan State was a large, public, land-grant university, one that included a new medical school. Caltech was a small, private, scientific institute that lacked not only a medical school but also the full panoply of colleges and schools that typically characterized research universities.[19]

Parity in performance in the various horsepower contests, in fact, told very little about similarities in institutions. Similarities in per capita measurements are thus more reliable guides. In NSF's 1968 ranking of institutions on the basis of federal R & D obligations, Michigan State had little resemblance to its immediate neighbors on the list—two private universities, Rochester and Yeshiva. Rochester's enrollment was only one-fifth the size of Michigan State's and its faculty was only one-third as large. Yeshiva, with only 3,700 students and a full-time faculty of 386, combined a liberal arts emphasis on Hebraic studies with the research-intensive Albert Einstein College of Medicine. When institutional R&D totals were interpreted in terms of faculty size, however, Michigan State was ranked between two universities—Purdue and Missouri—with similar attributes of size, institutional mission, type of control, and levels of research enterprise. Similarly, the schools immediately preceding and following Caltech in a 1968 per capita ranking of R&D funding—MIT and Johns Hopkins, respectively—were small, private, elite institutions, dominated like Caltech by large scientific research enterprises.

The chief virtue of a per capita method of measuring the various research outputs of institutions is not that it produces another and better grand ranking of research universities. Rather, controlling for size permits comparisons that illuminate the most important differences and similarities among an expanded group of research universities without conflating quality and quantity. Using this method we can compare institutions that are similar in mission and constituency (private elite campuses, state flagships, land-grant institutions, scientific and technical institutes, urban Catholic universities, regional groups) and can emphasize how patterns of research performance change over time. These per capita measurements do involve rank-ordered comparisons. Their chief purpose, however, is not to establish or validate an academic pecking order but to help construct a better understanding of the development of American research universities in the postwar era.

In this study we measure faculty achievement across the academic spectrum of creative work, including science and technology, the social and behavioral sciences, and the arts and humanities. Given the practical and financial limits of this study, which includes more than two hundred institutions and measures research productivity over a twenty-five-year period, from 1965 through 1990, we have selected five indicators of faculty research achievement which are aggregated by institution: (1) federal R&D support obligated to the institution; (2) journal articles published by institutional researchers (including articles published in proceedings, symposia, and anthologies); (3) articles published in top-rated science journals; (4) articles published in top-rated social science journals; and (5) fellowships and grants in the arts and humanities. Faculty research productivity is measured over different time periods, with the comparisons clustering around the years 1968, 1974, and 1988. Because data for top-rated science and social science journals was not available until the mid-1970s, our analysis for the 1960s relies on three measures: federal R&D for 1968, publications in science journals in 1968, and fellowships in the arts and humanities during 1965–74. A per capita index of productivity was determined by dividing the results by the number of full-time instructional faculty on each campus. Research performance was then measured and compared, both within institutions and between them, as it changed over time.

The use of per capita measurements and comparisons, like any other method, carries advantages and disadvantages. Among the advantages are the following: First, such measurements avoid the distortions common to horsepower rankings. Second, they permit comparisons across Carnegie (or other) categories or by size, region, functional emphasis, or type of control. They highlight important differences between types of institutions and illuminate the consequences of those differences. For example, per capita comparisons throw into bold relief a surprisingly large advantage in research productivity enjoyed by private universities over their public competitors, especially among Carnegie-classified Research I and II institutions. Similarly, they illuminate the powerful multiplier effect that medical schools have on scientific research on their parent campuses, and they identify the research consequences of multiple missions in state university systems. Finally, they facilitate internal as well as external comparisons of institutional strength and weakness.

Despite their advantages, per capita methods carry disadvantages as well. These are discussed more fully below, in the Note on Method and Sources, but they require a caveat here. First, in per capita comparisons, small numbers of full-time faculty produce high scores for research productivity. Errors in determining the number of full-time faculty are thus magnified. In 1987 the U.S. Department of Education's National Center for Education Statistics (NCES) conducted a National Survey of Postsecondary Faculty that provided more complete information than did the annual surveys of the AAUP and the ACE's periodic editions of *American Universities and Colleges*.[20] Thanks to the NCES survey, comparisons based on full-time institutional faculty for the late 1980s may be made with greater confidence. But the various index ratings for the 1960s and 1970s, especially the ranked comparisons of individual institutions, are offered with greater caution.[21]

A second disadvantage of per capita comparisons of institutional productivity is that measures aggregated at the level of institutions, rather than at the level of discipline or profession, incur a loss of precision. Per capita measures based on faculty productivity across the academic spectrum inescapably combine apples and oranges. Such measures, used to chart changes over time involving more than two hundred institutions, cannot peer very deeply into specific institutions. They are effective for sorting weaker research institutions from stronger ones, with some specificity as to field. But unlike most previous assessments, these per capita measures do not identify strengths at the level of particular departments or graduate programs.

Third, both the method and the evidence carry a scientific bias that does not adequately reflect the full range of knowledge-creation in universities. The most commonly used and readily accessible measures of research effort, such as federal R&D funding and publication counts, carry a pronounced scientific bias.[22] Since 1960, federal support for academic research other than basic and applied science—designated by NSF as social science and "other nonscience"—has rarely exceeded 3 or 4 percent of total federal R&D funds for universities. We devised the top–social science index and the arts and humanities (A&H) index to compensate for this bias. Finally, per capita comparisons are inherently reductionist. They homogenize universities, flattening their institutional personalities and collapsing their histories. This has been an essential cost for conducting this study, but it is a substantial one.

Public-Private Differences and Their Research Consequences

Despite their limitations, per capita comparisons illuminate important characteristics of the American system of higher education that other methods have obscured. One of the most striking of these is the relative advantage in research productivity enjoyed by the leading private universities. As we have seen, when measures such as R&D dollars are divided by the number of full-time instructional faculty, the strongest productivity scores are produced by institutions such as Caltech, which have high dollar totals and low numbers of faculty.[23] The distribution of faculty resources in 1968 is displayed in table 3.3.

There were sharp differences, however, in the distribution of faculty between public and private institutions. As would be expected, in 1970 a higher Carnegie category was associated with lower student-faculty ratios. Research I and II private universities offered the lowest (best) student-faculty ratios, Doctoral private campuses offered the highest (worst) ratios, and the public universities fell in between.

TABLE 3.3

Average Numbers of Full-Time Students and Full-Time Instructional Faculty, and Student-Faculty Ratio, by Carnegie Category and Public/Private Status, 1968

Carnegie Category	Average Student Enrollment	Average Full-time Faculty	Student-Faculty Ratio
Public			
Research I	28,200	1,326	21.3
Research II	18,480	826	22.4
Doctoral I	12,390	478	25.9
Doctoral II	13,720	506	27.1
Private			
Research I	11,560	759	15.2
Research II	8,620	419	20.6
Doctoral I	11,600	388	30.0
Doctoral II	7,830	214	36.6

Source: Carnegie Commission, *Classification of Institutions of Higher Education* (1973); faculty data from AAUP *Bulletin* (Mar. 1968).

TABLE 3.4

Average Federal R&D Funding, Number of Full-Time Instructional Faculty, and R&D Per Capita Funding, by Carnegie Category and Public/Private Status, 1968

	Average Federal R&D	Average Full-time Faculty	Average R&D Index
Public Institutions			
Research I	$15.3 million	1,326	$11,540
Research II	4.8 million	826	5,810
Doctoral I	1.8 million	478	3,750
Doctoral II	801,000	506	1,585
Private Institutions			
Research I	$21.5 million	759	$28,350
Research II	5.1 million	419	12,230
Doctoral I	2.1 million	388	5,290
Doctoral II	447,000	214	2,090

Source: Full-time faculty data from AAUP *Bulletin* (Mar. 1968); R&D data from National Science Foundation, *Federal Support of Research and Development at Universities and Colleges and Selected Nonprofit Institutions, Fiscal Year 1968.*

Did these differences in faculty staffing between public and private institutions produce comparable results in federal R&D funding? The answer is that the average per capita R&D funding—the R&D index—for faculty at private institutions in 1968 exceeded the R&D average for public institutions in every Carnegie class (table 3.4). But the significant public-private difference is found among Research institutions. Among Research I institutions the mean R&D index for private universities, $28,350 per faculty member in 1968, is almost two and a half times as large as the $11,540 average for public institutions. Among Research II institutions it is more than twice as large for private campuses ($12,230) as for public campuses ($5,810). Private institutions' advantage in R&D funding tails off in the Doctoral classes, but it remains substantial.

Controlling for institutional size sharply reorders the rankings commonly found in the various horsepower ratings, such as the NSF's annual top-hundred list of federal R&D winners. For example, in 1968 Ohio State was ranked nineteenth in federal R&D obligations, with $16.4 million; Duke, with $16.2 million, was ranked twentieth. At Duke, the full-time faculty of 693 in 1968 produced an R&D index of $23,410. At Ohio State, with 1,548 faculty, the R&D index was $10,590. When public and private universities' R&D indexes for 1968 are ranked, Ohio State and Duke fall within one position of the median in the Research I class. On average, the faculty at private universities in 1968 won two and one-third times as many federal R&D dollars as their public counterparts. The private sector shows a similar margin of superiority when compared on the basis of per capita journal publications.

Technically, federal research grants represent competitive success in winning the *means* of research, not competitive success in publishing the *results* of research in scientific and scholarly journals. The publication of journal articles is an essential step in the knowledge-creation process. Journal publications were chosen as the second indicator of research achievement for several reasons. Since 1665, when Henry Oldenberg, secretary of the Royal Society in London, published the first issue of *Philosophical Transactions,* scholarly—especially scientific—journals have performed a crucial mediating role in the growth of knowledge. As the privately owned organs of scientific, scholarly, and professional societies and associations, these journals have historically been free of control by government or by commercial enterprises. They have provided not only a formal, effective, and self-documenting medium of communication but also a means of filtering, evaluating, and unifying information.[24] In 1968 the *Science Citation Index* monitored 1,968 journals and indexed 308,536 articles.[25] A count of science articles published during 1968 by faculty at each institution in our study demonstrated that, for example, researchers at Texas A&M published 540 articles in science journals. With a full-time instructional faculty of 710 in 1968, Texas A&M faculty thus produced a per capita publications index of .76—the median score among public Research I institutions. Table 3.5 shows the mean science publications indexes for public and private institutions by Carnegie category.

On average, Research I public institutions in 1968 produced 50 percent fewer per capita science publications than did private institutions in the same category. The private advantage declined, however, in lower Carnegie categories. At the Doctoral II level the average publications index for public institutions was 83 percent of that for private ones. With regard to the publication index (of scientific arti-

TABLE 3.5
Average Science Publications Index, by Carnegie Category and Public/Private Status, 1968

Carnegie Category	Public Institutions	Private Institutions
Research I	.76	1.51
Research II	.48	.84
Doctoral I	.24	.38
Doctoral II	.10	.12

Source: Data from Institute for Scientific Information, *Science Citation Index.* See also Note on Method and Sources.

cles only in 1968), the margin of private advantage, strong among Research-class universities but weaker at the Doctoral level, is similar to the difference seen in the R&D index. The apparent superiority of private over public universities in per capita research productivity is reduced when measured by journal publications, but it remains significant.

Not surprisingly, there is a positive correlation between R&D funding and journal publication.[26] Some universities, however, have developed R&D funding patterns that are not matched by publications productivity. New Mexico State, a Doctoral I institution in 1968, provides an example of a campus with high R&D awards unmatched by publication output. In 1968 the Las Cruces campus received approximately half its R&D funding from NASA, in the form of funds to provide technical support for the White Sands Missile Range. This funding placed New Mexico State first among the thirty-three Doctoral I universities on the 1968 per capita R&D index ranking. Yet New Mexico State ranked below the median for its class (eighteenth of thirty-four) in per capita science publications. At the University of Alaska, a Doctoral II institution where in 1968 Defense Department funds helped to drive the R&D index at the Fairbanks campus to the top of the Doctoral II class, the R&D index was twenty-five times the average for the seventeen public Doctoral II institutions. Yet Alaska's science publications index (.08) ranked below the median for Doctoral II public universities.

Alaska represented an extreme case, and New Mexico State an unusual one, of weak correspondence between research dollars and published results. But often the differing needs of federal agencies have produced varied patterns of project support to universities, and consequently federal R&D awards have varied by agency and program in their potential for producing published research results. Research grants from agencies such as the NIH and the NSF, for example, have typically produced higher yields in published articles than have project grants from agencies with missions in agriculture, defense, commerce, and education. Where practical applications are emphasized, research results are often disseminated through in-house project reports rather than through refereed publications, and research is closely tied to development. In some cases, R&D awards from the Pentagon yielded a weak payoff in publications productivity. One reason for this was that publication of the results of classified research was not permitted. By 1968, however, in an atmosphere of rising antiwar protest, the federal government was shifting much of its classified research from university campuses to the federal contract research centers or to military and intelligence facilities.[27] A second reason for a weaker publications output was Pentagon funding for development work—the D in R&D—as found not only at Alaska and New Mexico State, but even more substantially at Johns Hopkins, Penn State, Utah State, Georgia Tech, and Texas-Austin. Similarly, at many land-grant institutions, especially in rural states, R&D funding from the Department of Agriculture supported applied programs that pro-duced fewer publications than did basic research projects.

Far removed from the practical world of R&D funding and science publications are the humanities. With rare exceptions in fields such as the history of science and medicine, sponsored research grants have been unavailable to arts and humanities faculty. Moreover, scholarly journals in the arts and humanities are relatively few in number and modest in circulation. Rather, books have been the scholarly staple of these fields. But in a study involving more than two hundred campuses, the books written by each institution's faculty cannot be identified adequately or compared in a practical way.[28] For these reasons we developed the A&H index, which includes fellow-ships won during 1965–74 from the NEH, the John Simon Guggen-heim Foundation, and the American Council of Learned Societies (ACLS) for research in humanities disciplines (table 3.6).[29] (Aggrega-tions of fellowships won during the 1980s will be discussed in a later chapter.)

In humanities scholarship, even more decisively than in R&D funding and scientific journal publications, the elite private univer-sities are in a world apart. For generations and in some cases for cen-turies, tradition has nourished the arts and humanities at the heav-ily endowed private universities. Because external funding has been scarce and this tradition has been expensive to maintain, private uni-versities in the Doctoral class have found it difficult to sustain. As a

TABLE 3.6
Average Arts-and-Humanities Index, by Carnegie Category and Public/Private Status, 1965–1974

Carnegie Category	Public Institutions	Private Institutions
Research I	.03	.07
Research II	.02	.04
Doctoral I	.02	.02
Doctoral II	.01	.01

Source: A&H index based on annual reports, 1965–1974, of the American Council of Learned Societies, John Simon Guggenheim Foundation, National Endowment for the Humanities. See also Note on Method and Sources.

consequence, in the 1960s we find in Research universities the greatest margins of private superiority in the A&H index, and in Doctoral universities we find virtually no difference between public and private institutions.

Overall, according to the 1960s data the margin of superiority in research performance shown by private Research institutions is so consistent and so large that it requires an explanation. Among private Research I universities, the R&D index is almost two and one-half times as large as that of their public counterparts, and the scientific publications index is twice as large (tables 3.4 and 3.5). An advantage in research productivity of the magnitude apparently enjoyed by private elite universities runs counter to previous ranking studies. Private institutions enjoyed only a modest advantage in the top-twenty rankings derived from the Cartter and Roose-Andersen studies (eleven private institutions and nine public ones were ranked). Indeed, in all of the reputational rankings, private and public institutions have been fairly well mixed in the academic pecking orders. How much of the apparent quality gap is real, therefore, and how much may be an artifact of per capita methods of measurement themselves?

In a widely cited essay on America's private universities published in *Minerva* in 1973, the sociologist Edward Shils attributed their unique success to the combined effects of "sovereignty, affluence, and tradition."[30] Commenting on these assets, the historian Roger Geiger observed, "Sovereignty has allowed these [private] universities to have their centers of initiative within themselves; their great wealth has given them the wherewithal to pursue their chosen goals; and their traditions have guided each institution in its own fashion toward its vision of academic excellence."[31] Beyond the unique traditions that gave each university a distinct institutional personality, however, lay a larger, shared tradition of the private elites. It nurtured high culture in the arts and humanities; emphasized pure science over applied technology; assumed leadership in the learned professions, especially medicine and law; and acknowledged the claims of spiritual life by supporting schools of divinity—as for example at Harvard, Yale, Chicago, Duke, Emory, and Vanderbilt.[32] Tradition also led private colleges and universities for generations, and in some cases for centuries, to maintain the social dominance of white male Protestant elites. To private universities sovereignty also meant the freedom to design an institutional future relatively unencumbered by missions imposed by external authorities, such as state bureaucrats and public governing boards.

As a consequence of this freedom and these traditions, prior to World War I private research universities in the United States had developed an organizational form that seemed preternaturally designed to fit the research economy of the 1960s. First, their sovereignty as private entities enabled them to move quickly to exploit targets of opportunity, and their prestige and prior service guaranteed access to the corridors of national power. Dean John Burchard of MIT, in his memoir of the World War II years, observed that "private institutions were almost without exception the first of the universities to enter into the war research program on any large scale."[33] This was implicit in their type of management, Burchard explained, "which made rapid change of policy and rapid decisions on details as easy as it is for a private corporation." The advantage of private entrepreneurial freedom was reinforced by the prestige factor, with its origin in the colonial colleges and its modern center in the Ivy League. Second, and less well understood than the prestige factor, was a structural advantage. The private research universities were organized in a way that maximized, far more than in the public universities, the proportion of campus faculty whose research fields were supported by the major federal funding agencies.

This important organizational difference between private and public universities was not immediately apparent from a comparison of their structures, because they shared a basic form—a kind of Standard Model—that was peculiar to American universities and reflected their distinctive history. The Standard Model had two main components. At the university's center was its largest school, the college of arts and sciences. As the campus unit with the highest number of students, especially undergraduates, "the college" produced the largest group of alumni and held the largest bloc of faculty. In turn, these faculty provided most of the advanced instruction in the graduate school. The Standard Model university's second component was an array of graduate and professional schools. Most frequently there was a core of schools in five areas: medicine, engineering, law, business, and education. Among these, the school of medicine, which had relatively few students but usually included a teaching hospital, was typically the campus giant in terms of operating budget, capital costs, faculty and staff personnel, and sponsored research expenditures.[34] By 1968, many medical schools were part of an academic health center that typically included two or three smaller schools specializing in other health professions (e.g., dentistry, nursing, optometry, pharmacy, public health, and allied health sciences).[35] Some of the larger public university campuses (e.g., Florida, North Carolina, and

69

Washington) included as many as four health professions schools.[36] In addition to maintaining core schools in the areas of medicine, engineering, business, law, and education, public universities, to meet student demand, established a second tier of schools across a broad array of elective fields. These included fields supported by the land-grant program (e.g., agriculture, veterinary medicine, forestry, fisheries, home economics, and physical education); public service fields (e.g., government and public affairs, criminal justice, and social work); the visual and performing arts (e.g., drama, fine arts, and music); other professional fields (e.g., architecture, divinity, journalism, and library science); and specialized fields (e.g., film, international relations, labor economics, hotel management, and marine science).

Because private universities were free to design their preferred mix of academic and professional programs, they typically included schools in the more prestigious fields, such as medicine, law, and business. As a corollary of this freedom of choice, however, they excluded many of the practical and applied program areas in which state institutions were obliged to provide instruction. At the state institutions, however, separate schools and colleges proliferated over the years to meet the demands of multiple public constituencies. Thus, the larger state universities have typically supported more graduate and professional schools than have their private counterparts. Among the twenty top-ranked universities aggregated from the Roose-Andersen study of 1970 (excluding the two scientific institutes, Caltech and MIT, which had a single-school structure), the average number of schools and colleges on public campuses was twelve, whereas on private campuses the average was eight.[37]

For research universities in the postwar era the major winners of federal R&D funding for medicine, the arts and sciences, and engineering have typically been large schools. Aside from medical schools, professional schools and colleges at both private and public universities, however, have generally been small units, often department-sized. Despite their status as schools headed by deans, they have rarely been large enough in relation to the host institution to affect significantly its research funding or its output of published scholarship.[38] In the Roose-Andersen sample of eighteen institutions (the top twenty minus MIT and Caltech), for example, law schools averaged only 34 full-time faculty members in 1968. Schools of business or management averaged 78. Rarely did professors of law or business engage in government-sponsored research. In 1968 and subsequently, the majority of schools and colleges in fields such as architecture, drama, divinity, fine arts, government affairs, home eco-

70

nomics, journalism, library science, physical education, and social work at major universities were closer in faculty size to arts-and-sciences departments such as history or English.[39] Professional schools that enjoyed international reputations for excellence were often surprisingly small. In 1968, for example, three top-ranked schools of journalism had full-time faculties averaging 33 (52 at Columbia, 28 at Missouri, and 19 at Northwestern). Pennsylvania's well-endowed Annenberg School of Communications had only 12 full-time faculty members. Full-time faculty numbered only 46 at Princeton's Woodrow Wilson school, 52 at Harvard's Kennedy school, 17 at Cornell's well-known school of hotel administration, and 20 at the University of Washington's College of Fisheries. At Yale in 1968, the renowned school of drama had only 40 full-time faculty. There was no significant outside sponsorship of research at Yale's school of drama or in the schools of art and architecture, divinity, law, and music, and sponsored research was only of modest significance in the schools of forestry and nursing.[40] Specialized schools such as these provided much of the distinctive appeal and reputation of public and private universities. But often their work was remote from the main competitive arenas of research funding and publication.[41]

Where the private and public universities most significantly differed in their structures was not in their number of schools but rather in their relative size and mix. The penalty that large public universities have paid for their large size has not come primarily from their organizational sprawl or from their greater number of graduate and professional schools. Nor has it come from their obligation to provide public service programs in areas such as home economics or physical education, although these attributes have indubitably influenced their overall per capita research performance. Rather, the large state universities have been disadvantaged in per capita research performance for two other reasons. First, the size and program distribution of their undergraduate enrollments has meant that the proportion of science faculty on campus was smaller than was the case at private universities. Second, a majority of them lacked medical schools, an asset at most private Research institutions that raised the proportion of science faculty on campus.

Consider first the swollen size of the arts-and-sciences faculty at public universities compared with that of private institutions. At state universities such as Michigan and Michigan State in 1968, for example, the number of full-time arts-and-science faculty required at each institution to teach the tens of thousands of undergraduates reached almost one thousand. As was typically the case in both private and

71

public universities, approximately one-third of the arts-and-sciences faculty (including behavioral psychologists) were scientists. Roughly another third held appointments in the arts and humanities, and the remaining third in the social sciences. Thus, as the undergraduate student body of an institution grew during the 1960s, roughly two-thirds of the additional faculty required to teach the undergraduate majors were hired in humanities and social science disciplines, fields that were weak in research funding and that found far fewer outlets than the sciences for publication in scholarly journals. The larger the undergraduate student body, the smaller, by a rough one-to-two ratio, was the relative size on campus of the well-funded and highly published science faculty. Turning this maxim around to express it positively and thus to capture a key element of private advantage: at private Research universities, because the undergraduate student body was relatively small and thus required a smaller arts-and-sciences faculty, there was on campus a higher percentage of faculty in the financially well-nourished fields of medicine, engineering, and the physical and natural sciences. In Standard Model universities, a best-mix formula for maximizing per capita research achievement could thus be adduced: high institutional productivity in research funding and publication was best achieved by maximizing the size of the medical faculty in relation to the arts-and-sciences faculty. In such an endeavor, private institutions held many advantages over their public counterparts.

Because Standard Model universities in both the public and private sectors evolved primarily as teaching and degree-granting institutions in the liberal arts tradition, their structures fit unevenly with the postwar research agenda. Most university students and faculty worked in fields that were given low priority in federal R&D funding decisions. In 1968 this included virtually all of the visual and performing arts, the humanities, and most social sciences, as well as popular fields such as business and law. Proportionally few students studied for degrees in science and engineering. In fiscal 1968, federal R&D funding to the nation's campuses, most from six leading funding agencies, totaled $1.4 billion (table 3.7).

The universities most likely to benefit from such funding offered graduate and research programs that fit this agency profile, especially the enticing array of biomedical funding offered by the NIH. The most successful universities in the funding competition would thus have been those with medical schools. In such universities the health science faculties, together with the institution's science and engineering faculty, constituted a majority or a near-majority of the research

TABLE 3.7
*Federal R&D Funding to Academic Institutions by Funding Agency, Dollar Amount, and
Percentage Distribution, Fiscal 1968*

Agency	R&D Funding (thousands)	% of Total
HEW (PHS)	$619,112	43.7
DOD	243,148	17.2
NSF	212,523	15.0
NASA	126,096	8.9
AEC	94,443	6.7
USDA	62,224	4.4
Other	58,287	4.1
Total	$1,415,833	100.0

Source: Data from National Science Foundation, *Federal Support of Research and Development at Universities and Colleges and Selected Nonprofit Institutions, Fiscal Year 1968.*

scholars and scientists on campus. In the intense postwar competition for research support, the supreme structural advantage of the private research universities was that most of them fit this mold. Almost none of their public competitors, however, did so.

This structural advantage of private institutions can be demonstrated by comparing the faculty staffing ratios in two groups of universities, one private and one public, drawn from the top-twenty 1970 Roose-Andersen ranking. The private group includes seven universities, all with medical schools: Chicago, Columbia, Harvard, Hopkins, Pennsylvania, Stanford, and Yale.[42] At these seven campuses in 1968, the health science faculty (including the faculties of medicine, dentistry, nursing, pharmacy, and public health) included an average of 39.1 percent of the campus's full-time instructional faculty. The arts-and-sciences college or its equivalent at the seven private campuses contained an average of 38.2 percent of the full-time faculty. Thus the medical and allied health faculty and the arts-and-sciences faculty at these elite private institutions were approximately equal in size. Of the arts-and-sciences faculty, approximately one-third were scientists—a ratio that was common to both private and public universities.[43] In private universities, the bloc of scientists holding appointments in "the college," when combined with the health science faculty centered in the medical school, typically comprised almost half of the full-time campus faculty.[44] Faculty in this group held appointments in research fields supported by the five federal agencies that together provided almost 92 percent of R&D obligations to the nation's campuses in fiscal 1968. Thus, even excluding the additional research leverage provided by schools of engineering

73

(and often private institutions included engineering programs either as separate schools or as departments), the majority of faculty at most private universities worked in disciplines well funded by federal agencies.

Among the top-ranked public universities, however, the size and combination of colleges and schools were such that the proportion of faculty members in fields well supported by federal funding was smaller. For the nine public universities on the Roose-Andersen top-twenty list of 1970 (Berkeley, Illinois, Indiana, Michigan, Minnesota, Texas, UCLA, Washington, and Wisconsin), faculty in medicine or the health sciences in 1968 made up, on average, only 12.6 percent of the total. On these large campuses, with their heavy undergraduate populations, the arts-and-sciences faculty accounted on average for approximately half (49.7%) of the full-time institutional faculty.[45] Thus, in comparison with the private universities, the public institutions had smaller health science faculties and larger faculties in the social sciences, the humanities, and the arts. At three leading public universities with medical schools (Minnesota, UCLA, and Wisconsin), health science faculty in 1968 accounted on average for only 17.5 percent of full-time faculty. By contrast, at private universities, where medical school and teaching hospital budgets alone often exceeded the operating budget for the rest of the campus, the proportion of full-time faculty in health-related fields often approached 40 percent. In general, the research budgets of public universities were less dominated by biomedical research than were those of private universities. But in an era of growing NIH leadership in federal research funding, the private sector's skew toward the health sciences carried significant advantages.

The Unique Multiplier Effect of Medical Schools

In light of the extraordinary postwar growth of research in academic health centers on American university campuses, it is striking how little the health science schools have to do with the rest of their host campuses, and vice versa. Faculty and administrators in the two campus environments, the arts-and-sciences environment and the academic health science environment, have rarely bridged the distance that separates them. The literature on higher education reflects this persistent division.[46] Yet understanding the modern research university requires that we bridge the gap. The presence of a medical school on campus had an unmatched multiplier effect on university research capability.

One key to explaining private institutions' structural advantage in receiving federal funding and producing research publications was found in the leverage offered by a medical school that was large relative to the size of the institution as a whole, *or* by an institutional mission that centered on science and engineering. In 1968, of the twenty-two private institutions in the Carnegie Research I category, all but four included medical schools. Of the four lacking medical schools, moreover, three (Caltech, MIT, and Rockefeller) were scientific institutes whose relatively small faculties and large research budgets set them in a class apart from other arts-and-sciences universities. The research awards and scientific publications of these three institutions customarily topped the per capita and aggregate charts. The fourth nonmedical private institution, Princeton, was an elite liberal arts university whose great strength in the physical sciences, mathematics, and engineering compensated heavily for the absence of NIH funding that medical faculties customarily receive. Of the thirteen private campuses classified by the 1970 Carnegie taxonomy as Research II, five (Boston, Emory, George Washington, Tufts, and Tulane) had medical schools. Another (Brown) was in the process of establishing a medical school program. Three (Carnegie Mellon, Illinois Institute of Technology, and Rice) emphasized science and technology, and one (Claremont Graduate School) was a consortium institution. Only two (Catholic and Syracuse Universities) were, like Princeton, arts-and-sciences universities without medical schools. In the public sector, by contrast, only seventeen of the thirty Research I universities and six of the twenty-seven Research II universities had medical schools. Thus, among the nation's ninety-two Research-class institutions in the late 1960s, two-thirds of the private universities included medical schools and three-fifths of the public universities did not.[47]

Medical schools brought their universities two principal advantages in the postwar competition for research support. One was the funding provided by the perennial generosity of Congress toward the NIH. The other was the unique structure and role of academic medical schools, a product of their historical development in the United States. The dominance of medical school research within most major universities is a relatively recent development. In colonial America, medical schools sought affiliation with liberal arts colleges in order to gain prestige and to confer degrees. In return, the colleges acquired a science faculty (often a weak one) and a medical curriculum at little or no cost. These marriages of convenience never produced close ties between American universities and the medical schools they acquired. Yet during the years between the Civil War and World War I, the era of professional consolidation for medicine, law, and the major academic disciplines, reforms within the leading universities profoundly influenced the medical profession by transforming medical education. The modernization associated with Abraham Flexner's famous report of 1910 depended heavily for its success on the reforms in scientific and clinical training pioneered at Johns Hopkins in the 1890s under the leadership of medical dean William Welch.[48] Turning away from the British model of medical education, which separated instruction in medical science at universities (Oxford or Cambridge) from clinical training at urban teaching hospitals (London or Edinburgh)—a model most notably associated with Harvard in the United States—Hopkins adapted to American circumstances a Berlin model that joined the medical school and the teaching hospital.

Prior to World War II, the basic science faculty at leading medical schools conducted modest research programs while the clinical faculty, composed almost entirely of part-time, volunteer physicians and surgeons in local private practice, had almost no research involvement. This changed, however, after 1945, when the NIH began its extraordinary expansion as the nation's biomedical research patron. In response to the flood of research funding from Washington, medical schools demonstrated a capacity unmatched elsewhere on the campuses for expanding research activities with little assistance (or control) from the parent university. As the costs of medical education soared, academic health administrators expanded sponsored research as a way to build their professional (especially clinical) staffs, increase scientific prestige, and maximize income from indirect cost recovery.

By 1968, there were eighty-seven American Medical Association–approved medical schools in the United States. Fifty-two of them were located on the campus of a parent university, fifteen were geographically distant from the parent institution, and ten were not university-affiliated.[49] The nation's thirty-five thousand medical students in 1968 were remarkably evenly divided, both in numbers and in student quality, between the forty-three private and the forty-four public institutions. Privately controlled medical schools (e.g., Columbia, Harvard, and Hopkins) dominated the elite ranks. Nevertheless, most of the schools facing accreditation or survival problems were also privately controlled.[50] Although medical schools, far more expensive and complex than other units in Standard Model universities, varied widely in size and organization, certain generalizations may be risked concerning the functional distribution of the medical faculty and its consequences for medical school research.

76

In 1968 the average university medical school employed approximately 250 full-time faculty. Several of the larger medical schools, especially at private universities, had full-time faculties twice that size—for example, Pennsylvania (560), Yeshiva (514), and Yale (481).[51] In a typical university medical school in 1968, roughly one-third of the full-time faculty taught basic science courses, primarily to "undergraduate" M.D. students during the first two years of their four-year curriculum.[52] In basic science departments, faculty generally were expected to participate in sponsored research, and the expanding coffers of the NIH provided ample resources. Typically, a majority of these basic science faculty held Ph.D.'s rather than M.D.'s (faculty with Ph.D.'s were less expensive to employ), although a small but increasing number held both degrees. Their daily routines and loyalties, shared with colleagues in arts-and-sciences departments in fields such as biology and chemistry, revolved around undergraduate science courses, advanced graduate instruction, and the omnipresent demands of conducting laboratory research, writing biomedical science papers, and submitting proposals to federal funding agencies. Unlike their faculty colleagues in arts-and-sciences departments, however, the pre-clinical faculty who taught medical students worked in an environment in which the degree they awarded, the M.D., outranked their own Ph.D.'s in prestige. In the pre-Flexner era, the Ph.D. had been king, and M.D. degrees had been widely suspect. By the end of the 1960s, however, the rapid expansion of doctorate-granting programs had weakened the prestige claims of academic Ph.D.'s, while the prestige—and income—of M.D.-holders had soared.[53]

The clinical faculty, composed entirely of physicians, was typically twice the size of the basic science faculty, and often larger. As practicing physicians and surgeons, members of the clinical faculty directed student training in the hospital wards, where medical education was applied to patient care and was less involved in research.[54] This, however, began to change during the late 1960s in response to three new developments. The first was the increasing emphasis in Congress, and hence in NIH programs, on practical results in scientific warfare against diseases. In the era of Rachel Carson's *Silent Spring,* growing public concern over the life-threatening effects of smoking, alcohol and other mind-altering drugs, birth control pills, obesity, and a host of environmental pollutants led federal mission agencies to emphasize the search for effective prevention, treatment, and cures, a quest that involved the clinical world of applied medical science and patient care.[55] The second new development was the revolution in computer science and technology, which provided powerful new tools for biostatistics, clinical epidemiology, radiation physics, and health policy. The third was the passage of legislation establishing Medicare and Medicaid in 1965. The new programs of government health insurance, joined by the growth of Blue Cross and Blue Shield and the provision of health insurance as an employee benefit, offered physicians and hospitals a sea of fee-for-service earnings from third-party insurers. The large fees associated with expensive clinical tests and procedures allowed academic health centers to expand their clinical research dramatically by adding clinical faculty supported by "soft money" research grant funds. The full impact of this fiscal revolution in the development of academic medical centers would not be felt until the 1970s and 1980s.[56] Nonetheless, in 1968 American medical schools enjoyed a cornucopia of external funding, and they responded creatively.

Faced with these financial opportunities and pressures, deans of medicine enjoyed far more budgetary flexibility than did their decanal colleagues elsewhere in the university. Medical school faculty were hired and paid through budgets that were largely free of the enrollment-based constraints that limited the size of faculties in other schools. The budgetary resources of medical school deans included the same range of external funding available to the deans of schools in the arts and sciences and engineering: for instance, tuition income, alumni gifts, direct cost subventions from research grants and contracts, and indirect cost recovery ("overhead") associated with the provision of research facilities.[57] Medical deans, however, could generate two or three times more sponsored research funding than could deans of arts and sciences or engineering. And access to the growing tide of third-party fees for clinical practice was an advantage uniquely enjoyed by schools of the health professions.[58] As a consequence of these funding advantages, which in turn reflected the prestige of the medical profession and the high priority assigned by political leaders and the general public to excellence in health care, medical schools could leverage a relatively small core of instructional faculty into often spectacular totals of research funding.[59]

By exploiting these distinctive attributes, schools of medicine became the true citadels of Clark Kerr's "unfaculty." On American university campuses, soft-money research appointments had long been standard arrangements in research institutes, where neither degrees nor faculty tenure were customarily awarded and where principal investigators were commonly expected to pay their own salaries by winning sponsored research grants.[60] Among degree-granting schools within universities, however, where faculty tenure was the norm, medical schools pioneered in creating nontenured posts for research faculty. The practice was also found—though nowhere as extensively as in medical schools—in schools of engineering as well as in other health professions schools, especially schools of public health, which emerged from the 1960s with an expanding research agenda in specialties such as biostatistics and epidemiology.[61]

The rapid expansion of soft-money appointments intensified the funding pressures within biomedical science. In the 1970s, when the number of faculty researchers increased, the luster of biomedical science was dimmed by growing complaints of rat-race competition and scientific fraud.[62] In the late 1960s, however, medical schools exploited their unparalleled leverage for research expansion. One consequence was to widen the research gap between private and public Research universities, because most of the private universities included medical schools and most of the public ones did not. Table 3.8 displays average index scores for federal R&D obligations (1968), science publications (1968), and arts-and-humanities awards (1965–74) for three groups of top-ranked universities. Many factors other than campus medical schools drive these numbers, including public-private differences in sizes of student bodies and faculties. But the medical school variable goes a long way toward explaining large institutional differences in research performance during the late 1960s in such a distinguished group of universities.[63]

Top-ranked public universities such as Michigan and Wisconsin, despite the excellence of their faculties and the comprehensive range of their schools and programs, reflect configurations that made it difficult for them to score as high as the private elite universities when judged in terms of per capita research productivity. Why? Because the majority of public university campuses, even more disadvantaged than Michigan and Wisconsin, lacked one or more of the research-intensive components—a medical school, an engineering school, or land-grant programs. Since the chartering of the College of William and Mary in 1693, America's public institutions of higher education have developed a unique variety of functional forms—normal schools, land-grant institutions, military and maritime academies, teachers colleges, polytechnic institutes, vocational and community colleges, state liberal arts colleges, and research universities with a central undergraduate liberal arts college. The diversity of campus forms mirrored the nation's size and variety, and reflected historical accident and geopolitical maneuver as well as systematic public planning. Indeed, much of the reform impulse in American higher education since

TABLE 3.8
Average Federal R&D Funding Index, Science Publications Index, and Arts-and-Humanities Index for Leading Public and Private Universities with Medical Schools, and Public Campuses without Medical Schools

Institution	1968 R&D Index (thousands)	1968 Science Publications Index	1968–74 A&H Index
Private, with medical school			
Chicago	$28,770	1.72	.08
Columbia	30,570	1.61	.16
Harvard	33,570	2.35	.11
Stanford	51,440	2.19	.09
Yale	20,480	1.40	.17
Average	$32,970	1.85	.12
Public, with medical school			
Michigan	$19,170	1.01	.05
Minnesota	12,140	.99	.02
UCLA	18,530	.82	.06
Washington	18,660	1.08	.03
Wisconsin	12,130	.86	.04
Average	$16,130	.95	.04
Public, without medical school			
UC Berkeley	$18,960	1.31	.09
Illinois	15,440	.96	.03
Indiana	4,990	.26	.06
Purdue	7,160	.72	.01
Texas	7,900	.38	.05
Average	$10,890	.73	.05

Source: Data from National Science Foundation, *Federal Support of Research and Development at Universities and Colleges and Selected Nonprofit Institutions, Fiscal Year 1968;* Institute for Scientific Information, *Science Citation Index* (1968); annual reports, 1965–1974, American Council of Learned Societies, John Simon Guggenheim Foundation, and National Endowment for the Humanities. See also Note on Method and Sources.

the 1960s has consisted of efforts by state coordinating boards and blue-ribbon commissions to diversify and specialize the missions of public institutions in the face of campus-level yearning for research university status.[64] In this contest, as in the past, private institutions, subject chiefly to financial constraints, have been able to select their missions and organize themselves accordingly. As a result, American private universities have increasingly come to resemble one another as the Standard Model has become their organizational norm.

Among the nation's public universities, however, institutions possessing the main research assets of Standard Model organization—a college of arts and sciences, accompanied by schools of medicine and engineering—have remained in the minority. The multiple public constituencies and roles of state institutions led them to develop several distinct models. Only the first of these, exemplified by Minnesota, where the state flagship is also the land-grant institution, approaches the structural balance of private Standard Model universities.[65] Public universities such as Minnesota and Wisconsin include such Standard Model components as schools of medicine, engineering, agriculture, and education. The second model is exemplified by the many state institutions that lack major components of the Standard Model. For example, in North Carolina, the state university's flagship campus (North Carolina–Chapel Hill) houses a medical school, but the state's land-grant institution (North Carolina State) does not.[66] A third model is illustrated by the University of Illinois, where the flagship campus is the state's land-grant institution, but the medical school is located elsewhere. The Illinois arrangement reflects the common nineteenth-century practice of establishing state universities in rural areas (such as Urbana) remote from the sinful distractions of cities such as Chicago. The Illinois model, combining flagship and land-grant status but lacking a medical school, finds a parallel in a host of other historic college towns: Fayetteville, Arkansas; Berkeley, California; Athens, Georgia; Baton Rouge, Louisiana; College Park, Maryland; Lincoln, Nebraska; Amherst, Massachusetts; New Brunswick, New Jersey; and University Park, Pennsylvania.

A fourth model is found in Kansas, where neither the flagship campus in Lawrence nor the land-grant institution in Manhattan includes a medical school. Indiana also falls into this category. The Kansas model is one associated historically with nonindustrial states—for example, Alabama, Colorado, Kansas, Mississippi, Oklahoma, and Oregon. These four state models, however, do not exhaust the possibilities. A fifth is seen in thinly populated states without any medical school—Alaska, Idaho, Montana, North Dakota, and Wyoming. Other models are found at campuses in the Carnegie classification's most numerous category, the comprehensive institutions, four-year state universities and colleges, which in 1970 included 453 institutions but which are outside the focus of this study. These campuses demonstrate the considerable degree of program segmentation that has historically characterized public institutions but not their private counterparts.

The combined impact on faculty research during the 1960s of the factors explored in this chapter—the organizational freedom enjoyed by private institutions, the multiplier effect of medical schools, and the structural constraints imposed on public universities—is illustrated by subdividing the Carnegie Research institutions on the ba-

TABLE 3.9

Average R&D Index and Publications Index for Eighty-eight Research-class Institutions, by Public/Private Status and Medical School Status, 1968, Ranked by Publications Index

Category (no. of institutions)	Avg. R&D Index	Avg. Publications Index
1. Private Research I, nonmedical (4)	$26,940	2.80
2. Private Research I, medical (17)	20,630	1.47
3. Private Research II, medical (6)	5,670	1.13
4. Public Research I, medical (16)	17,040	.93
5. Private Research II, nonmedical (6)	5,330	.73
6. Public Research I, nonmedical (14)	12,380	.59
7. Public Research II, medical (6)	5,350	.58
8. Public Research II, nonmedical (19)	4,880	.44

Source: Data from National Science Foundation, *Federal Support of Research and Development at Universities and Colleges and Selected Nonprofit Institutions, Fiscal Year 1968;* Institute for Scientific Information, *Science Citation Index* (1968). See Note on Method and Sources.

Note: The institutions in each category, ranked by average publications index, are as follows: (1) Caltech, MIT, Princeton, Rockefeller; (2) Case Western, Chicago, Columbia, Cornell, Duke, Harvard, Johns Hopkins, Miami, NYU, Northwestern, Pennsylvania, Rochester, Stanford, Southern California, Vanderbilt, Yale, Yeshiva; (3) Boston, Brown, Emory, George Washington, Tufts, Tulane; (4) Arizona, Florida, Iowa, Kentucky, Michigan, Minnesota, Missouri, North Carolina–Chapel Hill, Ohio State, Pittsburgh, UC Davis, UCLA, UC San Diego, Utah, Wisconsin, Washington; (5) Brandeis, Catholic, Carnegie Mellon, Illinois Tech, Rice, Syracuse; (6) UC Berkeley, Colorado, Georgia, Hawaii, Illinois, Purdue, Maryland, Michigan State, Rutgers, North Carolina State, Penn State, Tennessee, Texas A&M, Texas; (7) Cincinnati, SUNY Buffalo, Temple, Virginia, Wayne State, West Virginia; (8) Arkansas, Auburn, Colorado State, Connecticut, Florida State, Georgia Tech, Indiana, Iowa State, Kansas, Kansas State, LSU, Mississippi, Nebraska, Oklahoma, Oklahoma State, Oregon, Oregon State, Virginia Tech, Washington State.

sis of public or private status and the presence or absence of a medical school. Table 3.9 displays for the eight resulting categories the mean R&D index and publications indexes for the eighty-eight Research campuses, ranked by publications index. The dominance of private institutions, and of those institutions with medical schools, is striking.

Ranked at the top, in a lofty category all their own, are the four nonmedical private institutions: Caltech, MIT, Princeton, and Rockefeller. Of these, all are scientific institutes except Princeton, which, in all respects save its lack of a medical school, belongs with the eighteen private arts-and-sciences universities in the second group. Together, these first two groups constitute the recognized aristocracy of American private higher education. Ranked third is a group of six private universities with medical schools in the Carnegie 1970 Research II class: Boston, Brown, Emory, George Washington, Tufts, and Tulane. Private institutions so dominate the per capita analysis that we do not reach a group of institutions with the stature of Michigan, UCLA, UC San Diego, Washington, and Wisconsin until the fourth-ranked group. This includes the sixteen public Research I universities that, like Minnesota, include a medical school.[67] The remaining private institutions—six Research II institutions without medical schools, including Brandeis—constitute the fifth-ranked group. All of the remaining thirty-nine public universities, ranked in the bottom half of the distribution, are public institutions. They include, in the sixth group, recognized institutions of high quality such as UC Berkeley and Illinois, and, in the eighth group, Indiana. Universities of that caliber were consensual choices for top-twenty status in the reputational surveys of the 1960s, with Berkeley topping the list. This achievement is therefore all the more exceptional, given the structural advantages enjoyed by private universities and by campuses that included medical schools.

By inviting us to explain large differences in relative per capita productivity, the public-private competition teaches lessons about the role of such determinants as institutional size and program structure. It should not, however, obscure the larger and more important point with which we began: American universities have excelled in creating knowledge because they have been forced to compete in a decentralized and pluralistic environment. Historically, the private and public sectors have exploited their different advantages—the private institutions, their sovereignty, affluence, and tradition; and the public universities, their democratic opportunity, republican utility, and taxpayer support. In modern memory the 1960s are etched in gold because this competition, fueled by expansionist federal funding policies, produced so many winners and so few losers. During 1958–68, total academic R&D expenditures more than tripled (in 1988 dollars), growing from less than $2 billion in 1958 to nearly $7 billion in 1968. The federal contribution to academic research increased fivefold, from $1 billion (in 1988 dollars) to $5 billion. The number of academic researchers (faculty and nonfaculty) in American doctorate-granting universities grew from twenty-five thousand in 1958 to forty-six thousand in 1968. Enrollment in public doctoral universities grew from 800,000 to 1.9 million, while private doctoral university enrollments grew from 440,000 to 650,000.[68] The golden 1960s were a hard act to follow.

During the next decade, however, the higher education environment was characterized by declines in public esteem, research support, academic employment, alumni giving, and campus morale, and by fear of shrinking enrollments. The folklore of higher education, dominated on the campuses by the culture of the arts and sciences, has etched the 1970s in modern memory as a decade of academic recession or even depression. Looking back, we can see more evidence of continuity and less of crisis. Nonetheless, the 1970s would test the capacity of an overexpanded system to adjust to uneven contractions in a competitive market.

4

■

THE STAGNANT DECADE REVISITED: RESEARCH UNIVERSITIES ADJUST TO THE 1970s

The ten years from 1968 to 1978 have been called the "age of survival," the "stagnant decade," and the "steady-state era" for American higher education.[1] During this period, shifting demographic, economic, and political conditions created far less favorable circumstances for universities and colleges than they had enjoyed during the previous decade-long "golden age." Uncertainties brought by inflation and economic crisis, declining university enrollments, and more restricted federal funding raised questions about how the nation's campuses might best proceed, or in some cases, survive. Research universities, forced to operate in a new context of shifting agency priorities, a renewed emphasis on targeted research, and the increasing costs of regulation, faced particularly difficult challenges. While the term *stagnant* may be appropriate as a descriptor for enrollment patterns or funding trends or faculty hiring, the years from 1968 to 1978 were anything but stagnant for higher education. Rather, the time might be more appropriately characterized as the age of adjustment.[2]

By the late 1960s there was widespread belief that, as a matter of necessity, the federal contribution to higher education would continue to rise. In 1968 the Association of American Universities reported that "American higher education is experiencing widespread financial pressures that constitute a threat to [its] nature and vitality." The Carnegie Commission's first report, *Quality and Equality*, called for an immediate doubling of federal support, and a tripling of federal funding by 1980.[3] In 1970 higher education's "new depression," whose main symptoms were budget deficits, declining applications, unsteady enrollments, mandatory cost reductions, and decreasing educational quality, was identified.[4] That same year, the President's Task Force on Higher Education reported a complementary finding—

that current levels of support did not provide an adequate base for maintaining or developing existing institutions, and even the Senate proposed emergency assistance in 1971.[5] The nation's faculty clearly felt the pinch. In its 1971–72 report the AAUP noted that "the shrinkage of funds devoted to faculty salary increases has been greater than the retardation of price increases [and] the economic status of the profession is worse than it was a year ago."[6]

Rapid demographic and social change fed a growing sense of dislocation. The 1960s boom in university enrollments had been accompanied by what some considered a cultural revolution at universities. The resulting campus turmoil during the decade's later years was followed by mounting popular distrust. A Gallup poll conducted in May 1970 (the same month that students were killed at Kent State and Jackson State) found that campus unrest was viewed as the nation's most serious problem, well ahead of the Vietnam War, racial strife, and the high cost of living.[7] The 1972 break-in at the Watergate complex and the eventual resignation of Richard Nixon in 1974 raised further questions about the integrity of institutions generally, and made government officials even more insistent on the accountability of those who benefited from their support.

The economic constraints facing the nation's colleges and universities during the 1970s have been well documented.[8] Financial difficulty caused in part by the overbuilding of facilities and programs in the preceding years was exacerbated during the first half of the decade by double-digit inflation, the oil embargo, which increased fuel costs, and economic recession. Government compliance requirements that accompanied the expansion of student aid programs, the enforcement of affirmative action policies, and the extension of health and safety standards sharply increased the universities' economic burden. At the same time, there was a shift in national priorities away from the unequivocal, *Sputnik*-inspired faith in science and the corresponding support for basic university research.

The abrupt contraction of federal spending for research—grounded in the increased costs of the war in Vietnam and extensive federal social programs—created a context in which many universities and colleges with rising aspirations and heavy fixed commitments were no longer supported, either by burgeoning enrollments or sufficient funding, as they had been during the 1960s. Public universities, suffering from a reduced tax base, threats to their autonomy from their governing or coordinating boards, and citizens' distrust of higher education, were also concerned about a qualitative leveling that might take place as increasing numbers of states organized higher education institutions into multicampus systems. State-supported campuses had good reason to fear an encroaching process of "delocalization," a transfer of decision-making power from authorities located on campus to those residing in agencies and governments external to the institution.[9] Private institutions in particular were compelled to concentrate on controlling their budgets. As their stock portfolios diminished in value, even financially secure private campuses were squeezed by decreases in alumni support and other private donations, the failure of endowments to keep pace with rising expenditures, and growing pressure from increasing enrollments at public universities. Under these stringent conditions of the 1970s, would elite universities maintain their lead? Would other institutions lose the momentum they had gained during the golden 1960s?

Campus Adjustments to Demographic Shifts

The slowing growth rate of the college-age population and the expectation, voiced by the Carnegie Commission in the early 1970s, that the rate of enrollment growth would decrease promised to have both a short-term and long-term effect on the nation's postsecondary campuses.[10] Between 1970 and 1978, enrollments in all institutions of higher education increased by 46 percent, or 2.7 million students.[11] In the first two years of the decade, however, only 350,000 new degree-seeking students enrolled, as compared with an increase of more than 1 million during 1968–70.[12] The rate of growth was further slowed by the termination of compulsory military service in the early 1970s, which removed selective service deferment as an incentive for college attendance. Enrollments continued to rise in Carnegie-classified comprehensive institutions and two-year colleges. But at doctorate-granting universities, enrollments had stabilized by 1973. That year, 2.5 million students enrolled in public doctorate-granting institutions, while enrollments increased to 700,000 on private doctoral campuses.

Slowing enrollments contributed to the recognition that there had been an overexpansion of expensive university programs, especially graduate programs, and that there were more students receiving bachelor's and advanced degrees than could be fully utilized by the available jobs. Stories about Ph.D.'s driving taxis or college graduates washing dishes were common, and long-standing beliefs about the economic returns of higher education were challenged by popular polemics such as *Education and Jobs: The Great Training Robbery* and

The Case against College.[13] Wary campuses cut back on graduate programs, and the number of Ph.D. degrees awarded, which had more than tripled during the 1960s (growing from 10,000 in 1961 to 31,500 in 1970), peaked at 33,000 in 1972–73 and then declined to 31,200 in the last year of the decade. Doctorates awarded to scientists and engineers followed a similar pattern, growing from 4,500 in 1960 to a peak of 14,300 in 1971, then declining to 11,700 by 1979.[14]

Faculty appointments also slowed. In 1969, the nation's campuses employed 546,000 full-time and part-time faculty; by 1976 their numbers had increased to 781,000.[15] It was clear, however, that as enrollment growth slowed these gains would not continue. Annual faculty hiring, averaging around 27,000 in the 1960s, was expected to fall to about 16,000 in the 1970s and to less than 10,000 by the early 1990s.[16] Yet when polled in 1978, officials at most Research I and II universities expected "little or no change" in the number of faculty, and the majority of officials at Doctoral I and II universities registered similar opinions.[17] A further consequence of the large-scale hiring of the 1960s was the growth of the tenured faculty. The ratio of tenured faculty to total faculty was 47 percent in 1969 and 65 percent in 1973, resulting in a kind of "tenure blockage." At the same time, the low proportion of faculty at the upper age levels meant that relatively few vacancies were created by retirement.[18]

In response to these conditions, and to build their research portfolios, universities hired even more researchers on short-term, soft-money contracts that did not carry the benefits of faculty status. This practice, which posed no serious problem during the growth years of the 1950s and 1960s, was by the 1970s producing a two-tiered academic employment system in which a group of "unequal peers," or "unfaculty" (to use Clark Kerr's term) emerged around the "real" faculty.[19] In 1978 there were about four thousand nonfaculty postdoctoral research staff in academic science and engineering, and this group was growing about two and a half times as rapidly as faculty.[20] There was also an increase in the use of part-time faculty, a group that constituted 22 percent of the total instructional staff in 1969 and 31 percent by 1976.

Owing to the pressures of a tight academic job market, the increasing use of postdoctoral researchers, and salaries that were not keeping pace with inflation, and aided by a 1971 National Labor Relations Board ruling that extended collective bargaining to private higher education, faculty at a number of institutions voted to be represented by collective bargaining agents.[21] Unionizing efforts were first successful in the public sector, particularly at community colleges and at relatively new institutions where there were few alternatives for faculty participation in institutional decision making. But faculty on private campuses also joined the ranks of the represented. By 1970, 7.5 percent of all colleges and universities had collective bargaining contracts in force, and eight years later the proportion had tripled.[22] Collective bargaining, virtually nonexistent in the early 1960s, had been instituted in one-fifth of the nation's colleges and universities by 1980.

Changes in Federal Policy and Funding during Nixon's Presidency

The major challenge for research universities, many heavily dependent on federal dollars, was how to manage a steady level of funding that contrasted with the lavish, increasing support they had received in the previous decade. Federal funding of academic research reached a peak between 1967 and 1968 and then declined until the mid-1970s. Between 1968 and 1971, the federal research budget fell more than 10 percent in real terms. Accounting for inflation, total federal awards to universities declined from $4.2 billion in 1968 to $3.9 billion in 1974 (in 1982 dollars), while academic research costs increased about 50 percent between 1967 and 1975.[23] Although the total amount available for university research grew slightly during this period, there was less available for each faculty member. When viewed in per capita terms, federal research funds decreased from $11,200 to $8,400, a 25-percent loss during the seven-year period. The percentage of faculty who received federal support also dropped, from 65 percent in 1968 to 57 percent in 1974.[24]

In addition, changes in the nature of the federal contribution greatly reduced the university's flexibility in building and supporting a research infrastructure. Funds for purchasing scientific equipment, constructing new laboratories, and maintaining existing facilities, reaching $126 million per year in the mid-1960s, averaged just $35 million per year during the 1970s. With the promise of fewer enrollments and a saturated academic job market, support for graduate studies declined dramatically. Fellowship support that had soared to $447 million in 1967 had dropped to $185 million ten years later.[25] By one estimate, the number of federal fellowships and traineeships fell from fifty-seven thousand in 1968 to forty-one thousand in 1970.[26] Research universities adjusted to the change in part by increasing the number of state-funded or institutionally funded teaching assistantships. By the mid-1980s about one-half of the nation's doctoral students received teaching assistantships, one-fifth received university fellowships, fewer than 10 percent received federal fellowships, and fewer than 5 percent held nonfederal national fellowships.[27]

Demographic realities and a rising concern for the disadvantaged led federal policy makers to focus on removing barriers to higher education. The theme was articulated in President Nixon's 1970 "Special Message to Congress on Higher Education," the first such presidential message devoted exclusively to the postsecondary arena. Nixon stated emphatically that "no qualified student . . . should be barred by lack of money." "That has long been a great American goal; I propose that we achieve it now," the president emphasized.[28] The Carnegie Commission agreed, and noted that the highest single priority for federal funding in the 1970s was to help fulfill the "two-century-old dream of social justice" in America: "the equality of opportunity to obtain a college education."[29]

The goal of equal educational opportunity thus was not new. The land-grant movement and the GI Bill had expanded collegiate opportunities significantly. During the prosperous 1960s, when the needs of students were compatible with the needs of institutions, more than two dozen education acts connected to the Great Society and the War on Poverty further expanded access. A string of new federal aid initiatives offered college work-study programs, educational opportunity grants, and partially subsidized guaranteed student loans.[30] But as financial conditions worsened and competition for limited federal resources intensified, the debate between those who favored aid to institutions and those who called for direct aid to students became more acerbic. The higher education community argued that the entire higher education system would be jeopardized unless the government adopted a formula-based program of basic support to institutions. Advocates of the alternative (including the Nixon White House, Department of Health, Education, and Welfare officials, and the leadership of the Carnegie Commission) believed that direct aid to students would make institutions more responsive to changing market pressures. Carnegie officials further feared that if the federal government provided support to institutions, the states would begin to reduce their funding.[31]

Following the 1971 ratification of the Twenty-sixth Amendment, which made 98 percent of the nation's college students eligible to vote, the promise of federal assistance finally was implemented with the Higher Education Amendments of 1972, landmark legislation designed to broaden access to higher education. Stating that students, not institutions, were the first priority for federal support, the legislation provided for a Basic Educational Opportunity Grant that gave financial assistance directly to low- and moderate-income students.[32] In addition to its student aid provisions, the 1972 legislation created accountability mechanisms that would have far-reaching implications. It authorized federal support of State Commissions for Postsecondary Education, the "1202 commissions" that would oversee administration of federal education programs, and established a National Commission on Financing Postsecondary Education charged with developing uniform standards for determining costs and alternative models for the long-range financing of postsecondary education.[33] In other provisions the amendments also authorized the General Accounting Office and authorized the commissioner of education to require institutions to provide information about the costs of educating their students. Title IX of the 1972 amendments, which prohibited discrimination in employment on the basis of sex, required campuses to conform to whatever enforcement and accountability criteria the U.S. Office of Education, and particularly its Office for Civil Rights, might require.[34]

The effect of the new federal student aid policy on the well-being of institutions was regarded by leaders in Congress and the Nixon administration as "a secondary consideration."[35] But its impact on research universities was far-reaching. The law produced a major shift in student aid from the graduate level to the undergraduate and vocational levels. By channeling students away from doctorate-granting and four-year institutions, the law exacerbated these institutions' enrollment problems. Loans became an important source of funds, shifting more of the burden of financing higher education to the student.[36]

At the same time, Congress displaced the White House as the major player in the higher education arena. This process was aided by President Nixon, who in 1973 abolished the presidential Office of Science and Technology and transferred its functions to the National Science Foundation, thus diminishing the science policy machinery that had been expanded by Presidents Eisenhower and Kennedy. For one observer there was no doubt that the reorganization "represent[ed] an official downgrading of science in the Executive Office of the President and the federal government."[37] As a result, not only student aid but also academic research increasingly were considered the province of the legislative branch. The nation's leading research universities, experiencing difficulties with student protest, were vulnerable to critics' charges that they were serving as holding companies for large laboratories or research programs that were not linked to their educational programs.[38] Congress extended distrust of universities to the agencies that funded university research, particularly the NSF. Senator William Proxmire's monthly "Golden Fleece" awards targeted NSF projects considered to be a waste of federal funds. By 1975, criticism of a precollegiate curriculum reform effort entitled "Man—A Course of Study" resulted in a House attempt, one that was ultimately defeated, to require final congressional approval on all NSF projects. Some members of Congress attacked NSF's system of peer review, claiming that it was not a reliable way to coordinate federal funding of research with the political goals of the government. The resulting NSF study of peer review, in part motivated by the agency's need to protect itself from the conflict between proponents of the egalitarian distribution of funds and those who backed the support of larger, prestigious schools, showed that peer review was basically unbiased.[39]

Although the shift in federal policy after 1968 emphasized student access and egalitarianism at the expense of the knowledge-creating role of universities, federal research funding during the 1970s was characterized as much by an overall decline as by shifting internal patterns. By 1970 the total federal research budget had grown smaller. Yet, continuing a trend begun after World War II, academic researchers continued to fare better than their counterparts in industry or federal laboratories. Between 1967 and 1976, for example, the federal R&D contribution to all research activities grew smaller, but support for academic research increased; university research funding from the federal government was 3 percent greater in 1976 than in 1967.[40] Even so, the proportion of university research funded by Washington would fall steadily, dropping from 70 percent of the total in 1970 to 67 percent by 1980 and 59 percent by 1990 (table 4.1). For public doctorate-granting universities the federal share de-

TABLE 4.1
Percentage Distribution of Funding for Academic R&D, by Sector, 1960–1990

Year	Federal Government	State/ Local	Industry	Academic Institutions	All Other[*]
1960	62.7	13.2	6.2	9.9	8.0
1970	70.5	9.4	2.6	10.4	7.1
1980	67.5	8.2	3.9	13.8	6.6
1990	59.0	8.2	6.9	18.5	7.5

Source: National Science Board, *Science and Engineering Indicators, 1993*, app. table 5.2.
[*]Includes foundations.

creased from 75 percent to 60 percent of their total research expenditures, and for their private counterparts it decreased from 82 percent to 77 percent.[41]

The cooling of the cold war associated with the 1972 Anti-Ballistic Missile Treaty, coupled with the U.S. pullout from Vietnam and the winding down of the U.S. space program following the Apollo mission, led to a decade of funding declines for military and space research. Among the most significant changes was the abrupt decline in DOD research funding resulting in part from the Mansfield Amendment, a rider to the Military Authorization Act of 1970 which prohibited the DOD from sponsoring research unless it had a "direct or apparent relationship to a specific military function." Technically a transitory one-year action that had no legal status beyond the year specified in the legislation, the Mansfield Amendment in fact had a more lasting effect.[42] In 1969 the DOD contributed more than 17 percent of the total federal academic R&D commitment, but the Pentagon portion fell to 8 percent by 1975 (table 4.2), a decrease from $279 million in 1969 to $184 million five years later. If universities had received in 1975 the same share of R&D funding from the DOD as they received in 1966, they would have received about $200 million more in 1975.[43]

The shift of DOD funds away from universities had an immediate and lasting impact on the leading research universities. With the overall decline in DOD funding and continued campus protest against university-administered classified research, many institutions reconsidered their relationship with the Pentagon and chose other arrangements for their defense laboratories. Stanford, for example, severed ties with the Stanford Research Institute (SRI); Michigan converted its Willow Run Laboratories to an independent nonprofit institute; and MIT lost substantial overhead allowances when the Draper Instrumentation Laboratory ceased to be affiliated with the university.

The decline in defense and space funding for academic R&D had

TABLE 4.2

Percentage Distribution of Federal Obligations for Academic R&D, by Agency, 1969–1979

Year	NIH	NSF	DOD	NASA	DOE[a]	USDA	Other
1969	35.0	13.9	17.2	6.5	6.6	4.1	16.7
1975	44.7	18.0	8.4	5.4	5.5	4.5	13.5
1979	45.4	15.9	11.3	3.6	6.7	5.1	12.1

Source: National Science Board, *Science and Engineering Indicators, 1989*, app. table 5.5.

[a]DOE = Atomic Energy Commission, 1969–73; Energy Research and Development Administration, 1974–76; Department of Energy, 1977–89.

the effect of increasing the relative contribution of the NSF. From a 1969 baseline of $213 million (current dollars), or 14 percent of the total federal R&D, the NSF share ranged from $435 million (18%) in 1975 to $537 million (16%) in 1978.[44] Among the reasons for the increase was a 1968 legislative mandate that broadened the NSF's authority to support applied research. Initiated in 1971, a major program known as Research Applied to National Needs (RANN)[45] received in 1972 almost $42 million, the largest single increase approved for a particular research program in a single year.

A government-wide emphasis on applied and special projects resulted in sharply contracted NSF funding for academic research facilities and other infrastructure needs. For example, support for university computing facilities dropped from $69 million per year at the beginning of the decade to $39 million two years later.[46] The NSF also absorbed several programs from other agencies, most notably NASA, which, after sharp cuts in the space program following the manned lunar landing, reduced the support it provided, which had reached $117 million in 1966, to $83 million in 1975, or from 6.5 percent in 1969 to 3.6 percent in 1979 (table 4.2). In addition, the NSF assumed responsibility for certain DOD programs (such as the Advanced Research Projects Agency materials research programs) curtailed by the Mansfield Amendment. In the field of physics alone, NSF support increased from $30 million in 1971 to $52 million in 1975, while combined DOD-NASA support for physics declined from $74 million to $44 million.[47] As for RANN, its prosperity was short-lived. By 1977 the program, discredited both because of its failure to meet national needs and because of the poor quality of its funded projects, was absorbed into NSF's established programs.

Declines in federal support for defense and space research and for building campus research facilities were partially offset by increases in biomedical and energy research funds. Support for biomedical research of all kinds continued to rise during the 1970s, thanks to initiatives such as the War on Cancer. The National Cancer Act of 1971 resulted in a threefold increase in appropriations for the National Cancer Institute (NCI)—from almost $200 million in 1970 to almost $600 million four years later. Increasing support for cancer research and for heart and lung disease research in 1972 accounted for 82 percent of the increases in HEW funds.[48] Housing these programs, the NIH continued as "the giant" of academic research funding, providing 35 percent of federal funding for academic research in 1969, averaging 45 percent during the 1970s, and providing almost 50 percent by 1989. The NIH became so dominant, some argued, that "every change in its policies, priorities, regulations and procedures must be of critical concern to every university."[49] NIH support of medical school research thus continued to prosper during the 1970s, increasing (in current dollars) from $518 million in 1970 to $1,077 million in 1975 and $1,493 million in 1978.[50]

Academic research losses in defense and space agency support were also offset somewhat suddenly by the energy crisis of the 1970s. Influenced by the price shock of the oil embargo in 1973, the portion of the federal R&D budget for energy would increase almost fivefold during the 1970s. In 1974 Congress passed the Federal Nonnuclear Energy Research and Development Act, abolishing the Atomic Energy Commission and dividing its functions between the new Energy Research and Development Administration (ERDA) and the Nuclear Regulatory Commission. Funding for energy-related academic R&D under ERDA, and later the Department of Energy, went from $94 million (6.8% of the federal R&D obligations) in 1970, to $132 million (5.5%), to $240 million (7%) in 1978.[51] The buildup of energy R&D offset nearly half of the decline in defense and space R&D, while health and energy expenditures together offset all but 20 percent of the decline.[52]

Internal shifts in federal funding reflected the government's emphasis on targeted research. Historically, federal support of research, including university research, was programmatic, designed to help mission agencies strengthen national defense, improve health care, win the space race, or stimulate economic growth.[53] Especially in the cold war climate of the early 1950s, federal funds for academic research were heavily weighted toward goals that would further the program of the sponsoring agency rather than toward the basic research agenda determined by individual scientists.[54] However, in the decade following *Sputnik,* both by the benefactions of the NSF, the "patron of pure science," and by the creation of NASA, federal agencies provided generous funding for basic research to scientists at an expanding group of institutions. Such a healthy climate for basic research and for the "kind of benign anarchy in which merit could be quickly recognized" contributed to the academy's inhospitable reception of the government's return to programmatic priorities in the decade that followed.[55]

By the late 1960s, "relevance" had become a salient criterion for political support as Congress began to ask what science could do for society. The NSF's RANN program was one example of the government's effort to redirect research toward applied public goals. Especially in biomedical fields, Congress became dissatisfied with the failure of basic research to produce concrete results. The NIH reorganization that gave special status to the National Cancer Institute and the National Heart and Lung Institute further increased attention to specific medical problems. The 1976 Senate hearings on biomedical research focused on a single theme: "Why don't you people at NIH spend less time `understanding' disease and spend more time preventing or curing it?" one senator asked. And another claimed, "I have never heard of anyone dying of microbiology."[56]

Changes in federal obligations for basic and applied research between 1969 and 1979 reflected the emphasis on funding targeted research. In 1969 more than three-fourths of the total federal academic R&D contribution went for basic research, compared with about one-fifth supporting applied research. By the mid-1970s, however, funding for applied research had increased to one-fourth of the total.[57] DOD support for basic research, for example, inhibited by the Mansfield Amendment, fell by 50 percent between 1969 and 1975. Responding to criticism about the lack of useful results, NIH in the 1970s funded more research in the form of contracts that required specified techniques and a timetable determined prior to the award; by 1975 contracts accounted for 25 percent of the $1.5 billion NIH awarded for R&D.[58] The federal emphasis toward programmatic research was reflected in the increasing frequency with which government agencies advertised for research bids by using Requests for Proposals (with their shorter turnaround time), as well as in the growth of federal contracts at the expense of grants and in the incentives given to coupling university research with industrial and governmental efforts, exemplified by RANN projects.

Campus Adjustments to Changing Research Support and the Costs of Accountability

During the 1960s, growing federal support had meant that universities both sought fewer nonfederal funding sources and relied on them less. The contribution by state governments to academic research, 13 percent of the total in 1963, dropped to less than 10 percent in 1970 and to 8 percent in 1990. Industry contributed around 3 percent between 1970 and the middle of the decade, and that figure grew to 4 percent by 1990. The share of university R&D supported by foundations and other nonprofit organizations, whose disposable income was reduced by "stagflation" and stock market losses, also declined. It became the responsibility of the academic institutions themselves to contribute increasingly to support their own research activities.

95

Motivated in part by the financial benefits of expanding research, universities steadily increased their support of research activities, from 10 percent of the total R&D costs in 1960 to more than 12 percent by 1980. By 1990 the university contribution would reach 18.5 percent (table 4.1).[59] In 1982 dollars, the academic contribution increased from $206 million in 1960 to $386 million in 1963, and jumped to $706 million in 1974. Public research universities, unable to rely on state appropriations and receiving a smaller percentage of federal dollars than their private counterparts, began to contribute more to their own research efforts. By 1980 their own allocation reached 17 percent of the total, as compared to less than 8 percent at private institutions.[60] A study of growth in research expenditures at a group of seventy-one leading universities demonstrated that between 1975 and 1979 the research expenditures of public institutions grew at a rate (about 11%) exceeding the rate of increase in federal grants and contracts (about 7.5%). At the leading private institutions a $12-million increase in federal grants and contracts was accompanied by a $9-million gain in university research expenditures.[61]

Increased congressional involvement, an emphasis on targeted research, and a general trend toward government regulation of the private sector all contributed to growing public intrusion into what Martin Trow called "the private life of higher education."[62] Before the mid-1960s, campuses were essentially exempt from almost all federally mandated social programs, including Social Security and unemployment insurance. With the adoption of federal civil rights legislation in 1964, however, Washington began to expand the web of social regulation. One decade later, universities "had lost their immunity to the burdens of an increasingly regulated society."[63] During the 1970s federal regulation of university affairs was extended to include mandates on equal employment and equal educational opportunity for women and minorities, toxic waste disposal, human and animal subjects of research, and access for the handicapped. By the end of the decade, federal agency regulations covered the hiring, promotion, and firing of university personnel, including faculty; wage and salary administration; pensions and benefits; plant construction and management; record keeping; research; admissions; athletics; fund raising; and in some cases, curricula.[64]

The issue of federal regulation took center stage as university officials recognized that the new federally mandated social programs significantly added to university operating costs and thus would compete for funding with research activities.[65] During the 1970s, campuses found that federal regulatory compliance demanded a staggering share of scarce dollars and administrative time and gave rise to layers of bureaucracy both in Washington and on the campus. In a widely quoted claim, Derek Bok noted that at Harvard, compliance with federal regulations consumed over sixty thousand hours of faculty time and cost almost $8.3 million in 1974–75.[66] The Internal Revenue Service threat to revoke the tax exemption of every private school, college, or university that did not conform to IRS definitions of public policy with respect to racial discrimination sent shudders through the academic community.

A series of studies measured higher education's cost of compliance with federally mandated requirements.[67] One of these studies, sponsored by the ACE, found that at six selected research universities, the combined costs of implementing government programs comprised 1 to 4 percent of the universities' operating budgets, and these costs increased much faster than did either instructional costs or total institutional revenues. Another study concluded that "implementing federal policies with respect to social justice, manpower, science, defense, and taxation has a far greater impact on higher education than does any explicit and coherent federal policy in support of higher education."[68] Another found that meeting regulatory costs absorbed as much as 7 to 8 percent of total institutional budgets.[69] Particularly alarming was the prospect that private institutions, unable to turn to state legislatures for increased funding, "may bear relatively heavier social program cost burdens."[70] University complaints focused on the burden of reporting and its incompatibility with university procedures,[71] and on the escalating standards of documentation without reimbursement of most of the increased costs.[72]

Of particular importance for research universities was the manner in which the government determined indirect costs or overhead, a process set by Congress in 1965 as a "negotiated reimbursement." Federal agencies' reimbursement of the indirect costs incurred by universities in support of sponsored research—the costs of heat, light, maintenance, security, accounting, libraries, and administration—was governed by OMB Circular A-21, first issued by the Bureau of the Budget in 1958.[73] The A-21 regulations forced universities to expand their administrative staffs and computer capabilities in order to comply with the required records management and audits. After intense negotiations between federal officials and university representatives, Circular A-21 was revised in 1978 and again in 1982. These compromises eased the transition from the recession-ridden 1970s into the more prosperous 1980s—postponing to the 1990s the more radical policy adjustments that soaring federal deficits would force.[74]

Perhaps most heavily affected by the growth of federal regulation of universities in the 1970s were medical schools and academic health centers. These centers faced not only the increasing regulatory complexities that burdened other university units but also new efforts by federal policy makers to come to grips with the intractable problems of health care delivery. In health professions schools the impact of federal regulations on curriculum, admissions policies, financial aid, and the management of academic health centers was substantial.[75] Beginning with the Health Professions Assistance Amendments of 1971, those institutions that agreed to increase the size of their entering classes became the beneficiaries of direct institutional support in the form of capitation grants. These grants provided supplementary per-student awards that helped to finance the high cost of medical training. Not surprisingly, the extension of federal benefits was soon accompanied by increasing regulation. In 1976 Congress revised the 1971 legislation to require that universities receiving capitation grants admit to their third-year classes American medical students studying abroad who had completed two years of medical training.[76] Despite protracted negotiations between academic leaders and Congress, the law signed by President Ford so threatened medical deans that several prestigious universities announced that they simply would forgo the capitation funds rather than comply.[77] Faced with declinations from institutions that trained 13 percent of the country's medical students, Congress reconsidered, and in 1977 it modified the regulations so that medical schools were not precluded from applying their own admissions criteria.

State governments and agencies also increased their regulations governing universities during the 1970s, often specifying how state appropriations would be spent and requiring more detailed information on enrollments, faculty salaries and workload, and expenses and operating costs. Under these circumstances, public research universities had much to lose as state legislators, many of whom had not attended the leading research institutions, became increasingly involved in the internal affairs of higher education. State officials unfamiliar with the training of anthropologists or historians or physicists nonetheless defined criteria for measuring such elements as "efficient graduate student productivity" and used them as a basis for recommending levels of university support.[78] Because the combined cost to universities of operating federal and state accountability programs escalated at the same time that financial support decreased, it became impossible for campuses to continue to expand their research activities and also fulfill the new social agenda.[79]

Dispersion of Research Support and Activity during the 1970s

Observing the changes in federal support during the late 1970s, Bruce Smith and Joseph Karlesky argued that persistent financial difficulties facing most institutions would alter the state of academic science. As competition for research funds became more intense, they claimed, the accumulated advantage of the established elite research universities would become more pronounced and institutions with less elaborate research programs would fall by the wayside.[80] Fifteen presidents of elite universities, arguing that "the best is vastly more important than the next best," proposed that "a stronger partnership between our federal government and our major research universities" should be renewed.[81] Cutbacks during the Nixon administration, including the termination of the NSF's Science Development Programs, the DOD's Project THEMIS, NASA's Sustaining University Program, and similar federal efforts to enhance the research activities at second- and third-tier institutions, had a ripple effect as institutions scrambled to find new sources of support. Thus, in the early 1970s many of the less prestigious institutions returned to what one observer called "the second-hand, spectator-type science" that had characterized their activities prior to World War II.[82]

The effort to extend and decentralize the nation's research capacity to second- and third-tier institutions, given high priority in the 1960s, was called into question in the 1970s.[83] In the context of scarce resources, some argued, it was important to concentrate efforts in the nation's best institutions (an argument repeated in the early 1990s), especially in light of the explosion of recently developed research and graduate training programs, many at less distinguished universities. To some contemporary reviewers, a retrenchment of such programs in the 1970s in fact might reflect a "healthy readjustment in a system that squeezed out inefficient performers."[84] Others questioned whether institutions below the top rank could keep pace in the increasingly costly and more competitive research market.

Despite concerns about distributing scarce federal research dollars too widely, not all aspiring institutions were excluded from the research competition. Many avoided difficulties by specializing in areas of research and graduate training in which they had a natural advantage due to the presence of local industry or special faculty skills. Following a trend that was begun after World War II and was sustained and advanced during the 1950s and 1960s through federal policy and university initiative, the nation's research activity became increasingly dispersed among the top one hundred research universities. In 1963, one-third of all federal funds for academic research went to ten top-ranked institutions including Michigan, Harvard, and Berkeley, but by the mid-1970s their share had declined to one-fourth. The top twenty institutions, awarded half the federal R&D total in 1963, received little more than 40 percent in 1975.[85] There were also changes in the regional distribution of federal academic research funds. During the 1970s universities in the Sunbelt received more federal research support, thereby reducing the share of the top-ranked regions and their institutions.[86] The share for New England and the Middle Atlantic states dropped from 15 percent to 12 percent of the total, while the share for the Rocky Mountain and Pacific Coast states increased from 12 percent to 15 percent. Public and private universities demonstrated different trends. Of the twenty second-tier research universities that increased their share of research dollars, fourteen were public and six were private. All four of those that climbed into the top ten were public.[87]

The wider dispersion of federal funds was not the rule for medical schools, however, as the NIH continued to lavish research funding on established R&D leaders. During the early 1960s the ten wealthiest medical schools in R&D funding received more than twelve times as much NIH support as the ten poorest. In 1967, two years after President Johnson's executive order directing agencies to increase the number of institutions capable of performing research of high quality, the top fourteen medical schools received 41 percent of the NIH awards, and in 1973 they received 44 percent.[88] In 1978–79 the research expenditures of the top twenty medical schools accounted for 50 percent of the $887 million in federal R&D funds received by 120 medical schools.[89] Nonetheless, during the 1970s the significant increase in NIH funding, distributed through traditional peer-review procedures that favored established leaders, contributed to a healthy climate for biomedical research on the nation's campuses. The funding of medical schools illustrates the mixed pattern of institutional adjustment during the 1970s, as shifting federal priorities and funding brought leaner years to some sectors of the campuses but continued prosperity to others.

The institutional base of federally funded academic R&D continued to broaden during the 1970s, but rarely at a uniform rate or in a consistent direction. In 1971, 565 academic institutions received federal support for their R&D activities. By 1981 this number had increased to 681. During this ten-year period, there was almost no change in the number of Carnegie-classified Research and Doctoral institutions that received federal research support. Rather, almost all of the increase occurred in other Carnegie categories—among comprehensive universities and colleges, liberal arts colleges, two-year institutions, junior and technical colleges, professional schools, and other specialized institutions. The largest relative increases were among institutions receiving academic R&D support for the computer sciences, mathematics, and the geological sciences. Social science and psychology generally saw a decline in the number of institutions receiving federal support.[90]

The continued growth of the academic profession also contributed to mixed patterns of university adjustment, not stagnation, during the 1970s. Although the growth rate of academic appointments peaked during the 1960s, growth in faculty size continued through the 1970s, though at a reduced rate and less uniformly. Between 1969 and 1979 the number of faculty increased by 46 percent, expanding at half the pace of the previous decade but expanding nonetheless.[91] At the same time the nation's faculty increased in quality. Whereas in the 1960s institutions responded to faculty shortages by hiring applicants who had not completed the requirements for a Ph.D., this happened less frequently in the tight job market of the 1970s. In 1969 about two of five faculty members had earned the doctorate; by 1979, three of five held this degree. The proportion of faculty interested in research also increased sharply. A national ACE survey found that by 1972–73 almost two-thirds of all college and university faculty reported spending some time weekly in research and writing; about three-fifths had published in journals, and two-fifths had published at least one book.[92] In 1969 nearly three-fourths of all college and university faculty reported that they had never published or edited a book or monograph; by 1975, however, that figure was down to two-thirds.[93] At doctorate-granting universities, more than 20 percent of the faculty spent seventeen hours or more per week engaged in research and scholarly writing. Two other national surveys of faculty in doctorate-granting departments, conducted in 1974 and 1975, showed that more than 80 percent of the respondents spent at least 20 percent of their time on research.[94]

During the 1970s, faculty with doctoral degrees were distributed over an increasingly differentiated institutional structure of higher education. In 1969 nearly half the ranked faculty members had held appointments at universities, approximately two out of five had taught at other four-year colleges, and one-sixth had been at community colleges. One decade later, the university sector claimed barely a third of all faculty, the four-year sector had increased its share to 46 percent, and the share of the two-year colleges had increased to 22 percent.[95] The availability of so many highly skilled, well-qualified applicants for faculty positions enabled less prestigious institutions, enjoying a buyer's market, to recruit faculty trained at the elite universities.[96] A greater number of faculty researchers thus were active at a wider variety of institutions. According to one assessment, between 1969 and 1975 Doctoral I and Doctoral II campuses showed the greatest increase in the proportion of faculty with a primary interest in research.[97]

A comparison of the average number of full-time instructional faculty at institutions in the Carnegie doctorate-granting categories demonstrates that, in general, the period from 1968 to 1974 was one of continued expansion, even in the private sector. According to faculty data published by the AAUP, at private institutions the average number of faculty increased by more than 50 percent in the Research I and II categories, 48 percent in the Doctoral II category, and 18 percent at Doctoral I campuses (table 4.3). More modest public sector increases, approximately 20 percent in the Research universities, reflected slower growth (and by implication higher student-faculty

TABLE 4.3
Percentage Increase/Decrease in Average Number of Full-Time Instructional Faculty, by Carnegie Category and Public/Private Status, 1968 and 1974

	1968	1974	Change (%)
Research I			
Public	1,326	1,563	17.8
Private	742	1,149	54.9
Research II			
Public	797	959	20.3
Private	382	604	58.1
Doctoral I			
Public	464	653	40.7
Private	363	429	18.0
Doctoral II			
Public	478	472	−1.3
Private	193	285	47.6

Source: AAUP Bulletin, Mar. 1968 and June 1974. See also Note on Method and Sources.

ratios), except in the Doctoral I category, where the average number of faculty increased by more than 40 percent.

Keeping in mind that there were moderate increases in faculty size during the 1970s, we turn to per capita evidence to document changes in faculty success in the receipt of federal funding and in publication productivity, as well as faculty performance in three more qualitative measures—publications in top-ranked science journals and top-ranked social science journals, and awards to scholars in the humanities and arts. The data discussed below reflect, explicitly, the continuing dispersion of research activity during the 1970s; implicitly, they reflect the renewed emphasis on targeted research, and the increased costs of federally mandated social programs and reporting regulations. While we organize our data on the basis of Carnegie categories, we must note the importance of exercising caution in assuming similarity in research performance across Carnegie designations.

Measuring Research Performance in the 1970s

Two conflicting trends characterized the performance of research universities in the 1970s. On the one hand, the oversupply of Ph.D. holders enabled institutions to improve their scholarly credentials by hiring and supporting active researchers. On the other, as more institutions and researchers competed for fewer resources, established leaders with research traditions enjoyed greater reserves of investment capacity and blue-chip prestige. What do per capita comparisons of research performance tell us about the way these forces played out during the 1970s? Does the evidence show that the dispersion of research talent contributed to narrowing the lead enjoyed by established elites or strengthened the challenge that emerging new research universities posed?

A comparison of the total average federal R&D dollars obligated to Research and Doctoral campuses in 1967–68 with awards to those campuses five years later demonstrates that in current dollars, faculty at a majority of these institutions (the one exception being Doctoral II private campuses) won increased amounts of federal R&D support (table 4.4). The greatest gains were made at Research I and II public universities, where faculty increased their total R&D awards by 52 percent and 40 percent, respectively, while the R&D funding awarded to their private counterparts increased by about 35 percent. Faculty at Doctoral institutions also gained, with public Doctoral I

TABLE 4.4

Average Total Federal R&D Obligations for 1967–1968 and 1973–1974 by Carnegie Category and Public/Private Status, and Percentage Increase/Decrease

	1967–68 R&D Obligations (thousands)	1973–74 R&D Obligations (thousands)	Increase/Decrease (%)
Research I			
Public	$15,300	$23,358	52
Private	20,907	28,967	38
Research II			
Public	4,673	6,533	40
Private	4,537	6,207	33
Doctoral I			
Public	1,702	1,990	17
Private	1,915	2,314	21
Doctoral II			
Public	757	1,038	37
Private	486	304	−37

Source: Data from National Science Foundation, *Federal Support Series, Fiscal 1968 and Fiscal 1974.* See also Note on Method and Sources.

Note: R&D awards are in current dollars.

campuses winning an additional 17 percent and Doctoral II campuses receiving 37 percent more. At private campuses Doctoral I faculty increased their federal R&D funding by 21 percent, although private Doctoral II faculty endured a 37-percent decrease.

Comparing per capita R&D obligations from these two periods reflects in part the decline of research market shares at the top-ranked campuses and the dispersion of research dollars beyond the traditional elite campuses.[98] At Research I and II public campuses, whose faculties grew by about 20 percent, the amount of R&D funding per faculty member increased by 30 and 15 percent, respectively (table 4.5).[99] But at private research campuses, where the average number of faculty increased by more than 50 percent, the average per capita research award *decreased* by more than 10 percent. Doctoral I public institutions received 17 percent fewer per capita R&D dollars, but Doctoral II public campuses, where faculty size remained stable, received 39 percent more federal R&D dollars per capita. Doctoral II private faculty experienced a 57-percent per capita decrease. These per capita R&D comparisons suggest that the public-private gaps had narrowed somewhat, especially at Doctoral II institutions.

All the same, federal R&D awards to Research institutions during 1974 show patterns similar to those demonstrated in 1968, with

TABLE 4.5

Average Per Capita Federal R&D Funding for 1967–1968 and 1973–1974, by Carnegie Category and Public/Private Status, and Percentage Increase/Decrease

Carnegie Category	1967–68 R&D Index[a]	1973–74 R&D Index[a]	Increase/ Decrease (%)
Research I			
Public	$11,540	$14,940	29.5
Private	28,190	25,220	−10.5
Research II			
Public	5,900	6,800	15.4
Private	11,870	10,290	−12.6
Doctoral I			
Public	3,670	3,050	−16.7
Private	5,000	5,390	7.8
Doctoral II			
Public	1,585	2,200	39.2
Private	2,515	1,070	−57.0

Source: Data from National Science Foundation, *Federal Support Series, Fiscal 1968 and Fiscal 1974.* Per capita compilations by the authors; see Note on Method and Sources.

[a]R&D indexes are in current dollars.

Research I and Doctoral I private institutions dominating the competition. At private institutions, faculty in three of four Carnegie categories received higher sums than did their public counterparts, in terms of both total dollars awarded and the amount per faculty member (tables 4.4 and 4.5). In the Research I group, faculty at private institutions were awarded almost 25 percent more total federal R&D funding (in current dollars) and almost 70 percent more per capita dollars. Their success can be attributed in large part to the many NIH-supported research activities at medical schools in their ranks. Faculty at Research II private institutions, receiving fewer federal dollars than their public counterparts, demonstrated a 10 percent higher per capita score. In the Doctoral categories, faculty at Doctoral I private schools also achieved higher per capita scores, but consistent with the decline in federal funding experienced by private Doctoral II institutions, these campuses were awarded about half the per capita amount won by public institutions.

Campus publication counts served as the second indicator of faculty research achievement. During the 1960s, studies in the sociology of science centered on the analysis of publication and citation rates.[100] And with the refinement of the Institute for Scientific Information's (ISI's) Science Citation Index (SCI) in the early 1970s, scholarly publication became an even more important index for research achievement.[101] There was also a dramatic increase in the amount of available journal space and the number of publications produced. According to one assessment, between 1962 and 1974 there was a 129-percent growth in the number of research articles in both science and social science fields.[102] Multiple authorship became the norm in the life sciences. The proportion of single-authored articles in the *New England Journal of Medicine,* for example, declined from 91 percent in 1916 to 49 percent in 1946, 29 percent in 1951, and 4 percent in 1976 and 1977.[103] Academic careerism accelerated publishing inflation and a dilution of quality. The ISI reported in the mid-1970s that approximately half of the articles published in scientific and scholarly journals were never cited by another researcher.

Predictably, between 1968 and 1974 faculty publication rates rose at institutions in all four of the Carnegie doctorate-granting categories.[104] A comparison of the number of science articles (the only type of article for which a count was available for the late 1960s) published during these two periods reflects such increases (table 4.6).[105] Science publication productivity basically doubled among Research I public faculty, and at Research I private campuses, faculty increased their productivity by 121 percent.[106] Research II public faculty published 90 percent more in 1974 than in 1968, and their private counterparts averaged an increase of 115 percent. At public and private Doctoral I institutions, there were increases of 100 to 200 percent, with the change most dramatic at Doctoral II private institutions. On these campuses, where R&D awards declined significantly (by 57 percent), faculty increased their science-publication productivity eightfold. A comparison of per capita science publication scores from 1968 and 1974 shows with greater clarity a closing of the gap, both within Carnegie categories and between them (table 4.7). By the 1970s there was less distance separating faculty in all four Carnegie doctorate-granting categories in both the public and private sectors, although faculty at private Research-class institutions continued to outpace their public counterparts.

In 1972, the ISI for the first time included social science publications in its computerized database, and in 1974 it added science publications to its electronic data files. (Humanities publications were added in 1980.)[107] These innovations made possible an assessment of faculty publication productivity across fields.[108] When per capita publications achievement across science and social science fields during 1973 and 1974 was examined, the overall pattern of higher success at private institutions was repeated in each Carnegie cate-

106

TABLE 4.6

Average Total Number of Science Publications for 1968 and 1974, by Carnegie Category and Public/Private Status, and Percentage Increase

Carnegie Category	1968	1974	Increase (%)
Research 1			
Public	1,003	1,996	99
Private	1,135	2,509	121
Research II			
Public	395	752	90
Private	312	672	114
Doctoral I			
Public	110	352	220
Private	135	275	103
Doctoral II			
Public	49	102	108
Private	23	226	882

Source: Data from Institute for Scientific Information, *Science Citation Index* (1968, 1974). See also Note on Method and Sources.

TABLE 4.7

Average Per Capita Science Publications Index, by Carnegie Category and Public/Private Status, 1968 and 1974

Carnegie Category	1968		1974	
	Public	Private	Public	Private
Research I	.76	1.51	1.28	2.13
Research II	.48	.84	.79	1.11
Doctoral I	.24	.38	.54	.61
Doctoral II	.10	.12	.19	.20

Source: Institute for Scientific Information, *Science Citation Index* (1968, 1974). Per capita compilations by authors; see Note on Method and Sources.

gory (table 4.8). Faculty at the elite Research I private institutions were 65 percent better than their public counterparts. But the scores of Research II private faculty were only slightly higher than those of their public counterparts, as were the scores of faculty at private Doctoral I campuses.

More interesting, perhaps, were high per capita publications scores produced at campuses not among the traditional leaders. In 1974 at a number of Research II campuses — Virginia, Carnegie Mellon, Brandeis, Tulane, and Vanderbilt — the number of publications per faculty member was higher than the scores at nineteen of twenty-nine Research I public institutions. While faculty at Doctoral I and II schools achieved generally lower per capita publication scores (table 4.8), those at two Doctoral I campuses, UC Riverside and Al-

107

TABLE 4.8
*Average Per Capita Publications Index, by Carnegie Category and
Public/Private Status, 1974*

Carnegie Category	Public	Private
Research I	1.7	2.8
Research II	1.1	1.5
Doctoral I	.81	.90
Doctoral II	.38	.86

Source: Data from Institute for Scientific Information, *Science Citation Index* (1974), and idem, *Social Science Citation Index* (1973–74). Per capita compilations by authors; see Note on Method and Sources.

Note: Index includes both science and social-science publications.

abama-Birmingham, produced per capita publication indexes that were higher than those of their colleagues at all other schools except at UC Berkeley, Princeton, and Johns Hopkins. The overall pattern of higher private sector publication indexes was repeated in each Carnegie category. Faculty at the elite private Research I campuses scored 65 percent higher than their public counterparts, and on Research II private campuses faculty averaged scores that were about 35 percent higher. In the Doctoral categories, faculty at private campuses received slightly higher scores. At Rice, a Doctoral I private campus, faculty achieved scores that were higher than those of their colleagues at all but four Research I public campuses and seven Research I private institutions. Faculty at another Doctoral I campus, Dartmouth, produced a per capita publications score that was higher than that of ten Research II private campuses, while faculty at the New School for Social Research, a Doctoral II private school, averaged a score that was comparable to that of fourteenth-ranked Washington University in the Research I private category.

It has been argued that to judge faculty research productivity according to publications counts addresses the quantity but not the quality of faculty research. Other indicators thus are needed to capture the quality of research output. Based on information that became available in the 1970s because of ISI's bibliometric advances, the first of these, the top-science index, documents the work of campus scholars publishing in forty-five leading natural and physical science journals (table 4.9).[109] This index (and the top–social science index discussed below) was calculated by dividing the total number of articles published by an institution's faculty in the leading science journals by the number of faculty on that campus.[110] The publications surveyed included such prestigious journals as *Cell, Nature, Physical Review,* and *Science* — the vehicles of choice for aspiring No-

TABLE 4.9

Average Per Capita Top-Science Publications Index, by Carnegie Category and Public/Private Status, 1974

Carnegie Category	Public	Private
Research I	.16	.29
Research II	.08	.10
Doctoral I	.05	.07
Doctoral II	.01	.01

Source: Data from Institute for Scientific Information, *Science Citation Index* (1974). Per capita compilations by the authors; see Note on Method and Sources.

TABLE 4.10

Twenty Leading Public and Private Research I and II Institutions Ranked by Top-Science Index, 1974

Rank	Public Institutions	Top-Science Index	Rank	Private Institutions	Top-Science Index
1	UC Berkeley	.59	1	Caltech	1.79
2	UC San Diego	.48	2	MIT	.89
3	Wisconsin-Madison	.29	3	Rockefeller	.81
4	Colorado	.25	4	Princeton	.69
5	SUNY–Stony Brook	.24	5	Stanford	.54
6	Purdue	.24	6	Brandeis	.47
7	Illinois-Urbana	.23	7	Cornell	.43
8	UCLA	.23	8	Harvard	.39
9	Utah	.22	9	Johns Hopkins	.37
10	Arizona	.20	10	Chicago	.35

Source: Data from Institute for Scientific Information, *Science Citation Index* (1974). Per capita compilations by the authors; see Note on Method and Sources.

bel laureates. (For a list of top-ranked journals and a discussion of how they were selected see the Note on Methods and Sources.)

Like per capita R&D awards and science publications during the 1970s, the top-science scores of faculty at private institutions outdistanced those of their public counterparts. Faculty indexes at Research-class private institutions were higher by about 40 percent. Of the five top-ranked Research I private institutions in this category— Caltech, MIT, Rockefeller, Princeton, and Stanford—only Stanford had a medical school. Fifth-ranked Stanford faculty attained a per capita top-science score comparable to that achieved by faculty at UC Berkeley, the Research I public leader (table 4.10). But faculty at UC San Diego, second-ranked in this category among public institutions, achieved a per capita top-science score that was higher than those of Harvard, Johns Hopkins, and Chicago faculty, ranked eighth through tenth among Research I private institutions.[111]

At the Research II level, faculty at private campuses demonstrated an average score that was about 25 percent higher than that of their public counterparts. In particular, the top-science score achieved by Brandeis (a Research II campus) was also higher than that of every Research I public institution except UC Berkeley and UC San Diego. Other Research II schools that in the 1970s demonstrated high top-science achievement were Carnegie Mellon (with scores higher than all but four of the Research I public institutions), Brown, Vanderbilt, and Tufts, in the private sector, and Virginia and Iowa State in the public sphere. The pattern of higher private achievement was repeated in the Doctoral I category, in which the scores of faculty at private institutions were 37 percent better than those of their colleagues at public institutions.

When the twenty leading public and private universities are ranked by top-science index, some patterns stand out. First, according to per capita measures, faculty at the top-ranked private universities, many located in the Northeast, published on a per capita basis about twice as much in top-science journals as their public counterparts. Elite, research-intensive scientific institutes such as Caltech, MIT, and Rockefeller (the latter excluded from this study because it was not a comprehensive university) have no real equivalent in the public sector. With their small full-time faculty, their huge budgets for sponsored research, and their heavy output of publications, they considerably boost the private per capita top-science scores. Second, and not surprising, when judged on the basis of per capita productivity in top-science journals many of the country's strongest public institutions are clustered in the Midwest and the West.

To document faculty publication in the social sciences during the 1970s, a top–social science index was constructed, based on publications in forty-four top-rated social and behavioral science journals, including *American Economic Review, American Sociological Review, Child Development,* and *Psychological Review.* (The Note on Method and Sources provides a detailed discussion about their selection.) Private sector faculty generally produced somewhat higher per capita scores than did their public counterparts, perhaps a surprising outcome considering the outstanding reputation of the major public research universities in social science fields (table 4.11). Among Research I private institutions, for example, faculty at Stanford, Princeton, Chicago, Yale, Cornell, and Northwestern achieved per capita totals that were higher than faculty scores at Berkeley, the public Research I leader (table 4.12). Other public Research I cam- . puses with exemplary faculty performances in the social sciences

110

TABLE 4.11

Average Per Capita Top–Social Science Publications Index, by Carnegie Category and Public/Private Status, 1974

Carnegie Category	Public	Private
Research I	.04	.06
Research II	.03	.05
Doctoral I	.02	.02
Doctoral II	.01	.02

Source: Institute for Scientific Information, *Social Science Citation Index* (1974). Per capita compilations by authors; see Note on Method and Sources.

TABLE 4.12

Twenty Leading Public and Private Institutions Ranked by Top–Social Science Index, 1974

Rank	Public Institutions	Top–Social Science Index	Rank	Private Institutions	Top–Social Science Index
1	UC Berkeley	.08	1	Stanford	.13
2	Indiana	.08	2	Princeton	.12
3	Washington (Seattle)	.07	3	Chicago	.11
4	Wisconsin-Madison	.07	4	Yale	.10
5	Illinois-Urbana	.06	5	Northwestern	.10
6	Kansas	.06	6	Washington (St. Louis)	.08
7	Michigan	.05	7	Harvard	.08
8	Texas-Austin	.05	8	Johns Hopkins	.07
9	Pittsburgh	.05	9	Duke	.07
10	UC San Diego	.05	10	Cornell	.05

Source: Data from Institute for Scientific Information, *Social Science Citation Index* (1974). See also Note on Method and Sources.

during the 1970s included Indiana, Washington, Wisconsin, Illinois, Kansas, Michigan, and Texas.

Faculty on private campuses in other doctorate-granting categories averaged per capita top–social science scores that were generally about 30 percent better than those of their public counterparts. Tufts faculty ranked second after Stanford, and Claremont Graduate School faculty ranked fourth behind their colleagues at Princeton when per capita social science scores for Research I and II private institutions were compared. Faculty at Carnegie Mellon, a Research II school, achieved a per capita social science score that would rank them with the top half of the Research I group, while Brown faculty produced a score identical to that of Johns Hopkins, ranked ninth among the private Research I campuses. Research II public faculty were led by Indiana, a few percentage points below UC Berkeley. Faculty at Kansas, Virginia, Washington State, and SUNY–Stony Brook

TABLE 4.13
Average Per Capita Arts-and-Humanities Index, by Carnegie Category and Public/Private Status, 1965–1974

Carnegie Category	Public	Private
Research I	.03	.07
Research II	.02	.04
Doctoral I	.02	.02
Doctoral II	.01	.01

Source: Annual reports, 1965–74, American Council of Learned Societies, John Simon Guggenheim Foundation, and National Endowment for the Humanities. See also Note on Method and Sources.

were among the overall top twelve when the performance of public Research I and II faculty was compared.

A particularly acute problem, the lack of comprehensive and reliable data documenting research achievement in the arts and humanities, led us to compile a separate arts-and-humanities (A&H) index.[112] Because journals are not a major forum for scholars in the arts and humanities, this per capita measure was derived by counting competitive grants and fellowships awarded to a given campus (1965–74) by the National Endowment for the Humanities, the John Simon Guggenheim Foundation, and the American Council of Learned Societies (table 4.13). (See the Note on Method and Sources for a discussion of how the index was calculated.) A second A&H data set constructed for 1980–89 will be discussed in chapters 6 and 7, below.

As expected, given the strength of the humanities in private collegiate traditions since the founding of the colonial colleges, the private advantage in per capita A&H awards was strikingly evident at private campuses, especially at Research I institutions. Scholars at Yale, Princeton, and Columbia, ranking first through third among Research I private institutions, achieved higher per capita A&H scores than did faculty at UC San Diego, the Research I public leader in A&H performance (table 4.14). Faculty at UC Berkeley, second among public Research I institutions in A&H scores, would rank just below Stanford (ranked eighth) in a comparative Research I competition. Most noticeably, in the public sector new institutional faces from the Sunbelt broke into positions of arts-and-humanities leadership. Five of the top ten public universities were campuses from the University of California system, and the South, where humanities traditions often were nurtured, was represented by Virginia, Texas-Austin, and UNC–Chapel Hill (table 4.14). Faculty at private Research I and II campuses attained average per capita A&H scores that were at least

TABLE 4.14
Twenty Leading Public and Private Institutions, Ranked by A&H Index

Rank	Public Institutions	A&H Index	Rank	Private Institutions	A&H Index
1	UC San Diego	.11	1	Yale	.17
2	UC Berkeley	.09	2	Princeton	.16
3	Virginia	.09	3	Columbia	.16
4	UC Riverside	.06	4	Brown	.12
5	UCLA	.06	5	Dartmouth	.12
6	SUNY–Stony Brook	.06	6	Harvard	.11
7	Indiana	.06	7	Johns Hopkins	.10
8	Texas	.05	8	Stanford	.09
9	North Carolina–Chapel Hill	.05	9	Chicago	.08
10	UC Santa Barbara	.05	10	Pennsylvania	.08

Source: Annual reports, 1965–74, American Council of Learned Societies, John Simon Guggenheim Foundation, and National Endowment for the Humanities. See also Note on Method and Sources.

twice as high as the Research I public faculty scores. Faculty at Doctoral public and private campuses achieved average scores that were the same as those of their counterparts at Research II public institutions.

The story of excellence in the arts and humanities, one that spans Carnegie categories, unfolds through an examination of faculty achievement at specific institutions. In a comparison of A&H indexes of all private sector campuses, for example, scholars at the Doctoral I Claremont Graduate School, advantaged in this process by a small consortium faculty, attained the highest per capita score. Faculty at Brown (Research II) and Dartmouth (Doctoral I) achieved A&H scores that ranked them fifth and sixth, respectively, just above Research I Harvard and Johns Hopkins. Faculty at Brandeis (Research II) also received a per capita score that ranked them twelfth between Stanford and Chicago. At Rice (classified as Research II in the 1970 Carnegie classification but Doctoral I in the 1976 revision), faculty attained the same A&H score as those at Vanderbilt. Faculty at Tufts and Emory, two other Research II private campuses, also achieved A&H scores that qualified them for the top twenty overall. In a Carnegie category in which six schools received no A&H awards, faculty at Doctoral II Clark achieved an A&H score that would rank them eighteenth among private doctorate-granting institutions.

In the public sector, faculty at the UC Research I campuses at San Diego, Berkeley, and Los Angeles and the Doctoral I campus at Riverside claimed four of the top five A&H places; faculty at the University of Virginia, in 1970 classified as a Research II campus, ranked third. Faculty at SUNY–Stony Brook (Doctoral I in 1970) and Indiana (designated as Research II in 1970) ranked sixth and seventh, respectively. Faculty at two other UC campuses, Santa Barbara and Irvine (both Doctoral I), and at Davis (Research I) also joined the A&H public top-ranked schools.

The per capita qualitative scores that document research activity across the academic spectrum indicate that by 1974, faculty at Research and Doctoral public and private institutions had expanded dramatically the quality and quantity of their scholarly work. In general, however, faculty at private sector institutions demonstrated a higher per capita performance. Those at elite private Research I universities continued to dominate in each category. On a per capita basis, they were the major recipients of federal dollars, they published the largest number of scholarly articles overall as well as in leading science and social science journals, and they achieved the highest arts-and-humanities scores. At the same time, when the per capita federal R&D awards received by faculty at these institutions in 1968 are compared with the 1974 per capita awards, there is a 10-percent per capita decrease. This comparison reflects the growth in quality of faculties at public and private Research and Doctoral universities, the steady level of federal funding, and the wider dispersion of federal R&D awards to more research campuses.

Faculty at the smaller Research II private institutions also demonstrated significant research prowess. Awarded lower federal R&D support than their colleagues at Research I private and public institutions, Research II private faculty were nevertheless highly competitive. These faculty averaged publications and top-science indexes that were comparable to those of faculty at Research I public institutions, and top–social science and A&H scores that were higher than those of their public Research I counterparts. In particular, faculty at Carnegie Mellon and Vanderbilt, Tufts, Brandeis, and Brown achieved scores in the three qualitative categories that rivaled those attained by their counterparts at Research I institutions.[113]

At the UC doctoral campuses, faculty during the 1970s achieved remarkably high scores in the three qualitative categories. Faculty per capita scores at Riverside and Santa Barbara led the Doctoral I campuses in all three qualitative categories and surpassed the per capita score of faculty at Berkeley, the Research I public leader, in the top–social science category. Santa Cruz faculty achieved impressive top–social science and A&H scores, and Irvine faculty attained a high A&H score. Faculty on private Doctoral campuses, particularly those at Dartmouth, the New School, and Clark, also achieved consistently high qualitative scores across the academic spectrum.

114

In comparing data from the 1960s and 1970s, we see patterns in the research behavior of groups and clusters of institutions. Such comparisons are useful in exploring the questions asked at the beginning of the chapter about whether the large gap in research performance separating elites and challengers was reduced between 1968 and 1974. This gap took two forms. One was furthered by the outstanding performance of faculty at private institutions. The other, as expected, was represented by the elite advantage—the margin by which the per capita achievement of faculty at Research-class institutions exceeded that of faculty at Doctoral-class institutions. Yet, clear evidence of "gap closing" and dispersion of research activity across institutional types is demonstrated in the more quantitative categories (the R&D and total publications indexes). But during the 1970s, evidence from the qualitative measures (the top-science, top–social science, and A&H indexes) documented the unmatched excellence of faculty at elite private universities in particular, and elite research universities generally. These academics' continuing success, aided by the power of prestige, influence with the editorial boards of the leading journals, an important role in peer-reviewed competition for grants and awards, and so on, was not fundamentally challenged.

Nevertheless, during the 1970s there is evidence that a number of rising research universities seriously engaged in the nation's academic research enterprise. We see this trend in spite of severe economic inflation, slowing academic enrollments and faculty hiring, and a decline in federal funding for academic research. We see this trend because of university adaptation to stringent economic conditions, wider dispersion of research dollars and faculty talent, a strengthening of programs hastily expanded in the 1960s, and the view that academic research was good university business. Given the domination of traditional elites in American higher education and the power of the Matthew effect in reinforcing their hegemony, the appearance in the 1970s of other emerging institutions at which faculty research performance equalled that of established elite institutions is perhaps surprising but certainly explicable.

By the end of the 1970s our universe of research universities, grown to include 213 institutions, experienced a reinvigorated research environment. At the same time, Congress began to increase federal investment in universities for basic as well as applied research, especially to support national defense and energy self-sufficiency. During the Reagan years, defense R&D once again soared, and a growing concern for American economic competitiveness in a global market led business leaders and state and local leaders to invest in universities as engines of regional economic development. In the peculiar way in which the thematic decades of federal higher education policy have begun two years early—the golden sixties beginning with the post-*Sputnik* investments of 1958, signs of the decelerating seventies starting in 1968—the defense-driven boom of the Reagan era began in 1978 under President Jimmy Carter.

5

■

THE GOLDEN AGE REDUX: FEDERAL FUNDING AND ACADEMIC RESEARCH IN THE 1980s

The turnaround in government funding of research which began in 1978 under Carter continued through the presidencies of Ronald Reagan and George Bush. Although the Reagan administration dismantled several Carter initiatives—for example, "industrial policy" planning, federal sponsorship of industry-university collaboration, and development of alternative energy sources—the growth of academic research funding begun under Carter was accelerated by the Republican administrations of the 1980s, especially in defense technology. Overall, the endurance of congressional structures and preferences, interest-group networks, and agency alliances produced more continuity than change in federal science policy. When the economy recovered in 1982, Congress passed and Reagan signed appropriations bills that raised federal academic R&D obligations from $4.5 billion in fiscal 1981 to $10.2 billion in fiscal 1991 (in 1987 dollars), an increase of 127 percent.[1]

Despite the reputation of the Reagan and Bush administrations for emphasis on defense R&D, the most powerful engine of academic research nonetheless remained the National Institutes of Health. The growth of NIH funding during the 1980s continued to strengthen biomedical research across the campuses in life science and behavioral science departments and in molecular and chemical engineering programs as well. But its greatest impact was in academic health centers. As we noted in chapter 4, research expanded in medical schools throughout the 1970s despite contractions in other areas. Medical schools in the 1980s enjoyed further advantages that flowed from a unique combination of assets, including generous NIH funding, a capacity to expand clinical as well as academic science research, and research subsidies from teaching hospitals in the form of reimbursements from private insurers, Medicare, and Medicaid for the provision of health care.

Federal Science Policy from Carter to Reagan

From the viewpoint of the universities, federal science policy functioned at three levels: (1) scientific advice provided to the president on fundamental matters of national security and welfare; (2) agency policies and program priorities concerning university-based research; and (3) policy that determined the levels of federal funding to be provided. The first level, which drew most public attention and dealt with issues of the greatest potential significance to the nation, had the least direct connection to the supply-and-demand functions of the academic research economy. The decline of the President's Science Advisory Committee from its peak of prestige under Eisenhower and Kennedy to its dismantlement under Nixon left a vacuum that denied university leaders the access to presidential power they had enjoyed prior to the turmoil over Vietnam. This absence of institutionalized access was partially addressed during the Ford administration by Vice President Nelson Rockefeller, whose efforts led Congress in 1976 to establish the Office of Science and Technology Policy (OSTP). During the Carter administration the president's science advisor, the geophysicist Frank Press of MIT, participated to varying degrees in policy reviews concerning major issues of national policy—the neutron bomb, missile basing, global warming, antisatellite weapons, strategic arms limitation, recombinant DNA, and nuclear reactor safety.[2] Carter's science and higher education policies had their greatest impact on campus research, however, at the more programmatic second and third levels, where they were tailored to domestic economic and social circumstances.

Growing economic competition from abroad, a high level of inflation and unemployment, and a slowdown in worker productivity were conditions inherited by Jimmy Carter. The early Carter years thus witnessed sharpening fears about the loss of international markets and domestic jobs, and subsequent calls to reindustrialize America. Trained in engineering, Carter protected basic science research while emphasizing applied development work—the *D* in R&D—especially in energy, space, and defense technology. Universities, traditionally involved in research but not heavily involved in product development, welcomed Carter's initiatives to strengthen their research infrastructure.[3] In 1978, a new National Science Foundation program to support the project grant system provided discretionary funds to more than three hundred colleges and universities. That same year a Commerce Department report on innovation inaugurated a new emphasis on the nation's economic competitiveness.[4] Even as part of his "Economic Program for the Eighties," Carter called for the expansion of federal programs for research and technology to help stimulate industrial revitalization and provided funds for research instrumentation to both the NSF and the NIH.[5] Congress in 1980 authorized NSF programs to increase participation by women, minorities, and minority institutions in scientific research.

At the level of federal R&D funding to the campuses, Carter directed the NSF and the mission agencies to build on existing programs in defense, energy, environmental protection, agriculture, space, and medicine. During 1977–80, the academic R&D obligations of federal agencies, essentially stagnant since 1972, increased by 16 percent (in constant dollars). And under the Carter administration, academic R&D for defense grew by 51 percent in actual dollars, a growth rate not matched during Reagan's presidency, despite its longer and larger defense buildup.

Federal science policy under Reagan generated intense controversy but involved issues that had little to do with university research. Disputes over acid rain, MX missile basing, the credentials of science advisor George Keyworth, and especially, in March 1983, Reagan's Strategic Defense Initiative (SDI), the "Star Wars" program, left the presidential science advisory system in disarray and greatly strained the administration's relations with the nation's scientific establishment.[6] At the level of scientific program priorities, Reagan and his conservative advisors opposed what had been Carter's emphasis on government leadership in industrial strategy and dismantled many of Carter's development and demonstration projects. Reagan's OMB director, David Stockman, and his successors were especially hostile to government-controlled development projects in energy (in fields such as synthetic fuels, solar energy, and conservation) and civilian commerce (cooperative auto research and industrial productivity innovation). The Reagan White House, viewing government economic intervention as dangerous and the academic culture as hostile, slashed agency budgets supporting research in the social sciences, the humanities, and the arts and discontinued university-government-industry joint ventures.[7]

Yet R&D policy per se was not a Reagan priority. The Reagan administration disapproved of government development programs and preferred applied over basic research, but it called for no major changes in the relationship between the federal government and universities. Like the Carter administration and its predecessors, the Reagan White House approved of the traditional mechanisms of peer-review competition for merit-based project grant research. And Congress, despite Republican control of the Senate during 1981–87, did not fundamentally alter the standard policies and procedures that had nourished the academic research economy since the 1950s. What Congress did accomplish during the Reagan years was to approve budget proposals that poured vast new sums into university research budgets. The renewed flood of R&D support was spent not only in defense, where proposals such as Star Wars attracted the most notice, but across the board among the major mission agencies. This even included the NSF, which at the beginning of the Reagan Revolution was recommended for closure by economist Milton Friedman and was called "nonessential" by budget director David Stockman.[8] Most important, the Reagan budgets filled the coffers of the NIH.

New Funding for Academic Research

In the surge of funding for academic research during the 1980s, federal agencies provided the largest amounts, but other funding sectors—industry, foundations, state and local governments, and the institutions themselves, chastened by the decline of federal support in the 1970s—provided even larger increases in research support. In 1988 dollars, total support for academic research nearly doubled, rising from less than $8 billion in 1978 to more than $13 billion in 1988.[9] The annual federal contribution increased from $5 billion (in 1988 dollars) to $8 billion, and support per academic investigator increased by 60 percent. From 1980 to 1990 the campuses enjoyed robust growth in research support from all five major funding sectors (table 5.1).

Private industrial firms, seeking commercial advantage from closer ties with leading universities and research faculty, tripled their level of financial support.[10] State and local political leaders, anxious to protect the competitiveness of regional economies, invested in university-based research parks modeled after Silicon Valley, Boston's Route 128, and North Carolina's Research Triangle.[11] Finally, the universities themselves more than doubled their investments in academic research.[12] In 1988 dollars, the annual contributions of universities to their own research enterprise rose from $1.2 billion in 1978 to $2.4 billion in 1988.[13] In response to the new funding, the

TABLE 5.1
Funding for Academic R&D, and Percentage Distribution, by Sector, 1980 and 1990

Funding Sector	1980		1990		% Increase 1980–90
	R&D Funding (millions)	Share (%)	R&D Funding (millions)	Share (%)	
Federal government	$5,813	67.5	$8,550	59.0	47
Academic institutions	1,186	13.8	2,667	18.5	124
State/local government	704	8.2	1,188	8.2	69
All other sources	571	6.6	1,081	7.5	89
Industry	334	3.9	1,006	6.9	201
Total	$8,608		$14,502		

Source: Data from National Science Board, *Science and Engineering Indicators, 1993,* app. table 5-2.
Note: Funding amounts are in 1982 constant dollars.

pool of trained academic researchers, underemployed in the 1970s, expanded to seize the new opportunities. Between 1978 and 1990 the number of academic scientists with doctorates increased by 41 percent.

On university campuses during the 1980s the renewed vigor of research budgets was accompanied, as it had been in the 1960s, by increased criticism of higher education. American universities felt the lash of public attacks to an extent not seen since the late 1960s, when public confidence in higher education had plummeted as the antiwar movement and radical protest led to widespread campus violence. Most public attention during the late 1980s was drawn to non-research conflicts on the campuses, especially those surrounding issues of "political correctness"—campus free speech codes, affirmative action policies in student admissions and faculty appointments and tenure, the policing of sexual harassment, and the definition of the literary canon. Complaints that universities rewarded research at the expense of teaching, a concern that considerably predated the 1980s, received renewed attention in populist books attacking the professoriate.[14] The controversies associated with university research in the 1980s included charges of conflict of interest stemming from faculty investments in commercial enterprises, federal agency investigations of scientific fraud, congressional attacks on campus abuses of indirect cost recovery, protests against the use of animals in research, and rising concern over the growing numbers of foreign students in doctoral programs and foreign scholars receiving faculty appointments in engineering, mathematics, and computer science.[15]

With regard to research funding on the campuses, however, in many areas of biomedical science and engineering the 1980s exceeded the bountiful years of the 1960s. By far the largest component of the federal R&D funding of the campuses was the continued and expanded NIH support for biomedical research. Under Reagan, the Pentagon's share of academic R&D support had increased from 12.8 percent of total federal R&D funding in 1981 to 16.7 percent in 1986. During the same period, however, the NIH share of academic R&D funding grew from 44.4 percent to 46.6 percent. This represented a five-year increase (in 1982 dollars) of $1,123 million in NIH funding for the campuses. During the 1980s, NIH support for campus research typically was larger by a factor of two than the combined academic R&D budgets of the Pentagon, NASA, and the Department of Energy.

The Unique Research Advantages of Academic Health Centers

The flowering of academic health center research in the 1980s was rooted in events of the 1970s. New arrangements for subsidizing research increased the prosperity enjoyed by campus health professionals while other university researchers complained of recession. For two reasons, it is important to understand how academic health professionals, and especially medical researchers, acquired and exploited these advantages. First, it explains the distinctive invulnerability of the medical school world, at least from the end of World War II to the beginning of the 1990s, to the sectoral recessions that have commonly afflicted other research fields. Second, it may help to explain a crisis in the health of the university research enterprise itself that is occurring in the 1990s, as changes in the nation's health care economy and the federal government's fiscal capacity threaten the underpinnings of academic medicine's half-century reign of prosperity. The consequences of these developments of the 1990s are still unclear, and we will return to them in the conclusion.

Two developments chiefly accounted for the prosperity of academic health centers during the 1970s. One was the uninterrupted growth in NIH funding. University research on defense technology and social issues lost public and congressional support after 1968, but biomedical research did not. Draft cards and American flags were not burned at the medical schools. As President Nixon struggled to withdraw from the unpopular war in Vietnam, he declared a popular "war" on cancer. During 1971–81, annual NIH obligations for academic research grew from $603 million to $2 billion, an increase in constant dollars of 55 percent. During the same period, R&D support from all other federal agencies grew by only 12 percent.[16] During 1972–82, federal support for graduate research assistants in all fields of science and engineering increased by only 5 percent in constant dollars, while support for graduate research assistants in the life sciences grew by 44 percent.[17]

The second development that nourished the health centers during the 1970s owed its provenance to an event that ostensibly had little to do with research universities, at least not directly: the passage of legislation creating Medicare and Medicaid in 1965. The Johnson administration, seeking to win the support, or at least to neutralize the opposition, of physicians, hospitals, and insurance companies, negotiated compromises in the Medicare bill that included an agreement to reimburse hospitals on the basis of their costs, as Blue Cross did, rather than according to a schedule of negotiated rates.[18] This provided an incentive for hospitals and physicians to maximize their reimbursement income by increasing their costs. Medicare, like Blue Shield, reimbursed physicians according to "customary" and "reasonable" fees that were "prevailing" in their area of expertise. These inflationary incentives were balanced by no effective cost-control mechanisms. Under this expanding fee-for-service system, one fueled by tax dollars provided by Medicare and Medicaid to reimburse hospitals and physicians for treating the elderly and the poor, medical costs soared.[19] Hospital bed occupancy increased sharply because high hospital costs produced large reimbursements from third-party insurers. Medical technology produced scientific marvels with large price tags—magnetic resonance imaging, CAT-scanning, laser surgery. Physicians who performed expensive clinical procedures—for example, angiograms and angioplasty, gastroscopy, and colonoscopy—generated fees in dollar amounts previously available mostly for surgeons. The clinical faculty in medical schools, especially those whose practice included medical procedures, began to generate enormous incomes.[20]

These developments accelerated the growth of worrisome trends in American medicine—trends such as runaway health care costs, increasing specialization by medical practitioners and decreasing availability of primary care, reliance on hospital care at the expense of ambulatory care and preventive medicine, and widespread problems of access to health insurance. Many of these problems, however, were felt more acutely in society at large than in the universities, where employees routinely received health care benefits and the academic employee pool was attractive to medical insurers. In the academic health centers, where biomedical research brought university prestige to the teaching hospitals, the portability of health insurance brought a flood of new patients and new revenue to the clinical faculty.

In the medical schools, by the mid-1970s the soaring fee income paid to clinical faculty by third-party insurers was stretching the faculty salary scale to morale-threatening dimensions. Basic science faculty, with salaries not greatly exceeding those paid to professors in chemistry and biology, anchored the low end of the medical school pay scale. In the middle were clinical faculty in fields such as psychiatry, primary care, and preventive health care, who supplemented their academic salaries with professional fees to a greater extent than did most basic science faculty but whose practice as clinical physicians required few procedures. At the high end of the income spectrum, joining the surgeons, was a growing battalion of highly paid clinical faculty in such fields as cardiology, oncology, and gastroenterology, where technically advanced procedures generated high fee-for-service income. By the 1980s professors of surgery commonly received twice as much in pay and benefits as did the most highly paid university presidents.[21] In response, medical deans and department heads negotiated "practice plans" that allowed clinical faculty (who would otherwise leave the academy for more remunerative private practice) to keep most of their new income but required them to contribute a portion of it to support the common research enterprise.

One important goal of the practice plans was to provide for a pooling of clinical fees to invest in strengthening academic medical education and research. Practice-plan income gave medical administrators a rapidly expanding source of discretionary revenue that was independent of traditional funding sources (sponsored research, tuition, gifts, and endowments). The cornucopia of practice-plan income paid the salaries of residents and fellows and subsidized undergraduate and graduate medical education. One of the most productive forms of investment was for new positions for clinical research faculty. These new clinical professors would generate even more income by winning sponsored research grants from government and industry and by generating their own clinical practice fees, which would be fed back into the health center budgets. Small wonder that as university campuses generally grew quiet during the 1970s, academic health centers continued to whine with the sounds of construction, taking on what University of Florida president John Lombardi called that familiar "imploded look, building piled on top of building."[22]

The dimensions of the revenue explosion due to the increase in professional fees during the 1970s are suggested by the medical school experience at Johns Hopkins, where the late-nineteenth-century American marriage between medical schools and teaching hospitals was originally consummated. At Johns Hopkins University the income from sponsored research at the university's school of medicine reached its zenith, as a percentage of the university's total expenditures, in 1970, at 76.5 percent (approximately two-thirds of this was from federal R&D support, and the remainder was from private foundations and industry).[23] Professional fees provided only 3 percent of medical school revenue at Hopkins in 1970. By 1990, however, professional fees had risen to 34 percent of the medical school budget at Hopkins. This was a tenfold increase in twenty years. In nominal (i.e., face-amount) dollars the increase was exponential—from $1.03 million in 1970 to $140 million in 1992.[24] In 1970, professional fees had ranked sixth among major revenue sources at the Hopkins medical school (behind government-sponsored research, and followed by research sponsored by private foundations and industry, endowment income, reimbursements other than professional fees, and indirect cost recovery). By 1990, however, practice-plan income had displaced government-sponsored research as the school's largest single source of revenue.[25]

Given the relative immunity of NIH funding from the retrenchment of federal support in the 1970s, research in the health professions would have considerably outpaced the other fields of university research even in the absence of significant growth by health science faculties. The unanticipated boom in fee-for-service revenue in the teaching hospitals, however, accompanied by practice-plan investment in new faculty positions, produced an extraordinary burst of growth in the nation's medical schools. The dimensions of this expansion can be demonstrated by examining the increase in the number and type of medical faculty at several leading medical schools between 1968 and 1988. The sample used here includes twelve universities with medical schools (six private and six public) ranked in the top twenty according to the National Research Council study of 1982 (as aggregated by Webster).[26] In 1968 these medical schools employed an average of 367 full-time faculty members, 108 of them in the basic science departments and 259 in clinical departments. In the 1960s, public and private medical schools did not differ significantly in faculty size. In both public and private institutions, the clinical faculty in 1968 was roughly two-and-a-half times as large as the basic science faculty. Public and private medical schools responded similarly to the opportunities offered by the bonanza in practice fees.

TABLE 5.2

*Average Number of Full-Time Faculty in Basic Science and Clinical Departments at
Selected Public and Private Medical Schools, 1968 and 1988*

	1968			1988						
	Basic Science	Clinical	Total	Basic Science		Clinical		Total	
				No.	% Increase	No.	% Increase	No.	% Increase
Public	111	251	362	166	52	746	197	912	152
Private	106	266	372	130	20	600	126	730	96
Average	108	259	367	148	37	673	160	821	124

Source: Data from Association of American Medical Colleges.

Note: The public institutions are Michigan, Minnesota, North Carolina–Chapel Hill, UCLA, Washington, and Wisconsin-Madison; the private institutions are Chicago, Columbia, Northwestern, Pennsylvania, Stanford, and Yale.

By 1988, the twelve medical schools in the sample had more than doubled the average size of their clinical faculties (table 5.2). Between the 1960s and the late 1980s, the size of the average basic science faculty had grown from 108 to 148, an increase of 37 percent. The average clinical faculty had grown from 259 to 673, an increase of 160 percent. Most of the faculty growth at the twelve medical schools, not surprisingly, came on the clinical side, where the practice fees, together with indirect cost recovery on expanding research budgets, provided the investment capital. By 1988 the average clinical faculty was more than *four* times as large as the basic science faculty.

What difference did this explosion in faculty size make in the research enterprise at university medical schools? Although basic science faculty members at American medical schools continued through the 1970s and 1980s to participate in sponsored research at a higher rate than clinical faculty, the clinical faculty grew so large, and the amount of clinical research funded by the NIH and private sponsors grew so rapidly, that by 1980 at most medical schools the clinical professors generated more sponsored research funding than did their basic science colleagues.[27] At the twelve universities in this sample, the NIH share of total federal R&D funding on campus increased from 50.4 percent in 1968 to 64 percent in 1988. Although NIH funds comprised a higher percentage of research support at private institutions, the NIH share grew faster at the six public institutions, where it increased by 30.3 percent between 1968 and 1988. By contrast, at four comparable public universities without campus medical schools — UC Berkeley, Illinois, Indiana, and Texas — the NIH share of federal research funding on campus during the same period decreased, from an average of 27 percent in 1968 to 20.8 percent in 1988. Academic health centers were booming everywhere, and cam-

126

puses without them—most of them in the public sector—were denied the chief engine of research expansion.

The great leap forward in clinical investigation was reflected in global patterns of scientific publication. The fundamental discoveries of basic research in molecular biology and cellular physiology, published in journals such as *Cell,* the *Journal of Biological Chemistry, Nature,* and *Science,* continued to dominate the Nobel awards and shape the star system in biomedical science. But research by the great new battalions of clinical scientists produced life-saving applications that won strong support from Congress and the federal funding agencies. American newspaper readers in the 1970s and 1980s became familiar not only with the *New England Journal of Medicine* but also with the *Journal of the American Medical Association,* and occasionally the British journal *Lancet,* publications whose reports on the results of clinical trials with new diagnostic tests or drug therapies offered immediate hope in the war against killers such as cancer, heart disease, and later, AIDS. In the international world of science journals, clinical medicine dominated all other fields of science and technology in the number of articles published annually. In 1987, for example, clinical medicine accounted for 49,904 (37%) of the 134,497 articles in U.S. science journals listed in the *Science Citation Index.*[28] Biomedical research accounted for 24,542 (18%) of the articles. Taken together, by 1987 clinical medicine and biomedical research accounted for *half* of all the scientific papers published in the world. Between 1973—when practice-plan revenue began to fuel the dramatic expansion on the clinical side of American medical schools—and 1987, the U.S. share of the world's scientific articles in clinical and biomedical science had increased from 47 percent to 55 percent.

Between 1945 and 1990 American medical schools were radically transformed. The focus of basic medical research had shifted from the level of organs and tissues, where M.D.-level training had historically been sufficient, to the level of intracellular mechanisms and molecular behavior, where Ph.D.-level training was standard. The clinical faculty, once largely a volunteer, part-time cadre of private physicians with little involvement in research, was transformed into a full-time faculty of clinical science whose members' number (and income) typically dwarfed that of their nonclinical colleagues. Congress, anxious to improve treatments and cures, was generous in its appropriations for clinical research. Because voters linked health care to the health of loved ones, Congress was quick to authorize new disease-based institutes within the NIH for cancer, heart disease, lung disease, arthritis, diabetes, and stroke (by 1970 there were six-teen NIH institutes) and to increase NIH funding accordingly. The fa-mous postwar promotional campaigns associated with Mary Lasker, Florence Mahoney, the American Cancer Society, and the March of Dimes produced in Congress a "categorical" approach that involved an unsystematic proliferation of research institutes but provided a rich shopping mall for extramural researchers.[29] In the 1960s, bio-medical research was still dominated by basic science faculty in the medical schools, where cracking the genetic code had fired the pub-lic imagination. By the 1980s, however, biomedical research was ful-ly twin-engined, and clinical research budgets often exceeded those in the basic sciences.[30]

In 1990 the NIH awarded research grants and contracts to 124 medical schools in the United States. A majority of these—69, or 56 percent—were located on the campus of a Standard Model arts-and-sciences university. We refer to these as "A&S campus medical schools," a group that included most of the nation's major centers of medical research. Twenty-two of the twenty-five medical schools that had the largest total NIH research awards were A&S campus medical schools; the remaining three were university medical schools located on separate health science campuses (UC San Francisco, Baylor College of Medicine in Houston, and the University of Texas Southwest-ern Medical School in Dallas). In 1990, 85 percent ($1.5 billion) of the 1.7 billion research dollars awarded to the twenty-five medical schools receiving the largest sums in NIH research grants and con-tracts was won by A&S campus medical schools. Table 5.3 shows the twenty-five medical schools that led in total NIH research funding in fiscal 1990. Table 5.4 shows a classification based on a per capita ranking of the seventy A&S campus medical schools.[31] We have clas-sified them into five categories on the basis of how much per capita research funding they received from the NIH in fiscal 1990.

Three attributes of table 5.4 invite comment. First, when the re-search productivity of medical school faculty is compared on a per capita basis, the private advantage is found to be more apparent than real. At first glance, the per capita rank order appears to support a private advantage: private medical schools predominate in Class I (those with awards above $100,000) and public medical schools in Class V (those with awards of less than $18,000). These two groups, however, account for only 27 percent of the total number of schools. Overall, the distribution of funding at public and private universities is relatively even, whether compared in total dollars received (table 5.3) or per capita awards (table 5.4). This mixed pattern suggests that

TABLE 5.3
Medical Schools Receiving the Largest NIH Research Grants and Contracts Ranked by Total Dollar Award, Fiscal 1990

Rank	Medical School	Number of Full-Time Faculty 1988–1989	Research Awards (thousands)
1	UC San Francisco*	995	$122,363
2	Johns Hopkins	1,073	111,619
3	Stanford	402	93,831
4	Washington (Seattle)*	1,241	92,825
5	Yale	671	89,580
6	Washington (St. Louis)	860	89,256
7	Duke	1,072	78,072
8	Columbia	840	76,881
9	Michigan*	776	70,168
10	Pennsylvania	871	69,104
11	UC San Diego*	523	66,118
12	Baylor (Houston)	1,128	63,150
13	UCLA*	1,287	62,151
14	Yeshiva	1,259	59,829
15	Rochester	728	57,596
16	North Carolina–Chapel Hill*	686	56,758
17	Alabama-Birmingham*	938	52,562
18	Chicago	591	52,363
19	Vanderbilt	639	51,129
20	Harvard	3,231	51,056
21	Minnesota*	944	49,671
22	New York University	876	47,958
23	Southern California	818	47,711
24	Texas-Dallas*	762	47,167
25	Iowa*	625	46,127

Source: Data from National Institutes of Health and Association of American Medical Colleges.
*Institutions marked with an asterisk are public institutions.

whereas the private advantage has been significant in the per capita research indicators discussed above, the public-private distinction is not very significant with respect to the medical schools, which tend to share common structures, professional hierarchies, and administrative procedures. On the average, private and public schools of medicine have not differed significantly in their ability to win research funding. The medical schools at Chicago and Michigan, Vanderbilt and North Carolina, for example, appear to be similar in this regard. The significant differences are found in the size of the medical school relative to its host university, and in the relative quality of the faculty.

Second, the slope of the curve that describes the distribution of NIH funding shown in table 5.4 is a relatively steep one. Medical schools have varied considerably in their per capita ability to win research funding. Stanford is in a class by itself. Even excluding the five top schools (Stanford, Yale, UC San Diego, Washington [St. Louis] and

TABLE 5.4

Arts-and-Sciences Campus Medical Schools Classified by
NIH Per Capita Funding, Fiscal 1990

Rank	Institution	NIH Funding
Class I (awards above $100,000)		
1	Stanford	$233,410
2	Yale	133,500
3	UC San Diego*	126,420
4	Washington (St. Louis)	104,980
5	Johns Hopkins	103,790
Class II (awards $60,000 to $100,000)		
6	Columbia	91,230
7	Michigan*	90,420
8	Chicago	88,600
9	Wisconsin-Madison*	83,210
10	North Carolina–Chapel Hill*	82,740
11	Vanderbilt	80,010
12	Pennsylvania	79,340
13	Rochester	79,120
14	Harvard	78,200
15	Washington (Seattle)*	74,800
16	Iowa*	73,800
17	Duke	72,830
18	Boston University	71,030
19	Vermont*	69,340
Class III (awards $35,000 to $60,000)		
20	Southern California	58,330
21	Arizona*	57,450
22	Alabama-Birmingham*	56,040
23	New York University	54,750
24	Minnesota*	52,620
25	Utah*	51,440
26	UC Los Angeles*	48,290
27	Yeshiva	47,520
28	Dartmouth	45,820
29	UC Davis*	44,850
30	Virginia*	43,390
31	Miami	42,450
32	Temple*	42,080
33	Case Western	40,420
34	Emory	38,900
35	Virginia Commonwealth*	38,460
36	Cincinnati*	38,280
37	Wayne State*	37,900
38	SUNY–Stony Brook*	37,850
39	Pittsburgh*	36,680
40	Ohio State*	36,640
Class IV (awards $18,000 to $35,000)		
41	Georgetown	33,430
42	Northwestern	32,740
43	UC Irvine*	30,060

TABLE 5.4—*Continued*

Rank	Institution	NIH Funding
44	Tulane	30,060
45	Missouri-Columbia*	29,200
46	New Mexico*	28,310
47	George Washington	28,240
48	Florida*	28,110
49	Nevada-Reno*	27,600
50	Saint Louis	27,470
51	SUNY-Buffalo*	26,250
52	Brown	25,830
53	Kentucky*	25,390
54	Illinois-Chicago*	22,550
55	Michigan State*	19,900
56	Tufts	18,650
Class V (awards less than $18,000)		
57	South Carolina*	14,020
58	Hawaii*	12,900
59	West Virginia*	10,800
60	Louisville*	10,300
61	Loyola (Chicago)	9,500
62	South Florida*	9,640
63	Missouri–Kansas City*	7,170
64	Texas Tech*	6,230
65	Southern Illinois–Carbondale*	5,080
66	Texas A&M*	4,520
67	Howard	3,520
68	Loma Linda	2,980
69	North Dakota*	2,880
70	South Dakota*	1,990

Source: Data from National Institutes of Health. Class divisions compiled by the authors; see also Note on Method and Sources.

*Institutions marked with an asterisk are public institutions.

Johns Hopkins), the distance in per capita research funding between the top and bottom tier of medical schools is huge. The average per capita NIH funding at the fourteen Class II medical schools (e.g., Columbia and Michigan) in 1990 was $79,600, compared with an average of $7,250 for the fourteen Class V schools (e.g., South Carolina and Hawaii). The median per capita award for the seventy A&S campus medical schools in 1990, Virginia Commonwealth's $38,460, was a robust figure, but the mere presence of a medical school on campus was no guarantee of high levels of performance in campus research.[32]

A third comment concerns Harvard. Harvard's practice of appointing an extraordinarily large number of medical faculty members (3,231 in 1988–89) from the staffs of several Boston teaching hospitals makes a per capita assessment misleading. The Harvard School

131

of Medicine ranked nineteenth nationally in total research funding received from the NIH in fiscal 1990, just below Vanderbilt (both with approximately $51.1 million in research awards). But whereas Vanderbilt's full-time medical faculty of 639 produced a per capita value of $80,010 (qualifying it for Class II), Harvard's per capita funding, when calculated in this fashion ($51.1 million divided by 3,231), would send Harvard to the bottom of the class. Harvard would rank fifty-fifth out of seventy! This is methodologically consistent, but the result is absurd. The NIH research funding won by Harvard's huge medical faculty greatly exceeds the total for the Harvard medical school per se.[33] By adjusting the method to take into account Harvard's unusual medical traditions, we can calculate a 1990 per capita NIH award of $78,200 for Harvard's army of 3,231 medical faculty.[34] By this calculation the Harvard medical school would rank fourteenth nationally among main-campus university medical schools. This ranking is a crude approximation, but it represents, we believe, a reasonable compromise. It also reminds us, and our readers, that systems of institutional comparison can camouflage the unique history, structure, and organizational personality that give institutions their distinctive character.

In the postwar era, medical schools have increasingly dominated the research funding of the university campuses that include them. This perhaps has been a mixed blessing. Because they lack campus medical schools, some great universities, such as Berkeley, Illinois, Indiana, and Texas, have been greatly disadvantaged in the competition for research funding from the nation's largest sponsoring agency, the NIH. As partial compensation, their research portfolios have remained more balanced. Nonetheless, the funding presence of the NIH has dominated the research agenda of postwar American universities. Even the original golden age of university funding in the 1960s arguably owed as much to Mary Lasker and the "iron triangle" alliances in the War on Cancer as to *Sputnik* and the cold war. During the 1980s, when defense funding from the Reagan administration helped sustain a second golden age of research spending on the campuses, NIH funding at Harvard and Yale still exceeded the combined R&D totals from the Department of Defense, the Department of Energy, and NASA by a factor greater than four. At Michigan and UCLA, where defense-related spending had historically been high, NIH funding during the 1980s still provided two-thirds of all federally sponsored research.

Medical schools have provided their host campuses with a research-intensive academic health center that has often included several other health professions schools. These academic health centers were traditionally dominated by the medical school and its powerful dean, and included a teaching hospital and one or more other health professions or allied health schools. None of the other health professions schools approached the medical school in research activity, but after 1960 research budgets expanded rapidly in health-related fields other than medicine — especially in public health, but also in dentistry and pharmacy, nursing, and allied health fields. The financial muscle and independence of academic health centers widened the distance between the college of arts and sciences, which by tradition claimed pride of place at the center of the university, and the health professions schools, where medicine remained *primus inter pares.* The clustering of health professions schools within academic health centers during the 1960s and 1970s was reflected administratively by new channels of reporting: increasingly, the deans of the health professions schools reported to the university president and trustees through a vice president or provost for health affairs. Because the university's deans of arts and sciences, engineering, law, business, and so forth continued to report through the regular provost or academic vice chancellor, this new trend reinforced the tension and separation between health professions faculty and traditional academic faculty.[35]

The Pecking Order of Academic Research Support

Between 1965, when Congress added the arts and humanities to the portfolio of federal funding, and 1990, the nation's priorities for academic research remained remarkably stable. Federal R&D spending had shaped a research economy characterized by political consensus, incremental growth, and a steep hierarchy among the competing research sectors. Federal research policy shifted in emphasis from applied research during the 1950s to basic research in the 1960s, then back toward applied research in the 1970s and 1980s. But throughout the postwar era there was little disagreement in Congress about research priorities for biomedical science and engineering, especially in health science and defense technology. Nor was there much challenge to the notion that the social sciences merited little more than maintenance support from taxpayers, and that support of the humanities and arts was not a federal priority. Table 5.5 shows the relative distribution in fiscal 1989 of total academic R&D funding. That year, total R&D obligations on American campuses reached $15 bil-

TABLE 5.5
Total Academic Funding (Including Federal R&D) by Field, Fiscal 1989

Field	Total R&D (millions)	Federal R&D (millions)	Federal R&D as % of Total R&D
Life sciences	$8,080	$4,773	59.1
Engineering	2,388	1,380	59.0
Physical sciences	1,643	1,195	42.7
Environmental sciences	983	645	65.6
Math/computer sciences	682	474	69.5
Social sciences	636	211	33.2
Psychology	238	156	65.5
Total	$14,987	$8,834	58.9

Source: Data from National Science Foundation.

TABLE 5.6
Fields of Study Ranked by Federal Academic R&D Funding, Fiscal 1989

Rank	Field	R&D Funding (millions)	Rank	Field	R&D Funding (millions)
1	Medical Science	$2,505	11	Psychology	$156
2	Biological Science	1,720	12	Mathematics	156
3	Physics	598	13	Atmospheric Science	125
4	Chemistry	424	14	Aeronautical/Astronautical Engineering	113
5	Electrical Engineering	389	15	Civil Engineering	104
6	Agricultural Science	346	16	Chemical Engineering	93
7	Computer Science	318	17	Astronomy	88
8	Oceanography	266	18	Sociology	53
9	Mechanical Engineering	210	19	Economics	51
10	Earth Science	186	20	Political Science	29

Source: Data from National Science Board, *Science and Engineering Indicators* (1991), app. table 5-5.
Note: Excludes "other science" categories.

lion. The federal government contributed approximately $9 billion of this amount—almost 60 percent. Both federal and nonfederal support (the funds provided by state and local government, business, foundations, and academic institutions), showed the same steep hierarchy by field. More than half (54%) of the total investment for academic research went to the life sciences. Engineering received the next largest amount, 16 percent of the total. The physical sciences ranked third, with 11 percent. The environmental sciences (7%), mathematics and computer science (5%), the social sciences (4%), and psychology (1.5%) were also supported. The federal funding hierarchy in support of academic science is shown in more detail in table 5.6.

134

The list looks like a report of common stock values, in which the relative positions have changed only marginally over the course of a thirty-year bull market. The blue-chip stocks were medical science, listed at $25, and biological science, listed at $17. Engineering, averaging $2, was led by electrical engineering at about $4. At the market's bottom were the social sciences. Economics and sociology were offered at half a dollar each. Political science brought only a quarter. In fields in which research demand in the private market was weak but national priorities were strong (atmospheric science, oceanography, mathematics, and physics), the federal government supported at least three-fourths of the research effort. In most fields, however, federal agencies accounted for closer to two-thirds of total academic R&D funding. The balance was provided by private interests, such as pharmaceutical companies, engineering firms, software developers, defense industries, and foundations. Federal funds accounted for 65 to 70 percent of the total academic R&D funding in fiscal 1989 in medical and biological science, chemistry, computer science, and electrical engineering. By the 1980s, but not before, psychology was among the fields receiving two-thirds of their research funding from federal agencies.

In the 1960s, academic psychology shared the low levels of research funding available to the other social sciences. As a health science discipline, however, psychology benefited from the clinical practice boom of the 1970s and 1980s. Prior to the 1970s most research funding for psychologists had been provided by the National Institute of Mental Health (NIMH) to support behavioral and physiological research. In the 1970s the Alcohol, Drug Abuse, and Mental Health Administration (ADAMHA), a new subagency within the Department of Health, Education, and Welfare (and after 1979 part of the Department of Health and Human Services [HHS]), became a second major sponsor of psychological research. By the 1980s ADAMHA had displaced the NIMH as the chief research-sponsoring agency for academic psychologists.

In patterns of research funding and professional employment, psychology in some ways resembled a field of medicine more than it resembled either the life sciences or the social sciences. The NSF, in its reports on science training and manpower, treated psychology separately from the social sciences. Among Ph.D.'s in the workforce at large in 1989 there were almost as many psychologists (60,600) as social scientists in all fields (70,000). In academic employment there were more than twice as many psychologists (21,400) as economists (10,500), whose discipline was the largest among the social sci-

135

ences.[36] Psychology had benefited greatly from the postwar growth of basic research in the biomedical sciences, and also from the post-Medicare boom in clinical practice. The growth during the 1970s of third-party reimbursement for psychological assessment and counseling services created a robust job market for graduate programs, especially in clinical psychology. Of the 60,600 Ph.D.-holding psychologists employed in the United States in 1989, almost half (28,100) worked in clinical practice. Only one-third (21,300) were employed by academic institutions, and only one-fifth (13,500) were employed in teaching.[37]

The academic psychologists, however, dined with the medical faculty and the life scientists at the generous research table of the Public Health Service. Between 1976 and 1989, federal academic support for psychological research increased by 108 percent in constant dollars. During the 1980s the number of Ph.D.-holding psychologists employed by academic institutions increased by 28 percent (from 16,600 to 21,300), and the number active in research increased by 53 percent. By 1990 this prosperity, which distanced the behavioral science of psychology even further from the social sciences, left the discipline with a respectable rank of eleventh among the twenty fields of science and engineering receiving the most federal R&D support.[38]

Ranked at the bottom of the twenty academic fields receiving the largest amounts of federal support (table 5.6) are the social sciences — chiefly economics, sociology, political science, anthropology, and linguistics, with history (mainly the history of science) included on the margin. The NSF, where the culture of basic science has historically shown little respect for the applied nature of social science research, allocated only 2 percent of its $1.3-billion R&D budget to social science research in fiscal 1989. Yet the NSF and HHS were the only agencies to provide some funding, however modest, to most of the social sciences (table 5.7).[39]

Only three mission agencies made significant use of social science research. Applied economic analysis was used in the Department of Agriculture, especially in the Economic Research Service, and also in the Labor Department's Bureau of Labor Statistics.[40] Sociologists were funded most extensively by HHS for research in health organizations, medical sociology, and welfare policy.[41] Federal support for social science research enjoyed a brief surge during the 1960s, when social unrest and racial violence prompted federal investment to solve these problems. The amount so invested, however, never exceeded 8 percent of total federal academic support. By 1976 the social science share had dropped below 6 percent, and by 1989 it had fallen to 2.5

TABLE 5.7

Federal Academic Research Support for the Life Sciences, the Social Sciences, and the Arts and Humanities, by Agency, Fiscal 1989

Field	Total	USDA	DOD	DOE	HHS	NASA	NSF
Life sciences	$4,677.9*						
Biological	2,555.9	$70.1	$45.8	$39.2	$2,206.9	$15.3	$149.8
Environmental Biology	108.6	47.1	9.3	.3	.5	1.9	40.0
Agricultural	180.9	141.9	.5	—	.3	.4	26.3
Medical	1,832.5	13.0	55.4	11.5	1,734.0	5.7	11.6
Social sciences	146.4						
Anthropology	7.1	—	—	—	.7	—	6.3
Economics	51.8	26.2	.1	.1	6.9	—	9.6
History	1.7	—	—	—	.1	.1	1.5
Linguistics	3.4	—	—	—	.8	—	2.7
Political science	7.0	—	.2	—	1.7	.1	3.2
Sociology	75.4	7.2	1.7	—	56.7	—	3.0
Arts & Humanities	91.5						
Arts (NEA)	54.3						
Humanities (NEH)	37.2						

Source: For the life and social sciences, National Science Foundation; for the arts and humanities, *Statistical Abstract of the U.S. 1992.*
*All figures are in millions of dollars.

TABLE 5.8

Federally Financed R&D Expenditures in the Social Sciences at the Twenty Leading Institutions, Ranked by Social Science Expenditures, 1986

Rank	Institution	Federal R&D (thousands)
1	Michigan	$14,757
2	Wisconsin-Madison	7,846
3	Harvard	7,422
4	Johns Hopkins	5,994
5	UC Berkeley	4,832
6	Pennsylvania	4,427
7	Brandeis	3,139
8	North Carolina–Chapel Hill	2,931
9	Michigan State	2,620
10	Washington (St. Louis)	2,364
11	Ohio State	2,358
12	Syracuse	2,357
13	SUNY-Albany	2,230
14	Rutgers	2,218
15	Arizona	2,201
16	Columbia	2,196
17	Texas Tech	2,057
18	Penn State	2,010
19	Princeton	1,989
20	Carnegie Mellon	1,935

Source: Data from National Science Foundation.

percent. During 1976–89, when federal academic R&D funding grew by 175 percent in constant dollars, support for social science research grew by only 7 percent.

Federal support for social science research has been so meager that the standard pattern of funding for mainstream research fields — in which two-thirds of the support is provided by federal agencies — is reversed for the social sciences. The social sciences received only 4.2 percent ($636 million) of the country's total academic R&D funding in 1989, and had to obtain two-thirds of that support from non-federal sources.[42] Table 5.8 shows the twenty leading universities ranked by federally financed R&D expenditures (in fiscal 1986) in the social sciences.

Last in the pecking order of sponsored academic research have been the arts and humanities. Despite the establishment of federal research fellowships and grants by the national endowments in the late 1960s, the arts and humanities have never been included in the NSF reports that document federal support for academic research. Periodic reports from the NSF and the National Research Council provide profiles of the number and status of the nation's academic scientists and engineers, including social and behavioral scientists, but equivalent information about academics working in the humanities and the fine and performing arts is difficult to find. A report from the U.S. Department of Education, based on a 1987 faculty survey, counted 378,732 full-time faculty in all fields in four-year institutions. Approximately 56 percent of them (211,342) were employed by the 213 institutions included in the four Carnegie Research and Doctoral categories of 1987.[43] Estimates from the National Center for Education Statistics suggest that approximately 24,600 humanities faculty and 12,900 arts faculty were found on the 213 Research and Doctoral campuses.[44]

Data on federal support for the arts and humanities in fiscal 1989 are shown in table 5.7. Since 1965 the arts and humanities have enjoyed the modest support of two federal agencies, the National Endowment for the Arts and the National Endowment for the Humanities, dedicated to their nurture. Though twins at birth in 1965, the two agencies developed different constituencies and leadership styles. Although both endowments remained small and isolated from the federal establishment of agencies active in academic research support, they nonetheless have had little to do with one another and have mounted no common defense while suffering from persistent attacks in Congress.[45]

The humanities endowment has supported scholarly research in the classics, literature, history, philosophy, and similar fields of humanistic learning. The NEH from its inception developed a core constituency of academics and channeled most of its research fellowships to college faculty.[46] This clientele pattern drew early criticism from Congress as elitist and irrelevant to public policy. Until the 1990s congressional conservatives (especially Republicans), rejecting taxpayer subsidy of the arts and humanities as illegitimate and of no practical value, were not strong enough in Congress to seriously endanger the continued existence of the endowments. During the 1970s the most formidable congressional criticism was led by a Democratic supporter of public funding for the humanities, Senator Claiborne Pell of Rhode Island, who chaired the authorizing committee for the NEH. This tension was heightened by the general hostility of the executive branch, during the Reagan-Bush years, to federal subsidies for the arts and humanities. As a consequence of all these factors, the NEH spent an increasing share of its budget on nonacademic programs (especially the state humanities councils) whose intended audience was the civic community rather than campus academics. Correspondingly, the agency's research grants and fellowship budgets, which nourished humanities scholarship on the campuses, declined from more than half of the NEH program budget in the early 1970s to less than a third in 1990.

Unlike the humanities endowment, the arts endowment developed a community-based constituency (e.g., visual and performing artists, drama groups, dance and opera companies, and community orchestras) with relatively few campus ties.[47] The NEA—after getting off to a rocky start with Congress in the era of guerrilla theater and *Hair!*—enjoyed a surprising period of respectability and congressional peace during the 1970s under the adroit, eight-year (1969–77) leadership of a Nixon appointee, Nancy Hanks. During the Reagan-Bush years, however, NEA support for controversial art, such as a Robert Mapplethorpe exhibit that included homoerotic photographs, brought conservative attacks that surpassed those leveled against the NEH. Thus, during the 1980s the humanities endowment, long criticized as elitist and irrelevant, was surpassed in congressional disdain by the arts endowment, which was attacked for subsidizing moral perversity. By the mid-1990s, when Republican control of Congress removed the protection traditionally provided by the Democratic leadership, both endowments faced the threat of termination through nonreauthorization and phase-out of appropriations.[48]

As the figure on p. 141 indicates, the budgets of the two endowments generally prospered from their inception as part of Lyndon

Johnson's Great Society until the end of the Carter administration. They then fell sharply in constant dollars under Republican administrations during the 1980s, and continued to decline through the Clinton administration. Between 1980 and 1990, even before the Republican capture of Congress in 1994, congressional appropriations for the NEA in constant dollars decreased by 43 percent. During the same period the NEH appropriation decreased by 52 percent, and the NEH's research grants and fellowship budget decreased by 51 percent. For campus scholars in the arts and humanities, the golden age of the 1960s corresponded with the first decade of the national endowments. For humanists, the 1980s was no golden age redux.

Research Growth and Dispersion in a Robust Research Economy

Yet even the humanities and arts faculties, at the bottom in the pecking order of external research support, were buoyed by the restored health of the research universities, especially after the economic upturn of 1982. During the 1980s, campus enrollments were strengthened by widening earnings differentials favoring college graduates. Faculty salaries showed the first substantial real gains since the 1960s, and universities enjoyed real increases in research support from all contributing sectors.[49] State and local governments and business leaders increased their university investment in order to boost regional economic competitiveness. Between 1980 and 1990, total academic R&D expenditures grew from $5.9 billion (in 1982 dollars) to $12.5 billion.

The hallmarks of the U.S. academic research system during the 1980s, as Roger Geiger and Irwin Feller and others have observed, were continued growth and dispersion.[50] The growth of the research economy during the postwar era had been cyclical, reflecting the tides of economic and demographic life. But the dispersion of research funding and activity through an expanding pool of competing institutions has been continuous. The share of total federal research support won by the ten leading recipient institutions had declined from 43.4 percent in 1952 to 27.7 percent in 1968, and to 20.1 percent in 1990.[51] Growth and dispersion were propitious conditions for aspiring research universities but were worrisome for established leaders. Federal policy makers and pace-setting foundations such as the Carnegie and Ford foundations had encouraged the development of new research universities during the decade following *Sputnik* but

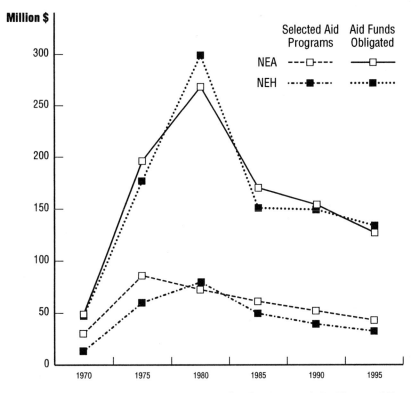

The budgets of the National Endowment for the Arts and the National Endowment for the Humanities, 1970–95. Chart by Tom Ventress.

had abandoned this position by the early 1970s. By 1990 the leadership of American science was warning that excessive dispersion was leading to quality dilution in academic research, a view also expressed by similar groups active in the 1970s. In 1991 a report by the Office of Technology Assessment, *Federally Funded Research: Decision for a Decade,* warned aspiring universities against trying to mimic the research university model.[52] In 1992 a report of the House Committee on Science, Space, and Technology described a Malthusian cycle in which an increase in research funds to universities "stimulates graduate enrollments, and leads to growth in the number of researchers that inevitably outstrips the ability of the federal government to provide adequate support."[53] That same year, the Government-University-Industry Research Roundtable, in a report titled *Fateful Choices,* warned against "overcapacity" produced by too many universities adopting the research model, and the Bush administration's President's Council of Advisors on Science and Technology opposed programs that would "increase the net capacity of the system of research-intensive universities."[54]

However, as Geiger and Feller noted, these dire judgments had been reached "without any reliable knowledge about the extent or nature of the dispersion of research among American universities."[55] Their study, concentrating on the dispersion of federal R&D research support, led them to conclude that the warnings against overcapacity and dilution had been largely misplaced. Dispersion arose not from overcompetition by aspiring institutions but from fundamental features of the academic research economy itself, and hence was self-limiting to a significant extent. Leading universities in the first tier of research institutions tended to operate at near-optimal levels of research production.[56] During expansionist periods such as the 1960s and 1980s, they thus tended to lose research shares to aspiring universities of the second tier. These latter institutions were characterized by status ambition, suboptimal research efforts, a willingness to invest in research expansion, and academic attributes (e.g., faculty quality, teaching loads, and physical facilities) that approached elite university norms. Just below was a large third tier of institutions whose characteristics generally prevented them from competing successfully as research universities even in periods of relative funding abundance. These characteristics included heavy teaching responsibilities, low faculty salaries, inadequate laboratories and libraries, mixed institutional missions, and an inability to retain successful research faculty.

The Geiger-Feller study, concluding that research dispersion in the 1980s had benefited institutions of above-average quality while not threatening the quality and effectiveness of academic research, complements and confirms our institutional comparisons of research achievement in the postwar era. In expansionist periods, established elite universities continued to perform at optimal levels of research quality and quantity. As Harvard president Derek Bok complained, the modern research-intensive university was inherently an "overextended organization."[57] Over time, the distinguished universities' relative losses in research share were often counterbalanced by the strength of their biomedical research agenda, which provided an expanding support base when other sources fluctuated. Most of the top-ranked universities included academic health centers and benefited from such centers' relative immunity to cyclical tides such as enrollment trends and shifting agency priorities. Elite universities were further protected against competitive decline by deeply institutionalized commitments to research quality, and by the Matthew effect, which continued to brighten the halo of their prestige.

Their competitors, the rising universities, typically made rapid gains during periods of adjustment as well as expansion. Who are these successful challengers? Which specific institutions surged ahead during the 1980s, and which fell behind? In the two chapters that follow we attempt to provide some answers, first for the public universities (chapter 6) and then for the private institutions (chapter 7). As a first step in doing so, we revise the useful but crude taxonomy of the Carnegie classifications. By eliminating weak or inappropriate competitors, we reduce the universe of comparison from 213 institutions to 203. We then reclassify these campuses into four categories, using as criteria their performance on the R&D and publications indicators. Finally, we rank institutions according to their combined faculty per capita performance in science, social science, and the arts and humanities. By comparing institutional research performance in a way that controls for size, we appropriately level the playing field skewed by Carnegie categories, size-driven hierarchies of academic horsepower, and reputational rankings. The results contain some startling surprises.

6

■

THE PUBLIC RESEARCH UNIVERSITIES

For a generation, students of higher education have paid their respects to the Carnegie Foundation for providing a standardized system of classification that could accommodate a complex universe of more than thirty-four hundred institutions. A chief goal of the institutional taxonomy developed by the Carnegie Commission in 1970 was to shift attention away from the elite research universities as models for institutional development. Kerr and his colleagues wanted to focus on the widening range of missions among the nation's postsecondary institutions and to authenticate those institutions' diversity. There is every reason to expect the Carnegie categories, revised most recently in 1994, to continue in useful service. Our concentration on the knowledge-creating role of universities and our controls for institutional size, however, lead logically to a different set of criteria for classifying the campuses, especially the doctorate-granting universities. In this chapter we introduce our own system of classification, based on per capita comparisons.

Because our most recent evidence of research achievement is drawn primarily from 1986–90, we begin with the Carnegie Commission's 1987 universe of 213 doctorate-granting universities. Like Carnegie, we separate public and private institutions, and we sort the campuses into four categories, which we designate as Research 1, 2, 3, and 4. Our definitions are based on per capita measures of research performance, as described below. The business of selecting cutoff scores to separate the four categories inescapably requires some arbitrary decisions, as it has done for the periodic Carnegie classifications. Our decisions were guided by the natural clustering of institutions and by our own desire to avoid status inflation. We have therefore set rigorous standards for admission to the first three of our

144

four categories. As a consequence, our top-ranked group is much smaller than Carnegie's, and our fourth-ranked group is much larger. The Carnegie Research I category, for example, included 70 institutions in 1987 and 88 in 1994. Our own Research 1 class includes only 55 institutions (32 public and 23 private). In the fourth doctorate-granting category, Carnegie designated 58 institutions as Doctoral II in 1987 and 60 in 1994, while our own Research 4 group includes 76 institutions (51 public and 25 private). Our results, not surprisingly, produce some striking shifts in research university status. More important than the revised pecking order, however, are the insights gained about the strengths and weaknesses of different types of universities as well as about individual institutions.

Reclassifying American Research Universities

Before reclassifying the Carnegie universe of Research and Doctoral universities into four groups, each subdivided into public and private categories, we first needed to remove institutions that in our judgment did not belong. There are relatively few of these. Using the 1987 Carnegie rule that, as a minimum, institutions in the doctorate-granting classes must "offer a full range of baccalaureate programs" and be "committed to graduate education through the doctorate degree," we have dropped from consideration as "research universities" several institutions that the Carnegie Commission included (for further discussion see the Note on Method and Sources).[1] UC San Francisco, which is exclusively a health professions campus, and Hahnemann University, the former Homeopathic Medical College of Philadelphia, are medical institutions rather than universities. Like the University of Maryland at Baltimore and Thomas Jefferson University in Philadelphia, they properly belong in Carnegie's category of specialized medical schools and health professions centers.[2]

Similarly, the SUNY College of Environmental Science and Forestry belongs in Carnegie's "other specialized institutions" category, in which Carnegie rightly placed the SUNY Maritime College, service academies, colleges of professional psychology, and graduate schools. For similar reasons we excluded three other consortium institutions that Carnegie included as separate doctorate-granting institutions: the City University of New York (CUNY) Graduate School, Claremont Graduate School, and Atlanta University. We also excluded Rockefeller University, a specialized graduate institution for biomedical science. Indisputably, Rockefeller and UC San Francisco are world leaders in biomedical research, but they lack the diversity of academic programs that characterizes more comprehensive universities. Finally, we have excluded three private institutions, all in Carnegie's Doctoral I category, because in our judgment they lacked the range of undergraduate and graduate programs and the full-time faculty core appropriate to a minimal definition of a university. These are International College, in California; Nova University, in Florida; and the Union for Experimenting Colleges and Universities, in Ohio.[3] These ten exclusions reduce the field from 213 institutions to 203 — 131 of them under public control and 72 of them private.

To emphasize the unique characteristics of research universities, we offer an alternative system of classification that is grounded in faculty research achievement. It relies on the first two per capita quantitative indicators, the federal R&D index and the publications index, indicators that are closely correlated.[4] The institutional per capita scores used to define these categories are drawn from data covering 1986–90.[5]

We begin reclassifying institutions with the public sector, which in 1990 enrolled more than 75 percent of the 3.4 million students then studying at the 203 institutions. The public sector not only is much larger in number of students and faculty but also is in many ways more complex. Public institutions, more susceptible to the forces of political control and accountability, have produced a greater variety of institutional types. Historical traditions and state and local political forces have reinforced traditional divisions of public mission — there are state flagships, land-grant institutions, state teachers colleges, regional universities, technical institutes, and health professions campuses.

In reclassifying Carnegie's Research and Doctoral universities we retained the four-group design of the Carnegie system, partly because we value continuity with Carnegie's four-tiered model and partly because public institutions are so numerous that a three-tiered hierarchy, workable for private institutions, becomes unwieldy. We have labeled our categories Research 1, 2, 3, and 4. Like teachers devising grading curves to fit the contours of test score distributions, we established cutoff scores on the two defining variables, the per capita R&D index and the per capita publications index, sorting the campuses into groups showing similar levels of performance. To classify a public institution in the Research 1 class, our criteria require an R&D index above $28,000 and a publications index above 2.0. (The criteria for Research 1 and 2 private institutions differ. See chapter 7, below.) To be included in the Research 2 group, faculty at public institutions must score above $14,000 in R&D and above 1.5 in publications. The threshold for Research 3 institutions (both public and private) is an R&D index of at least $9,000 and a publications index of at least 1.0. The Research 4 group contains all the remaining institutions.

Research 1 Public Universities

When these criteria are applied to the public sector, thirty-two universities were included in our Research 1 group. Six of these are not included in the Carnegie Research I category. The thirty-two Research 1 universities are identified in table 6.1, rank-ordered by the per capita publications index.

At first glance our Research 1 list looks familiar, yet also rather odd. Clustered toward the top, where we expect to find them, are the traditional elites among the great American public universities—UC Berkeley, Michigan, Wisconsin—the "roundup of the usual suspects" from the periodic reputational surveys. Most of the other top-ranked public campuses from the reputational studies are present as well—UCLA, UC San Diego, Illinois, Minnesota, North Carolina, Purdue, Texas, and Washington (Seattle).[6] Similarly, most of the leading public medical schools are located on the Research 1 campuses. Nineteen of the thirty-two Research 1 public universities have medical schools, and sixteen of the twenty medical schools were categorized as either Class I (UC San Diego), Class II (Washington, Wisconsin, Michigan, North Carolina, and Iowa), or Class III (table 5.4). Only three of the group's medical schools are in Class IV, all of them located on "second-flagship" campuses (UC Irvine, SUNY-Buffalo, and Illinois-Chicago). None is in Class V.

What is different about the list is the presence among these elite schools of several new institutional faces, beginning with UC Riverside. Indeed, *all eight* general campuses of the University of California system, not just the big, nationally ranked, metropolitan trio of Berkeley, UCLA, and San Diego, are represented in the Research 1 group. Also notable is the inclusion of three campuses from the SUNY system, and Alabama-Birmingham. Finally, there are the institutional faces we no longer see. Eighteen universities included in the Carnegie 1987 Research I category are missing from our Research 1 group, eight of them members of the Association of American Universities.[7]

The changes brought by reclassification represent four patterns.

TABLE 6.1
Per Capita Publications and R&D Funding Indexes for Research 1 Public Institutions, Ranked by Publications Index, 1986–1990

Rank	Institution	Publications Index	R&D Index
1	UC Riverside	6.19	$33,540
2	UC San Diego*	5.93	226,090
3	UC Los Angeles*	4.92	94,140
4	UC Berkeley	4.77	80,200
5	Wisconsin-Madison*	4.31	90,590
6	UC Irvine*	4.08	78,940
7	SUNY–Stony Brook*	3.94	58,060
8	Michigan*	3.75	87,120
9	Iowa*	3.75	66,710
10	SUNY-Albany	3.73	28,920
11	UC Davis*	3.70	53,510
12	North Carolina–Chapel Hill*	3.42	67,910
13	Minnesota*	3.41	72,180
14	Pittsburgh*	3.36	61,280
15	Washington*	3.30	100,170
16	North Carolina State	3.24	28,830
17	Alabama-Birmingham*	3.10	70,430
18	UC Santa Cruz	3.02	33,220
19	Colorado	2.95	86,610
20	Utah*	2.92	64,930
21	Virginia*	2.91	45,390
22	Illinois-Urbana	2.75	47,520
23	SUNY-Buffalo*	2.73	34,690
24	Arizona*	2.72	50,630
25	Indiana	2.72	29,490
26	Maryland–College Park	2.61	43,210
27	UC Santa Barbara	2.42	49,430
28	Ohio State*	2.40	32,240
29	Texas-Austin	2.31	35,990
30	Illinois-Chicago*	2.31	29,160
31	Penn State	2.29	40,590
32	Purdue	2.28	36,770
	Average	3.26	60,760
	Median	3.17	52,070

Source: Unless otherwise noted, data in all the tables in this chapter derive from the authors' calculations. See Appendixes and Note on Method and Sources.

Note: The publications index is for 1986–88; the R&D index is for 1988–90.

*Campus includes medical school.

One of them, the public-private difference, does not arise until the newly reclassified private universities are brought into the comparison. (See chapter 7, below.) A second pattern emphasizes the advantages of campuses with medical schools over those without them. Among the thirty-two public universities in the new Research 1 group, for example, the twenty with medical schools have a mean R&D index of $72,350, while those without medical schools have a mean R&D index of $41,030. We have discussed the dynamics of both private sector advantage and medical advantage at some length in previous chapters, and we shall return to those important themes. Of more immediate interest is a third pattern, the emergence of new research universities, and a fourth, the declining success of other institutions in the research competition. In both the emerging and declining categories, there are some surprises.

No aspect of our revised class of Research 1 universities is more arresting than the inclusion of all eight general campuses of the University of California. Historically, most state university systems have nurtured the flagship campus and protected it from competition. The University of California was no exception; prior to World War II the faculty and administration in Berkeley regarded the aspirations of the Los Angeles campus with open contempt.[8] While Berkeley has always remained first among equals in California, the Master Plan adopted by the state legislature in 1960 established a tripartite system that reserved the research and doctoral-training mission to the multicampus UC system.[9] The UC system was premised on a one-university principle—meaning, for faculty at all UC campuses, a common salary scale, common promotion and tenure criteria, common standards for graduate programs, and a systemwide faculty senate. The goal was to provide UC campuses of top quality to serve all major metropolitan regions, rather than to continue favoring the San Francisco Bay area. Thus UCLA, with its important medical and engineering complex, in the 1950s and 1960s became the nation's first true "second flagship," surpassing even UC Berkeley in total awards of federal R&D dollars (excluding dedicated federal contract facilities, such as Lawrence Livermore and Los Alamos laboratories).

In 1973, when the Carnegie Commission first published the classification system it had devised in 1970, the San Diego and Davis campuses, like UC Berkeley and UCLA, were designated as Research I institutions. In 1974, UCLA joined Berkeley as a member of the AAU. In 1982, the National Research Council assessment found UC San Diego in a tie (with Indiana) for tenth rank in graduate program quality among the nation's public institutions. In 1987, Carnegie's revised Research I group included UC Irvine, a relatively small university whose robust research budget was dominated by its medical school.

The eye-catching additions to the Research 1 ranks in our classification of research universities, however, are the UC campuses at Santa Barbara, Riverside, and Santa Cruz. The speed with which these institutions rose from modest beginnings is astonishing. Santa Barbara, a former normal school like UCLA and then a state college, joined the UC system in 1944 and became a general campus in 1958.[10] Santa Barbara was classified by Carnegie as a Research II campus in the 1987 revision and as a Research I campus in 1994. Riverside, a former citrus experiment station, awarded its first baccalaureate degree in 1954 and offered no graduate instruction until the 1960s. Santa Cruz, founded as a UC campus in 1962 and designed primarily with its residential undergraduate colleges in mind, awarded its first baccalaureate degree in 1967. In the 1987 Carnegie classification, Riverside and Santa Cruz were Doctoral I institutions; in 1994 both were shifted to Carnegie's Research II category. None of these three smaller UC campuses enjoyed the research-boosting presence of a medical school. Yet by 1990 Santa Barbara was winning $50 million in federal R&D annually and ranked among the top six public institutions nationally in all three of our qualitative per capita indicators. Santa Cruz produced the highest top–social science index of all the nation's public doctorate-granting universities, and Riverside produced the highest per capita publications index. In 1995 Santa Barbara won membership in the AAU. Much of the UC success may be attributed to the distinctive allure of California's climate, economy, and cultural mystique in the postwar era. But considerable credit must also go to the state's visionary higher education policy, as codified in the 1960 Master Plan.[11]

Of the three remaining entrants in our Research 1 class that were excluded from the 1987 Carnegie Research I category, two are State University of New York campuses—SUNY-Albany and SUNY-Buffalo. When the original Carnegie classifications were published in 1973, the Research I category included six of New York's private universities but none of the state's public institutions. In New York, as in most other northeastern states, private universities overshadowed their public counterparts. SUNY, established in 1948 to coordinate the development of a stronger public sector, governed a wide variety of institutions (a separate City University of New York system was established in 1961). By 1990 there were sixty-four SUNY campuses, many of them two-year colleges. Included in the SUNY system were the four statutory colleges of land-grant provenance on Cornell's Ithaca campus (the colleges of agriculture and life sciences, human ecology, industrial and labor relations, and veterinary medicine). In the SUNY system only four campuses were designated for research university development: Albany, Binghamton, Buffalo, and Stony Brook. Albany, growing from normal school origins like UC Santa Barbara, was a state college until 1963. Buffalo was a financially struggling private university with a medical school that the state rescued in the early 1960s.[12] Stony Brook, like UC Irvine, was a new campus of the 1960s, established to serve the rapidly growing Long Island area. Developed from the outset as a research campus that included a medical school, Stony Brook was located close to the Brookhaven National Laboratory. In the 1987 Carnegie classifications all four of the SUNY research campuses were given research university status—Stony Brook was categorized as Research I, Albany and Buffalo as Research II, and Binghamton as Doctoral I; in the 1994 classification Buffalo was shifted to Research I. Unlike the UC system, with its tripartite protection, its one-university principle, and its history of public prestige in higher education, the SUNY system attempted to arbitrate the political wars of academic status internally, grooming only four of its campuses to compete for research prominence at the national level.

The final entrant in the Research 1 group not to have been included in the 1987 Carnegie Research I category, Alabama-Birmingham (UAB), represents a third pathway for emerging new research campuses. The development of UAB illustrates a postwar urban strategy designed to compensate for a nineteenth-century American bias against establishing major state universities in cities. In this familiar scenario, a state's historic flagship campus, secluded in a university town to shield students from the sins of the city, is too distant from the state's major urban center(s) to satisfy metropolitan leaders. In cities such as Atlanta, Baltimore, Birmingham, Boston, Chicago, Dallas, Kansas City, Los Angeles, Milwaukee, New Orleans, Richmond, St. Louis, and Tampa, civic leaders demanding their "own" state university threw their political weight behind campaigns to build a "second flagship" in the underserved metropolis. UCLA, for example, overcame bitter resistance from Berkeley through the sheer crush of demography and the rallying of civic elites in the Los Angeles basin, ultimately forcing the debate that culminated in the unique UC system.

In Alabama, several circumstances accelerated the rapid development of the Birmingham campus. Civic leaders there shrewdly used the Hill-Burton Act of 1946 and the urban renewal provisions of the federal housing law of 1949 to develop a downtown medical campus.[13] At Alabama's flagship campus in Tuscaloosa, political strength and athletic prowess had traditionally exceeded the school's academic reputation, and this created opportunities that were exploited not only by UAB but also by the new campus built near the federal space science center in Huntsville. Finally, the development of UAB's arts-and-sciences programs (the first baccalaureate degree was awarded in 1970) coincided with the extremely favorable financial conditions enjoyed by academic medical centers in the 1970s.[14] The Carnegie classification of 1994 shifted UAB from Doctoral II to Research I, but the flagship campus at Tuscaloosa remained in the Doctoral I category. In no other American state has a new, urban campus of the state university so surpassed the traditional flagship as a research university.

The most successful post-*Sputnik* example of the second-flagship phenomenon in a traditional, flagship-dominated system, however, is Illinois-Chicago, another of our Research 1 campuses. There, in 1982, an "instant" research university of formidable dimensions was created to serve Chicago by the shotgun merger of the state university's academic health center and the newer arts-and-sciences campus at Chicago Circle. (The shotgun, held by the political and business leaders in the state university's governing network, was pointed at the heads of two opposing blocs — the medical center authorities in Chicago, who preferred their traditional autonomy, and the equally traditional protectors of the powerful flagship downstate in Urbana-Champaign.)[15]

Research 2 Public Universities

At a glance, we may recognize the thirty-two public universities in the Research 1 category either as established leaders whose presence we expect, or as rising stars whose presence may surprise us. The twenty-six public universities identified as Research 2 institutions (table 6.2) offer a more mixed variety of institutional types. They are clearly a more research-intensive group than the twenty-six public institutions classified as Research II by the Carnegie Commission in 1987 or in 1994. Faculty scores at Research 2 institutions exceed $14,000 in average per capita R&D and 1.5 in per capita publications. The Research 2 group's average per capita R&D index ($24,910) and publications index (1.81) exceed those of the 1987 Carnegie Research II group ($20,500 and 1.64, respectively). Twenty of the twenty-six schools we classify as Research 2 are Research I institutions in the 1994 Carnegie classification. All twenty-six are research universities of considerable achievement, and many are large and complex. At first glance a thoroughly mixed lot, they sort themselves into several subgroups.

First, consider the medical school variable. Whereas two-thirds of the Research 1 public universities include medical schools, three-

TABLE 6.2
Per Capita Publications and R&D Indexes for Research 2 Public Institutions,
Ranked by Publications Index, 1986–1990

Rank	Institution	Publications Index	R&D Index
1	Louisiana State	2.34	$16,560
2	Missouri-Columbia*	2.17	19,490
3	Rutgers–New Brunswick	2.12	22,460
4	Wayne State*	2.04	27,030
5	Texas A&M*	2.04	25,480
6	Oregon	2.03	23,800
7	Washington State	1.95	22,200
8	Oregon State	1.94	60,660
9	Cincinnati*	1.93	32,040
10	Florida*	1.89	23,230
11	Massachusetts	1.86	31,470
12	Kentucky*	1.85	17,410
13	Kansas	1.83	17,580
14	Mississippi	1.72	16,470
15	Houston	1.71	16,650
16	Georgia	1.66	21,970
17	Delaware	1.65	16,560
18	Michigan State*	1.62	23,940
19	New Mexico*	1.61	24,210
20	Georgia Tech	1.61	46,850
21	Virginia Commonwealth*	1.60	37,630
22	Hawaii-Manoa*	1.59	32,840
23	Colorado State	1.59	37,120
24	Florida State	1.56	27,290
25	Iowa State	1.52	14,540
26	Virginia Tech	1.50	19,620
	Average	1.81	24,910
	Median	1.78	23,510

*Campus includes medical school.

fifths of the Research 2 public group do not. The paucity of medical schools in the Research 2 class explains much about the ability of those campuses to attract federal research support. Six of the twenty-six public Research 2 institutions have per capita publications indexes of at least 2.0, high enough to qualify them for Research 1 status. But faculty on those campuses did not receive enough federal R&D funding to achieve the $28,000 per capita cutoff necessary for inclusion in the Research 1 category. Most Research 2 public universities lacked medical schools, and the ten medical schools on Research 2 campuses mostly were small.[16] More important, none of these ten medical schools ranked above the median in per capita research funding from the NIH (table 5.4). Three of the medical schools were included in Class III (Cincinnati, Virginia Commonwealth, and

Wayne State), five in Class IV (Florida, Kentucky, Michigan State, Missouri, and New Mexico), and two in Class V (Hawaii and Texas A&M). By contrast, although nineteen of the thirty-two Research 1 universities in the public sector include medical schools, only three are in Class IV (UC Irvine, Illinois-Chicago, and SUNY-Buffalo) and none are in Class V.[17]

Second, consider the regional variable. The Research 2 group includes ten southern institutions (according to a definition of the South as the eleven former Confederate states). Their mean publication index, 1.81, is not impressive in comparison with the publication productivity of the leading public universities and reflects lower levels of research achievement at many southern universities. Southern campuses comprise 39 percent of the Research 2 class but only 16 percent of the Research 1 group. Southern colleges and universities since the Civil War have been crippled by the impoverishment of the region, the weakness of the public schools, and the racial caste system.[18] Generally lacking the industrial base that nourished traditions of campus research elsewhere in the nation, the South remained intellectually isolated by its defense of Jim Crow. Southern state governments and university trustees enforced racial segregation until well into the 1960s, a practice that clashed with mainstream academic values and hampered faculty recruiting. As a consequence, southern universities have been underrepresented among the nation's highly ranked institutions. Of the forty institutions ranked among the top twenty-five in seven national comparisons of graduate programs since 1925, only three — UNC–Chapel Hill, Texas-Austin, and Duke — have been southern institutions.

Finally, there is the unique American variable of land-grant status. This tradition has commonly produced a pattern of mission specialization where the state land-grant university is neither a flagship nor a medical institution. Campuses that exemplify this pattern in the Research 2 group include Colorado State, Iowa State, Oregon State, Virginia Tech, and Washington State. These functional divisions have skewed the academic mission of land-grant campuses toward practitioner programs (e.g., in agriculture, veterinary science, engineering and mechanical arts, military science, home economics, business and industrial relations, forestry, health education, physical education, and nursing) in which academic and scientific publishing traditions have been understandably weak. Two such land-grant state universities, Michigan State and Texas A&M, established medical schools during the baby boom expansion of the 1960s.[19] Another nonflagship land-grant university without a medical school,

North Carolina State, has shown unusually balanced research strength across the academic spectrum. Together with North Carolina–Chapel Hill and Duke, North Carolina State has become an important institutional anchor for the Research Triangle. Most land-grant institutions in this tradition, however—usually competing for status against a rival flagship campus—have suffered. Characteristic of this pattern is a tendency for the faculty to generate strong per capita R&D indexes, tapping the advantage of federal program funding in engineering and agriculture (much of the latter awarded by formula rather than through peer-reviewed competition), but then to demonstrate weaker performances in publications and in the more qualitative indicators measuring research achievement in science, social science, and the arts and humanities.

The disadvantage due to the skewing of the academic mission toward practitioner programs, commonly found in land-grant institutions without flagship or medical status, can be demonstrated by comparing the per capita research indicators of Oregon's state universities, the flagship campus in Eugene and the land-grant campus in Corvallis. Neither campus housed the state university's medical, dental, and nursing schools, which are located at the Oregon Health Sciences University in Portland. Judged by the R&D and publications indexes, Oregon State, with its engineering and agricultural programs, appears to be the stronger of the two institutions. Oregon State, with a faculty publications index of 1.94, narrowly misses the Research 1 cutoff of 2.0, and with an R&D index of $64,200 easily surpasses the R&D minimum ($28,000) for Research 1 status. Faculty at the flagship campus in Eugene, by contrast, in 1988–90 achieved an R&D index of only $23,800 but met the Research 1 criterion with a publications index of 2.03. Adding three qualitative indicators to the comparison, however, reflects a different pattern:

Index	Oregon State	Oregon
R&D	$60,660	$23,800
Publications	1.94	2.03
Top-science	.29	.21
Top–social science	.32	.88
A&H	.17	.60

While Corvallis faculty outdistanced the Eugene faculty in the top-science category, University of Oregon scholars performed at a significantly higher level in the social science and humanities indexes. In the top-science category, Oregon State enjoyed a structural advantage over Oregon because the latter (like Indiana but unlike most other state flagships) had neither a medical school nor a school of engineering. In most states with separate flagship and land-grant campuses, land-grant universities are hampered by their legislated program structure. When the land-grant campus is competing with a flagship campus that includes a medical school, as for example in Iowa or North Carolina, the land-grant disadvantage is intensified. A comparison of faculty scores at Iowa State, a traditionally strong land-grant university and AAU member, with those of Iowa, a state flagship that includes both a medical school and a school of engineering, demonstrates this disadvantage in four of five categories:

Index	Iowa	Iowa State
R&D	$66,700	$14,540
Publications	3.75	1.52
Top-science	.25	.23
Top–social science	.76	.22
A&H	.48	.13

The dimensions of this structural and programmatic disadvantage are suggested by comparing a group of land-grant universities with their flagship counterparts according to per capita scores on the five research indicators. In table 6.3 the average index scores for six land-grant universities in the Research 2 group—Colorado State, Iowa State, Michigan State, Texas A&M, Virginia Tech, and Washington State—are compared with those of their state flagship counterparts, all Research 1 institutions.

As table 6.3 demonstrates, flagship campuses in such states hold strong advantages over their land-grant counterparts. Two-thirds of the flagships but none of the land-grant universities included medical schools. Moreover, flagship traditions nourished the social sciences and the humanities in ways that land-grant traditions did not. Partly for these reasons, as measured by the five index scores the flagship campuses in these states outperformed their land-grant counterparts by a factor of almost three in winning research dollars and humanities awards and in publishing in top-ranked social science journals. In these state rivalries, where the academic competition was often less intense than the athletic competition, structural factors and academic traditions generally favored the flagship institutions.

Almost two-thirds of the universities in the Research 2 class are land-grant institutions, and they give the group its distinctive flavor. In addition to the seven land-grant universities that are not flagship campuses, the Research 2 class includes eight flagship universities with land-grant designation, four of them with medical schools.[20] In

TABLE 6.3

Average Per Capita Indexes of Research Achievement for Selected State Flagships and Land-Grant Institutions, 1980–1990

Institutions	R&D Index	Publications Index	Top-Science Index	Top–Social Science Index	A&H Index
Flagship institutions					
Colorado	$86,610	2.95	.549	.093	.042
Iowa*	66,700	3.75	.248	.076	.048
Michigan*	87,120	3.75	.318	.164	.058
Texas	35,990	2.31	.311	.090	.041
Virginia*	45,390	2.91	.289	.064	.045
Washington*	100,170	3.30	.371	.104	.028
Group mean	$70,330	3.16	.348	.099	.044
Land-grant institutions					
Colorado State	$37,120	1.59	.194	.014	.005
Iowa State	14,540	1.52	.232	.022	.013
Michigan State*	23,940	1.62	.142	.047	.016
Texas A&M*	25,480	2.04	.199	.051	.009
Virginia Tech	19,620	1.50	.082	.035	.021
Washington State	22,200	1.95	.155	.033	.024
Group mean	$23,820	1.70	.167	.035	.015

*Campus includes medical school.

the latter institutions, where land-grant programs are combined with medical schools, the agricultural component of land-grant research is reduced in significance. Among Research 1 schools of this type (Arizona, UC Davis, Minnesota, and Wisconsin), research funding from the U.S. Department of Agriculture (USDA) in 1990 was on average only 5 percent of total federal R&D funding. Among land-grant universities with medical schools in the Research 2 group (Florida, Hawaii, Kentucky, Michigan State, and Missouri), USDA funding was on average 18 percent of federal R&D funding. At Research 2 land-grant universities without medical schools (Colorado State, Iowa State, Oregon State, Virginia Tech, and Washington State), the USDA average is 27 percent.

In general, at land-grant institutions approximately half of the USDA R&D funding is allocated by formula under the Hatch Act of 1887, and the other half is awarded competitively through standard peer-review processes. We excluded the USDA's formula-based funds from our R&D index, much as we excluded the Defense Department's "development" funding because it was allocated outside the competitive peer-review process. It should be noted that many land-grant universities, including those in the Research 2 class, win two-thirds or more of their USDA research funding through competitive programs. In fiscal 1990, for example, Hawaii won 74 percent of its USDA

157

research funding through competitive programs. Others winning a high percentage of their research funds from the USDA through competitive proposals include Oregon State (73%), Florida (68%), Michigan State (66%), and Colorado State (63%).[21] Our evidence suggests that land-grant universities relying heavily on formula funding from the USDA are less productive in publishing research results.

A final attribute of the Research 2 group is that the large urban state systems—those of California, Illinois, New York, and Pennsylvania—are little represented there. Yet the public Research 2 universities, with an average full-time faculty in 1987 of 1,141, did not differ significantly in faculty size from the public Research 1 schools, with a full-time faculty average of 1,251 (table 6.4). The chief differences between the first and second tier of public research universities lie elsewhere—in tangible attributes such as geography, structure, and medical mission; and in intangible factors such as institutional history, campus culture, and academic leadership. Nonetheless, state institutions with large faculties show a general advantage in research competition even when the indicators are controlled for size.

Public universities, unlike their better-endowed private counterparts, have relied heavily on enrollment growth to build the critical mass of faculty and graduate students necessary to support ambitious programs of research and graduate study. Although, for the most part, by the 1990s the major public universities had reduced their enrollments somewhat since the student explosion of the 1960s, two-thirds of the Research 1 universities and a majority of the Research 2 group still employ more than a thousand full-time faculty. A few public universities combine small faculties with high research productivity, especially in the UC and SUNY systems, in which selected smaller campuses have been nurtured as research universities. Elsewhere, however, a more Darwinian environment has prevailed, especially since the 1960s. On the whole, it has remained difficult for medium-sized and small public institutions to compete against mature research campuses, with their accretion of bureaus and institutes, intramural research funds, sponsored research offices, endowed chairs, promotion and tenure incentives, academic health science centers, and perhaps most important, reputations as the home of research faculty. Although this study controls for size, and thus highlights research achievement at smaller institutions, the advantages of larger size in the public sector are significant. Political and business leaders seeking economic development from their university campuses would in all likelihood prefer a Michigan State, win-

TABLE 6.4

Average Per Capita Indexes of Scholarly Achievement for Public Research Universities, by Graham-Diamond Category, 1980–1990

Graham-Diamond Category	No. of Full-time Faculty	R&D Index	Publications Index	Top-Science Index	Top–Social Science Index	A&H Index
Research 1	1,251	$60,760	3.26	.350	.097	.039
Research 2	1,141	24,910	1.81	.147	.047	.022
Research 3	750	15,750	1.47	.090	.040	.018
Research 4	604	6,650	.79	.044	.027	.015

ning $50 million a year in federal R&D funding, to a UC Riverside or Santa Cruz, ranked higher in per capita federal funding, but at total levels of $12 million. It should be no surprise that the four Research classes we devised show positive correlations between size and research achievement. Table 6.4 lists the mean values for the number of full-time faculty and for the five per capita indicators for each of these four classes in the public sector.

Research 3 and 4 Public Universities

The relationships demonstrated in table 6.4 are remarkably symmetrical. Index scores decline in rough correspondence with institutional size and complexity. The typical institution for the Research 1 group was a Standard Model state flagship, such as Arizona; for the Research 2 group, it was a nonflagship land-grant university, such as Michigan State. The Research 3 institutions, however, ranked by their publications indexes (table 6.5), appear to have little in common. These twenty-two universities met the Research 3 criteria of an R&D index above $9,000 and a publications index above 1.0.

Three of the twenty-two (Connecticut, New Mexico State, and Tennessee), were classified by Carnegie in 1987 as Research I institutions, and five more (Arizona State, Nebraska, Temple, Utah State, and West Virginia) were reclassified from Research II to Research I status in 1994. According to our per capita calculations, however, they failed to meet the criteria ($14,000 R&D and 1.5 publications) for the public Research 2 class. New Mexico State, for example, one of seven land-grant universities in the Research 3 class, easily met the Research 1 criterion for R&D funding with a per capita index of $51,150.[22] But New Mexico State faculty produced a publication index of 1.01, which barely met the publications requirement (of 1.0) for the Research 3 category. In addition to New Mexico State, seven of

159

TABLE 6.5

Per Capita Publications and R&D Funding Indexes for Research 3 Public Institutions, Ranked by Publications Index, 1986–1990

Rank	Institution	Publications Index	R&D Index
1	Missouri-Rolla	2.39	$12,810
2	Tennessee	2.00	13,244
3	Clemson	1.94	9,130
4	Wyoming	1.75	13,670
5	Arizona State	1.65	13,020
6	South Carolina*	1.62	13,890
7	William and Mary	1.57	10,190
8	Nebraska	1.51	12,850
9	Oklahoma	1.47	14,522
10	Temple*	1.46	18,170
11	Connecticut	1.45	22,463
12	Colorado School of Mines	1.39	20,410
13	Kansas State	1.38	12,760
14	Utah State	1.35	19,120
15	Maryland–Baltimore County	1.23	9,930
16	Arkansas	1.23	10,770
17	Rhode Island	1.22	24,140
18	Auburn	1.22	11,010
19	West Virginia	1.12	13,670
20	Idaho	1.09	15,290
21	North Dakota State	1.01	11,550
22	New Mexico State	1.01	51,150
	Average	1.47	15,750
	Median	1.42	13,460

*Campus includes medical school.

the twenty-two Research 3 schools met the Research 2 criterion in R&D funding but not in publications. Eight others met the Research 2 standard in publications (the highest per capita performance in the Research 3 class was exhibited by faculty at Missouri-Rolla, a scientific and technical institution) but not in R&D funding. The faculty per capita scores of three schools—Connecticut, Oklahoma-Norman, and Temple—barely missed the Research 2 publications cutoff. Only three Research 3 universities (South Carolina, Temple, and West Virginia) have medical schools, and those medical schools are relatively small.[23]

Few states with large populations are home to Research 3 schools. Some Research 3 institutions were initially established as "branch" campuses of the state university, but most evolved as distinct institutions within multicampus systems. One such institution, Maryland–Baltimore County (UMBC), established in 1966 to provide Baltimore with an arts-and-sciences campus of the University of

Maryland, represented a new postwar genre, one of the many new metropolitan campuses of the 1950s and 1960s that had "second-flagship" ambitions.[24] New branch campuses were established in Boston, Chicago, Dallas, Milwaukee, St. Louis, and other cities. Other Research 3 schools, such as the University of Missouri–Kansas City (created from the University of Kansas City, a private institution founded in 1929) were developed from established institutions that were absorbed by the state university in response to political and economic pressures from major underserved cities. For many of these new urban universities in multicampus systems, the aspirational role model was UCLA. Yet by 1990, outside of the California and New York systems, with their special designations for research campuses, UMBC was the only new metropolitan campus of the baby-boom era to place out of the crowded Research 4 class.[25]

The Research 4 class is a large category containing fifty-one institutions (table 6.6). Almost half of these are regional universities, their names frequently denoting their geographic affiliations. Many are institutions of modest size and ambition that by dint of their history and location are unlikely to develop major research agendas. Eight of the Research 4 schools are flagship universities in states with small populations: Alabama, Maine, Montana, Nevada, New Hampshire, North and South Dakota, and Vermont. Seven are established urban institutions, state universities serving Akron, Atlanta, Cleveland, Louisville, Memphis, Portland, and Toledo. Seven (Maine, Mississippi State, Montana State, Nevada, New Hampshire, Oklahoma State, and Vermont) are land-grant universities. Three are state technical schools (Louisiana Tech, Tennessee Tech, and Texas Tech). Faculty at several of the Research 4 universities won substantial R&D funding—for example, $40,200 per faculty member at Vermont, $28,100 at Texas-Dallas, and $24,640 at New Hampshire. Seven include medical schools. The unusual presence among these long-established institutions is the cluster of relatively new urban branch campuses—in Milwaukee, St. Louis, Dallas, Arlington, and New Orleans—where ambitions soared in the expansive 1960s, when service to urban constituencies was high on the national agenda.

The Stunted Career of the "Second Flagships"

This study, based as it is on dependent variables that measure per capita research productivity, does not provide much direct evidence to explain why some institutions have been more successful than oth-

161

TABLE 6.6

Per Capita Publications and R&D Funding Indexes for Research 4 Public Institutions, Ranked by Publications Index, 1986–1990

Rank	Institution	Publications Index	R&D Index
1	Texas Woman's	3.28	$1,490
2	Missouri–St. Louis	2.50	5,950
3	Northern Colorado	1.41	1,260
4	Texas Tech*	1.30	7,700
5	Cleveland State	1.23	6,780
6	Montana	1.22	7,330
7	New Orleans	1.22	3,920
8	Middle Tennessee State	1.17	620
9	SUNY-Binghamton	1.16	5,720
10	North Carolina–Greensboro	1.12	2,120
11	Southern Illinois	1.10	6,260
12	Western Michigan	1.04	1,310
13	Alabama-Tuscaloosa	1.03	4,360
14	Oklahoma State	1.00	8,500
15	Georgia State	.98	5,290
16	Louisiana Tech	.96	1,410
17	South Florida*	.92	11,420
18	Ohio University	.92	6,540
19	Texas-Arlington	.91	2,830
20	Old Dominion	.87	10,480
21	North Texas	.82	2,690
22	Maine-Orono	.81	8,910
23	Akron	.79	4,290
24	East Texas State	.78	0
25	Toledo	.78	3,710
26	Miami (Ohio)	.76	1,800
27	Florida Atlantic	.72	4,760
28	Nevada-Reno*	.71	19,130
29	Texas-Dallas	.70	28,100
30	Northern Illinois	.69	2,870
31	Rutgers-Newark†	.68	NA*
32	South Dakota*	.68	1,380
33	Wisconsin-Milwaukee	.65	7,160
34	Northern Arizona	.64	4,850
35	Kent State	.63	4,480
36	Bowling Green	.61	1,330
37	New Hampshire	.61	24,640
38	Louisville*	.60	7,970
39	Mississippi State	.57	17,100
40	Vermont*	.56	40,200
41	Memphis	.56	3,680
42	North Dakota*	.53	17,740
43	Portland State	.47	5,340
44	Illinois State	.35	1,550
45	Indiana State	.31	510
46	Montana State	.31	12,480
47	Southern Mississippi	.27	1,420
48	Ball State	.25	200
49	Idaho State	.16	1,370
50	Tennessee Tech	.16	18,470
51	Missouri–Kansas City*	.14	6,200
	Average	.79	6,650
	Median	.76	4,760

*Campus includes medical school.
†The NSF did not report R&D data separately for the Rutgers-Newark campus.

ers. Most of the factors associated with high-powered public research universities—for example, large academic health science centers, comprehensive doctoral programs, substantial endowments, numerous organized research units, lighter teaching responsibilities, promotion and tenure systems that reward research, and institutional traditions of research prowess—have not been strongly represented among Research 4 institutions. During the 1960s, however, many of the new urban campuses advanced claims to a new research mission designed to find solutions to the growing problems of the nation's cities. The career of the aspiring second flagships closely parallels the curve of the baby boom that triggered the wave of urban institution-building. In Wisconsin and Louisiana the state research universities established branch campuses in the mid-1950s in Milwaukee and New Orleans. By the end of the 1960s similar campuses had been established, through a combination of the creation of new institutions and the absorption of existing ones, in Missouri at St. Louis and Kansas City, in Texas at Arlington and Dallas, and at North Carolina–Greensboro, Rutgers-Newark, and South Florida at Tampa.[26]

Often the new campuses of the state university system were granted authority to build new doctoral programs, often in spite of the objections of nearby state colleges and private institutions.[27] By 1990, however, after a generation of program building, there was little evidence, outside of the distinctive incubator systems in California and New York, of the spread of incipient research institutions, at least not in the accelerated tradition of postwar UCLA. In California, the research-intensive standards achieved by UCLA were approached with surprising speed by new metropolitan UC campuses in San Diego and Irvine. Both of these campuses, complete with medical schools, demonstrated, almost in the fashion of private elite universities, the virtues of combining a small (by public university standards) arts-and-sciences faculty with a research-intensive medical school. On the East Coast the SUNY system accomplished the same feat at Stony Brook, and in the Midwest, Illinois created an instantly powerful second flagship in Chicago. The UC and SUNY systems, which groomed new campuses for rapid research development, and the two-campus consolidation at Illinois-Chicago were exceptions to the general maxim that the evolution of public research universities in America has been a slow, Darwinian process in which the dominant flagship campuses developed formidable defenses. Most challengers spent much of their energy on the struggle for survival. A gap thus widened between the small number of successful challengers, such as UC San Diego and SUNY–Stony Brook, and the larger body of struggling new second-flagship contenders.[28] Symptomatic of the uphill struggle faced by aspiring second flagships, for example, was the slow development of Wisconsin's Milwaukee campus, where the growth of research relative to the standard set in Madison did not begin to approach the pace of research-campus development in the UC or SUNY systems.

Although our evidence does not enable us to explain why some institutions performed significantly better than others, we may base some plausible speculations on general historical trends. The new urban universities, lacking the alumni support and political and business ties of established institutions, and the financial magnet of a medical center, were especially vulnerable to the academic recession of the 1970s. Flagship university administrators and faculty rallied to protect their exclusive degree programs and their privileged state appropriations against aspiring claims from newer schools. State colleges, winning university status by mobilizing their political resources, objected to program expansion at the new research campuses (although the new titles and status won by the public regional universities were often unaccompanied by new doctoral programs or research missions). Tripartite systems of higher education, modeled after the California Master Plan of 1960 and adopted by urban-industrial states such as Illinois and Maryland during the 1960s, tended to break down politically.

The newer urban campuses of the research university systems, with their visions of a UCLA-like future, represented a threat to established institutions. The ambitions of upstart challengers often prompted a combined assault by resentful (and also ambitious) state colleges and universities, by established private institutions, and by the flagship campus itself, where leaders rallied against the threat of branch campuses whose new doctoral programs and aspiring research faculty claimed the prestige of the state's research university. California's tripartite system survived these assaults, sustained by a rare combination of forces that included the historic prestige and constitutional status of the University of California, and the relative weakness (at that time) of the state college and private sectors. In most states, however, the new urban campuses were politically weak, and the fragmenting forces included not only the hostility of flagships, state colleges and regional universities, and private institutions but also, in the southern and border states, opposition from historically black institutions.[29] During the 1970s new statewide coordinating bodies, created to reduce inefficiency and program duplication, slowed program growth and sought to impose corporate models of planning and specialization on the competitive scramble.[30] Under these circumstances, unanticipated in the golden age of expansion, the new urban campuses tended to reach middling size, but for most of them there were slow and uncertain rates of ascent in research achievement.

It should bring little surprise that these new institutions founded or expanded in the golden age generally failed to become mature research universities in the image of the young UCLA. Despite the frustration of these dreams during the 1970s and 1980s, we should acknowledge the several research assets these schools carried into the 1990s. One was generally younger faculty, trained at leading public and private universities and inculcated with the values of an academic research culture. The dispersion of thousands of such young faculty after 1970, with increasing numbers of women and racial minorities among them, amplified the research ambitions and improved the research performance of hundreds of campuses, old and new alike. Another advantage was an academic reward structure that mirrored that of the reluctant mother flagship, thereby encouraging the spirit, if not always the reality, of California's one-university credo. Finally, and as a consequence of these influences, both the newer campuses and many of the established institutions showed a strengthened respect for creative work in all academic fields, including not just the prestigious and well-funded sciences but also the arts and humanities.

Arrayed against these ecumenical forces were the more muscular claims of science and technology. During the 1970s and 1980s the traditional respect for the equal worthiness and universality of knowledge across the academic spectrum warred against the reality of highly skewed incentives. From federal agencies, private foundations, business firms, and wealthy benefactors, universities received massive subsidies for medicine, natural science, and engineering, while modest support was provided for the social sciences, and only occasional gestures of affirmation for the humanities and the arts. Recognizing the realities of the research support system, we have used in this study five indicators, of which three are biased toward science and technology. Our criteria for classifying 203 institutions into a hierarchy of four research groups reflect this bias by keying the decision to two indicators—R&D dollars and journal publications—in which science and technology dominate. Our three more qualitative indicators, however, show equal respect for the sciences and engineering, the social and behavioral sciences, and the arts and humanities. By combining the three qualitative rankings for each of the four classes, giving them equal weight, we are balancing an initial bias toward science and technology with a counterbias toward the equality of all forms of scholarly knowledge. In the following sections we construct for each of our four Research classes such a combined ranking, premised upon the assumption of equal value among three broad fields: science and engineering, the social and behavioral sciences, and the arts and humanities.

Ranking the Public Research Universities

In this section we offer a combined ranking of the thirty-two public Research 1 universities by summing their rank orders in the science, social science, and arts-and-humanities indexes (table 6.7). For example, faculty at the University of Texas–Austin had ratings of 16-16-16. This campus ranked sixteenth in science, sixteenth in social science, and sixteenth in the humanities. This remarkably well-balanced performance produced for Texas faculty a combined score of 48, which ranked Texas as the median institution (sixteenth of thirty-two) among the Research 1 group.

One's eye is pulled immediately toward the surprises in the prestigious Research I category, such as the tied-for-second ranking of UC Santa Barbara and SUNY–Stony Brook. Campuses in the UC and SUNY systems occupy nine of the top twenty places. This remarkable pattern will receive further attention below. But it should be noted here how closely the rank order in table 6.7 corresponds to that found in most previous national reputational studies. UC Berkeley still claims top honors among the nation's great public universities. When compared to contemporary grand rankings, other traditional leaders are rank-ordered with only a moderate reshuffling Our per capita method places UCLA fourth, Wisconsin and Michigan in a tie for fifth, Illinois seventh, UC San Diego and Indiana eighth, North Carolina–Chapel Hill thirteenth, Washington (Seattle) fourteenth, Texas sixteenth, and Minnesota tied with Arizona for twenty-first. Other previous national comparisons and reputational surveys that concentrated on assessing the quality of graduate faculty and their doctoral programs favored large universities with comprehensive graduate offerings and established traditions of leadership. In contrast, our assessment of per capita research achievement, by reducing the advantages of size and reputation, eases the entry of new contenders.

Our ranking method also rewards institutional balance in the creation of new knowledge. The great American universities, those

TABLE 6.7

*Research 1 Public Universities Ranked by Combined Index Rankings for Top-Science,
Top–Social Science, and Arts and Humanities*

Rank	Institution	Combined Rank	Rank on Qualitative Indexes		
			Top-Science	Top–Social Science	A&H
1	UC Berkeley	11	2	8	1
2	UC Santa Barbara	15	6	7	2
2	SUNY–Stony Brook	15	5	2	8
4	UCLA	23	7	13	3
5	Wisconsin-Madison	25	9	5	11
5	Michigan	25	15	3	7
7	Illinois-Urbana	28	8	11	9
8	UC San Diego	30	1	19	10
8	Indiana	30	22	4	4
10	Colorado	34	4	15	15
11	UC Santa Cruz	39	32	1	6
12	UC Riverside	40	29	6	5
13	North Carolina–Chapel Hill	44	20	10	14
14	Washington (Seattle)	46	10	14	22
15	UC Irvine	47	3	26	18
16	Texas-Austin	48	16	16	16
17	SUNY-Albany	52	24	9	19
18	Maryland–College Park	54	14	20	20
19	Iowa	55	21	22	12
20	Virginia	56	18	25	13
21	Arizona	61	11	29	21
21	Minnesota	61	19	17	25
23	Pittsburgh	62	26	12	24
24	Utah	65	13	24	28
25	Illinois-Chicago	66	31	18	17
26	UC Davis	70	17	30	23
27	Purdue	71	12	28	31
28	Penn State	75	25	21	29
29	SUNY-Buffalo	77	23	27	27
30	Ohio State	80	27	23	30
31	North Carolina State	85	28	31	26
32	Alabama-Birmingham	94	30	32	32

perennially found on the top-ten lists, have been strong across the academic spectrum of the sciences, social sciences, and humanities. Our combined rankings thus reward institutions with uniformly high scores on the qualitative indicators for science, social science, and humanities and penalize specialized institutions, such as scientific and technical institutes, that concentrate their research effort. In our study, the best pattern is represented by three low numbers, representing high ranks and showing balanced research strength. For example, UC Berkeley's rank-ordered positions are 2-8-1: the campus is second among the nation's strongest public universities in science,

eighth in social science, and first in the humanities. Similar low, evenly balanced rankings were achieved by faculty at UC Santa Barbara
(6-7-2), SUNY–Stony Brook (5-2-8), UCLA (7-13-3), Wisconsin (9-5-
11), and Illinois (8-11-9). And three of these six—Berkeley, Santa Barbara, and Illinois—won their high science rankings without the benefit of medical schools. Indeed, five of the ten top-ranked universities
in the Research 1 category lacked medical schools.

This is an encouraging message—that medical schools are usually helpful, but are not essential, to top rank among research universities. The rankings for UC San Diego (1-19-10) and UC Irvine (3-
26-18) reveal a strong reliance on biomedical research as the driving
force behind their rapid ascent. But Colorado (4-15-15) and Illinois-
Urbana (8-11-9) placed among the top ten institutions in science and
engineering without the benefit of a medical center on campus. When,
as in our system of ranking, the three academic arenas are vested with
equal value, superior performance in the social sciences and the arts
and humanities can compensate for the absence of a medical-school
boost. This pattern is characteristic of UC Riverside (29-6-5) and UC
Santa Cruz (32-1-6) as well as SUNY-Albany (24-9-19), universities
where the top-science indicator is relatively weak but where their
combined ranking places the institutions in the top twenty of their
Research class. By contrast, seven of the ten bottom-ranked universities in the Research 1 category had medical schools. It is instruc-
tive to note that Alabama-Birmingham, which ranked tenth among
the thirty-two Research 1 institutions in per capita R&D funding and
seventeenth in publications, was less competitive when judged according to the three qualitative indicators (30-32-32).

In the ranking of the twenty-six Research 2 universities (table
6.8), the four top institutions show high scores that are evenly balanced across the academic spectrum—Oregon (6-2-1), Massachusetts (4-3-3), New Mexico (10-5-4), and Delaware (5-8-10). Kansas
(19-1-6), ranked fifth, demonstrates a relative weakness in science
that is shared by Rutgers, Missouri, Kentucky, and Mississippi. A
mirror-image of the Kansas pattern is found among a third group of
Research 2 institutions, where high ranking in science is accompanied by low ranking in social science and the humanities. This pattern, common among land-grant universities, can be seen in the
strong showing in science at Oregon State (1-20-15), Iowa State (2-
24-20), and Colorado State (8-26-26). Not surprisingly, at Georgia
Tech (3-22-25), the emphasis on engineering and applied science
produced a similar pattern.

The Research 2 class (and to some extent the Research 1 class)

TABLE 6.8

Research 2 Public Universities Ranked by Combined Index Rankings for Top-Science, Top–Social Science, and Arts and Humanities

Rank	Institution	Combined Rank	Rank on Qualitative Indexes Top-Science	Top–Social Science	A&H
1	Oregon	9	6	2	1
2	Massachusetts	10	4	3	3
3	New Mexico	19	10	5	4
4	Delaware	23	5	8	10
5	Kansas	26	19	1	6
6	{ Houston	31	12	14	5
6	{ Rutgers–New Brunswick	31	25	4	2
8	Missouri	34	20	7	7
9	Hawaii	35	9	17	9
10	Oregon State	36	1	20	15
11	Washington State	38	11	19	8
12	Texas A&M	39	7	9	23
13	Wayne State	40	13	15	12
14	Michigan State	42	14	11	17
15	{ Iowa State	46	2	24	20
15	{ Kentucky	46	23	10	13
15	{ Mississippi	46	26	6	14
18	Louisiana State	49	17	16	16
19	Georgia Tech	50	3	22	25
20	Georgia	52	22	12	18
21	Virginia Tech	53	24	18	11
22	Florida State	55	18	13	24
23	Florida	57	15	21	21
24	Colorado State	60	8	26	26
25	{ Virginia Commonwealth	63	16	25	22
25	{ Cincinnati	63	21	23	19

reflects the relative weakness of state universities located in the South. Only five of the thirty-two Research 1 institutions are located in the South, and only two of these, UNC–Chapel Hill and Texas-Austin, are ranked in the top half of their group. In the Research 2 class, southern universities predominate below the median. Comments on the Research 2 universities should not end with a discussion of weakness, however. This is a group of large, complex research institutions, by the late 1980s averaging more than eleven hundred faculty members and by 1990 winning more than $28 million annually in federal research grants.

The ranking of twenty-two Research 3 institutions (table 6.9) tends to show a more even academic balance across the sciences, social sciences, and humanities than do the rankings of the first two classes. The average Research 3 institution employed 735 full-time faculty in the late 1980s and received $11.8 million in federal R&D

TABLE 6.9
Research 3 Public Institutions Ranked by Combined Index Rankings for Top-Science,
Top–Social Science, and Arts and Humanities

Rank	Institution	Combined Rank	Top-Science	Top–Social Science	A&H
1	Arizona State	13	4	1	8
2	Nebraska	18	9	6	3
2	South Carolina	18	8	5	5
4	Wyoming	22	3	12	7
4	Maryland–Baltimore County	22	17	3	2
6	Utah State	23	2	17	4
7	Connecticut	27	13	2	12
8	Temple	29	11	8	10
8	Tennessee	29	6	9	14
10	Oklahoma	33	10	7	16
11	Arkansas	35	16	4	15
12	Kansas State	36	14	13	9
12	North Dakota State	36	5	10	21
12	Rhode Island	36	7	11	18
15	New Mexico State	37	12	14	11
16	Colorado School of Mines	41	1	18	22
17	Idaho	43	18	19	6
17	William and Mary	43	22	20	1
19	West Virginia	53	20	16	17
20	Clemson	54	19	22	13
21	Auburn	55	21	15	19
22	Missouri-Rolla	56	15	21	20

funding. The group includes few medical schools and technical institutions to drive up the science ratings, the Colorado School of Mines (1-18-22) being the chief exception. Most of the state flagships in this class lack medical schools (the exceptions are South Carolina and West Virginia). The College of William and Mary (22-20-1), with its strength concentrated in the humanities, constitutes a kind of polar opposite to the Colorado School of Mines. Once again, southern and border institutions are prevalent among the lower-ranked campuses.

The fifty-one public institutions in the Research 4 class cover such a wide spectrum of type and size that drawing generalizations is risky. Their rank order suggests few patterns (table 6.10). The first-ranked institution in this group, the University of Texas–Dallas, shows impressive scores across the board on the qualitative top-science, top–social science, and A&H per capita indicators (3-3-1). These scores are produced, however, by the smallest institutional faculty (187) in the class and the second-smallest faculty size among all 203 institutions (the Colorado School of Mines, with 175, was the smallest).

TABLE 6.10
Research 4 Public Institutions Ranked by Combined Index Rankings for Top-Science,
Top–Social Science and Arts and Humanities

			Rank on Qualitative Indexes		
Rank	Institution	Combined Rank	Top-Science	Top–Social Science	A&H
1	Texas-Dallas	7	3	3	1
2	Montana	20	10	7	3
3	SUNY-Binghamton	21	2	13	6
4	North Carolina–Greensboro	31	16	6	9
5	Kent State	39	22	2	15
6	Alabama-Tuscaloosa	43	15	18	10
7	Tennessee Tech	48	1	1	46
7	Portland State	48	18	19	11
9	Idaho State	52	4	4	44
10	Texas-Arlington	54	5	29	20
11	Vermont	57	31	22	4
12	Georgia State	64	27	8	29
13	Missouri–St. Louis	65	48	15	2
13	Cleveland State	65	38	14	13
13	Southern Mississippi	65	8	32	25
16	Southern Illinois	66	29	11	26
17	Texas Woman's	67	13	9	45
18	East Texas State	71	9	12	50
19	North Texas State	72	24	5	43
19	South Dakota	72	12	23	37
21	Bowling Green State	73	20	34	19
22	Memphis	75	36	25	14
23	Maine	76	21	27	28
24	Wisconsin-Milwaukee	77	33	39	5
24	Texas Tech	77	26	20	31
24	Toledo	77	14	16	47
27	Western Michigan	79	11	33	33
28	Miami (Ohio)	81	34	17	30
29	Florida Atlantic	85	25	24	36
29	Illinois State	85	28	36	21
29	Middle Tennessee	85	6	28	51
32	South Florida	86	17	30	39
33	Northern Illinois	87	44	31	12
34	Missouri–Kansas City	91	35	38	18
35	Montana State	93	45	40	8
36	Rutgers-Newark	94	49	10	35
37	Akron	96	32	26	38
38	Oklahoma State	97	19	44	34
39	Ohio University	98	37	45	16
40	New Hampshire	100	47	46	7
41	Nevada-Reno	102	7	47	48
42	Louisville	103	46	35	22
43	Northern Colorado	109	39	43	27
43	North Dakota	109	40	21	17
45	Northern Arizona	112	43	37	32
46	Louisiana Tech	121	23	49	49
47	Ball State	123	50	50	23
47	Mississippi State	123	20	34	19
47	New Orleans	123	51	48	24
47	Old Dominion	123	30	51	42
51	Indiana State	124	42	41	41

Second-ranked Montana shows strength across the board (10-7-3) and demonstrates, like Wyoming in the Research 3 class, the problem of insufficient recognition experienced by small universities in thinly populated states. The third-ranked university in the Research 4 public class, SUNY-Binghamton, shows some potential for following an upward trajectory toward the bright young stars in the new-campus firmament, such as the newer UC campuses, or Stony Brook. Lacking both a metropolitan location and a medical school, Binghamton nonetheless offers doctoral programs across the academic spectrum and shows balanced strength (2-13-6) in all three qualitative categories. Probably more important, Binghamton enjoys its designation as one of SUNY's four university research centers. The evidence since the 1960s, however, suggests that the crucial protection and nurture derived from flagship traditions, or from designation as new university research campuses in state systems such as UC and SUNY, have not developed fully for the second-flagship aspirants in the Research 3 and 4 groups: Maryland–Baltimore County (Research 3), and Missouri–St. Louis, Missouri–Kansas City, North Carolina–Greensboro, SUNY-Binghamton, Texas-Arlington, Texas-Dallas, and Wisconsin-Milwaukee (all in the Research 4 class).

Most public institutions in the wide-ranging Research 4 class, however, are not postwar branch campuses. Rather, the majority, tracing their founding to the nineteenth century, have enjoyed few special advantages in the increasingly intense competition for research laurels. This group includes small state flagships that have not produced strong research and doctoral programs (Alabama, Montana, Maine, and New Hampshire) and four institutions with small medical schools (North Dakota, South Dakota, Nevada, and Vermont). The appearance in the Research 4 group of eight universities with medical schools—five falling below the group's median top-science score—should remind us that schools of medicine are not automatic research boosters. Additionally, the costs of institutional imbalance in our method of ranking are suggested by the depressing effect of one weak qualitative indicator score, especially for a university whose strength lies in science and social science but not in the humanities—for example, Idaho State (4-4-44). Moreover, institutions showing strength in specialized mission fields—for example, Georgia Tech (3-22-25), in the Research 2 group—are penalized by a method that assigns equal weight to research performance in all three of the principal academic areas.

In general, however, the public universities in the Research 4 class, reasonably well balanced in their per capita research output, simply did not produce enough research relative to the brisk competition. The reasons for this, of course, include each institution's history, location, academic culture and leadership, and financial and political resources—not to mention such imponderables as athletic success, famous graduates, and quirks of fortune. Our evidence, most of it external, does not begin to address these matters, which were different for each institution. However, they have in common their status as public institutions, established by statute (with some, like California and Michigan, given constitutional status) to perform stipulated functions, serve particular constituencies, and offer approved programs. Bound by an increasingly complex network of legislative obligations and constraints, state boards and commissions, statewide coordinating authorities, and federal agencies and regulations, the public institutions were obliged to compete for students, faculty, and financial support with hundreds of private institutions that enjoyed far greater freedom of action. How well those private universities competed is the subject of the next chapter.

7

■

THE PRIVATE RESEARCH UNIVERSITIES AND RISING INSTITUTIONS

We first compared the research performance of public and private universities in chapter 3, when discussing the 1968 distribution of federal R&D funds to academic institutions. The per capita campus productivity reflected by federal R&D obligations and scientific publications showed a surprising margin of advantage for private institutions. Among the institutions classified as Research I in the 1970 Carnegie taxonomy, the average per capita R&D index of private universities was 144 percent higher than that of their public counterparts, and the average publications index was 97 percent higher. The private advantage in per capita research productivity was strongest at the Research I level and weakest at the Doctoral II level.[1] In the qualitative measures, faculty at private universities on average exceeded the productivity of their public counterparts in all three areas, showing the greatest margin in the arts and humanities and the least in the social sciences.

Was the perceived advantage enjoyed by private research universities also weakening with time? During the 1960s most expansion in higher education occurred in the public sector, even among elite research universities. In the two decades following *Sputnik*, the Association of American Universities extended the prestige of its membership to nine public universities but added only four private institutions.[2] During the difficult 1970s, private institutions generally suffered more than public institutions from inflation, falling enrollments, rising tuition, increasing energy costs, and declines in endowment income. Because student enrollment and faculty job growth were concentrated in public sector institutions during the 1970s, the dispersion of high-quality research faculty throughout the public sector meant that faculty at private institutions faced increasingly stiff

174

competition from public university researchers for research support from government, business, and foundations. During the 1970s and 1980s the nation's higher education establishment, including the leading private foundations (especially the various Carnegie entities), the network of higher education associations (especially the AAU and the American Council on Education), and the Education Commission of the States sponsored a series of conferences and reports on the problems afflicting the private sector.[3]

Paradoxically, during the postwar era the private and public sectors in American higher education may have increased their functional differentiation while growing more alike in their administrative procedures. With respect to their goals, one study reported that during the boom years of the 1960s "the private universities emphasized goals which suggested an elitism, an emphasis on the liberal arts, pure research, and a concern with the preservation of cultural heritage. The public universities were characterized by a strong egalitarianism, applied research, a concern with serving the population in their immediate area, and other service activities."[4] However, the rapid growth of federal aid to higher education following *Sputnik*, and the growth of state aid to private institutions, especially in the Northeast, brought in their wake increased government regulation that imposed similar requirements and constraints on all recipient institutions. As a consequence, public and private research universities increasingly grew to resemble one another in their administrative structures and procedures. In response to federal requirements, they developed common patterns of regulatory policing and reporting on student loans and grants, research protocols (especially concerning human and animal subjects), environmental protection measures, affirmative action requirements, public accountability in spending tax funds, and rights to privacy in record-keeping.[5] Private institutions, in their tuition and research programs, increased their reliance on federal and state tax dollars. Many leading public universities, faced with declining state contributions during the economic recessions of the 1970s and 1980s, increased their reliance on tuition and voluntary giving. In light of these mixed, post-*Sputnik* trends influencing public-private differentiation and convergence, did public-private differences in research productivity widen or narrow?

The per capita data from 1986–90 compiled for this study suggests that public universities had narrowed the private institutions' margin of advantage.[6] Moreover, among institutions classified as Doctoral I in the 1987 Carnegie taxonomy, the private advantage had been greatly reduced, and among Doctoral II institutions it had almost disappeared.[7] However, in the qualitative indicators measuring performance in science, social science, and the arts and humanities, the Research I and II private universities largely maintained their margin of superiority.[8] Comparisons over time by Carnegie category are problematic because many institutional classifications were changed. In particular, the Carnegie system's modest statistical thresholds for Research I status have produced an increasingly swollen category of Research I institutions—fifty-two in 1970, seventy in 1987, and eighty-eight in 1994. One purpose of our reclassification of the public universities in the previous chapter was to use per capita analysis to construct a more rigorous taxonomy, one based on faculty research achievement. In this chapter we apply this method to the private universities, among which, on most per capita indicators, the point-spread between Carnegie Research I and Doctoral II private institutions was twice as wide as among public institutions.[9]

Reclassifying the Private Universities

In the previous chapter, when we reclassified 131 public campuses according to their R&D and publications indexes, we reduced the top category of public research universities sharply from 45 institutions in the Carnegie Research I class to 32 in the new Research 1 public group. This process of reclassification assigned 26 public institutions to the Research 2 category, 22 to Research 3, and 51 to Research 4 (as compared with 26 public institutions in the Carnegie Research II class, 30 in Doctoral I, and 33 in Doctoral II). In chapter 6 the qualifying criteria we selected to identify the elite public Research 1 group were an R&D index of at least $28,000, and a publications index of at least 2.0. Because faculty at the leading private universities produced index scores considerably higher than those of most of their public counterparts, our classifying criteria were set higher for the private sector in the Research 1 and 2 categories. In the Research 3 and 4 categories, in which public and private index scores tended to converge, the cutoff scores were the same for the public and private sectors.[10]

To account for the higher index scores of the leading private universities, we set the criteria for Research 1 status for private institutions at $58,000 in per capita R&D funding, and a publications index of 3.0. Using this standard and the classification method described in chapter 6, we classified twenty-three private universities as Research 1 institutions (table 7.1). The resulting distinguished group has a familiar look. It includes all eleven private universities ranked

TABLE 7.1

Per Capita Publications and R&D Funding Indexes for Research 1 Private Institutions,
Ranked by Publications Index, 1986–1990

Rank	Institution	Publications Index	R&D Index
1	Caltech	15.44	$278,290
2	Harvard*	7.46	92,260
3	Stanford*	6.73	250,560
4	Yale*	6.57	156,570
5	Chicago*	6.10	99,060
6	Johns Hopkins*	6.05	264,100
7	Pennsylvania*	5.84	114,100
8	Washington (St. Louis)*	5.65	116,610
9	Duke*	5.21	120,770
10	Columbia*	5.09	122,360
11	Princeton	4.62	72,270
12	Northwestern*	4.00	59,740
13	Cornell	3.96	66,040
14	MIT	3.95	193,770
15	Rochester*	3.93	130,830
16	Brown*	3.84	60,430
17	Yeshiva*	3.59	173,470
18	Vanderbilt*	3.59	83,750
19	Emory*	3.36	75,380
20	Case Western*	3.33	92,570
21	Carnegie Mellon	3.21	107,470
22	Southern California*	3.15	82,510
23	Tufts*	3.08	64,420
	Mean	4.97	$119,100
	Median	4.00	107,470

Source: Unless otherwise noted, data in all the tables in this chapter derive from the authors' calculations. See Appendixes and Note on Method and Sources.

Note: The publications index is for 1986–88; R&D index for 1988–90.

*Campus includes medical school.

among the top twenty according to the 1982 National Research Council study, and it includes thirteen of the seventeen institutions that were members of the billion-dollar-endowment club as of June 1994.[11] All but three of the twenty-three private Research 1 campuses are included in Carnegie's twenty-five-member Research I private category of 1987.

Before we comment on three newcomers in the new Research 1 private category, and also on the four Carnegie Research I campuses not included, several attributes displayed in table 7.1 are worth noting. First, the rank order of institutions according to their scores on the publications index is similar to the top-twenty ranking of private universities found in the major reputational surveys of graduate education since the 1960s, including the Cartter (1966), Roose-Andersen (1970), and National Research Council (1982) studies. Second, roughly 80 percent (eighteen of twenty-three) of the Research 1 private universities include medical schools. (Among public sector Research 1 schools 60 percent [nineteen of thirty-two] include medical schools.) Medical schools heavily influence the first two of the five indicators—federal R&D obligations and total journal publications. As we noted in chapter 3, the existence of medical schools among many of the larger, most respected private universities contributes significantly to the private advantage in research performance.

Third, irrespective of the inclusion of a medical school on campus, elite private institutions tend to combine small faculty complements with powerful networks of "unfaculty" researchers and organized research units (ORUs). Four of the twenty-three private Research 1 institutions (including the top-ranked campus in journal publications, Caltech) produced impressive research scores without medical schools. Caltech, with only 245 full-time faculty, demonstrates the extraordinary multiplier potential of ORUs. The presence of such research institutes at Caltech produced a concentration of publishing researchers that considerably augments the publications of Caltech's regular full-time faculty.[12] A similar pattern of scientific and engineering excellence and ORU enrichment is found at the other three Research 1 campuses that do not have medical schools—MIT, Princeton, and Carnegie Mellon.

Finally, the Research 1 group includes two institutions—Brown and Emory—classified by Carnegie in 1987 as Research II, and one—Tufts—classified as Doctoral I.[13] All three of these institutions have relatively small faculties. The full-time faculty in 1987 numbered 539 at Brown, 647 at Emory, and 585 at Tufts. (The average number of full-time faculty for the twenty-three private Research 1 institutions in 1987 was 858.)[14] While these three universities were added to the new Research 1 class, four Carnegie Research I institutions were excluded. Boston University, the University of Miami, and New York University (NYU) were reclassified as Research 2 campuses, and Howard was reclassified as Research 4. (We did not include the prestigious Rockefeller University, the Claremont and Atlanta graduate schools, Hahnemann, International, Nova, and the Union Institute because these campuses did not meet our minimal criteria for a comprehensive doctorate-granting university.)

Our new Research 2 private class (table 7.2) includes ten institutions. Universities in this group have a per capita R&D index above $20,000 and a per capita publications index above 2.0. The Research 2 class includes three Carnegie Research I universities: Boston, Mi-

TABLE 7.2
Per Capita Publications and R&D Funding Indexes for Research 2 Private Institutions,
Ranked by Publications Index, 1986–1990

Rank	Institution	Publications Index	R&D Index
1	Georgetown*	3.29	$39,690
2	Boston*	3.05	52,730
3	New York University*	2.78	53,130
4	Tulane*	2.69	56,430
5	Dartmouth*	2.68	60,280
6	Miami*	2.65	73,930
7	Brandeis	2.50	51,970
8	George Washington*	2.50	41,820
9	Notre Dame	2.48	20,980
10	Rice	2.23	37,820
	Mean	2.74	$50,320
	Median	2.67	52,350

Note: The publications index is for 1986–88; the R&D index is for 1988–90.
*Campus includes medical school.

ami, and NYU. Also included are three schools classified in 1987 as Carnegie Doctoral I institutions: Dartmouth, Notre Dame, and Rice. Whereas Boston, Miami, and NYU had relatively large faculties (1,028 at Boston, 1,462 at NYU, and 821 at Miami in 1987), the faculty was relatively small at Dartmouth (440), Notre Dame (572), and Rice (384). In the Research 2 private group only Brandeis, Notre Dame, and Rice were without medical schools.

The criteria for inclusion in the Research 3 private class (table 7.3) are the same as those for the Research 3 public class: an R&D index of at least $9,000 and a publications index of at least 1.0. Only three of the fourteen universities in this category have medical schools (St. Louis, Loma Linda, and Loyola in Chicago). Two of the fourteen were classified as Research II in the 1987 Carnegie classification (Rensselaer and Syracuse), and six were in Carnegie's Doctoral II group (Clark, Clarkson, Drexel, Loma Linda, Polytechnic, and Southern Methodist). With the exception of Syracuse, which had 930 full-time instructional faculty in 1987, these are small universities. The average faculty size for the fourteen Research 3 schools in 1987 was 371, and four had fewer than 200 full-time faculty. This diverse group combines clusters of distinctive institutional types, including Roman Catholic schools (Catholic, Loyola-Chicago, and Saint Louis), Protestant-affiliated campuses (Loma Linda, with Seventh-Day Adventist affiliations; and Southern Methodist), technical institutions (Rensselaer, Polytechnic, and Drexel), and specialized institutions such as Columbia Teachers College, with only 134 full-time faculty. On the

179

TABLE 7.3

Per Capita Publications and R&D Funding Indexes for Research 3 Private Institutions,
Ranked by Publications Index, 1986–1990

Rank	Institution	Publications Index	R&D Index
1	Rensselaer	1.89	$47,910
2	Saint Louis*	1.76	28,140
3	Loma Linda*	1.69	9,940
4	Columbia Teachers College	1.67	10,190
5	Syracuse	1.62	19,110
6	Clark	1.43	9,190
7	Lehigh	1.29	24,850
8	Polytechnic	1.27	32,670
9	Southern Methodist	1.26	23,830
10	Clarkson	1.25	21,100
11	Catholic	1.24	12,780
12	Denver	1.13	14,100
13	Loyola-Chicago*	1.10	9,900
14	Drexel	1.00	15,900
	Mean	1.39	$20,180
	Median	1.28	17,510

Note: The publications index is for 1986–88; the R&D index is for 1988–90.
*Campus includes medical school.

whole, the Research 3 schools were successful in winning federal re-search funding (almost half the group met the Research 2 criterion for R&D awards), but their record of publication in scientific and scholarly journals was modest.

Most diverse is the Research 4 group (table 7.4). Defined as insti-tutions receiving less than $9,000 in per capita R&D funding and scoring lower than 1.0 in per capita publications, these twenty-five private campuses generally did not compete successfully with the top research universities for students, faculty, and extramural support. Institutions such as Howard, Brigham Young, and the New School for Social Research have no counterpart in the public sector. Howard, chartered in the District of Columbia by Congress in 1867 to offer a college education in the liberal arts and sciences to freedmen, and the only Research 4 campus with a medical school, has historically en-joyed a unique combination of private control and public funding.[15] Although the federal government has funded most of Howard's oper-ating budget, the university's federal R&D funding has remained small. In 1990 Howard was ranked eighth nationally in total federal obligations ($186.6 million), but only $15.5 million of this (8%) was for R&D awards.[16] Howard's medical school, which emphasizes pri-mary medical care rather than research, was ranked sixty-seventh

TABLE 7.4

Per Capita Publications and R&D Funding Indexes for Research 4 Private Institutions,
Ranked by Publications Index, 1986–1990

Rank	Institution	Publications Index	R&D Index
1	New School	1.55	$ 1,890
2	Tulsa	1.36	3,670
3	San Francisco	1.35	1,850
4	Marquette	1.25	4,270
5	Fordham	1.19	3,170
6	Boston College	1.10	7,510
7	American	1.10	4,190
8	Stevens Tech	.95	11,350
9	Texas Christian	.89	4,460
10	Northeastern	.81	10,950
11	Howard*	.76	11,900
12	Florida Tech	.72	8,960
13	Brigham Young	.68	3,140
14	Hofstra	.61	420
15	Baylor (Waco)	.60	2,670
16	St. John's	.60	860
17	Adelphi	.56	1,010
18	Duquesne	.51	350
19	Biola	.51	0
20	Drake	.37	60
21	Pepperdine	.32	1,560
22	U.S. International	.23	270
23	Andrews	.20	320
24	Mississippi College	.17	100
25	Illinois Tech	.02	15,110
	Mean	.79	$ 4,850
	Median	.68	2,670

Note: The publications index is for 1986–88; the R&D index is for 1988–90.
*Campus includes medical school.

(out of seventy medical campuses included in this study) in NIH per capita research funding in fiscal 1990. Brigham Young, a large university (with 29,000 students and 1,220 full-time faculty in 1987) affiliated with the Church of Jesus Christ of Latter-Day Saints, has stressed undergraduate and graduate education but not research.[17] The New School for Social Research, chartered in the 1930s to provide an institutional home for scholars who had fled from European totalitarianism, built a faculty that published intensively but concentrated on the social sciences.[18]

There are more Roman Catholic and Protestant-affiliated universities in the Research 4 group than in any other classification. Reflecting these religious and denominational loyalties, five of the Research 4 schools had endowments among the largest hundred in the nation, and three of the top five were church-affiliated (Boston College, Texas Christian, and Baylor).[19] The average faculty size of Research 4 institutions was 381, slightly larger than the Research 3 average of 371. However, the average R&D index for the private Research 4 group, $4,850, was not only considerably smaller than the private Research 3 average ($20,180) but also smaller than the average ($6,650) for the public Research 4 universities. As can be seen by comparing the mean per capita values for the four private Research categories (table 7.5) with the corresponding values for public institutions (table 6.4), the "private advantage" disappears when we reach the Research 4 class, where the advantage in research productivity instead shifts to the public sector.

In chapter 5 we noted that the presence of medical schools on university campuses was generally associated with high scores on the R&D and publications indexes and the top-science index but not with high arts-and-humanities scores. This is not surprising. Biomedical journals dominate scientific publishing, but health science faculties contribute only indirectly if at all to an institution's A&H index, and their numbers, by increasing the number of institutional faculty, may lower that index somewhat. In the private sector, most of the larger campuses include medical schools. Partly for this reason, the twenty top-ranked private institutions' average performance on the top-science index was substantially stronger than the average for the twenty top-ranked public universities.

Table 7.6 shows twenty-five leading institutions in the private sector and twenty-five in the public sector ranked according to the top-science index. Faculty at the median private institution, Pennsylvania, produced a top-science index of .47. The median public institution in top-science performance was Utah, with an index of .35. As judged by median scores on the top-science index, the top-ranked private universities were approximately one-third stronger than their public counterparts.

Most of the elite private institutions (table 7.6) include large campus medical schools; in the case of Yeshiva, the medical school largely explains the institution's high ranking.[20] Nine institutions without medical schools, however, including three of the top five (Caltech, MIT, and Princeton), are among the top twenty-five in top-science achievement. Caltech's top-science score is predictably spectacular. More striking, perhaps, is the inclusion, in this select group of scientific powers, of several arts-and-sciences universities without medical schools—such as Princeton, ranked fifth, a campus that earned its scientific laurels without the benefit of the medical multiplier. Un-

TABLE 7.5

Average Per Capita Indexes of Scholarly Achievement for Private Research Universities, by Graham-Diamond Category, 1980–1990

Graham-Diamond Category	Avg. No. of Full-Time Faculty	R&D Index	Publications Index	Top-Science Index	Top–Social Science Index	A&H Index
Research 1	858	$119,100	4.97	.608	.142	.075
Research 2	683	50,320	2.74	.212	.074	.052
Research 3	371	20,180	1.39	.023	.124	.046
Research 4	381	4,850	.79	.013	.036	.024

TABLE 7.6

Fifty Leading Public and Private Universities, Ranked by Top-Science Index

Rank	Private Institution	Top-Science Index	Rank	Public Institution	Top-Science Index
1	Caltech	3.36	1	UC San Diego	1.07
2	Stanford	1.21	2	UC Berkeley	.92
3	MIT	1.16	3	UC Irvine	.56
4	Harvard	.93	4	Colorado	.55
5	Princeton	.83	5	SUNY–Stony Brook	.54
6	Johns Hopkins	.75	6	UC Santa Barbara	.53
7	Yale	.65	7	UCLA	.51
8	Cornell	.60	8	Illinois-Urbana	.45
9	Washington (St. Louis)	.55	9	Wisconsin-Madison	.42
10	Chicago	.54	10	Washington (Seattle)	.37
11	Columbia	.49	11	Arizona	.37
12	Brandeis	.48	12	Purdue	.35
13	Pennsylvania	.47	13	Utah	.35
14	Duke	.46	14	Maryland–College Park	.33
15	Rochester	.46	15	Michigan	.32
16	Rice	.44	16	Texas-Austin	.31
17	Yeshiva	.43	17	UC Davis	.31
18	Northwestern	.42	18	Virginia	.29
19	Carnegie Mellon	.38	19	Minnesota	.29
20	Rensselaer	.36	20	Oregon State	.29
21	Case Western	.36	21	UNC–Chapel Hill	.26
22	Notre Dame	.33	22	Iowa	.25
23	Vanderbilt	.27	23	Colorado School of Mines	.25
24	Tufts	.27	24	Indiana	.24
25	Southern California	.27	25	SUNY-Buffalo	.24
	Mean	.66		Mean	.42
	Median	.47		Median	.35

like the primarily scientific institutions (Caltech, MIT, and Rensselaer), Princeton by the late 1980s carried less than 40 percent of its full-time faculty in its science and engineering departments.[21] Cornell, whose medical school is located in New York City (and thus is not considered in the Ithaca campus scores) shows the same kind of scientific strength as Princeton.[22] Brandeis, founded as recently as

183

1948 and obliged by its location in metropolitan Boston to compete in an academic market dominated by Harvard and MIT, achieved distinguished levels of research performance with astonishing speed.[23] A final addition to this list of the top twenty-five is Notre Dame, classified in the Research 2 category, without a medical school, but building a strong claim in the sciences and other fields as the nation's leading Catholic research university.[24]

Seventy percent of the twenty-five leading private institutions in the social sciences are also top-ranked in science (tables 7.6 and 7.7). Among public institutions the overlap is 68 percent.[25] Among private universities, the new social science leaders include Brown, Emory, NYU, Tulane, and three institutions classified by Carnegie in Doctoral categories: Clark, Denver, and the New School. It is not surprising that the New School, with a small faculty (235) and a concentration on social theory and research, would rank among the leaders in per capita social science publications. The presence of Clark (with 161 full-time faculty in 1987) and Denver (with 354 full-time faculty) among the top twenty-five demonstrates the ability of small institutions, often lacking the resources to compete at a high level in expensive fields such as science and engineering, to build competitive programs (according to per capita assessments) in the social sciences and the humanities. On the whole the rankings of the top twenty-five institutions in science and social science, in both the public and private sectors, include the same core of powerful institutions while modestly rearranging their order. The private advantage over the public sector, however, is smaller with respect to social science research. The median private institution in social science was Rochester, with a top–social science index of .128. Among public universities the median institution was Pittsburgh, with a social science index of .111. Thus, a comparison of per capita median top–social science scores among the leading twenty-five institutions gives the private universities a modest 14-percent margin over their public counterparts.

In the arts and humanities, private liberal arts colleges and universities in the United States have historically nurtured the classic tradition. Even the private scientific institutes have shown a concern for learning in the humanities—witness MIT's drive in the 1940s to strengthen the humanities and social sciences.[26] In the private sector there is no equivalent of the sixty-nine land-grant institutions (including the sixteen historically black institutions supported under the 1890 land-grant program), in which emphasis was placed on engineering, applied science, and professional education.[27] Since the 1960s, as political and market pressures have reduced investments

TABLE 7.7
Fifty Leading Public and Private Universities, Ranked by Top–Social Science Index

Rank	Private Institution	Top–Social Science Index	Rank	Public Institution	Top–Social Science Index
1	Chicago	.281	1	UC Santa Cruz	.188
2	Stanford	.236	2	SUNY–Stony Brook	.180
3	Duke	.193	3	Michigan	.164
4	Northwestern	.188	4	Indiana	.163
5	Harvard	.181	5	Wisconsin-Madison	.160
6	Yale	.169	6	UC Riverside	.145
7	Princeton	.168	7	UC Santa Barbara	.137
8	Pennsylvania	.164	8	UC Berkeley	.129
9	Columbia	.158	9	SUNY-Albany	.114
10	Carnegie Mellon	.156	10	UNC–Chapel Hill	.113
11	Washington (St. Louis)	.145	11	Kansas	.112
12	Johns Hopkins	.129	12	Illinois-Urbana	.111
13	Rochester	.128	13	Pittsburgh	.111
14	Brown	.115	14	UCLA	.108
15	Vanderbilt	.115	15	Washington	.104
16	New York University	.109	16	Colorado	.094
17	Caltech	.102	17	Texas-Austin	.090
18	Brandeis	.097	18	Minnesota	.090
19	Tulane	.091	19	Oregon	.088
20	New School	.089	20	Illinois-Chicago	.087
21	Case Western	.089	21	UC San Diego	.085
22	Cornell	.089	22	Maryland–College Park	.084
23	Clark	.087	23	Massachusetts	.082
24	Emory	.087	24	Pennsylvania State	.080
25	Denver	.079	25	Rutgers–New Brunswick	.080
	Mean	.138		Mean	.116
	Median	.128		Median	.111

in the humanities at both state and private institutions, the strong private universities appear to have increased their lead.

Table 7.8 shows twenty-five leading private and public universities ranked by the A&H index. Because the humanities do not require expensive investments in physical plant and support personnel, and because well-trained faculty in the arts and humanities have been relatively plentiful and inexpensive compared with faculty in the sciences and engineering and in the "harder" behavioral and social sciences, small universities have found room to compete successfully.

The median private institution in A&H performance, Duke, has an index score (.072) that is roughly a third higher than that of the median public university, Maryland–Baltimore County (.055). Despite the increased representation of smaller universities, the continuity among top-ranked institutions, especially in the private sector,

TABLE 7.8

Fifty Leading Public and Private Universities, Ranked by Arts-and-Humanities Index

Rank	Private Institution	A&H Index	Rank	Public Institution	A&H Index
1	Princeton	.184	1	UC Berkeley	.088
2	Yale	.157	2	UC Santa Barbara	.066
3	Brandeis	.138	3	Texas-Dallas	.064
4	Chicago	.109	4	UCLA	.063
5	Brown	.109	5	William and Mary	.063
6	Harvard	.107	6	UC Riverside	.063
7	Columbia	.107	7	Indiana	.062
8	Stanford	.103	8	UC Santa Cruz	.060
9	Pennsylvania	.091	9	Oregon	.060
10	Dartmouth	.086	10	Michigan	.058
11	Rochester	.077	11	Missouri–St. Louis	.058
12	Notre Dame	.074	12	SUNY–Stony Brook	.056
13	Duke	.072	13	Maryland–Baltimore County	.055
14	New York University	.069	14	Rutgers–New Brunswick	.054
15	Johns Hopkins	.069	15	Illinois-Urbana	.050
16	Northwestern	.058	16	UC San Diego	.050
17	Cornell	.058	17	Wisconsin-Madison	.048
18	Tufts	.050	18	Iowa	.048
19	Tulane	.050	19	Montana	.047
20	Vanderbilt	.050	20	Vermont	.047
21	Marquette	.050	21	Virginia	.045
22	Catholic	.049	22	Massachusetts	.045
23	Rice	.048	23	North Carolina–Chapel Hill	.043
24	Fordham	.047	24	Wisconsin-Milwaukee	.042
25	Emory	.047	25	Colorado	.042
	Mean	.083		Mean	.055
	Median	.072		Median	.055

is high across the academic spectrum. More than three-fifths of the top-ranked private campuses in the arts and humanities are also top-ranked in the social sciences. Among the elite private universities, those ranked high in one field will usually be leaders in the other areas as well. For the humanities, however, this is less true below the top-twenty level. The institutions ranked twenty-first to twenty-fifth include three Roman Catholic universities (Marquette, Catholic, and Fordham) whose success in this category, together with twelfth-ranked Notre Dame, demonstrates the traditional emphasis on the humanities in Catholic universities.

Ranking the Private Research Universities

Following the same procedure we used to rank the public universities, we summed the institutional rankings for science, social science, and arts and humanities in each of the four private Research categories and ranked the private campuses in ascending order of their total scores (table 7.9). The familiar list does not differ sharply from the ranking of private institutions produced by the 1982 National Research Council study. Stanford led both parades. The top seven places in both rankings included Chicago, Columbia, Harvard, Princeton, Stanford, and Yale—the predictable leading cohort from decades of reputational rankings. There are fewer surprises here than we found in the previous chapter when we ranked, on the basis of per capita research achievement, the leading public universities.

The greatest American universities are powerful in all major academic areas, irrespective of whether they are publicly or privately controlled or whether or not they house medical schools. Thus, UC Berkeley scored second among the top tier of public institutions in the top-science index, eighth in the top–social science index, and first in the A&H index. Wisconsin bent the other way but showed a relatively balanced set of rankings: 9 in top-science, 5 in top–social science, and 11 in humanities (table 6.7). Yet a kind of disequilibrium seems to operate in the public sector, partly in response to political factors that forced a dispersion in mission assignments (and differences in schools' flagship status, land-grant designation, medical mission, professional school mix, and technical emphasis). Economists and business executives might call this market specialization, and deem it a virtue. But one consequence of this phenomenon is that a Berkeley-type balance is relatively rare among the leading public universities. More common are wide variations in academic strength. In science, for example, the three-index rankings show patterns of relative strength at UC Irvine (3-26-18) and weakness at UC Riverside (29-6-5). Other patterns show SUNY-Albany's strength (24-9-19) and UC San Diego's relative weakness (1-19-10) in the social sciences. High rank in the arts and humanities is often paired with strength in either science or social science, but rarely with both.[28]

Unlike the variegated public universities, most of the leading private institutions are Standard Model universities. They are centered on a college of arts and sciences, include a research-intensive medical school, and manifest a relatively even balance in scholarly strength across the academic spectrum. The closely matched three-index rankings that indicate academic balance are found not only among the top-ranked campuses—for example, Stanford (2-2-7), Princeton (5-7-1), Harvard (4-5-5), and Yale (7-6-2). Among private universities, such balanced academic portfolios are common throughout the Research 1 distribution—for example, eighteenth-ranked

187

TABLE 7.9

Research 1 Private Universities Ranked by Combined Index Ranking for Top–Science,
Top–Social Science, and Arts and Humanities

			Rank on Qualitative Indexes		
Rank	Institution	Combined Rank	Top–Science	Top–Social Science	A&H
1	Stanford	11	2	2	7
2	Princeton	13	5	7	1
3	⎰ Chicago	14	10	1	3
3	⎱ Harvard	14	4	5	5
5	Yale	15	7	6	2
6	⎰ Columbia	26	11	9	6
6	⎱ Duke	26	13	3	10
8	Pennsylvania	28	12	8	8
9	Johns Hopkins	29	6	12	11
10	Northwestern	32	16	4	12
11	⎰ Caltech	36	1	16	19
11	⎱ Rochester	36	14	13	9
13	Cornell	39	8	18	13
14	⎰ Brown	41	23	14	4
14	⎱ Washington (St. Louis)	41	9	11	21
16	MIT	43	3	20	20
17	Carnegie Mellon	44	17	10	17
18	Vanderbilt	49	19	15	15
19	Tufts	56	20	22	14
20	⎰ Case Western	57	18	17	22
20	⎱ Emory	57	22	19	16
22	Southern California	60	21	21	18
23	Yeshiva	61	15	23	23

Vanderbilt (19-15-15), twentieth-ranked (tie) Case Western (18-17-22), and twenty-first-ranked Southern California (21-21-18). Because our approach weighs equally the three academic areas of index comparison, leading scientific institutions such as MIT (3-20-20) and Caltech (1-16-19) are ranked lower in our study than in other ratings.[29]

However, certain institutions are ranked higher in our comparison than in recent reputational rankings. According to our per capita measures, Duke and Northwestern move into the private top ten. Johns Hopkins, seen in the 1970s as declining, and tied for thirtieth place according to the 1982 National Research Council study, here returned to the top-ten ranks among private institutions. Reputational surveys, by capturing shared perceptions of institutions' rising and falling status in the academic pecking order, reinforce and prolong the reputations they survey. The objective evidence of per capita research productivity upon which our comparisons are based, however, lends no support to the perception of a Johns Hopkins in sunset. Evidence of fresh upward movement, however, is shown by faculty at Rochester and Brown. Emory—which, like Brown, was reclassified by the Carnegie classification of 1994 from Research II to Research I status—moves into the top twenty-five. According to this per capita assessment, Tufts, shifted by the 1994 Carnegie classification from Doctoral I to Research I, has a strong claim to honors as the private sector's most improved institution.

Finally, a word about Harvard. Often ranked first or second in reputational surveys or overall institutional rankings, Harvard may with some justice claim that our per capita method slightly undermeasures the research achievements of its faculty, especially outside the medical sciences. We agree in part. Harvard's practice of including on the medical faculty such a large number of professionals from its teaching hospitals and research institutes in Boston inflates the campus denominator of full-time faculty.[30]

The ten institutions in the private Research 2 group are shown in order of their combined ranks in table 7.10. The Research 2 private campuses average $50,300 in per capita R&D funding and 2.7 in per capita publications, as compared with the Research 1 per capita average of $119,000 in per capita R&D funding and 5.0 in publications (table 7.5). Three (Boston, Miami, and NYU) are large universities that fell short of the Research 1 per capita R&D criterion of $58,000 despite the substantial funding of their medical schools.[31] Top-ranked in the Research 2 class, Brandeis, enjoying the advantages that fall to a small university that has maintained high standards of faculty scholarship since its 1948 founding, compiled almost perfect per capita index ranking scores—first in science, second in social science, and first in humanities. NYU, despite its medical school and its strong reputation in the performing arts (an area of creative work not well represented in this study), showed considerable strength in the social sciences (8-1-4).[32]

The equivalent averages for the private Research 3 universities are half again as small as those of their Research 2 counterparts—$20,200 in per capita R&D funding and a publications index of 1.4. The fourteen Research 3 institutions are rank-ordered in table 7.11 according to their combined index scores. Once again, the rankings are revealing. As is often the case, campuses with their main strength in the humanities often have religious affiliations. For example, among the fourteen private Research 3 institutions, first-ranked in the humanities was Catholic University (10-3-1), and second was Southern Methodist (11-6-2). Small universities without extensive scientific establishments often excel in the social sciences and the humanities: for example, Clark (8-1-4) and Denver (9-2-6). Technical in-

TABLE 7.10

Research 2 Private Universities Ranked by Combined Index Ranking for Top-Science, Top–Social Science, and Arts and Humanities

Rank	Institution	Combined Rank	Rank on Qualitative Indexes		
			Top-Science	Top–Social Science	A&H
1	Brandeis	4	1	2	1
2	Notre Dame	11	3	5	3
3	{ Dartmouth	12	4	6	2
3	{ Rice	12	2	4	6
5	New York University	13	8	1	4
6	Tulane	17	9	3	5
7	Boston University	19	5	7	7
8	Miami	23	6	8	9
9	Georgetown	24	7	9	8
10	George Washington	30	10	10	10

TABLE 7.11

Research 3 Private Universities Ranked by Combined Index Rankings for Top-Science, Top–Social Science, and Arts and Humanities

Rank	Institution	Combined Rank	Rank on Qualitative Indexes		
			Top-Science	Top–Social Science	A&H
1	Clark	13	8	1	4
2	{ Syracuse	14	6	5	3
2	{ Catholic	14	10	3	1
4	Denver	17	9	2	6
5	Clarkson	18	2	11	5
6	Southern Methodist	19	11	6	2
7	Lehigh	22	4	8	10
8	Loyola (Chicago)	23	12	4	7
9	Rensselaer	24	1	12	11
10	Drexel	25	7	10	8
11	Saint Louis	26	5	7	14
12	Polytechnic	29	3	13	13
13	Columbia Teachers College	35	14	9	12
14	Loma Linda	36	13	14	9

stitutions are of course skewed toward the sciences (as shown by rankings of 1-12-11 at Rensselaer, and 3-13-13 at Polytechnic). Universities with small medical schools where faculty are little involved in research may show little strength in the sciences (12-4-7 at Loyola-Chicago and 13-14-9 at Loma Linda). The medical schools at both of these universities fall in the lowest category in NIH research funding (Class V—less than $18,000), while the medical school at Saint Louis University is Class IV ($18,000-$35,000) (table 5.4).

The private Research 4 category, unlike its public counterpart, includes no equivalent of the new urban universities—the ambitious

TABLE 7.12

Research 4 Private Universities Ranked by Combined Index Rankings for Top-Science,
Top–Social Science, and Arts and Humanities

| | | | Rank on Qualitative Indexes | | |
Rank	Institution	Combined Rank	Top-Science	Top–Social Science	A&H
1	Marquette	8	4	3	1
2	Boston College	12	3	6	3
3	American	18	8	5	5
4	Northeastern	21	1	9	11
5	Fordham	22	16	4	2
6	Tulsa	26	20	2	4
7	Stevens Tech	29	2	19	8
8	New School	30	14	1	15
9	Howard	33	9	15	9
10	Illinois Tech	34	6	16	12
11	⎰ St. John's	35	15	10	10
11	⎱ Texas Christian	35	5	13	17
13	⎧ Duquesne	39	12	14	13
13	⎨ Hofstra	39	22	11	6
13	⎩ San Francisco	39	13	7	19
16	Brigham Young	40	10	12	18
17	Adelphi	43	21	8	14
18	Drake	47	19	21	7
19	Florida Tech	52	7	25	20
20	⎰ Andrews	58	17	18	23
20	⎱ Baylor	58	11	22	25
22	Pepperdine	59	18	20	21
23	U.S. International	62	23	17	22
24	Biola	65	25	24	16
25	Mississippi College	71	24	23	24

competitors of the state flagships, aspiring to follow the path of UCLA. The twenty-five private campuses (table 7.12) are all long-established institutions, although some have been renamed.[33] Few of these institutions are well endowed. Caught between the expanding public sector with its lower tuitions, on the one hand, and the more prestigious private universities on the other, most of the campuses in this category have struggled to find a market niche. These are primarily teaching institutions, not research universities, and the prevalence of religious affiliations among them testifies to a number of distinctive missions.

Many of the Research 4 private universities are urban Catholic institutions with roots in nineteenth-century immigrant communities.[34] This description fits three of the five top-ranked institutions — Marquette, Boston College, and Fordham. In the Research 4 category, as elsewhere in this assessment, top-ranked institutions nourish balanced strength across the academic spectrum — for example, the three index rankings at Marquette (4-3-1), at Boston College (3-6-3), and at American University (8-5-5). A more typical pattern at private Research 4 institutions, however, was emphasis on excellence in the humanities and the social sciences—for example, at Fordham (16-4-2) and Tulsa (20-2-4). Not surprisingly, the New School ranked first in the top–social science category (14-1-15). Also predictably, scientific prowess, uncommon in the Research 4 group, is found chiefly at technical institutes such as Stevens Institute (2-19-8) and Florida Tech (7-25-20), as well as at Northeastern, with its strength in engineering (1-9-11). Only one Research 4 university, Howard, included a medical school.

The Continuing Success of Elite Public and Private Research Universities

The evidence in this study suggests that in all fields of research performance, including the arts and humanities, faculty at most of the nation's more than two hundred doctorate-granting universities had increased considerably their levels of per capita research achievement in the three decades following *Sputnik.* Most of the major incentives affecting university behavior during the postwar era—federal science policy, competition for prestige, campus fiscal pressures, and service to the industrial economy—combined to increase campus research efforts. As the tide of research support and activity rose, levels of university effort rose with it. Private elite institutions, which enjoyed substantial leads in per capita measures of performance in all research fields in the 1960s, still maintained large margins of superiority in most academic fields in the early 1990s. The leading state flagships similarly strengthened their already substantial advantages over most public sector competitors. The great public universities, led by perennially high-ranked institutions such as UC Berkeley and Michigan, performed at per capita levels of research achievement superior to that of all but perhaps a score of their private competitors. The success stories of these perennial leaders are well known and well earned, but they have obscured the story of rising research universities in the public and private sectors—the brightening stars in the academic firmament. By their number and success they testify against the defeatist corollary implicit in the Matthew effect: that the rich institutions get richer while the lesser institutions fall further behind.

We have charted the progress of these rising universities as individual institutions throughout this study. Many have been well regarded in public opinion but others often have been little known. In some instances they have suffered from the prestige of powerful neighbors who have screened them from sight. In the shadow of Harvard and MIT, for example, it has been difficult to see Brandeis; in the bright light cast by Berkeley and UCLA, it was hard to see the beacon from Santa Barbara. By comparing per capita measurements of research achievement over time, however, we can identify a cadre of rising institutions in the public and the private sectors. Their individual and collective performance supports the optimistic proposition that in the postwar era, America's research universities demonstrated not only a surge to global leadership by traditional elites, but also the bracing success of new challengers.

Rising Research Universities in the Public Sector

To identify rising public universities we pooled the fifty-eight institutions in the Research 1 and Research 2 public groups and ranked them according to their combined scores on the per capita top-science, top–social science, and A&H indexes. Rising public universities (table 7.13) are defined as institutions included in the top thirty-three in the combined Research 1 and 2 pool but not previously ranked among the nation's top twenty-five in any of the three major comparative studies conducted during 1960–82 (Cartter [1966], Roose-Andersen [1970], National Research Council [1982]).[35] Twenty-one rising institutions in the public sector are thus identified and ranked:

1.	UC Santa Barbara	12.	Virginia
2.	SUNY–Stony Brook	13.	Arizona
3.	Colorado	14.	Pittsburgh
4.	UC Riverside	15.	UC Davis
5.	UC Santa Cruz	16.	Utah
6.	Oregon	17.	Kansas
7.	UC Irvine	18.	New Mexico
8.	Maryland–College Park	19.	Illinois-Chicago
9.	Massachusetts-Amherst	20.	SUNY-Buffalo
10.	Iowa	21.	Rutgers-New Brunswick
11.	SUNY-Albany		

These twenty-one rising public institutions fall into two groups. Approximately half are state flagship universities, most of them mem-

TABLE 7.13

Nationally Ranked and Rising Public Research Universities Ranked by Combined Index for Top-Science, Top–Social Science, and Arts-and-Humanities Indexes

Rank	Institution	Previous National Reputational Ranking*
1	UC Berkeley	1
2	*UC Santa Barbara*	
3	*SUNY–Stony Brook*	
4	UCLA	8
5	Michigan	8
6	Wisconsin-Madison	8
7	Illinois-Urbana	13
8	Indiana	21
9	UC San Diego	21
10	*Colorado*	
11	{ *UC Riverside*	
11	{ North Carolina–Chapel Hill	20
13	Texas-Austin	16
14	Washington (Seattle)	19
15	{ *UC Santa Cruz*	
15	{ *Oregon*	
17	*UC Irvine*	
18	{ *Maryland–College Park*	
18	{ *Massachusetts-Amherst*	
20	{ *Iowa*	
20	{ *SUNY-Albany*	
21	*Virginia*	
23	Minnesota	16
24	*Arizona*	
25	*Pittsburgh*	
26	{ *UC Davis*	
26	{ *Utah*	
28	*Kansas*	
29	*New Mexico*	
30	*Illinois-Chicago*	
31	*SUNY-Buffalo*	
32	*Rutgers–New Brunswick*	
33	Purdue	25

Italics denotes rising institution.

*Previous rankings by David S. Webster, "America's Highest Ranked Graduate Schools, 1925–1982," *Change* 15 (May–June 1983): 23, based on data from National Research Council, *An Assessment of Research-Doctorate Programs in the United States* (Washington, D.C.: National Academy Press, 1982). See also Appendixes and Note on Method and Sources.

bers of the prestigious AAU: Arizona (admitted to AAU membership in 1985), Colorado (1966), Iowa (1909), Maryland (1969), Kansas (1909), SUNY-Buffalo (1989), Oregon (1969), Rutgers (1989), Virginia (1904), and UC Santa Barbara (1994). The remaining three flagship campuses in this cluster of rising institutions are Massachusetts, New Mexico, and Utah, which are not AAU members but are competitive with AAU institutions. Their overall performance on the indicators of per capita research achievement measured in this study surpassed the level achieved by more than a half-dozen public AAU universities.[36]

Even more striking, however, is the profile of a second group of rising public universities. These nine—the University of California campuses at Davis, Irvine, Riverside, Santa Cruz, and Santa Barbara; the SUNY campuses at Albany, Buffalo, and Stony Brook; and the University of Illinois–Chicago—are, with the exception of formerly private Buffalo, essentially *new* postwar research universities. Albany and Santa Barbara were former normal schools elevated to research university status in the modern era (Santa Barbara in 1944,[37] Albany in 1963); Riverside, a former citrus experiment station, joined the University of California in 1954. Three of the nine were founded in the postwar period—SUNY–Stony Brook (1957), and the UC campuses at Irvine and Santa Cruz (1965). The University of Illinois at Chicago was created through a consolidation of the medical center and the Chicago Circle campuses in 1982. All nine institutions are designated research campuses within multicampus state university systems in large urban-industrial states.[38] Two of these new institutions, UC Santa Barbara and SUNY–Stony Brook, are outranked in combined per capita research achievement only by Berkeley among the nation's public campuses. These emerging new research universities occupy five of the top seven positions among rising new institutions.

The twenty-one rising universities, led by the new research campuses, have shown strong growth in the per capita measures of performance since the 1960s. Between 1968 and 1988 the six top-ranked rising institutions in the public sector—UC Santa Barbara, SUNY–Stony Brook, Colorado, UC Riverside, UC Santa Cruz, and Oregon—received an average per capita increase in constant R&D dollars of 121 percent. In general, during the period 1960–90 the twenty-one rising public universities surpassed the average performance levels of Research 1 public institutions, but gained more slowly on the nationally ranked institutions. Several of the new institutions, however, especially within the University of California and SUNY systems, not only gained on the elite public campuses but actually surpassed them in per capita research performance. In the academic ratings game for the 1990s, even if smaller campuses such as UC Riverside and UC Santa Cruz were excluded through some threshold requirement of critical mass, UC Santa Barbara and SUNY–Stony Brook pose strong challenges for inclusion among the nation's top ten public research universities. And in a top-twenty rating, similar challenges arise both from the universities in multicampus systems (UC Irvine and SUNY-Albany) and the rising flagships (Colorado, Oregon, Mary-land–College Park, Massachusetts, Iowa, Virginia, Arizona, Utah, Kansas, New Mexico, Rutgers). In the private sector, however, the rising institutions offered a less formidable challenge to the established leaders.

Rising Research Universities in the Private Sector

To identify the rising private universities we combined the thirty-three institutions in the Research 1 and Research 2 private groups and ranked them according to their combined per capita scores on the top-science, top–social science, and arts-and-humanities indexes (table 7.14). The rising private universities are defined as institutions included among the top twenty-five in this study but not previously ranked in the three major comparative studies of 1960–82. This procedure identified eleven rising universities in the private sector, ranked as follows:

1. Brandeis
2. Rochester
3. Washington University
4. Carnegie Mellon
5. Vanderbilt
6. Notre Dame
7. Rice
8. Dartmouth
9. Emory
10. Tufts
11. Tulane

What are the chief attributes of this group? First, all but Brandeis, founded in 1948, are long-established institutions. With the exception of colonial Dartmouth (1769) and twentieth-century Rice (1912), all were founded in the nineteenth century. The rising private institutions are similar to the flagship institutions among the rising public universities. Both groups have gained research momentum since the 1960s and are contenders for national standing. But they lack the kind of accelerated development seen in new-model public institutions such as UC Santa Barbara and SUNY–Stony Brook. Instead, they demonstrate (Brandeis excepted) a traditional, incremental mode of steady improvement, one that earlier enabled the University of Washington (Seattle) and Purdue, in the public sector, and Brown and Duke, in the private sector, to break into the national rankings by the 1960s.[39]

By the end of the 1980s, the rising private institutions had not narrowed the lead enjoyed by the nationally ranked private universi-

TABLE 7.14

Nationally Ranked and Rising Private Research Universities, Ranked by Combined Index for Top-Science, Top–Social Science, and Arts-and-Humanities Indexes

Rank	Institution	Previous National Reputational Ranking*
1	Stanford	2
2	Princeton	6
3	Chicago	7
3	Harvard	3
3	Yale	3
6	Columbia	11
7	Duke	25
7	Pennsylvania	14
9	*Brandeis*	
9	Johns Hopkins	30
11	Northwestern	18
12	*Rochester*	
13	Caltech	15
14	Cornell	11
15	Brown	25
16	*Washington (St. Louis)*	
17	*Carnegie Mellon*	
18	MIT	5
19	*Vanderbilt*	
20	*Notre Dame*	
21	*Rice*	
21	*Dartmouth*	
23	New York University	21
24	*Emory*	
24	*Tufts*	
24	*Tulane*	

Italics denotes rising institution.

*Previous rankings by Webster, "America's Highest Ranked Graduate Schools, 1925–1982," 23, based on data from National Research Council, *Assessment of Research-Doctorate Programs in the United States*. See also Appendixes and Note on Method and Sources.

ties. As a group they performed at a middle level. Functionally they were similar to the rising flagships in the public sector, institutions such as Colorado, Oregon, and Maryland–College Park, competing in a zero-sum game to gain national ranking.

Though stronger than their public counterparts when judged according to the qualitative per capita scores in top-science, top–social science, and the arts and humanities, the rising private institutions have not been able to close the gap. Since the 1960s, the rising private universities have gained ground mostly in the arts and humanities. This feat was achieved in part because the top-ranked private universities were already so strong in the humanities that they could scarcely win a larger share of the expanding pool of fellowships and awards. Among the six rising universities listed among the top twenty private institutions (table 7.14), one, Washington University (St. Louis), had been nationally recognized in graduate education prior to World War II, and another, Rochester, had been ranked in a postwar reputational survey.[40] Three others converging on the threshold of national ranking represented three different institutional traditions: Carnegie Mellon, the institutional merger of philanthropic sponsorship in science and the humanities; Vanderbilt, northern industrial philanthropy in the defeated South; Notre Dame, Roman Catholic excellence in an American academic culture historically dominated by Protestant elites. Brandeis, ranked first in combined scores among the rising private institutions, remained sui generis. A postwar institution drawing on Jewish financial support and cultural traditions, Brandeis was competitive in research achievement soon after its founding.

In summary, the trends produced a trade-off. The success of the private sector, enjoying historic advantages of excellence as demonstrated throughout this study, also underscores the strong influence of the Matthew effect. Rising private universities, enjoying a widening lead in research performance over most other doctorate-granting institutions, nonetheless found it difficult to narrow the lead of the private elite institutions. By contrast, public sector institutions, disadvantaged by fragmentation in mission assignment and political jurisdiction but advantaged by enrollment and sectoral expansion, have nonetheless demonstrated a superior capacity for building internationally competitive new research universities.[41] The Matthew effect, reinforcing the proven capacities of the great state universities, has not prevented the emergence of successful new public challengers.

On the whole, this trade-off echoes themes of the American past. Its mixture of advantages and disadvantages appears to provide a kind of equilibrium mechanism, helping, in the absence of a centralized, national system of higher education, to balance the scales of competition between public and private institutions in an expanding market economy. Yet these traditions reach forward from World War II to encompass changes unprecedented in the history of American higher education.

■

Conclusion

The story of American research universities since World War II is a modern success story of knowledge-creation with an unlikely provenance. In the introduction and chapter 1 of this book we described and offered some explanations for the sudden leap to global leadership by American universities, which previously had found little respect in world opinion. In telling that story we claim little originality. It is a story of American exceptionalism, resting on evidence showing that the nation's distinctive history produced a unique combination of political beliefs, governing institutions, and social norms. Some practices or traits regarded as characteristically American produced rewards early in our history but later extracted high costs—for example, the aggressive exploitation of natural resources, the widespread arming of civilians, and the constitutional subordination of equality to property rights. The historic American preference for decentralized authority and weak governmental institutions has exacted a price—vigilante justice, chattel slavery, incompetent militias, debased currencies, fraudulent securities, medical quackery, and poisoned food and drugs. In higher education, however, the nation's historic proliferation of weak institutions in a decentralized environment paid surprising dividends in the modern era of market competition.

Ironically, this positive view of American institutional development, coinciding with the soaring prestige of American research universities since the 1950s, has found its mature scholarly expression in an era in which claims to American exceptionalism have otherwise been widely attacked.[1] During the past two decades students of higher education have used historical and cross-national comparisons to provide fresh evidence of the uniqueness of American institutions.

Joseph Ben-David, Burton Clark, Roger Geiger, Clark Kerr, Edward Shils, Martin Trow, and other scholars have described the emergence of a unique American "system" of higher education characterized by decentralization, market competition, and institutional pluralism. Yet despite the variety of institutional forms in American higher education, especially in the public sector, American university campuses developed a common structural model that differed significantly from Old World forms. The American university, governed by a lay board of trustees, was typically centered on a large college of arts or letters and science (or equivalent divisional schools) and its graduate school, surrounded by a ring of smaller professional schools and situated on a campus with dormitories full of undergraduate students who by European standards were weakly prepared. By comparison with the national university systems found in most countries, the American system of higher education was institutionally a nonsystem, a product largely of historical happenstance and constitutional federalism. For more than two centuries, higher education in America remained fragmented, financially undernourished, intellectually provincial, and culturally parochial.

Then came World War II, the Manhattan Project, the cold war, and the revolution in federal science policy. The wartime achievement of Vannevar Bush and his colleagues in the atomic bomb project was crucial in linking the capacities of research universities to national survival. But the secret of American success in producing new knowledge lay in government funding of the research at a variety of public and private universities. The effective American formula for building research universities thus contained four key ingredients: (1) a decentralized system of colleges and universities; (2) competition in a widening market for students, faculty, and financial resources; (3) institutional pluralism (a strong private sector competing with diverse state systems); and (4) federal funding characterized by multiple agency sponsorship and peer review competition.

Given the postwar fuel of federal research dollars and the mechanism of multiple-agency funding, many of the weaknesses of American higher education were transformed into strengths. In a decentralized and highly competitive market governed mainly by peer review, campus researchers defined their own projects and shopped for funding in a thickening maze of government agencies, private associations, commercial firms, and sponsoring foundations. In the competitive world of knowledge-creation, the key to success was found not in Bush's original model of an omnibus federal science agency but rather in the proliferation of federal funding agencies.

Federal science policy was symbolized not by the strategic planning of the NSF but by the market bazaar of the NIH. In the American political game of pluralistic bargaining, the prestigious leaders of academic science successfully played by two sets of rules. In the outside game, academic and scientific associations lobbied Congress and the agencies to create expanding and overlapping research programs, such as the proliferating institutes of the NIH, in the name of national defense, public health, scientific progress, and economic competitiveness. In the inside game, however, the prestigious leaders of academic science, determined to enforce merit standards and prevent corruption through political influence, established peer-review screening by nongovernment professionals. On the whole, this system, fueled by postwar economic expansion, worked remarkably well. In the half-century since the defeat of the Axis, the university-based research economy in the United States performed far more efficiently than did the centralized, government-directed systems in most other nations.

The postwar success of American research universities has inspired a large literature, not surprisingly, and we stand appreciatively on the shoulders of a great battalion of scholars whose studies dominate our footnotes. Our per capita method of comparing institutional development over time, however, is more novel. For all its daunting methodological challenges and imprecision, the method allows us to compare the research performance of more than two hundred institutions since the 1960s. As our narrative of postwar expansion developed, its contours were shaped with surprising force by three themes. The first of these is the persistence and strength of the public-private difference. Expressed less neutrally: the leading private universities have consistently outperformed the best public universities in per capita research productivity. The unique historical role of elite private institutions in American higher education has been a source of both pride and resentment. On the one hand, the well-endowed private elite institutions, by bidding up the stakes in ongoing market competition, have raised the level of academic support and performance in public universities. On the other hand, private universities, enjoying a large measure of freedom from the bureaucratic and regulatory constraints of the public sector, have nonetheless relied heavily on government tax and fiscal policies to fund research, build and equip the research infrastructure, and subsidize high tuitions.

The second theme is the power of the medical multiplier. It emphasizes both the unmatched growth of biomedical research in the postwar era, and the unprecedented expansion after the 1960s of income derived from clinical practice. This combination gave medical schools a unique, dual advantage. Having evolved as separate dukedoms on university campuses, medical schools and the academic health science centers that surrounded them were the chief beneficiaries of the extraordinary rise of the NIH as the nation's preeminent research sponsor. In 1963, the NIH provided 36.6 percent of all federal R&D funding to the campuses, while the Pentagon ranked second with 26.4 percent; by fiscal 1994, the NIH share had soared to 52 percent, and the NSF was second with 14 percent. When Medicare and Medicaid accelerated the growth of third-party reimbursements for medical and surgical practice, medical schools within a decade doubled the size of their research budgets and tripled the size of their clinical faculty.

The third theme involves the structure and governance of higher education. It centers on the emergence of new elite institutions, especially in the state systems, and on the role of institutional strategies and public policy in building them.[2] In an era of increasing concern for economic competitiveness within a global economy driven by technological advances, university development became too important for political and business leaders to leave to the academic administrators and their lay trustees. In the wake of the campus expansion of the 1960s, political and business leaders developed state-level versions of industrial policy for higher education, designed to implement both cost-cutting consolidations and strategic plans to involve universities in regional economic development. Studies of state-level efforts since the 1960s to coordinate and control higher education have compared the two main approaches—the use of consolidated governing boards (or "superboards," as adopted, for example, in Wisconsin and North Carolina) and the use of statewide coordinating boards—and found little correlation between models of governance and indicators of university performance or economic growth.[3] Between forms of governance and output indicators there are too many intervening variables—state population size, economic base, per capita wealth, distribution of income, racial and ethnic diversity, political culture, higher education traditions, and prestige. Because our evidence concentrates on measures of research performance, we do not address these complex questions directly in this study. But we were struck by three patterns of successful institution-building that occurred within multicampus state systems. Most impressive was the extraordinary research performance of the entire University of California system under the hierarchical, tripartite plan

202

adopted in 1960. Also effective was the consolidated approach followed in the SUNY system, in which four campuses were designated as research centers. Finally, the rapid development of Illinois-Chicago and Alabama-Birmingham, public campuses that made major leaps in research performance, demonstrates institution-building possibilities in major cities whose economies are little helped by flagships in other locations.

The Advantages of Private Elite Universities

We first encountered the magnitude of the private advantage when comparing institutional data from the 1960s. Faculty at universities in the Carnegie Research I category produced an average per capita R&D index roughly two and a half times as high as that of their public counterparts. The average publications index of the private Research I schools was twice as high. Even in the Doctoral II category the average publications index for private institutions, 20 percent higher than the public Doctoral II average, was still substantial. The Carnegie categories, however, because they included more public than private universities and because they changed institutional membership with each revision (1970, 1976, 1987, 1994), proved inadequate for comparing institutional changes over time. A more coherent profile of the changing private advantage among elite institutions is provided by a sample of ten universities, five public and five private, all including medical schools. The private institutions chosen for this purpose are Chicago, Columbia, Pennsylvania, Stanford, and Yale; the public institutions are UCLA, Michigan, Minnesota, Washington, and Wisconsin.[4]

Using this sample of universities and comparing post-1960 changes in the average index scores of the public and private elite campuses, we find that the margin of private advantage declined but nonetheless remained significant. By 1968 the average R&D index of the five public universities in the sample had increased from 54 percent to 60 percent of the private group's average. During the same period, the average publications index of the five public universities increased from 55 percent to 65 percent of the private group's average. With regard to the three qualitative indicators, the top-ranked public universities were less successful in gaining on the private schools. Between 1974 and 1988 the average top-science index of the public campuses increased only slightly, from 55 percent of the elite private group average to 57 percent. The public universities fared only marginally better on the top–social science index, increasing their average score from 60 percent to 62 percent of the private group average. The private advantage, as measured by per capita comparisons during the postwar years, has always been weakest in the social sciences and has remained strongest in the arts and humanities. During the decade 1965–74 the average A&H index of the five selected private universities was almost two times as high as the public group average. For the decade 1980–89 the private A&H margin, while reduced, remained a robust 150 percent. What can we conclude from these striking and persistent differences?

First, we cannot conclude too much. As we observed in chapter 3, part of the difference in per capita performance between private and public universities is an artifact of the method of institutional measurement itself. Controlling for institutional size by dividing scores by the number of full-time instructional faculty on each campus in effect penalizes state institutions for teaching large numbers of undergraduates and for undertaking certain public service obligations. These include the historic land-grant missions, such as agriculture, physical education, and home economics, and also the substantial investment of faculty resources in undergraduate instruction in preprofessional fields such as business, education, accounting, administration, management science, and social work, which are not heavily involved in sponsored research or journal publication. Nonetheless, the margins of private superiority in research achievement demonstrated among the nation's leading research universities remain too large to attribute entirely to structural differences or methodological artifacts. On a per capita basis the leading private universities even show a consistent margin of superiority at the departmental level, where structural artifacts are less significant.

Using counts of journal articles from the 1982 National Research Council assessment, we selected a sample of leading public and private universities and compared the number of journal articles published by individual researchers in selected major disciplines (table C.1). By comparing faculty performance only in major disciplines—fields that are represented in almost all universities, such as economics, chemistry, history, and physics—we screen out most of the structural distortions caused by institutional size and minimize the influence of structural variables such as schools of medicine or agriculture. We selected eight private and eight public universities from the twenty top-ranked institutions as aggregated by Webster from the NRC study of 1982.[5] The private universities chosen are Chicago, Columbia, Harvard, MIT, Pennsylvania, Princeton, Stanford, and Yale.

TABLE C.1

Per Capita Publications of Faculty at Sixteen Selected Public and Private Universities, by Discipline and Academic Area, 1978–1979

Academic Area	Discipline	Public Institutions	Private Institutions	Private as % of Public
Behavioral and social sciences	Economics	2.47	3.47	141
	History	1.90	2.32	122
	Political science	2.26	2.48	110
	Psychology	3.80	4.36	115
	Average	2.61	3.16	122
Biological sciences	Biochemistry	9.27	9.74	105
	Cell/molecular	9.61	15.42	161
	Microbiology	5.56	6.68	120
	Physiology	1.37	2.04	149
	Average	6.45	8.47	134
Mathematical and physical sciences	Chemistry	4.60	5.66	123
	Geoscience	6.00	5.13	86
	Mathematics	1.37	2.39	175
	Physics	4.46	7.83	176
	Average	4.11	5.25	140
Engineering	Electrical	1.23	1.34	109
	Chemical	.95	.67	71
	Civil	.54	.53	98
	Mechanical	.84	.75	89
	Average	.89	.82	92

Source: Data from National Research Council, *Assessment of Research-Doctorate Programs in the United States* (Washington, D.C.: National Academy Press, 1982), and David S. Webster, "America's Highest Ranked Graduate Schools 1925–1982," *Change* 15 (May–June 1983): 23. See also Appendixes and Note on Method and Sources.

Note: The public institutions were UC Berkeley, Illinois-Urbana, Michigan, Minnesota, Texas-Austin, UCLA, Washington, and Wisconsin-Madison; the private institutions were Chicago, Columbia, Harvard, MIT, Pennsylvania, Princeton, Stanford, and Yale.

The public institutions are Berkeley, Illinois, Michigan, Minnesota, Texas, UCLA, Washington, and Wisconsin.

Selecting four representative disciplines apiece from the social and behavioral sciences, from the biological sciences, from the physical and mathematical sciences, and from engineering, we divided the total number of published articles identified by the NRC study in each discipline by the total number of full-time instructional faculty in that discipline. This produced for the public and private groups an average number of published articles for each discipline and academic area.[6] The results are summarized in table C.1. In three of the four fields compared, the faculty in the private elite universities outperformed their public counterparts by a substantial margin. Only in engineering did the public institutions enjoy an edge. Moreover, the

205

comparison excludes the arts and humanities, areas of traditional strength in private universities.[7] Because these per capita comparisons are based on selected graduate programs rather than on entire institutions, the scores of public universities are not lowered by faculty who teach in areas that are not research-intensive.

In 1995 the NRC published *Research-Doctorate Programs in the United States,* a comparative study of more than 3,600 graduate programs in forty-one fields at 274 institutions.[8] The NRC's 1995 study, like its predecessors, relied primarily on reputational surveys to rank graduate programs. But like the 1982 NRC assessment, it included data showing the publication of journal articles by program faculty.[9] Table C.2 extends to the period 1988–92 the comparisons shown in table C.1 for 1978–79. They show the elite public universities reducing the lead of their private counterparts in physical and life science publications, and the private campuses overtaking their public counterparts in engineering publications. But overall the comparisons show a continued pattern of private research superiority as judged by faculty publication of scientific and scholarly articles.

Our research method and data demonstrate this important phenomenon of private advantage but do not explain it. A good part of the explanation for the advantages enjoyed by private elite American research universities is captured by the trilogy of attributes identified by sociologist Edward Shils—"sovereignty, affluence, and tradition."[10] For the great private universities, this translates into historic prestige, large endowments, and the freedom to shape their own academic and professional programs, largely unencumbered by political constraints.[11] To this we would add a fourth factor, one less lofty but equally compelling. This is the need of private universities to balance the budget. In the leading private institutions, many of which observe a fiscal regimen of "each tub on its own bottom," the buck stops on the desk of the academic dean, who must generate income to match expenditures. This burden of balancing the financial ledgers—the other side of the coin of private sovereignty—is carried by all private colleges and universities, the majority neither heavily endowed nor crowned with prestige. In private institutions, faculty hiring and especially tenure decisions carry long-term consequences that cannot be shifted to the shoulders of the state taxpayers. Our data shed no light on this question of management incentives. But it is plausible to surmise that in matters of faculty hiring and tenure, private university deans may have been more cost-conscious decision makers than their public counterparts. Given the smaller size of private faculties,

TABLE C.2

Per Capita Publications of Faculty at Sixteen Selected Public and Private Universities, by Discipline and Academic Area, 1988–1992

Academic Area	Discipline	Public Institutions	Private Institutions	Private as % of Public
Behavioral and social sciences	Economics	3.20	4.24	133
	History	.88	1.11	127
	Political science	1.66	2.13	128
	Psychology	5.76	6.67	116
	Average	2.87	3.54	123
Biological sciences	Biochemistry	12.5	15.7	125
	Physiology	10.1	12.5	124
	Average	11.3	14.1	125
Mathematical and physical sciences	Chemistry	15.2	20.6	136
	Geoscience	7.3	7.8	107
	Mathematics	4.3	4.4	102
	Physics	11.0	9.7	88
	Average	9.5	10.6	108
Engineering	Electrical	9.6	12.2	127
	Chemical	15.5	13.4	87
	Civil	4.6	5.4	117
	Mechanical	6.61	7.3	111
	Average	9.1	9.6	106

Source: Data from National Research Council, *An Assessment of Research-Doctorate Programs* (1995); Webster and Skinner, "The Newest Comprehensive Rating of Ph.D. Programs," *Change* (May–June 1996).

Note: The public institutions were UC Berkeley, UCLA, Illinois-Urbana, Michigan, Minnesota, Texas-Austin, Washington, and Wisconsin-Madison; the private institutions were Chicago, Columbia, Harvard, MIT, Pennsylvania, Princeton, Stanford, and Yale.

the burden of tenured mediocrity or incompetence weighs more heavily as a long-term cost.

There is an emperor-wears-no-clothes quality to the sensitive question of private superiority.[12] It is a topic not much discussed in public forums. Evidence documenting the greater research productivity (on average) of private faculty at universities belonging to the Association of American Universities, for example, has been readily at hand in the postwar era, yet it has been largely ignored. This omission contrasts with the intense scrutiny otherwise directed by academics at the periodic comparisons of graduate program quality, such as the NRC studies of 1982 and 1995. Most such studies, and the grand rankings compiled from their combination of objective and reputational data, have slightly favored the private universities. But overall the periodic grand rankings have maintained a prudent mix among public and private elites.[13]

This posture of avoiding invidious comparisons between public and private institutions has been maintained in the higher education community for several good reasons. Leaders of private universities have been politically circumspect, anxious to avoid class antagonisms and populist resentments. Leaders of public universities, sharing an interest with their private counterparts in research-mission solidarity, have concentrated on raising levels of support from all sources to help them meet the high standards set by the well-endowed private elites. The public and private research universities have thus danced a mutually rewarding *pas de deux.* Over the generations, the leading private universities have used their unique position to bid up the level of competition in the hiring of faculty. University administrators in Urbana, Austin, or Berkeley cannot recruit or retain top faculty if their offers fall too far shy of the marks set in Cambridge, Evanston, or Palo Alto. The appropriate French aphorism is thus not *C'est la même chose,* it is *Vive la différence.* Private leadership in research productivity, as an incentive for public standard-raising, provided one of the main incentives for competition in the rise of the American research university.

The Medical Multiplier

Whereas the elite private universities have been influencing public university standards since the nineteenth century, university-based medical schools have participated fully in this upward-bidding process only since World War II. Prior to the Flexner reforms of the Progressive era, medical schools on university campuses were often little more than diploma mills, and their students were often considerably weaker academically than the baccalaureate students. Before the Hill-Burton Act of 1946, which launched a multi-billion-dollar flow of federal grants for hospital and medical school construction, and before the meteoric rise shortly thereafter of the NIH, which invested more billions in biomedical research on the campuses, medical school faculties had consisted mostly of a small cadre of preclinical researchers and a larger complement of part-time faculty, clinical practitioners not involved in research. Most university medical schools prior to the 1950s even *looked* like the rest of the campus — gothic, or redbrick Victorian, stolid, ivied, and old.[14]

Medical schools, however, had never really been *of* the campus. Unlike the other professional schools in the university, whose faculty typically have not built bridges and airplanes, run corporations or law firms, or published newspapers, faculty in medical schools have treated patients in hospitals, earning most of their income from their professional practice. Unlike other graduate and professional school deans, deans of medicine increasingly have circumvented the normal chain of campus authority by reporting to the university president not through the provost or academic vice chancellor but through parallel medical channels that reflect the autonomy demanded by medicine's financial independence from the central university administration. The arms-length relationship between universities and their medical schools has long been mirrored in the scholarly literature on higher education, in which specialists in medical science and education, on the one hand, and students of arts-and-sciences universities, on the other, have addressed their work to separate audiences. This traditional dualism was reinforced by the postwar flood of federal funding, which further strengthened medical schools' ties to federal funding agencies and their own teaching hospitals, and further weakened the schools' already insubstantial financial ties to university administrations.

Between 1945 and 1965, the size of full-time faculties at university medical schools quadrupled. By 1968, at leading private universities the medical school faculty had typically grown to three-quarters the size of the arts-and-sciences faculty, and the NIH was providing almost two-thirds of the federal R&D funding for the entire campus. In 1973, when college and graduate school enrollments fell into a steady state and the oil embargo helped trigger a decade of national (and academic) recession, medical schools were beginning a second great surge of growth. The first wave of growth, extending from 1945 to 1965, had been fueled by the Hill-Burton program, by NIH funding, and by the nationwide expansion of M.D. training. After 1970, Hill-Burton funding for construction tailed off and the number of students receiving M.D. training contracted. NIH funding, however, continued to expand. Most important, third-party reimbursements to teaching hospitals through Medicare and Medicaid and other programs of medical insurance provided a vast new pool of funding for academic medical centers. The spectacular growth of American academic medicine since 1960 is shown in table C.3.

The resultant program expansion included a sustained boom in clinical research, pursued by thousands of new professors of clinical medicine whose positions were funded largely through professional practice plans. Between 1968 and 1988, the size of the full-time faculty at leading university medical schools, having doubled since 1945, doubled once again. By 1990, the research funding provided

TABLE C.3
The Growth of Academic Medicine

Measure of Growth	1960	1970	1980	1992
Support from NIH (millions)	$1,320	$3,028	$5,419	$8,407
Average medical school budget (millions)	$24.1	$64.6	$91.9	$200.4
No. of full-time medical school faculty				
Basic science	4,023	8,283	12,816	15,579
Clinical	7,201	19,256	37,716	65,913
Average base compensation (thousands)				
Basic-science faculty	NA	$81.8*	$75.4	$86.4
Clinical faculty	NA	$140.2†	$132.6	$177.0
Revenues from faculty-practice plans (millions)	$61.0	$398.9	$1,704.7	$8,291.0
No. of matriculated medical students	30,288	40,487	65,189	66,142
No. of house staff	37,562	51,015	61,819	88,602

Source: Adapted from John K. Iglehart, "Rapid Changes for Academic Medical Centers," *New England Journal of Medicine* 331 (17 Nov. 1994): 1394.
    Note: Financial data are in 1992 dollars. NIH denotes National Institutes of Health, and NA denotes not available. Data are from the American Association of Medical Colleges.
    *Average compensation, in 1993 dollars, for a professor.
    †Data are for 1978.

by the NIH to medical schools typically comprised 40 percent of all federal R&D support at major public sector medical universities such as UC San Diego, Michigan, and Washington. At major private sector medical universities, such as Duke, Yale, and Washington (St. Louis), the NIH share of campus R&D funding typically exceeded two-thirds of federal R&D support.

    Clearly, the presence of a research-intensive medical school has been a great asset to universities in the campus enterprise of creating knowledge. Medical schools, jealous of their fiscal and administrative autonomy, have not been convenient cash cows for their parent universities, but they have been effective campus rainmakers. Their powerful magnet of funding for research, education, training, construction, and medical practice has pumped lifeblood into universities and their communities, which otherwise have been hard hit by rising costs and falling revenues. Moreover, it is not clear that the unusual independence of medical schools or academic health centers from central university control has been harmful to the parent universities. University presidents since the 1960s have routinely called for greater academic and intellectual integration between their health science divisions and the rest of the university.[15] Other than occasional program links in bioethics or medical jurisprudence, however, there appears to have been little reduction in the traditional distance between the university's medical center and the rest of the campus.

Despite this persistent dualism, the presence of a medical school has been a crucial element in the successful emergence since 1945 of a brace of strong new research universities, especially in the public sector. The prototype for the new public elite institutions, UCLA, made its major surge upward beginning in the late 1940s and used its medical school advantage, together with strong engineering programs serving the growing aerospace and electronics industry in the Los Angeles basin, to surpass UC Berkeley in federal R&D funding by the 1960s. Other breakthrough campuses, especially in the public sector, also relied heavily on the research muscle of medical schools. Examples include three other UC campuses (Davis, Irvine, and San Diego), SUNY-Buffalo and SUNY–Stony Brook, the merged Illinois-Chicago, and Alabama-Birmingham. However, several strong challengers with impressive research credentials emerged without the benefit of a medical school—for example, the UC campuses at Santa Barbara, Riverside, and Santa Cruz, and the SUNY campus at Albany. For many emerging research universities, medical schools were clearly a powerful asset. But they were neither a necessary nor a sufficient condition for breaking away from the pack in research achievement. The patterns of research growth seen in our evidence suggest that, in the public sector, breakthrough institutions were accelerated by state policies that designated specific institutions as research campuses and protected their mission. Competition between public and private institutions and across state lines invigorated the research enterprise. But competition within state systems, especially in large urban states, worked best when confined to two to four campuses—the giant California system, with its nine UC campuses, was the exception that proved the rule.

Models of Excellence in the Public Sector

In the era preceding *Sputnik,* since the 1934 ACE-sponsored Raymond Hughes study that ranked among its top dozen institutions UC Berkeley, Wisconsin, Michigan, Minnesota, and Illinois (in that order), reputational leadership among public universities was the exclusive reserve of the great flagships.[16] In 1959, UCLA broke into the national rankings when the Keniston study of graduate programs ranked it fourteenth among the nation's leading universities. After 1960, as UCLA's reputation continued to improve, two strong land-grant universities, Purdue (ranked twenty-fourth according to the Cartter ratings of 1966) and Michigan State (ranked twenty-fourth according to the Roose-Andersen ratings of 1970), broke into the national rankings. In 1982, UC San Diego was ranked twenty-first according to the NRC study. Nonetheless, among public universities the flagships continued to dominate the traditional ratings game. Although the per capita comparisons used in this study sharply challenge the accepted status of some of the nation's universities, our evidence shows also that the majority of America's most prestigious universities, those commonly reappearing in the periodic top-twenty rankings, deserve their elite reputations.

In the public sector, five of the traditional leaders are included among the top seven in our combined rankings. UC Berkeley is ranked first, and UCLA, Michigan, Wisconsin, Illinois, and Indiana are ranked fourth through eighth (table 6.7). Among private universities, the top five institutions listed in our combined ranking in chapter 7—Stanford, Princeton, Chicago and Harvard (tied for third), and Yale—bring no surprises, other than perhaps in the order of their ranking (table 7.9). The South, long relegated to the margins in reputational surveys, showed an upward surge in our combined rankings for public institutions, with UNC–Chapel Hill tied for eleventh, and Texas-Austin ranked thirteenth. Similar strength was shown by three western flagships not customarily found in the top-twenty-five rankings—Colorado (tenth), Oregon (tied for fifteenth), and Arizona (twenty-fourth). The flagship formula, building on established institutional strength, is a time-tested strategy. Although our findings challenge the perceived standing of many public universities, for most American states the flagship model has historically been effective in concentrating scarce resources to build high-quality programs.[17]

The unmatched success of California's tripartite system, however, posed its own challenge to the traditional state posture of flagship protection and aggrandizement. In our combined ranking of the public Research 1 and 2 universities (table 7.13), UC campuses occupied three of the first four positions among public universities, and six of the top fifteen. UC Santa Barbara was in second place and San Diego was ninth, followed by Riverside (tied for eleventh), Santa Cruz (tied for fifteenth), and Irvine (seventeenth). This is a stunning tribute to the effectiveness of California's tripartite system in raising all boats within the system, like a rising tide. UC Berkeley, the greatest of the western flagships, continued under the tripartite system to confirm the Matthew effect—as did UCLA, itself an established elite campus by 1960.[18] At the same time, the system brought to rapid maturity UC campuses as different as San Diego and Santa Cruz. Berkeley remains the state's glittering crown jewel. UCLA towers as the pioneer of second-flagship-building that strengthened the original flagship through competition and growth rather than diminished it in a zero-sum game. UC San Diego has become, arguably, the national exemplar of accelerated hothouse incubation.[19]

By the 1980s all three of these powerful UC campuses—Berkeley, UCLA, and San Diego—enjoyed AAU membership, national rankings, and world acclaim. The real test for the UC *system* was the progress of the smaller and less visible campuses. Perhaps the system's unprecedented achievements in building research universities are best symbolized by Santa Barbara. Born of humble, normal-school origins, lacking schools of medicine, business, and law, Santa Barbara surged from state-college obscurity in the 1950s to approach, but not quite enter, the spotlight of national prominence in the 1980s, and AAU membership in the 1990s. Santa Barbara thus represents the hidden success stories of postwar American higher education, screened by larger and older institutions whose greater name recognition is a proxy for higher status. But these hidden stories may tell us much about the postwar development of research universities, more than we are likely to learn from merely observing the continuing achievement of the nation's elite institutions.

Judged by the comparative results, California designed the nation's most effective state system for building research universities. The UC system evolved by fits and starts, winning constitutional autonomy for the campus at Berkeley in an eleventh-hour reprieve in 1879, periodically whiplashed by soaring enrollment pressures accompanied by collapsing revenues, and alternating between strategies of opposing the regional colleges and attempting to absorb them. California's tripartite system, institutionally a legacy of the Progressive era, was codified in the Master Plan of 1960. It sheltered the UC campuses, differentiating their roles by geography and function but encouraging competition between them. By excluding the California State University and College (CSUC) campuses (twenty of them by 1990, many with enrollments exceeding twenty-five thousand) from the doctoral-research mission, the Master Plan guaranteed periodic attacks from the large CSUC constituency to remove the research barrier. The prestige of the University of California was so great, however, that the UC constituency was able to defeat all attempts to dismantle the tripartite system.[20]

213

In New York, where many of the prestigious institutions were private, the land-grant university was Cornell, and the state lacked a flagship tradition, a different strategy was followed. The SUNY system, created in 1948, included community colleges and four-year colleges of arts and sciences but designated the campuses at Albany, Binghamton, Buffalo, and Stony Brook as university centers. This arrangement meant that political conflict over institutional status and resources was intramural rather than occurring on an intersystem level, as was the case in tripartite systems and in states with separate land-grant and flagship systems (for example, Texas and Texas A&M).[21] According to the data compared in this study, the SUNY system, though lacking many of the geographic and economic advantages enjoyed by the UC system, can claim significant successes, particularly since in New York private elite institutions historically have been privileged. Most striking is the rapid ascent of SUNY–Stony Brook, which is ranked third behind UC Santa Barbara in our combined ranking of Research 1 and 2 public universities. The SUNY-Albany campus was tied for twentieth nationally. Neither Stony Brook nor Albany was a member of the AAU, although SUNY-Buffalo, ranked thirty-first in our comparison, was admitted to AAU membership in 1989.

Corrosive Forces at the Turn of the Twenty-first Century

The year 1995 marked the fiftieth anniversary of the publication of *Science—The Endless Frontier,* Vannevar Bush's ambitious proposal to President Truman for a federally funded program of university-based research. Yet Americans in the 1990s remained ambivalent about their universities. The growing world acclaim for the research prowess of American universities has been accompanied by increasing attacks by social and academic critics. The sins of which the universities have been accused include frivolous courses and research, grade inflation, student cheating, faculty sinecures, corruption in intercollegiate athletics, fraternity hazing, animal abuse in research, student abuse of alcohol and drugs, scientific fraud, and bloated administrations. Of more recent vintage are complaints against padded research accounts that milked taxpayers by inflating contract and grant overhead; soaring default rates in student loans; faculty conflict of interest in commercial ventures; and campus "political correctness" that approached self-parody. The latter featured news reports on campus speech restrictions, codified rules of sexual conduct, and curricular attacks on Western Civilization; the proliferation — often surrounded by conflict and litigation — of interdisciplinary programs and tenure-granting departments to study African Americans, women, Chicanos, Native Americans, gays and lesbians; and an expanding list of proscribed "isms" in thought and utterance (e.g., racism, sexism, ageism, looksism, and able-ism).[22]

Few of these negative issues, however, were novel to the 1980s or 1990s. More complaints involved the university's teaching role and the quality of student life in the campus environment than the university's research mission. American colleges and universities had grappled with these types of controversies for generations. Given the rising demand for college credentials since the 1960s, backed by rising estimates of the income return from investment in college degrees, the attacks seemed serious but not alarming. Despite sharp post–cold war reductions in defense expenditures by the federal government during the early 1990s, cuts severe enough to batter the economy even of previously prosperous California, Congress did not require commensurate reductions in defense research on the campuses.[23] The shift in federal science policy away from the "big science" model associated with expensive particle accelerators, a change punctuated by congressional cancellation of the Superconducting Supercollider in 1993, was a gradual process, reaching back at least to 1980 (and in some ways to the Vietnam War).[24] This provided time for adjustments in the academic research economy, which in any event was fueled primarily by sponsored research in the health sciences, not in defense technology.[25] Forces of "research drift" and "teaching drift," in Burton Clark's analysis, had been fragmenting the "research-teaching-study nexus" in modern universities throughout the globe since World War II.[26] These divisive trends, corroding the bonds of the nineteenth-century "Humboldtian ideal" that tied research to advanced education, had been a staple of academic criticism since at least the 1960s.

However, universities during the 1990s faced several trends of more recent origin that drew less attention in the media but that posed perhaps greater long-range threats to the academic research economy. Most of these worrisome trends reflected new developments in federal policy. One such trend, for example, involved national health policy. The election of Bill Clinton to the presidency in 1992 brought increased attention to fundamental changes in the nation's health care economy, in which market changes were driven by a need to control soaring costs. This process, with its emphasis on preventive medicine and health maintenance organizations, primary and outpatient care, and the use of salaried staff physicians in capitation systems rather than fee-for-service providers in referral systems, threatened to erode the highly favorable terms of third-party reimbursement enjoyed by academic health centers and their teaching hospitals.[27]

How could the teaching hospitals of university medical schools, with their expensive specialized equipment and their highly paid clinical faculty, compete with cost-cutting competitors in a future health care environment characterized not by traditional deference to prevailing fees but rather by cost-consciousness on the part of insurance officials and government regulators? What would happen to the scientifically advanced but also elaborate and costly infrastructure of research at academic medical centers if the clinical practice plans, which had fueled the extraordinary expansion of clinical faculty since 1970, were dried up at their source?[28] By the 1990s, rapid changes in the health care market favored large for-profit providers at the expense of high-cost teaching hospitals.[29] University medical centers, squeezed by the lower costs of managed care providers and by cuts in Medicare and Medicaid that bled the teaching hospitals, scrambled to arrange mergers with more affluent community hospitals. Medical school deans faced a decline of subsidies to medical education and research, subsidies traditionally provided by teaching hospitals through third-party reimbursements set at high fee-for-service levels and by government grants for education and training.

A second example of threatening trends since the 1980s is the prospect of a prolonged downward spiral in federal R&D funding and other research support as expenditures on entitlement programs, debt service, and deficit reduction squeeze out discretionary spending by the mission agencies. By the mid-1990s Republican control of Congress threatened not only generally to speed federal budget reduction but specifically to eliminate NSF support for the social sciences and to slash drastically or eliminate entirely the National Endowment for the Arts and the National Endowment for the Humanities.[30]

In addition to a historic reversal of the federal government's crucial support role in the academic research economy, there were other threatening trends in federal science policy. Government funding of "overhead," or the indirect costs that universities incurred by supporting sponsored research (e.g., the cost of laboratory space, utilities, and accounting), had remained a contentious issue throughout the postwar era. Nonetheless the universities and federal funding agencies over the years had negotiated institutional rates that by

1991 averaged 60 percent at private universities (the funding agency paid the university an additional sixty cents for every dollar awarded for direct costs such as salaries, equipment, and supplies) and 47 percent at public universities.[31] Although deans of graduate studies and research routinely deplored the inadequacy of their institutional overhead rate, university administrators cherished the abundance, predictability, and fungibility of overhead dollars. When federal aid for the construction and renovation of research facilities withered after the 1960s, many universities replaced their deteriorating or obsolescent physical plant by in effect mortgaging construction bond issues against anticipated future overhead dollars. By the early 1990s, however, news reports of overhead abuse by prestigious institutions, symbolized by overhead charges that included a yacht at Stanford, led to a congressional crackdown.[32] Universities accustomed to tens of millions in federal R&D funding faced the prospect of a prolonged bleeding process as government leaders, hounded by intractable deficits, hunted for budget savings. The prospect of a long decline in overhead rates as well as in the (direct cost) research grants and contracts themselves threatened to undermine the fiscal stability of the major research campuses.

Yet another threatening trend in relations between the federal government and universities was a congressional practice called "academic earmarking." The term refers to congressional appropriations bills that direct federal agencies to pay for specified projects, typically construction and programs that benefited institutions in districts represented by senior members of Congress, especially those on appropriations committees. The earmarking of funds in appropriations bills, long practiced in federal assistance to agriculture, found its way to the campuses in the late 1970s, when enterprising institutions in the Boston area (Tufts, Boston University, Boston College, and Northeastern), often assisted by Washington lobbyists specializing in what journalists began to call "academic pork," won earmarking favors from powerful Massachusetts members of Congress (House speaker Thomas P. O'Neill, House Rules Committee chairman Joseph Moakley, and Senator Edward Kennedy).[33] Academic earmarks rose from $10.7 million for 7 projects in fiscal 1980 to $708 million for 499 projects in 1992, when 209 campuses were specified in 13 appropriations bills.

Because earmarking threatened the heart of the peer-review process, in which jury panels of scientists rated proposals in merit-based competition for agency funding, it was attacked by the major organizations representing academic science, led by the AAU. In

217

1993, AAU president Joe B. Wyatt, chancellor of Vanderbilt, pointed out in testimony before the House Committee on Science, Space, and Technology that no federal agencies had asked to support the earmarked projects, no peer review panels had recommended them, and no congressional authorizing committees had held hearings on them or debated their merits; and that because of earmarking, hundreds of campus research proposals that had won support recommendations in stiff competition would not be funded.[34] The counterattack against academic "pork," led in Congress by California Democrat George E. Brown Jr., chairman of the House Science Committee, slowed the growth of earmarked funding in the mid-1990s, when the practice accounted for almost 10 percent of the $10-billion federal budget for academic R&D support. Although institutions benefiting from earmarking defended it as a way to aid have-not campuses in a peer-review environment unfairly dominated by elite universities, the practice nonetheless directed millions of federal dollars to several AAU universities (UC San Diego, Columbia, Michigan State, Pittsburgh, and Washington University) with well-placed sponsors in Congress.[35] As a large-scale funding mechanism, academic earmarking is too recent a phenomenon to have affected significantly the performance rankings in this study.

A more generalized threatening trend is the continuing and expanding reach of government regulators into the internal affairs of universities. Since the 1960s, institutions of higher education have adjusted incrementally to new forms of social regulation by government — in policies regarding admissions and employment, hazardous chemicals, human and animal research subjects, access for the handicapped, and workplace safety. By the 1990s, regulatory intrusions by agencies and courts had reached into new areas of dispute, including charges of "reverse" discrimination against whites and Asians by public universities and historically black colleges, accusations of religious discrimination against church-affiliated institutions, claims of sexual harassment, and accusations of racism in research projects supported by federal funds. A case illustrating the volatility of racial issues involved cancellation of NIH funding in the early 1990s for a University of Maryland–College Park conference on "Genetic Factors in Crime" in response to complaints from African Americans that the conference would promote racism.[36] As government regulation increased, campuses increasingly were caught between conflicting pressures. In New York, for example, the sixty-four campuses of the SUNY system, required by state antidiscrimination law to ban military recruiters because the armed forces discriminat-

218

ed against homosexuals, faced a new congressional requirement (in the 1995 defense authorization) that institutions banning military recruiters would lose their eligibility for Pentagon research grants.[37] As the "rights revolution" brought more groups and categories of behavior under statutory and constitutional protection, and the growth of public law litigation brought increasing numbers of lawsuits against educational institutions, universities faced deepening involvement in regulatory disputes and court challenges.

In the 1990s, especially problematic in this regard was the still-unresolved question of desegregation, or more generally, of college obligations in equal protection law. Federal court rulings involving college desegregation in Mississippi, Louisiana, and Alabama, responding to suits filed by African American plaintiffs, raised the prospect that desegregation requirements might further fragment the state systems of higher education in the South.[38] In such states a redistribution of graduate and professional degree programs, faculty teaching loads and salary scales, and state budgets for research support and physical plant among the formerly white and black campuses might shift research and degree programs from historically white to black institutions, and in the process weaken the strongest research campuses. The prospect of continued racial conflict over the fate of campuses and programs added uncertainty to the efforts of research universities that in many southern rural states were in any event relatively weak by national standards. In Texas, similar lawsuits charged in state courts that areas with large Mexican American populations were underserved by prestigious research campuses and by graduate and professional programs.[39] In New York, students and professors sued the state for spending more per student on SUNY campuses, where most students were white, than on CUNY campuses, where two-thirds of the students came from minority groups.[40] In California, the UC system was thrown into turmoil when the Regents in 1995 voted to terminate affirmative action preferences for minorities in admissions, employment, and contracts.[41] In 1996, the U.S. Court of Appeals for the Fifth Circuit rejected the use of race or ethnicity as admissions criteria in a case involving the University of Texas law school.[42] By the mid-1990s, few of these challenges had produced a clear result. But they underscored the fragility of universities — especially but not exclusively the public institutions — when divisive issues of cultural conflict were injected by lawsuits and regulatory decrees into their decision-making processes.

Finally, although the above list of selected problematic topics concentrates, as does this book, on the research role of American universities, we acknowledge the relevance and seriousness of growing public complaints that the nation's universities, especially but not exclusively the large public institutions, have sacrificed their students on the altar of research prestige. Such complaints were featured in the student protest movement at Berkeley and other leading campuses in the 1960s. Yet students have continued to fight for admission to the great state flagships. More difficult to assess is the charge, plausible on its face and prominently featured in the Carnegie-sponsored policy studies of the 1970s, that too many American universities cheated their students by adopting a research model although they lacked the capacity—in faculty quality, financial resources, or institutional mission—to create significant new knowledge. Most observers of higher education can name several universities whose claims to research prowess are questionable, and others whose claims are not credible. Opinions differ sharply in the higher education community over whether and in what ways the learning environment and the liberal arts culture have been damaged since the 1960s by the dominance of the research model among American universities. This debate has produced a robust literature since Christopher Jencks and David Riesman published *The Academic Revolution* in 1968, although emphasis in the 1990s has shifted toward "culture war" themes.[43] Few, if any, empirical studies measure the effects of research activity on teaching effectiveness and compare the results across institutions. Our own data, although perhaps useful for selecting candidates for such inquiries, throw no light on the institutional relationship between research commitment and teaching effectiveness.

The Resilience of American Higher Education

Since 1945, American higher education has adapted to a series of unprecedented changes. The late 1940s brought the GI Bill veterans to campus; the 1950s brought a revolution in federal science policy driven by the cold war. The "golden age" of the 1960s was Janus-faced—buoyed on the one hand by the baby boom, massive expansion, and a cornucopia of federal assistance, but later in the decade torn by campus turmoil over civil rights, student power, and the Vietnam War. The 1970s, negatively associated with enrollment declines, faculty overproduction, and economic stagflation, also brought federal tuition aid, an end to the draft, and a continuing flood of funding to the academic health centers. In the 1980s, stiffening economic competi-

220

tion in a global market brought new efforts to coordinate the sprawl of higher education, including state-level consolidations and attempts to replicate the research parks associated with Stanford, the Harvard-MIT axis, and the North Carolina Research Triangle. These changes confronted a higher education community that at the same time was struggling to adjust to long-term changes that were less visible but in many ways more profound. These included the expansion, specialization, and fragmentation of knowledge; the extension of "postsecondary" education to engage a majority of the citizenry; the increasing intrusion of government regulation; the large increase in enrollment of women, minorities, and older students; and the inflow of foreign-born students and academic professionals.

Yet in the face of such vast and often contradictory changes, American research universities have generally prospered, and at the century's end they continue to hold a strong hand. In the knowledge-based economy of the future, the universities are proven engines for knowledge-creation. Partly for this reason, and partly for less lofty, credentialist reasons, in terms of lifetime income American universities and colleges offer students a growing return on investment.[44] The leading American universities are an international magnet, far outpacing competitors in attracting top students, professional staff, and academic faculty. Moreover, because the language of intellectual and creative discourse in these institutions is English, which is now the lingua franca of science and technology and the global language of international publishing, American universities enjoy an enormous advantage in the size of their recruiting pool.[45] For all these reasons, American research universities seem well positioned to face a future that assuredly will bring further waves of unanticipated change.

This study has emphasized the competitive advantages provided by the decentralized and pluralistic system of higher education in the United States, but few students of higher education will miss the irony implicit in the market analogy. The American university, pictured as an agile knowledge-merchant in an expanding bazaar, seems in many ways the opposite of the modern competitive firm. Unlike commercial enterprises, with their unambiguous profit motives and their steep hierarchies of control for production and marketing, colleges and universities are, in the language of organizational analysis, loosely coupled systems.[46] They are characterized by ambiguous goals, multiple constituencies and functions, and horizontal and collegial structures. Despite the organizational complexity and technical precocity of the modern American university, in many ways it remains a remarkably traditional collection of sheltered students, tenured pro-

221

fessors, departmental baronies, isolated centers and institutes, and disconnected support staff, an institution in which the expository lecture and the printed page still dominate the learning process, much as they did in centuries past. That such an organism should remain nimble enough to survive and even prosper in the volatile postwar environment in higher education testifies to the nation's inadvertent good fortune in inheriting, by the close of World War II, a decentralized and pluralistic system that then was held in rather low esteem in Europe.[47]

Despite the successful adjustment of American universities to the Darwinian pressures of the postwar era, however, there are no guarantees for the future. A fundamental tension abides between universities, which are rooted in tradition, and market forces, which are potentially radical. Academic medical centers, the resplendent beneficiaries of the golden years between 1950 and 1990, have since been battered by a cyclone of market forces. Rapid changes in communications technology, by threatening the need for traditional classroom instruction or for campus faculty organized in academic departments, may put universities and market forces on a collision course. Indeed, the radical impact of digital technology and Internet expansion in the 1990s is challenging many of the assumptions underpinning the traditional apparatus for judging the quality of academic science and scholarship—peer-reviewed journals, citation indexes, conventions governing copyright and plagiarism, and the concept of "publication" itself.[48]

However uncertain the future, during the half-century following World War II the competitive system of American research universities and the pull of market forces maintained a balance that led the nation's leading institutions to a position of world leadership. Moreover, during the three decades following *Sputnik* the defeatist corollary of the Matthew effect—that unto those who already have shall be given—was disproved by the emergence of new institutions among the ranks of the nation's leading research universities. The thirty-two rising universities (twenty-one public and eleven private) identified in chapter 7 testify to the effectiveness of the pluralistic, decentralized, and competitive American system during the second half of the twentieth century. How well that system accommodates the changes accompanying the nation into the twenty-first century, only time will tell.

Appendix A

Institutional Data for 203 Research Universities

■

Table Appendix.1

Institutional Data for Research 1 Public Institutions, 1980–1990

Institution (N=32)	No. of Full-time Faculty	Federal R&D Funding (thousands)	Total Publications	Publications in Top-Science Journals	Publications in Top–Social Science Journals	A&H Awards
Alabama-Birmingham*	921	$64,868	2,857	153	13	9.0
Arizona*	1,503	76,103	4,089	550	81	46.5
UC Berkeley	1,477	118,452	7,049	1,365	190	130.0
UC Davis*	1,095	58,595	4,054	337	59	30.0
UC Irvine*	587	46,336	2,397	330	37	22.5
UC Los Angeles*	1,778	167,374	8,741	897	192	112.0
UC Riverside	351	11,774	2,174	60	51	22.0
UC San Diego*	692	156,451	4,101	739	59	34.5
UC Santa Barbara	729	36,034	1,761	385	100	48.0
UC Santa Cruz	383	12,723	1,158	48	72	23.0
Colorado	864	74,834	2,552	475	81	36.0
Illinois-Chicago*	1,433	41,781	3,312	193	124	57.0
Illinois-Urbana	1,977	93,950	5,434	892	220	99.5
Indiana	1,256	37,036	3,421	305	205	78.0
Iowa*	1,125	75,043	4,214	279	85	53.5
Maryland–College Park	1,308	56,516	3,416	432	110	40.5
Michigan*	1,886	164,310	7,069	600	309	109.5
Minnesota	1,725	124,517	5,889	499	155	42.5
North Carolina State	1,164	33,554	3,768	204	32	28.5
UNC–Chapel Hill*	1,368	92,898	4,679	352	154	59.0
Ohio State*	2,083	67,148	5,004	407	140	27.0
Pennsylvania State	1,578	64,048	3,613	325	129	22.0
Pittsburgh*	1,426	87,382	4,788	282	158	37.0
Purdue	1,446	53,170	3,293	503	85	16.0
SUNY-Albany	641	18,539	2,393	138	73	24.0
SUNY-Buffalo*	962	33,370	2,631	227	57	23.5
SUNY–Stony Brook*	740	42,966	2,913	397	133	41.5
Texas-Austin	1,894	68,173	4,384	589	171	78.5
Utah*	941	61,099	2,749	325	61	18.0
Virginia*	1,153	52,334	3,353	334	74	52.0
Washington*	1,999	200,242	6,599	741	208	56.0
Wisconsin-Madison*	1,561	141,406	6,729	658	249	75.0
Mean	1,251	76,032	4,081	438	121	48.5
Median	1,282	64,458	3,691	369	105	41.0

*Campus includes medical school.

TABLE APPENDIX.2
Institutional Data for Research 1 Private Institutions, 1980–1990

Institution (N=23)	No. of Full-time Faculty	Federal R&D Funding (thousands)	Total Publications	Publications in Top-Science Journals	Publications in Top–Social Science Journals	A&H Awards
Brown*	539	$32,570	2,072	86	62	58.5
Caltech	245	68,182	3,783	823	25	8.0
Carnegie Mellon	495	53,196	1,589	187	77	20.0
Case Western*	734	67,947	2,442	264	65	8.5
Chicago*	940	93,118	5,730	512	264	102.5
Columbia*	1,197	146,464	6,093	588	189	127.5
Cornell (Ithaca)	1,469	97,019	5,814	885	130	85.0
Duke*	823	99,396	4,291	381	159	59.5
Emory*	647	48,770	2,174	152	56	30.5
Harvard*	1,485	137,002	11,074	1,374	269	159.5
Johns Hopkins*	814	214,976	4,922	613	105	56.0
MIT	1,041	201,715	4,110	1,209	79	30.0
Northwestern*	958	57,233	3,828	398	180	55.5
Pennsylvania*	1,155	131,781	6,743	544	189	105.5
Princeton	659	47,625	3,043	549	111	121.5
Rochester*	743	97,209	2,917	341	95	57.5
Southern California*	1,318	108,750	4,153	358	97	50.5
Stanford*	921	230,767	6,202	1,116	217	94.5
Tufts*	585	37,683	1,799	159	34	33.0
Vanderbilt*	768	64,317	2,755	209	88	38.5
Washington (St. Louis)*	904	105,416	5,108	494	131	24.0
Yale*	903	141,383	5,936	586	153	141.5
Yeshiva*	389	67,478	1,398	167	20	2.5
Mean	858	102,174	4,260	522	122	63.9
Median	823	97,019	4,110	494	105	56.0

*Campus includes medical school.

TABLE APPENDIX.3

Institutional Data for Research 2 Public Institutions, 1980–1990

Institution (N=26)	No. of Full-time Faculty	Federal R&D Funding (thousands)	Total Publications	Publications in Top-Science Journals	Publications in Top–Social Science Journals	A&H Awards
Cincinnati*	1,218	$39,023	2,346	166	26	11.0
Colorado State	919	34,116	1,462	178	13	4.5
Delaware	900	14,902	1,487	202	46	19.5
Florida State	982	26,799	1,528	126	45	7.5
Florida*	2,320	53,897	4,375	321	71	26.5
Georgia	1,679	36,879	2,783	154	77	26.0
Georgia Tech	545	25,532	877	125	14	4.0
Hawaii-Manoa*	1,081	35,501	1,724	189	39	24.5
Houston	853	14,206	1,460	127	39	34.5
Iowa State	1,303	18,951	1,982	303	28	17.5
Kansas	929	16,329	1,701	102	104	36.0
Kentucky*	1,315	22,893	2,432	111	62	26.0
Louisiana State	1,452	24,042	3,399	191	53	24.5
Massachusetts-Amherst	1,303	41,000	2,426	294	107	58.5
Michigan State*	2,079	49,776	3,358	295	98	34.0
Mississippi	407	6,703	702	25	27	7.5
Missouri-Columbia*	989	19,276	2,147	101	58	28.5
New Mexico*	888	21,498	1,429	142	64	36.0
Oregon	684	16,276	1,387	138	60	41.0
Oregon State	665	40,339	1,287	192	21	11.5
Rutgers–New Brunswick	1,350	30,324	2,862	102	110	72.5
Texas A&M*	1,563	39,822	3,183	312	79	14.0
Virginia Commonwealth	1,027	38,643	1,643	97	24	14.5
Virginia Tech	1,507	29,565	2,265	124	52	31.5
Washington State	737	16,364	1,438	114	24	17.5
Wayne State*	978	26,438	1,998	140	38	20.0
Mean	1,141	28,427	2,065	168	53	25.0
Median	1,008	26,619	1,853	141	49	24.5

*Campus includes medical school.

TABLE APPENDIX.4

Institutional Data for Research 2 Private Institutions, 1980–1990

Institution (N=10)	No. of Full-time Faculty	Federal R&D Funding (thousands)	Total Publications	Publications in Top-Science Journals	Publications in Top–Social Science Journals	A&H Awards
Boston University*	1,028	$54,210	3,132	235	69	47.5
Brandeis	320	16,630	800	154	31	44.0
Dartmouth*	440	26,523	1,178	108	30	38.0
George Washington*	634	26,516	1,584	52	29	5.0
Georgetown*	661	26,233	2,173	105	31	19.0
Miami*	821	60,694	2,172	150	43	11.5
New York University*	1,462	77,675	4,061	228	159	101.0
Notre Dame	572	11,999	1,418	189	39	42.5
Rice	384	14,524	855	167	30	18.5
Tulane*	508	28,666	1,364	61	46	25.5
Mean	683	34,367	1,874	145	51	35.3
Median	603	26,520	1,501	152	35	31.8

*Campus includes medical school.

Institutional Data for Research 3 Public Institutions, 1980–1990

Institution (N=22)	No. of Full-time Faculty	Federal R&D Funding (thousands)	Total Publications	Publications in Top-Science Journals	Publications in Top–Social Science Journals	A&H Awards
Arizona State	1,358	$17,676	2,243	177	104	27.5
Arkansas	743	8,005	912	47	39	7.5
Auburn	1,073	11,811	1,304	43	21	2.5
Clemson	691	6,309	1,339	33	6	8.5
Colorado School of Mines	175	3,572	243	43	3	0.0
Connecticut	1,130	25,383	1,641	87	78	17.5
Idaho	484	7,398	529	28	6	11.0
Kansas State	904	11,533	1,247	67	26	16.5
Maryland–Baltimore County	329	3,267	406	20	20	18.0
Missouri-Rolla	252	3,228	602	17	3	0.5
Nebraska-Lincoln	990	12,724	1,490	93	51	35.0
New Mexico State	557	28,490	560	45	16	9.5
North Dakota State	426	4,922	429	55	15	0.0
Oklahoma-Norman	737	10,703	1,083	65	37	7.0
Rhode Island	657	15,860	804	78	23	4.5
South Carolina	1,059	14,706	1,716	111	55	26.5
Temple*	1,313	23,861	1,913	108	60	23.0
Tennessee	1,160	15,363	2,320	146	41	14.0
Utah State	515	9,846	696	77	9	13.5
West Virginia*	929	12,697	1,045	43	17	8.5
William and Mary	405	4,128	637	13	5	25.5
Wyoming	614	8,396	1,076	83	18	13.0
Mean	750	11,813	1,102	67	30	13.2
Median	714	11,118	1,061	60	21	12.0

*Campus includes medical school.

Institutional Data for Research 3 Private Institutions, 1980–1990

Institution (N=14)	No. of Full-time Faculty	Federal R&D Funding (thousands)	Total Publications	Publications in Top-Science Journals	Publications in Top–Social Science Journals	A&H Awards
Catholic	355	$4,537	440	27	25	17.5
Clark	161	1,463	231	15	14	4.0
Clarkson	194	4,092	242	44	2	5.0
Columbia Teachers College	134	1,366	224	0	3	1.0
Denver	354	4,992	401	30	28	7.5
Drexel	408	6,487	410	52	9	6.0
Lehigh	379	9,419	488	67	10	5.5
Loma Linda*	204	2,027	344	4	0	3.0
Loyola (Chicago)*	640	6,337	702	14	42	10.5
Polytechnic	143	4,672	181	32	0	0.5
Rensselaer	374	17,920	705	136	2	5.0
Saint Louis*	425	11,958	747	59	20	1.0
Southern Methodist	491	11,702	618	35	29	21.0
Syracuse	930	17,775	1,506	128	57	33.5
Mean	371	7,482	517	46	17	8.6
Median	365	5,665	425	34	12	5.3

*Campus includes medical school.

TABLE APPENDIX.7

Institutional Data for Research 4 Public Institutions, 1980–1990

Institution (N=51)	No. of Full-time Faculty	Federal R&D Funding (thousands)	Total Publications	Publications in Top-Science Journals	Publications in Top–Social Science Journals	A&H Awards
Akron	774	$3,320	612	23	20	6.0
Alabama-Tuscaloosa	762	3,325	784	47	25	16.0
Ball State	877	179	218	1	3	11.0
Bowling Green	714	952	439	40	13	10.5
Cleveland State	515	3,493	631	11	20	9.5
East Texas State	246	0	193	19	11	0.0
Florida Atlantic	363	1,727	263	17	10	3.0
Georgia State	745	3,938	727	24	35	8.0
Idaho State	359	490	59	36	20	1.5
Illinois State	781	1,209	277	25	12	11.0
Indiana State	656	334	204	7	8	4.0
Kent State	706	3,164	447	39	45	12.0
Louisiana Tech	392	554	378	20	2	0.0
Louisville*	724	5,770	436	4	13	10.0
Maine-Orono	482	4,293	389	27	12	5.5
Memphis	729	2,680	405	18	19	12.5
Miami (Ohio)	756	1,363	572	22	25	8.0
Middle Tennessee State	444	277	518	43	11	0.0
Mississippi State	828	14,157	474	11	10	5.5
Missouri-Kansas City*	550	3,413	78	14	8	8.5
Missouri-St. Louis	287	1,708	717	1	11	16.5
Montana	359	2,630	437	25	17	17.0
Montana State	469	5,854	145	4	6	13.5
Nevada-Reno*	386	7,385	274	36	4	0.5
New Hampshire	562	13,849	342	3	6	18.0
New Orleans	493	1,932	600	0	4	6.0
North Carolina–Greensboro	526	1,116	587	32	26	11.5
North Dakota*	459	8,141	241	7	14	7.5
North Texas	688	1,849	567	33	36	4.0
Northern Arizona	477	2,313	303	5	7	5.0
Northern Colorado	434	548	614	7	5	5.0
Northern Illinois	1,056	3,029	726	11	22	21.0
Ohio University	637	4,166	587	14	7	10.5
Oklahoma State	963	8,188	965	56	11	8.5
Old Dominion	587	6,150	510	18	2	3.5
Portland State	439	2,346	208	26	14	9.0
Rutgers-Newark	398	0	272	1	18	3.5
South Dakota*	320	442	217	21	9	2.5
South Florida*	1,076	12,288	995	64	25	8.0
Southern Illinois	1,024	6,409	1,127	32	46	12.0
Southern Mississippi	1,140	1,620	307	93	23	13.5
SUNY-Binghamton	488	2,789	565	88	21	18.0
Tennessee Tech	358	6,611	58	70	27	1.0
Texas Tech*	858	6,611	1,114	32	27	9.0
Texas Woman's	257	384	843	16	12	1.0
Texas-Arlington	619	1,749	565	61	15	9.0
Texas-Dallas	187	5,254	130	21	11	12.0
Toledo	615	2,283	477	38	23	1.5
Vermont*	629	25,283	352	19	18	29.5
Western Michigan	733	959	763	50	14	7.5
Wisconsin-Milwaukee	854	6,112	557	25	12	36.0
Mean	604	4,012	476	27	16	9.1
Median	587	2,680	447	22	13	8.5

*Campus includes medical school.

APPENDIX A

TABLE APPENDIX.8

Institutional Data for Research 4 Private Institutions, 1980–1990

Institution (N=25)	No. of Full-time Faculty	Federal R&D Funding (thousands)	Total Publications	Publications in Top-Science Journals	Publications in Top–Social Science Journals	A&H Awards
Adelphi	305	$307	170	1	6	1.5
American	385	1,614	422	18	18	8.0
Andrews	146	46	29	1	1	0.0
Baylor	539	1,441	322	6	2	0.0
Biola	120	0	61	0	0	0.5
Boston College	540	4,056	594	36	25	19.5
Brigham Young	1,220	3,833	824	32	19	4.5
Drake	208	12	76	1	1	3.5
Duquesne	271	96	138	3	4	1.5
Florida Tech	106	950	76	6	0	0.0
Fordham	486	1,542	578	4	25	23.0
Hofstra	404	170	248	1	7	7.0
Howard*	968	11,517	737	29	13	9.0
Illinois Tech	264	3,988	4	15	3	1.5
Marquette	480	2,050	601	31	25	24.0
Mississippi College	130	13	22	0	0	0.0
New School	235	444	364	2	21	1.0
Northeastern	771	8,445	625	105	15	5.0
Pepperdine	202	234	65	1	1	0.0
Saint John's	605	523	361	5	11	5.0
San Francisco	210	389	284	2	6	0.5
Stevens Tech	149	1,692	142	16	1	1.5
Texas Christian	393	1,752	348	24	6	1.5
Tulsa	268	984	365	1	16	9.5
U.S. International	108	29	25	0	1	0.0
Mean	381	1,845	299	14	9	5.1
Median	271	950	284	2	6	1.5

*Campus includes medical school.

APPENDIX B

PER CAPITA SCORES FOR 203 RESEARCH UNIVERSITIES

■

TABLE APPENDIX.9
Per Capita Data for Research 1 Public Institutions, 1980–1990

Institution (N=31)	No. of Full-Time Faculty	Per Capita R&D	Per Capita Publications	Per Capita Publications in Top-Science Journals	Per Capita Publications in Top–Social Science Journals	Per Capita A&H Awards
Alabama-Birmingham*	921	$70,432	3.10	0.1661	0.0141	0.0098
Arizona*	1,503	50,634	2.72	0.3659	0.0539	0.0309
UC Berkeley	1,477	80,198	4.77	0.9242	0.1286	0.0880
UC Davis*	1,095	53,511	3.70	0.3078	0.0539	0.0274
UC Irvine*	587	78,937	4.08	0.5622	0.0630	0.0383
UC Los Angeles*	1,778	94,136	4.92	0.5045	0.1080	0.0630
UC Riverside	351	33,544	6.19	0.1709	0.1453	0.0627
UC San Diego*	692	226,085	5.93	1.0679	0.0853	0.0499
UC Santa Barbara	729	49,429	2.42	0.5281	0.1372	0.0658
UC Santa Cruz	383	33,219	3.02	0.1253	0.1880	0.0601
Colorado	864	86,613	2.95	0.5498	0.0938	0.0417
Illinois-Chicago*	1,433	29,156	2.31	0.1347	0.0865	0.0398
Illinois-Urbana	1,977	47,521	2.75	0.4512	0.1113	0.0503
Indiana	1,256	29,487	2.72	0.2428	0.1632	0.0621
Iowa*	1,125	66,705	3.75	0.2480	0.0756	0.0476
Maryland–College Park	1,308	43,208	2.61	0.3303	0.0841	0.0310
Michigan*	1,886	87,121	3.75	0.3181	0.1638	0.0581
Minnesota	1,725	72,184	3.41	0.2893	0.0899	0.0246
North Carolina State	1,164	28,826	3.24	0.1753	0.0275	0.0245
North Carolina–Chapel Hill*	1,368	67,908	3.42	0.2573	0.1126	0.0431
Ohio State*	2,083	32,236	2.40	0.1954	0.0672	0.0130
Pennsylvania State	1,578	40,588	2.29	0.2060	0.0817	0.0139
Pittsburgh*	1,426	61,278	3.36	0.1978	0.1108	0.0259
Purdue	1,446	36,770	2.28	0.3479	0.0588	0.0111
SUNY-Albany	641	28,922	3.73	0.2153	0.1139	0.0374
SUNY-Buffalo*	962	34,688	2.73	0.2360	0.0593	0.0244
SUNY–Stony Brook*	740	58,062	3.94	0.5365	0.1797	0.0561
Texas-Austin	1,894	35,994	2.31	0.3110	0.0903	0.0414
Utah*	941	64,930	2.92	0.3454	0.0648	0.0191
Virginia*	1,153	45,389	2.91	0.2897	0.0642	0.0451
Washington*	1,999	100,171	3.30	0.3707	0.1041	0.0280
Wisconsin-Madison*	1,561	90,587	4.31	0.4215	0.1595	0.0480
Mean	1,251	60,756	3.26	0.3501	0.0966	0.0388
Median	1,282	52,073	3.17	0.3094	0.0901	0.0406

*Campus includes medical school.

229

Table Appendix.10
Per Capita Data for Research 1 Private Institutions, 1980-1990

Institution (N=23)	No. of Full-Time Faculty	Per Capita R&D	Per Capita Publications	Per Capita Publications in Top-Science Journals	Per Capita Publications in Top–Social Science Journals	Per Capita A&H Awards
Brown*	539	$60,427	3.84	0.1596	0.1150	0.1085
Caltech	245	278,294	15.44	3.3592	0.1020	0.0327
Carnegie Mellon	495	107,467	3.21	0.3778	0.1556	0.0404
Case Western*	734	92,571	3.33	0.3597	0.0886	0.0116
Chicago*	940	99,062	6.10	0.5447	0.2809	0.1090
Columbia*	1,197	122,359	5.09	0.4912	0.1579	0.1065
Cornell (Ithaca)	1,469	66,044	3.96	0.6025	0.0885	0.0579
Duke*	823	120,773	5.21	0.4629	0.1932	0.0723
Emory*	647	75,379	3.36	0.2349	0.0866	0.0471
Harvard*	1,485	92,257	7.46	0.9253	0.1811	0.1074
Johns Hopkins*	814	264,098	6.05	0.7531	0.1290	0.0688
MIT	1,041	193,770	3.95	1.1614	0.0759	0.0288
Northwestern*	958	59,742	4.00	0.4154	0.1879	0.0579
Pennsylvania*	1,155	114,096	5.84	0.4710	0.1636	0.0913
Princeton	659	72,269	4.62	0.8331	0.1684	0.1844
Rochester*	743	130,833	3.93	0.4590	0.1279	0.0774
Southern California*	1,318	82,511	3.15	0.2716	0.0736	0.0383
Stanford*	921	250,561	6.73	1.2117	0.2356	0.1026
Tufts*	585	64,415	3.08	0.2718	0.0581	0.0564
Vanderbilt*	768	83,746	3.59	0.2721	0.1146	0.0501
Washington (St. Louis)*	904	116,611	5.65	0.5465	0.1449	0.0265
Yale*	903	156,570	6.57	0.6489	0.1694	0.1567
Yeshiva*	389	173,465	3.59	0.4293	0.0514	0.0064
Mean	858	119,096	4.97	0.6079	0.1416	0.0745
Median	823	107,467	4.00	0.4710	0.1290	0.0579

*Campus includes medical school.

Per Capita Data for Research 2 Public Institutions, 1980–1990

Institution (N=26)	No. of Full-Time Faculty	Per Capita R&D	Per Capita Publications	Per Capita Publications in Top-Science Journals	Per Capita Publications in Top–Social Science Journals	Per Capita A&H Awards
Cincinnati*	1,218	$32,039	1.93	0.1363	0.0213	0.0090
Colorado State	919	37,123	1.59	0.1937	0.0141	0.0049
Delaware	900	16,558	1.65	0.2244	0.0511	0.0217
Florida State	982	27,290	1.56	0.1283	0.0458	0.0076
Florida*	2,320	23,231	1.89	0.1384	0.0306	0.0114
Georgia	1,679	21,965	1.66	0.0917	0.0459	0.0155
Georgia Tech	545	46,848	1.61	0.2294	0.0257	0.0073
Hawaii-Manoa*	1,081	32,841	1.59	0.1748	0.0361	0.0227
Houston	853	16,654	1.71	0.1489	0.0457	0.0404
Iowa State	1,303	14,544	1.52	0.2325	0.0215	0.0134
Kansas	929	17,577	1.83	0.1098	0.1119	0.0388
Kentucky*	1,315	17,409	1.85	0.0844	0.0471	0.0198
Louisiana State	1,452	16,558	2.34	0.1315	0.0365	0.0169
Massachusetts-Amherst	1,303	31,466	1.86	0.2256	0.0821	0.0449
Michigan State*	2,079	23,942	1.62	0.1419	0.0471	0.0164
Mississippi	407	16,469	1.72	0.0614	0.0663	0.0184
Missouri-Columbia*	989	19,490	2.17	0.1021	0.0586	0.0288
New Mexico*	888	24,209	1.61	0.1599	0.0721	0.0405
Oregon	684	23,795	2.03	0.2018	0.0877	0.0599
Oregon State	665	60,660	1.94	0.2887	0.0316	0.0173
Rutgers–New Brunswick	1,350	22,462	2.12	0.0756	0.0815	0.0537
Texas A&M*	1,563	25,478	2.04	0.1996	0.0505	0.0090
Virginia Commonwealth	1,027	37,627	1.60	0.0944	0.0234	0.0141
Virginia Tech	1,507	19,618	1.50	0.0823	0.0345	0.0209
Washington State	737	22,204	1.95	0.1547	0.0326	0.0237
Wayne State*	978	27,033	2.04	0.1431	0.0389	0.0204
Mean	1,141	24,908	1.81	0.1473	0.0465	0.0219
Median	1,008	23,513	1.78	0.1425	0.0458	0.0191

*Campus includes medical school.

Per Capita Data for Research 2 Private Institutions, 1980–1990

Institution (N=10)	No. of Full-Time Faculty	Per Capita R&D	Per Capita Publications	Per Capita Publications in Top-Science Journals	Per Capita Publications in Top–Social Science Journals	Per Capita A&H Awards
Boston University*	1,028	$52,733	3.05	0.2286	0.0671	0.0462
Brandeis	320	51,969	2.50	0.4813	0.0969	0.1375
Dartmouth*	440	60,280	2.68	0.2455	0.0682	0.0864
George Washington*	634	41,823	2.50	0.0820	0.0457	0.0079
Georgetown*	661	39,687	3.29	0.1589	0.0469	0.0287
Miami*	821	73,927	2.65	0.1827	0.0524	0.0140
New York University*	1,462	53,129	2.78	0.1560	0.1088	0.0691
Notre Dame	572	20,977	2.48	0.3304	0.0682	0.0743
Rice	384	37,823	2.23	0.4349	0.0781	0.0482
Tulane*	508	56,429	2.69	0.1201	0.0906	0.0502
Mean	683	50,318	2.74	0.2122	0.0742	0.0563
Median	603	52,351	2.67	0.2041	0.0682	0.0482

*Campus includes medical school.

Per Capita Data for Research 3 Public Universities, 1980–1990

Institution (N=22)	No. of Full-Time Faculty	Per Capita R&D	Per Capita Publications	Per Capita Publications in Top-Science Journals	Per Capita Publications in Top–Social Science Journals	Per Capita A&H Awards
Arizona State	1,358	$13,016	1.65	0.1303	0.0766	0.0203
Arkansas	743	10,774	1.23	0.0633	0.0525	0.0101
Auburn	1,073	11,007	1.22	0.0401	0.0196	0.0023
Clemson	691	9,130	1.94	0.0478	0.0087	0.0123
Colorado School of Mines	175	20,411	1.39	0.2457	0.0171	0.0000
Connecticut	1,130	22,463	1.45	0.0770	0.0690	0.0155
Idaho	484	15,285	1.09	0.0579	0.0124	0.0227
Kansas State	904	12,758	1.38	0.0741	0.0288	0.0183
Maryland–Baltimore Co.	329	9,930	1.23	0.0608	0.0608	0.0547
Missouri-Rolla	252	12,810	2.39	0.0675	0.0119	0.0020
Nebraska-Lincoln	990	12,853	1.51	0.0939	0.0515	0.0354
New Mexico State	557	51,149	1.01	0.0808	0.0287	0.0171
North Dakota State	426	11,554	1.01	0.1291	0.0352	0.0000
Oklahoma-Norman	737	14,522	1.47	0.0882	0.0502	0.0095
Rhode Island	657	24,140	1.22	0.1187	0.0350	0.0068
South Carolina*	1,059	13,887	1.62	0.1048	0.0519	0.0250
Temple*	1,313	18,173	1.46	0.0823	0.0457	0.0175
Tennessee	1,160	13,244	2.00	0.1259	0.0353	0.0121
Utah State	515	19,118	1.35	0.1495	0.0175	0.0262
West Virginia*	929	13,667	1.12	0.0463	0.0183	0.0091
William and Mary	405	10,193	1.57	0.0321	0.0123	0.0630
Wyoming	614	13,674	1.75	0.1352	0.0293	0.0212
Mean	750	15,749	1.47	0.0896	0.0396	0.0175
Median	714	13,456	1.42	0.0815	0.0322	0.0163

*Campus includes medical school.

Per Capita Data for Research 3 Private Institutions, 1980–1990

Institution (N=14)	No. of Full-Time Faculty	Per Capita R&D	Per Capita Publications	Per Capita Publications in Top-Science Journals	Per Capita Publications in Top–Social Science Journals	Per Capita A&H Awards
Catholic	355	$12,780	1.24	0.0761	0.0704	0.0493
Clark	161	9,087	1.43	0.0932	0.0870	0.0248
Clarkson	194	21,093	1.25	0.2268	0.0103	0.0258
Columbia Teachers College	134	10,194	1.67	0.0000	0.0224	0.0075
Denver	354	14,102	1.13	0.0847	0.0791	0.0212
Drexel	408	15,900	1.00	0.1275	0.0221	0.0147
Lehigh	379	24,852	1.29	0.1768	0.0264	0.0145
Loma Linda*	204	9,936	1.69	0.0196	0.0000	0.0147
Loyola-Chicago*	640	9,902	1.10	0.0219	0.0656	0.0164
Polytechnic	143	32,671	1.27	0.2238	0.0000	0.0035
Rensselaer	374	47,914	1.89	0.3636	0.0053	0.0134
Saint Louis*	425	28,136	1.76	0.1388	0.0471	0.0024
Southern Methodist	491	23,833	1.26	0.0713	0.0591	0.0428
Syracuse	930	19,113	1.62	0.1376	0.0613	0.0360
Mean	371	20,175	1.39	0.1238	0.0464	0.0233
Median	365	17,506	1.28	0.1103	0.0367	0.0156

*Campus includes medical school.

TABLE APPENDIX.15
Per Capita Data for Research 4 Public Institutions, 1980–1990

Institution (N=51)	No. of Full-Time Faculty	Per Capita R&D	Per Capita Publications	Per Capita Publications in Top-Science Journals	Per Capita Publications in Top–Social Science Journals	Per Capita A&H Awards
Akron	774	$4,289	0.79	0.0297	0.0258	0.0078
Alabama-Tuscaloosa	762	4,364	1.03	0.0617	0.0328	0.0210
Ball State	877	204	0.25	0.0011	0.0034	0.0125
Bowling Green	714	1,333	0.61	0.0560	0.0182	0.0147
Cleveland State	515	6,783	1.23	0.0214	0.0388	0.0184
East Texas State	246	0	0.78	0.0772	0.0447	0.0000
Florida Atlantic	363	4,758	0.72	0.0468	0.0275	0.0083
Georgia State	745	5,286	0.98	0.0322	0.0470	0.0107
Idaho State	359	1,365	0.16	0.1003	0.0557	0.0042
Illinois State	781	1,548	0.35	0.0320	0.0154	0.0141
Indiana State	656	509	0.31	0.0107	0.0122	0.0061
Kent State	706	4,482	0.63	0.0552	0.0637	0.0170
Louisiana Tech	392	1,413	0.96	0.0510	0.0051	0.0000
Louisville*	724	7,970	0.60	0.0055	0.0180	0.0138
Maine-Orono	482	8,907	0.81	0.0560	0.0249	0.0114
Memphis State	729	3,676	0.56	0.0247	0.0261	0.0171
Miami (Ohio)	756	1,803	0.76	0.0291	0.0331	0.0106
Middle Tennessee State	444	624	1.17	0.0968	0.0248	0.0000
Mississippi State	828	17,098	0.57	0.0133	0.0121	0.0066
Missouri–Kansas City*	550	6,205	0.14	0.0255	0.0145	0.0155
Missouri-St. Louis	287	5,951	2.50	0.0035	0.0383	0.0575
Montana	359	7,326	1.22	0.0696	0.0474	0.0474
Montana State	469	12,482	0.31	0.0085	0.0128	0.0288
Nevada-Reno*	386	19,132	0.71	0.0933	0.0104	0.0013
New Hampshire	562	24,642	0.61	0.0053	0.0107	0.0320
New Orleans	493	3,919	1.22	0.0000	0.0081	0.0122
North Carolina–Greensboro	526	2,122	1.12	0.0608	0.0494	0.0219
North Dakota*	459	17,736	0.53	0.0153	0.0305	0.0163
North Texas	688	2,688	0.82	0.0480	0.0523	0.0058
Northern Arizona	477	4,849	0.64	0.0105	0.0147	0.0105
Northern Colorado	434	1,263	1.41	0.0161	0.0115	0.0115
Northern Illinois	1,056	2,868	0.69	0.0104	0.0208	0.0199
Ohio University	637	6,540	0.92	0.0220	0.0110	0.0165
Oklahoma State	963	8,503	1.00	0.0582	0.0114	0.0088
Old Dominion	587	10,477	0.87	0.0307	0.0034	0.0060
Portland State	439	5,344	0.47	0.0592	0.0319	0.0205
Rutgers-Newark	398	0	0.68	0.0025	0.0452	0.0088
South Dakota*	320	1,381	0.68	0.0656	0.0281	0.0078
South Florida*	1,076	11,420	0.92	0.0595	0.0232	0.0074
Southern Illinois	1,024	6,259	1.10	0.0313	0.0449	0.0117
Southern Mississippi	1,140	1,421	0.27	0.0816	0.0202	0.0118
SUNY-Binghamton	488	5,715	1.16	0.1803	0.0430	0.0369
Tennessee Tech	358	18,466	0.16	0.1955	0.0754	0.0028
Texas Tech*	858	7,705	1.30	0.0373	0.0315	0.0105
Texas Woman's	257	1,494	3.28	0.0623	0.0467	0.0039
Texas-Arlington	619	2,826	0.91	0.0985	0.0242	0.0145
Texas-Dallas	187	28,096	0.70	0.1123	0.0588	0.0642
Toledo	615	3,712	0.78	0.0618	0.0374	0.0024
Vermont*	629	40,196	0.56	0.0302	0.0286	0.0469
Western Michigan	733	1,308	1.04	0.0682	0.0191	0.0102
Wisconsin-Milwaukee	854	7,157	0.65	0.0293	0.0141	0.0422
Mean	604	6,648	0.79	0.0441	0.0265	0.0151
Median	587	4,758	0.76	0.0373	0.0258	0.0117

*Campus includes medical school.

Table Appendix.16
Per Capita Data for Research 4 Private Institutions, 1980–1990

Institution (N=25)	No. of Full-Time Faculty	Per Capita R&D	Per Capita Publications	Per Capita Publications in Top-Science Journals	Per Capita Publications in Top–Social Science Journals	Per Capita A&H Awards
Adelphi	305	$1,007	0.56	0.0033	0.0197	0.0049
American	385	4,192	1.10	0.0468	0.0468	0.0208
Andrews	146	315	0.20	0.0068	0.0068	0.0000
Baylor (Waco)	539	2,673	0.60	0.0111	0.0037	0.0000
Biola	120	0	0.51	0.0000	0.0000	0.0042
Boston College	540	7,511	1.10	0.0667	0.0463	0.0361
Brigham Young	1,220	3,142	0.68	0.0262	0.0156	0.0037
Drake	208	58	0.37	0.0048	0.0048	0.0168
Duquesne	271	354	0.51	0.0111	0.0148	0.0055
Florida Tech	106	8,962	0.72	0.0566	0.0000	0.0000
Fordham	486	3,173	1.19	0.0082	0.0514	0.0473
Hofstra	404	421	0.61	0.0025	0.0173	0.0173
Howard*	968	11,898	0.76	0.0300	0.0134	0.0093
Illinois Tech	264	15,106	0.02	0.0568	0.0114	0.0057
Marquette	480	4,271	1.25	0.0646	0.0521	0.0500
Mississippi College	130	100	0.17	0.0000	0.0000	0.0000
New School	235	1,889	1.55	0.0085	0.0894	0.0043
Northeastern	771	10,953	0.81	0.1362	0.0195	0.0065
Pepperdine	202	1,158	0.32	0.0050	0.0050	0.0000
Saint John's	605	864	0.60	0.0083	0.0182	0.0083
San Francisco	210	1,852	1.35	0.0095	0.0286	0.0024
Stevens Tech	149	11,356	0.95	0.1074	0.0067	0.0101
Texas Christian	393	4,458	0.89	0.0611	0.0153	0.0038
Tulsa	268	3,672	1.36	0.0037	0.0597	0.0354
U.S. International	108	269	0.23	0.0000	0.0093	0.0000
Mean	381	4,849	0.79	0.0357	0.0239	0.0134
Median	271	2,673	0.68	0.0095	0.0153	0.0055

*Campus includes medical school.

NOTE ON METHOD
AND SOURCES
■

The central argument of this book is that new research universities did emerge after 1945 to successfully challenge the hierarchy of traditional elites. Their story is a part of the continuous expansion of the nation's academic research enterprise from a concentrated group of elite institutions to a wide variety of campuses in diverse locations. Its magnitude is reflected in the Carnegie classification of doctorate-granting institutions, which grew from 173 campuses in 1970 to 236 in 1994, and in the National Research Council's 1995 study of research-doctorate programs, which included 3,634 Ph.D. programs at 274 institutions.[1] The Carnegie classification system provided a standard taxonomy, and the comparative assessments of graduate programs provided national benchmarks of program quality. Yet both the Carnegie classifications and the graduate program studies have contributed to the conflation of quantity and quality in the assessment of faculty research achievement in American higher education.

The Carnegie categories provided a common frame of reference and a set of definitions that emphasized the variety of roles in post-secondary education. But the Carnegie taxonomies, especially for Research and Doctoral institutions, were determined by crude variables of institutional size, the number of doctoral degrees awarded, and total federal support received. The periodic assessments of graduate programs, especially those sponsored by the American Council on Education (1966, 1970) and the National Research Council (1982, 1995), included a large number of institutions and academic fields, emphasized data specific to the faculty and graduate training of discipline-based programs, and avoided grand institutional rankings. But the national program rankings produced by these studies were based on subjective reputational surveys that were biased toward

235

large programs and prestigious institutions.[2] Reliance on quantitative accumulations and reputational surveys has been a persisting weakness in studies rating the research prowess of faculty at American institutions of higher education.

For these reasons, we determined to measure scholarly research activity in a manner that accounted for the size of an institution's faculty. Previous studies of research universities placed a premium on quantitative superlatives—for example, the highest dollar value of grants received, the greater number of advanced degrees awarded, the largest number of fellowships and publications. In contrast, this study documented research activity by dividing the various indicators of aggregate faculty performance by the number of full-time instructional faculty on a given campus. This produced a per capita measure that permitted comparison of universities of different size and type as their performance changed over time.

There are three components to the method: a universe of institutions identified by Carnegie as doctorate-granting universities; a set of five objective indicators for measuring research performance; and the number of full-time instructional faculty on each campus. Results were presented and comparisons drawn in terms of the Carnegie classifications (devised in 1970, first published in 1973, and then revised in 1976, 1987, and 1994) that grouped universities on the basis of federal dollars received and/or the number of doctorates awarded. These categorizations varied somewhat over three decades as some universities were "promoted" to higher groups while others were "dropped" to lower ranks. In 1987, 213 institutions were classified by Carnegie as Research or Doctoral institutions. For these 213 institutions we collected data on research indicators that spanned 1965–90.

To measure research performance we selected five indicators: federal R&D obligations, journal publications in all fields, journal publications in top-rated science and top-rated social science journals, and arts and humanities awards. The data concentrated on three benchmark periods: 1968, 1973–74, and the mid-1980s to 1990. Data availability dictated that, for the earlier periods, the assessment of research productivity was compiled according to similar, although not identical, measures. The five indicators were selected and refined through a pilot study that assessed faculty scholarship at Maryland's public and private institutions.[3] To attain measurements that could be compared across institutional types and sizes, totals in each category were standardized according to the number of full-time instructional faculty on each campus.[4]

The first indicator, the number of federal R&D dollars obligated to an institution, was published, beginning in 1968, in the National Science Foundation's annual series *Federal Support to Universities, Colleges, and Selected Non-Profit Institutions.*[5] For the late 1980s, federal R&D funds for 1988, 1989, and 1990 were averaged for each institution.[6] Four types of federal support were excluded from these institutional totals. First, we excluded all nonresearch funds, including awards for construction grants, repair, renovation and modernization of research facilities, library grants, training grants, and the like. Second, we excluded R&D funds for federal contract research laboratories, such as the Jet Propulsion Laboratory (Caltech) and the Lawrence Radiation Laboratory (Berkeley), that were not funded through the standard peer-review process.

Third, since our primary focus is on research, we excluded from campus R&D averages all Defense Department development contracts — the *D* in R&D — exceeding a total value of $500,000.[7] For the period 1988–90 this reduced the average federal R&D total of thirty-eight institutions, thirty of them by amounts less than $4 million. Experiencing the greatest reduction when the Pentagon *D* was removed from federal R&D was Johns Hopkins, which, if DOD contracts for naval weapons development at its Applied Physics Laboratory were included, would rank first in total federal R&D funding received. The development contract deductions for 1990 exceeding $3 million were, in descending order (in millions): Johns Hopkins, $223.2; Penn State, $37.6; Utah State, $29.6; Georgia Tech, $27.8; Texas, $19.3; New Mexico State, $11.0; Carnegie Mellon, $7.6; and Pittsburgh, $7.5.[8] Fourth, formula-based funding for agriculture research from the USDA, allocated to land-grant institutions separately from peer-review competition, was deducted from the R&D totals.[9] Of the forty-eight land-grant institutions affected, the majority (thirty-one) received less than $4 million annually in Hatch Act formula aid, and none received more than $5.5 million. In 1990, for example, three universities (North Carolina State, Penn State, and Texas A&M) received between $5 million and $5.5 million in formula-based funding, and eleven received between $4 and $5 million (Cornell, UC Davis, Illinois-Urbana, Iowa State, Kentucky, Michigan State, Minnesota, Ohio State, Purdue, Tennessee, and Wisconsin).

The second indicator measured the ratio of campus researchers publishing in scholarly journals in a sample year or years. Publication data were obtained from the Institute for Scientific Information's Science Citation Index and its parallel data collections for the social sciences and for the arts and humanities. All three databases captured authored "source items" — scientific and scholarly articles, research notes, and book reviews in journals and chapters in proceedings, anthologies, and collections published throughout the world.[10] Publications authored by campus researchers in the sciences, the social sciences, and the arts and humanities were documented, and then combined, producing a total number of publications for each institution. The publication data gathered for 1987 reflected a ratio of science to social science to arts and humanities of 80:15:5.[11] For this reason, for the natural and physical science fields in which the majority of journal publications occurred, publications from one year (1987) were counted; for the social sciences, in which research is often published in books, journal publications from two years (1986 and 1987) were recorded. For the arts and humanities, in which books predominate over journal articles, a three-year publication record (1986, 1987, 1988) was used.

While federal R&D obligations and the total number of publications were quantitative measures, two other measures captured the quality of publication output. To identify scholars publishing in leading journals, forty-five journals in the sciences and forty-four journals in the social sciences were selected. Our journal selection was guided by three goals. We wanted, first, to choose the most frequently read and cited journals; second, to include most of the major academic fields; and third, to exclude certain professional and applied areas that were unlikely to be represented on many university campuses—for example, clinical medicine, law, business (but not management), agriculture, social work, and architecture.

To meet the first goal—selecting the most frequently read and cited journals—we used frequency of citations as a criterion. We began with the ISI-identified top "Journals Ranked by Times Cited" but modified this list to accommodate our second goal—the inclusion of most of the major scientific and scholarly fields.[12] Because ISI's top fifty journals in citation frequency are heavily clustered in biomedical science and physics, journals in many academic fields are excluded from the list, especially social science journals in political science, geography, and history. Using citation frequency as a guide, we made our own judgments, selecting, for example, five journals in chemistry, six in physics, and one each in astronomy and entomology. Such a compromise best balanced our desire to cover most of the scholarly spectrum of journal publication while sampling more extensively in the fields with heavy traffic. This method, which allowed us to capture the broadest spectrum of fields represented at most research universities, produced a list of forty-five top-ranked journals from the sciences as well as a list of forty-four top-ranked social science journals. The science journals and the fields covered were as follows:

Field	Journal
Astronomy	*Astrophysical Journal*
Biochemistry and molecular biology	*Annual Review of Biochemistry* *Cell* *Journal of Biochemistry* *Journal of Molecular Biology*
Biophysics	*Biochimica et Biophysica Acta*
Biology	*Developmental Biology* *Life Sciences* *Microbiology*
Botany	*Annual Review of Plant Physiology*
Chemistry	*Analytical Chemistry* *Angewandte Chemie-International* *Journal of the American Chemical Society* *Journal of Organic Chemistry* *Journal of Physical Chemistry*
Computer science	*Communications of the ACM*
Ecology	*Ecology*
Engineering	*Journal of Catalysis* *IEEE Journal of Quantum Electronics*
Entomology	*Journal of Insect Physiology*
Environmental science	*Environmental Science and Technology*
Genetics	*Annual Review of Genetics*
Geology	*Geological Society of America Bulletin*
Geoscience	*Journal of Geophysical Research*
Mathematics	*Annals of Mathematics*
Mechanics	*Journal of Fluid Mechanics*
Metallurgy	*Acta Metallurgica*
Multidisciplinary science	*Nature* *Proceedings of the National Academy of Science* *Science*

| Neuroscience | *Brain Research* |
| | *Neuroscience Research* |

| Oceanography | *Limnology and Oceanography* |

| Optics | *Optics Letters* |

Physics	*Applied Physics Letters*
	Communications in Mathematical Physics
	Nuclear Physics
	Physical Review B
	Physical Review Letters
	Review of Modern Physics

| Polymer science | *Macromolecules* |

| Statistics | *Journal of the American Statistical Association* |

| Toxicology | *Annual Review of Pharmacology and Toxicology* |

| Water resources | *Water Resource Research* |

| Zoology | *Animal Behavior* |

The social science journals and the fields covered were as follows:

Field	Journal
Administration and management	*Academy of Management Journal*
	Academy of Management Review
	Administrative Science Quarterly
	Harvard Business Review
	Industrial & Labor Relations Review
	Management Science
Anthropology	*American Journal of Physical Anthropology*
Economics	*American Economic Review*
	Econometrica
	Journal of Finance

	Journal of Financial Economics
	Journal of Political Economy
	Review of Economic Statistics
	Review of Economic Studies
Education	*American Educational Research Journal*
	Educational Research
	Review of Educational Research
	Sociology of Education
Geography	*Annals of the Association of American Geographers*
History	*American Historical Review*
	Journal of American History
Political science	*American Journal of International Law*
	American Political Science Review
	World Politics
Psychology	*American Psychologist*
	Artificial Intelligence
	Child Development
	Cognitive Psychology
	Exceptional Children
	Journal of Abnormal Psychology
	Journal of Consulting and Clinical Psychology
	Journal of Personality and Social Psychology
	Psychological Bulletin
	Psychological Review
	Psychosomatic Medicine
	Reading Research Quarterly
Public opinion	*Public Opinion Quarterly*
Sociology	*Americal Journal of Sociology*
	American Sociological Review
	Demography
	Journal of Gerontology
	Social Forces
	Social Problems
Women's studies	*Signs*

A computer search of the ISI data bank identified the number of faculty at each campus who had published articles in these top-ranked science and top–social science journals during 1986–88.

To compensate for the low rates of journal publication in the arts and humanities and to measure excellence in these fields, a separate arts-and-humanities (A&H) index was constructed. The data sources for this index consisted of competitive grants and fellowships awarded during two ten-year periods, 1965–74 and 1980–89, documented in annual reports published by four funding sources: the National Endowment for the Humanities, the National Endowment for the Arts (for the 1980s only), the John Simon Guggenheim Foundation, and the American Council of Learned Societies. These awards were counted as follows: annual fellowships were counted as 1, and half-year fellowships, grants-in-aid of research, and summer fellowships were counted as .5.

These indicators left largely unrepresented the world of the scholarly book. Theoretically, book publications can be measured by checking the names of individual faculty authors against the computerized database of *Books in Print*. No database, however, identifies the institutional affiliation of book authors. Moreover, the process of sorting out book authors and editors, and co-authors and co-editors, and of identifying academic fields requires so many subjective judgments that such a method was rejected as impractical for this study.[13] However, our own study comparing the productivity of faculty in the history and political science departments of sixteen randomly selected universities indicated a product-moment correlation of .71 with the arts-and-humanities indexes for those schools. In humanities and social science disciplines in which book publication is frequent, faculty who win competitive fellowships tend to show high publications activity, and the A&H index may serve as a rough proxy measure for book productivity.

For the 1980s, faculty data were provided by the 1987 faculty and staff salary survey of the National Center for Education Statistics.[14] The number of medical school faculty on each campus, excluded from the NCES survey, was obtained from the American Association of Medical Colleges (AAMC) and added to the campus totals.[15] Similarly, medical faculty were added to the published American Association of University Professors 1969 and 1974 faculty data reports, which had excluded them. Only those medical schools located on the arts-and-sciences campuses were included in the calculation of full-time faculty. For example, medical faculty at the University of Kentucky, located at the Lexington campus, were included, while medical faculty at the University of Oregon, which has its arts-and-sciences campus in Eugene and its medical school in Portland, were not included.

Counting medical faculty is problematical. At most medical schools, the majority are practicing clinical physicians whose work routines, professional associations, hospital affiliations, and sources of income have little in common with those of most university faculty. Moreover, during the period studied their numbers rose sharply, responding to unprecedented increases in hospital funding for patient care. For basic science (preclinical) faculty, by contrast, professional routines are similar to those of science faculty elsewhere on campus, and faculty growth has more closely paralleled the expansion of medical education. For these reasons we included basic science faculty in the count of full-time instructional faculty and excluded clinical faculty.

The documentation of faculty research achievement for the University of California, Santa Barbara (UCSB) during the late 1980s demonstrates how the per capita measures were calculated. In the first category, federal R&D obligations, UCSB received federal grants for 1988, 1989, and 1990 which averaged to $36,034,000 per year. This result was translated to a per capita measure by dividing it by 729, the number of full-time instructional faculty for UCSB in 1987. The average per capita federal R&D award was thus $49,429. In the second category, journal publications, UCSB faculty published a total of 1,761 articles (ISI source items) in the sciences (total for 1987), the social and behavioral sciences (total for 1986 and 1987), and the arts and humanities (total for 1986, 1987, and 1988). Dividing by 729 produced an index of 2.42 publications per faculty member. The three indicators that represent quality of faculty scholarship were calculated as follows: UCSB authors published 385 articles in the top-ranked science journals, for a top-science index of .528. Social and behavioral sciences faculty published 100 articles in the top-ranked journals in their fields, producing a top–social science index of .137. Finally, UCSB scholars received forty-eight arts and humanities fellowship awards during 1980–89, yielding an A&H index of .0658. (See Appendixes A and B.)

The data sources described above provide a snapshot of research productivity in the 1980s. To provide a baseline from the 1960s, and to document scholarly research activity during the 1970s, further evidence was needed. The measures used to identify scholarly output during the 1980s could not be replicated exactly for the earlier time periods. While federal R&D obligations have been compiled and published annually since 1968, ISI's computerized data collections did not begin until 1972 for the social sciences, until 1974 for the sciences, and until 1980 for the humanities and arts. Thus, other similar indicators had to be used to capture research productivity during the 1960s and 1970s. For the 1960s, federal R&D obligations from 1968 and a count of journal articles in the sciences published during 1968, available from the ISI in print format, were used.

To document productivity during 1973–74, five measures were recorded for each campus: federal R&D obligations for 1973 and 1974, averaged; the number of journal publications in science and the social sciences recorded by the ISI during 1973 and 1974; the number of publications in top-ranked science journals during 1973 and 1974; and the number of publications in top-ranked social science journals during these years. The fifth measure, the A&H index, was replicated for the period 1965–74. The A&H index for these years excluded NEA grants, which during the agency's early years were awarded primarily to community organizations (orchestras, dance and opera companies, theater groups, museums, etc.) rather than to campus arts faculty. For both the 1960s and 1970s, the resulting scores were divided by the number of instructional faculty, published annually by the AAUP.[16] Data for preclinical medical school faculty, excluded from the AAUP survey but obtained from the Association of American Medical Colleges for the periods surveyed, were added to the AAUP totals. Readers interested in institutional and per capita data for the 1960s and 1970s should contact the authors.

On the basis of these per capita measures, for our concluding analysis in chapters 6 and 7 we reclassified institutions to reflect their level of research performance. We eliminated 10 of the 213 institutions because they were consortium-based or too specialized to qualify as comprehensive research universities. The eliminated institutions were, in the public sector, UC San Francisco (UCSF), CUNY Graduate School, and SUNY College of Environmental Science and Forestry; in the private sector, Atlanta University, Claremont Graduate School, Hahnemann, International College, Nova, Rockefeller, and the Union for Experimental Colleges and Universities. Two of these, UCSF and Rockefeller, are among the most powerful and prestigious research institutions in the world. But their research and graduate programs largely exclude the social sciences, arts, and humanities. These exclusions reduced the universe from 213 (the number classified as Carnegie doctorate-granting institutions in 1987) to 203, 131 public and 72 private universities.

On the basis of the first two per capita indicators—federal R&D obligations and total publications by campus authors—we then reclassified these 203 institutions into four categories. In the public sector, we classified as Research 1 universities 32 institutions whose R&D index exceeded $28,000 and whose publications index exceeded 2.0. Twenty-six public institutions scoring above $14,000 in R&D and above 1.5 in publications were categorized as Research 2 universities. The criteria dividing 22 Research 3 and 51 Research 4 public universities (all the rest) were a per capita R&D index of at least $9,000 and a per capita publications index above 1.0. In the private sector, to take into account the higher per capita scores produced by the approximately 30 leading private institutions, we set higher criteria for Research 1 private status: an R&D index of at least $58,000 and a publications index exceeding 3.0. Twenty-three private institutions met this test. Ten private universities were placed in the Research 2 class, which was defined as institutions with an R&D index above $20,000 and a publications index of at least 2.0. Because private universities at the Research 3 and 4 levels generally did not differ significantly from their public counterparts in per capita research performance, we used the same criteria for public and private institutions: an R&D index of at least $9,000 and a publications index above 1.0. Fourteen private institutions were included in the Research 3 category and 25 were classified as Research 4.

Like any other research method, the documentation of scholarly achievement according to per capita measures has both strengths and limitations. First, an important contribution of this study is the aggregation of research performance at the institutional rather than the departmental or graduate program level. While a small number of earlier studies interpreted departmental rankings in institutional terms, most targeted the academic department as the unit of analysis. As noted in chapter 3, while single-field comparisons served well the needs of faculty and department chairs, they were less useful to academic administrators and trustees, or to business and political leaders who wished to build engines of economic development. By translating total scores into per capita measures, this study provides a picture of across-the-board institutional prowess. Also avoided was the bias of standard horsepower rankings of institutional totals (based on, e.g., R&D expenditures, grant and contract dollars awarded, the number of faculty receiving grants and prizes, etc.) that tended to conflate quality with quantity and favored the larger, more elite institutions. Controlling for institutional size, this study highlighted the exemplary performance of faculty at a number of previously overlooked smaller institutions.

Second, this study used both quantitative and qualitative measures. The per capita determination of R&D awards and the ratio of publications per faculty member are primarily quantitative measures. However, the documentation of articles in top-ranked science and social science journals is a more qualitative assessment. Similarly, the arts and humanities awards demonstrate success in a research competition in which the number of winners is severely limited. With the documentation of prestigious arts and humanities awards from the NEH, the NEA, the ACLS, and the Guggenheim Foundation, the study also identified those institutions at which faculty demonstrate impressive productivity in these less intensively funded fields.

A third strength of the research design was the decision to assess change over time, as well as to recognize the importance of historical circumstance. Factors such as the distribution of federal dollars to support programmatic research in the sciences, or the institutional response to external constituencies, reflected in these data, must be taken into account when interpreting faculty research achievement. In contrast to many earlier rankings, which were narrowly focused, this study, in looking at more than two hundred institutions, conforms to a research tradition exhibited by the 1995 NRC study, a tradition that defines research achievement at a wider variety and greater number of institutions. To have been included in the Roose-Andersen 1970 survey, for example, an institution must have awarded at least one hundred doctorates in the most recent ten-year period. Even once a university was included in the survey universe, a department was considered only after awarding at least one doctorate in the ten-year period. According to these criteria, the non-rated universities included UC Santa Barbara, Dartmouth, and the CUNY Graduate School. The more inclusive approach of this research project documents the dispersion of research dollars and publishing scholars across the nation and recognizes the achievement of faculty at smaller, less widely known research universities.

Like all other research designs, this one contains some inherent limitations. The most obvious results from the difficulty of defining and measuring "research productivity." The number of variables is potentially so large that, according to one observer, to calculate a total productivity factor is not just difficult: it is impossible.[17] An appropriate definition of *scholarship* provides another challenge. The exclusive use of awards and publications clearly excludes other valued forms of scholarship.[18] Often faculty who do not conduct research leading to publication are engaged in activity they consider to be scholarly.[19]

During the 1980s there was also a factor of inflation resulting from increased multiple authorship. In sociology, for example, the number of single-authored articles dropped from 69 percent to 2 percent between 1936 and 1982.[20] Describing a similar phenomenon, the historians Robert Fogel and Stanley Engerman in 1983 wrote with pride about an article in economic history that involved no fewer than ten authors.[21] In addition, there was an increasing amount of available journal space during the 1970s and 1980s.[22]

Another limitation lies in the fugitive nature of much of the data.[23] In particular, the designation of an institution's faculty—the denominator on which the per capita measure is based—was self-reported by the institutions to the NCES 1987 salary survey. Each institution, working with an NCES definition, thus determined just what constituted the number of "full-time instructional faculty" positions. For the periods 1968–69 and 1973–74, full-time instructional faculty data was reported to the AAUP for its annual reports on the economic status of the profession. As noted, information about medical faculty was obtained separately from the AAMC and added to the NCES and AAUP counts. There were also additional difficulties regarding the number of faculty at specific institutions. Cornell University, for example, reported data for the endowed colleges but not the statutory colleges.[24] In this case and other cases, institutions had to be contacted directly to determine their full-time instructional faculty.

Nor was parallel information available for each decade. The documentation of faculty publications during the three decades serves as an illustration. Available through the ISI, the record of scholarly publication in science journals was documented only in print format during 1968, with computer data banks established in 1972 for the social sciences and in 1974 for science publications. Scholarly articles in the humanities and the arts were computer-documented beginning in 1980. Thus it is not possible to track growth in parallel publication productivity over the twenty-year period. In addition, because of the absence of additional data, the per capita documentation of only two measures in 1968—federal R&D obligations and science publications—gives only a limited sense of faculty research productivity in the late 1960s. Information about arts and humanities awards received by an institution's faculty during 1965–74 somewhat adds to the picture.

Data collection for universities classified as Doctoral I and II by Carnegie posed another problem. Many of these institutions are part of larger university systems, and statistics such as full-time-equivalent faculty and federal R&D obligations often are reported for the system as a whole. In these instances, communication with individual institutions was necessary to identify award amounts and numbers of faculty. The reporting of R&D obligations for those institutions with medical schools posed a different kind of challenge. In some cases, these awards were added to an institution's total even when the medical school was in a different location. Disaggregation required identifying the medical school awards on the basis of NIH reports and subtracting the awards from campus totals. Finally, it should be noted that while publication data from indexes and abstracts is likely to be more accurate than self-reported counts, published indexes and abstracts are not without error.[25] With respect to inevitable errors in ISI databases, it is plausible to assume that measurement errors are distributed randomly throughout the database.

The difficulty of defining, measuring, and comparing research achievement among institutions is acknowledged in a substantial literature. Nonetheless, arguing over the campus pecking order has long been a favorite pastime of academics, and judging from the market success of the annual ratings produced by *U.S. News and World Report*, rankings are important to the public as well. While per capita rankings may confirm or intensify traditional hierarchies of academic and scholarly prestige, they also level the research playing field so that the achievements of faculty at smaller, leaner, and often newer institutions are not obscured by those of the established leaders.

N O T E S
■

Introduction

1. The term *research university* refers loosely to four-year institutions offering the doctoral degree and requiring research achievement as well as teaching performance (and campus service) for faculty advancement and tenure. In this book the term refers to those institutions designated in the Carnegie classification system as belonging to the Research I and II and Doctoral I and II categories. A modern variant, used increasingly since the late 1970s, is *research-intensive university.*

2. Robert M. Rosenzweig, *The Research Universities and Their Patrons* (Berkeley: University of California Press, 1982), 1.

3. Ibid., 1–3.

4. David S. Webster, "America's Highest Ranked Graduate Schools, 1925–1982," *Change* 15 (May–June 1983): 14–24.

5. J. Fredericks Volkwein, "Changes in Quality among Public Universities," *Journal of Higher Education* 60 (Mar.–Apr. 1989): 136–51; William G. Bowen and Neil L. Rudenstine, *In Pursuit of the Ph.D.* (Princeton: Princeton University Press, 1992), 62–68.

6. See, e.g., the discussion of reputational rankings in National Research Council, *Research-Doctorate Programs in the United States* (Washington, D.C.: National Academy Press, 1995), 21–23.

7. Robert Merton, "The Matthew Effect in Science," *Science* 159 (1968): 156–63; idem, "The Self-Fulfilling Prophecy," in *Social Theory and Social Structure* (New York: Free Press, 1968), 475–90; Jonathan Cole and S. Cole, *Social Stratification in Science* (Chicago: University of Chicago Press, 1973), 191–209; Jonathan Cole and J. Lipton, "The Reputations of American Medical Schools," *Social Forces* 55 (1977): 3–4.

8. Examples include Paul Von Blum, *Stillborn Education: A Critique of the American Research University* (Lanham, Md.: University Press of America, 1986); Marcel C. Lafollette, *Stealing into Print: Fraud, Plagiarism, and Misconduct in Scientific Publishing* (Berkeley: University of Cal-

ifornia Press, 1992); Sheila Slaughter, *The Higher Learning and High Technology* (Albany: State University of New York Press, 1990); Page Smith, *Killing the Spirit: Higher Education in America* (New York: Viking Press, 1990); Charles J. Sykes, *Profscam: Professors and the Demise of Higher Education* (New York: Regnery Gateway, 1988); Bruce Wilshire, *The Moral Collapse of the University* (Albany: State University of Albany Press, 1990).

9. Roger L. Geiger, *To Advance Knowledge: The Growth of American Research Universities, 1900–1940* (New York: Oxford University Press, 1986); idem, *Research and Relevant Knowledge: American Research Universities since World War II* (New York: Oxford University Press, 1993).

10. Stephen R. Graubard, "The Research University: Notes toward a New History," in *The Research Universities in a Time of Discontent,* ed. Jonathan R. Cole, Elinor G. Barber, and Stephen R. Graubard (Baltimore: Johns Hopkins University Press, 1994), 361–90.

11. Allan M. Cartter, *An Assessment of Quality in Graduate Education* (Washington, D.C.: American Council on Education, 1966); Kenneth D. Roose and Charles J. Andersen, *A Rating of Graduate Programs* (Washington, D.C.: American Council on Education, 1970); Lyle V. Jones, Gardner Lindzey, and Porter E. Coggeshall, eds., *An Assessment of Research-Doctoral Programs in the United States* (Washington, D.C.: National Academy Press, 1982); National Research Council, *Research-Doctorate Programs in the United States.* Technically, the studies published by the National Academy Press in 1982 and 1995 were sponsored by the Conference Board of Associated Research Councils.

12. See David S. Webster, *Academic Quality Rankings of American Colleges and Universities* (Springfield, Ill.: Thomas, 1986).

13. For example, the National Research Council's 1995 study covered 3,634 doctoral programs in forty-one academic fields at 274 universities. Its program rankings were determined largely by subjective ratings of the quality of program faculties, based on a reputational survey of approximately eight thousand faculty members. The published report included objective data on program faculty, including their journal publications and citations.

14. Determining faculty size is often problematic, especially when dealing with campus medical schools (for a detailed discussion see the Note on Method and Sources). The research indicators we employ to attain institutional measures lack the precision provided by program-specific comparisons. The latter may be calculated with considerable precision—for example, the average federal R&D award per chemistry professor or the average number of journal articles per law professor. Another attempt to develop institutional measures is the Research Activity Index (RAI), which annually ranks institutions according to fourteen statistical variables (such as expenditure of R&D dollars, number of full-time scientists and engineers, number of Ph.D.'s awarded). The RAI, however, does not control for institutional size. See Larry L. Leslie and Kenneth G.

Brown, "Beyond R&D Expenditure Ranking: The Scale of Research Activity in American Universities," *NACUBO Business Officer* (Apr. 1988): 36–40; Randall Groth, Kenneth Brown, and Larry L. Leslie, "Research Activity in Major Research Universities: An Alternative Ranking System," *SRA Journal* 23 (spring 1992): 23–33.

15. Robert Kelley, *Transformations: The University of California, Santa Barbara, 1909–1979* (Santa Barbara: Associated Students of UCSB, 1981).

Chapter 1: Origins of the American Research University

1. Elinor G. Barber, ed., *Foreign Student Flows,* Institute of International Education Research Report no. 7 (Washington, D.C.: IIE, 1984), 19.

2. By 1976 only four nations counted their Nobel laureates in more than one digit: the United States had won 105 Nobel prizes, Great Britain 58, Germany 50, and France 21. See Harriet Zuckerman, *Scientific Elite: Nobel Laureates in the United States* (New York: Free Press, 1977), 25–35. When Zuckerman wrote, all seventy-seven Nobel laureates affiliated with American universities and research institutes were men. The two American female laureates — Gerty Cori (medicine, 1947) and Maria Coeppert Mayer (physics, 1963)—had died in 1957 and 1972, respectively. The literature of science and science policy prior to the 1970s is relentlessly masculinist. The Jacques Cattell Press and R. R. Bowker Company changed the title of *American Men of Science* to *American Men and Women of Science* only in 1973, for the twelfth edition.

3. Henry Rosovsky, *The University: An Owner's Manual* (New York: Norton, 1990), 29.

4. Ibid., 30. The poll to which Rosovsky referred was reported in the *Wall Street Journal,* 5 May 1986. The inclusion of Tokyo and the Sorbonne among the world's top ten, Rosovsky wrote, would be difficult to defend on objective grounds.

5. Jaroslav Pelikan, *The Idea of the University: A Reexamination* (New Haven: Yale University Press, 1992); Noel Annan, "Hint: It's More than One Idea," *New York Times,* 24 May 1992.

6. James Bryce, *The American Commonwealth,* 3d ed. (New York: Macmillan, 1893), 667. Bryce noted that Ohio's closest claim to a university, the state institution at Columbus, had only thirty-two teachers and thirteen graduate students. Almost half of its 386 undergraduate students were in the college preparatory department.

7. Abraham Flexner, *Universities: American, English, and German* (New York: Oxford University Press, 1931); Thorstein Veblen, *The Higher Learning in America* (New York: Viking, 1935).

8. In Germany and Switzerland, universities controlled by subnational governments—the German *länder* and the Swiss cantons— showed some resemblances to American state universities, but private

institutions played no significant role in the European systems. For a comparison of higher education systems in Germany, Japan, Switzerland, and the United States which emphasizes the public-private and centralized-decentralized dichotomies, see A. J. Heidenheimer, "Government and Higher Education in Unitary and Federal Political Systems," *Encyclopedia of Higher Education*, ed. Burton R. Clark and Guy Neave (Oxford: Pergamon Press, 1992), 924–34.

9. See generally Burton R. Clark, *The Higher Education System: Academic Organization in Cross-National Perspective* (Berkeley: University of California Press, 1987).

10. Bryce, *American Commonwealth*, 666. Bryce reported that of the 118,581 students enrolled in American colleges and universities in 1890, 44,133 were studying in the collegiate department and 39,415 were in the preparatory department.

11. The forgoing summary is inherently reductionist, doing little justice to the variety that enriches the comparative study of higher education. Policies and traditions in the British university system, for example, often fall somewhere between the continental model and the American one. Moreover, since the 1960s there has been some international convergence toward the American model. See Burton R. Clark, *Places of Inquiry: Research and Advanced Education in Modern Universities* (Berkeley: University of California Press, 1995), pt. 2; Heidenheimer, "Government and Higher Education," 924–34.

12. For an emphasis on distinctive national traditions in higher education, see Barbara B. Burn et al., *Higher Education in Nine Countries* (New York: McGraw-Hill, 1971); Clark, *Places of Inquiry*, pt. 1.

13. Clark, *Higher Education System*, 28–71; Joseph Ben-David, *Fundamental Research and the Universities: Some Comments on International Differences* (Paris: Organisation for Economic Cooperation and Development, 1968), 29–44.

14. Burton R. Clark, ed., *The Academic Profession: National, Disciplinary, and Institutional Settings* (Berkeley: University of California Press, 1987), 375; Clark, *Places of Inquiry*.

15. Joseph Ben-David, *The Scientist's Role in Society: A Comparative Study* (Englewood Cliffs, N.J.: Prentice-Hall, 1971), 139–68; Martin Trow, "Aspects of Diversity in American Higher Education," in *On the Making of Americans*, ed. Herbert Gans et al. (Philadelphia: University of Pennsylvania Press, 1979), 271–90.

16. Martin Trow, "American Higher Education: Exceptional or Just Different?" in *Is America Different? A New Look at American Exceptionalism*, ed. Byron E. Shafer (Oxford: Clarendon Press, 1991), 140. Our discussion of American exceptionalism is indebted to Trow's insightful comparative analysis.

17. Edward Shils, "The American Private University," *Minerva* 11 (1973): 6.

18. Roger L. Geiger, *Private Sectors in Higher Education: Structure*,

Function, and Change in Eight Countries (Ann Arbor: University of Michigan Press, 1986), 161–95.

19. In order of their founding, the nine colonial colleges were Harvard, 1636; William and Mary, 1693; Yale, 1701; the College of New Jersey (later Princeton), 1746; King's College (Columbia), 1754; the College and Academy of Philadelphia (University of Pennsylvania), 1755; Rhode Island College (Brown), 1764; Queen's College (Rutgers), 1766; and Dartmouth, 1769.

20. Richard Hofstadter and Walter P. Metzger, *The Development of Academic Freedom in the United States* (New York: Columbia University Press, 1955), 115–51.

21. Christopher J. Lucas, *American Higher Education: A History* (New York: St. Martin's, 1994), 103–82.

22. John S. Whitehead and Jurgen Herbst, "How to Think about the Dartmouth College Case," *History of Education Quarterly* 26 (fall 1986): 333–49.

23. Like the colonial colleges, many institutions founded in the nineteenth century subsequently changed their names, often several times. For example, Duke, founded as Brown's Schoolhouse in 1838, was known as Trinity College from 1859 to 1924; Tulane, established as the Medical College of Louisiana in 1834, adopted its present name in 1884. For the sake of readability, short and familiar names will be used for educational institutions throughout—e.g., Berkeley, Caltech, Chicago, Michigan, Stony Brook, UCLA—except where a longer form is needed for clarity.

24. Earle D. Ross, *Democracy's College: The Land-Grant Movement in the Formative Stage* (Ames: Iowa State College Press, 1942). In some states, land-grant designation went to private institutions. These states included Connecticut (Yale's Sheffield Scientific School), Massachusetts (the Massachusetts Institute of Technology), and New York (Cornell); and in Kentucky and Oregon land-grant funds went to denominational colleges that remained under church control. In 1890 a "second Morrill Act" provided funds on a state matching basis to establish agricultural and mechanical colleges for African Americans.

25. Raymond M. Hughes, *A Study of the Graduate Schools of America* (Oxford, Ohio: Miami University Press, 1925). In 1934 Hughes conducted a second study with similar results: Hughes, *Report of the Committee on Graduate Instruction* (Washington, D.C.: American Council on Education, 1934).

26. Frederick Rudolph, *The American College and University: A History* (New York: Knopf, 1962); Laurence R. Vesey, *The Emergence of the American University* (Chicago: University of Chicago Press, 1965); Geiger, *To Advance Knowledge.*

27. The founding member institutions of the AAU in 1900 were Catholic University, Clark, Columbia, Cornell, Harvard, Johns Hopkins, Princeton, Stanford, California, Chicago, Michigan, Pennsylvania, Wisconsin, and Yale. Between 1904 and 1925 the AAU admitted twelve new

members: Virginia (1904); Illinois, Minnesota, and Missouri (1908); Indiana, Iowa, Kansas, and Nebraska (1909); Ohio State (1916); Northwestern (1917); North Carolina (1922); and Washington University (1923).

28. Trow, "American Higher Education," 144–47; Lucas, *American Higher Education*, 165–70, 210–15.

29. Raymond Walters, *Four Decades of U.S. Collegiate Enrollments* (New York: Society for the Advancement of Education, 1960); Calvin B. T. Lee, *The Campus Scene, 1900–1970* (New York: McKay, 1970).

30. Prior to World War II and the development of multicampus public university systems in California, Illinois, New York, and other urban-industrial states, the major research campuses were commonly referred to by their state name—"California" (or "Cal") meant the Berkeley campus, "Illinois" meant the University of Illinois at Urbana, "Texas" the Austin campus, and so forth. Because multicampus systems brought some confusion over campus designations, increasing use was made of the term *flagship*, an informal designation referring to the historic "main" campus, as distinct from subsequent expansion campuses. For the sake of simplicity, we generally follow this convention throughout the text. For example, "Wisconsin" refers only to the Madison campus, but Wisconsin-Madison may be used for clarification when the discussion also involves Wisconsin-Milwaukee. For some large multicampus state systems, abbreviations are used—e.g., UC San Diego, SUNY-Albany.

31. This development widened the difference between graduate students studying for masters and doctoral degrees in the arts and sciences and engineering, and professional students training for practice in fields such as medicine, law, architecture, and divinity. For the latter, advanced study was generally full-time, involved no teaching duties, and required greater financial investment (often leading to substantial indebtedness upon graduation) but required fewer years of study.

32. James Axtell, "The Death of the Liberal Arts College," *History of Education Quarterly* 11 (winter 1971): 339–52. In the 1880s student enrollments were larger at Williams than at Cornell and Indiana, and were as large at Amherst as at Wisconsin and Virginia.

33. Criticism of the corporate model of American higher education found an early voice in Veblen's *The Higher Learning in America* (1935), and since the 1960s a robust literature has attacked academic careerism and the entrepreneurial university. For a recent synopsis, see Lucas, *American Higher Education*, 267–97.

34. See, e.g., Hofstadter and Metzger, *Academic Freedom*, 115–51; Jurgen Herbst, *From Crisis to Crisis: American College Government, 1636–1819* (Cambridge: Harvard University Press, 1982); Clark Kerr and Marian L. Gade, *The Guardians: Boards of Trustees of American Colleges and Universities* (Washington, D.C.: Association of Governing Boards of Universities and Colleges, 1989).

35. Trow, "American Higher Education," 148.

36. Roger L. Geiger, "Organized Research Units—Their Role in the De-

velopment of University Research," *Journal of Higher Education* 61 (Jan.–Feb. 1990): 2.

37. Ben-David, *Fundamental Research and the Universities*, 19–27; Derek J. de Sola Price, *Little Science, Big Science* (New York: Columbia University Press, 1963), 96.

Chapter 2: The Revolution in Federal Science Policy

1. Alexander J. Morin, *Science Policy and Politics* (Englewood Cliffs, N.J.: Prentice-Hall, 1993).

2. Roger L. Geiger, *To Advance Knowledge: The Growth of American Research Universities, 1900–1940* (New York: Oxford University Press, 1986).

3. See James Phinney Baxter III, *Scientists against Time* (Boston: Little Brown, 1946); Irwin Stewart, *Organizing Scientific Research for War: The Administrative History of the Office of Scientific Research and Development* (Boston: Little Brown, 1948); Carroll Purcell, "Science Agencies in World War II: The OSRD and Its Challengers," in *The Sciences in the American Context*, ed. Nathan Reingold (Washington, D.C.: Smithsonian Press, 1979).

4. Daniel J. Kevles, "The National Science Foundation and the Debate over Postwar Research Policy, 1942–1945," *Isis* 68 (1977): 5–26.

5. Bruce L. R. Smith, *American Science Policy since World War II* (Washington, D.C.: Brookings Institution, 1990), 40–52; Jeffrey K. Stine, *A History of Science Policy in the United States, 1940–1985*, Task Force on Science Policy, House Committee on Science and Technology, 99th Congress, 2d sess. (Washington, D.C.: U.S. Government Printing Office, 1986), 15–24.

6. Vannevar Bush, *Science—The Endless Frontier: A Report to the President on a Program for Postwar Scientific Research* (Washington, D.C.: U.S. Government Printing Office, 1945); idem, *Pieces of the Action* (New York: Morrow, 1970), 64–68; Kevles, "National Science Foundation," 16–18; J. Merton England, "Dr. Bush Writes a Report: *Science—The Endless Frontier,*" *Science* 191 (1976): 41–47.

7. Bush, *Science—The Endless Frontier,* 19; James L. Penick Jr. et al., eds., *The Politics of American Science, 1939 to the Present* (Chicago: Rand McNally, 1965), 54–64.

8. J. Merton England, *A Patron for Pure Science: The National Science Foundation's Formative Years, 1945–57* (Washington, D.C.: National Science Foundation, 1982); John T. Wilson, *Academic Science, Higher Education, and the Federal Government, 1950–1983* (Chicago: University of Chicago Press, 1983), 1–30.

9. On the politics of federal policy in the postwar years, see J. Leiper Freeman, *The Political Process: Executive Bureau–Legislative Committee Relations* (New York: Random House, 1955); Douglass Cater, *Power in Washington* (New York: Vintage, 1964).

10. U.S. Advisory Commission on Intergovernmental Relations, *Categorical Grants: Their Role and Design* (Washington, D.C.: U.S. Advisory Commission, 1978), 15–31.

11. On agency-committee relationships in federal education policy, see Hugh Davis Graham, *The Uncertain Triumph: Federal Education Policy in the Kennedy and Johnson Years* (Chapel Hill: University of North Carolina Press, 1984), 190–93.

12. The ONR enjoyed the advantage of inheriting an unexpended appropriation of $40 million from wartime construction funds. The navy's entrepreneurs in government-sponsored research, like their enterprising counterparts at the NIH, used the OSRD contract model, including merit competition for research awards, to sponsor a broad array of research relationships in the universities and in research institutes such as the Woods Hole Oceanographic Institute and the Scripps Institution of Oceanography. The research sponsored by the navy included many pure-science projects that had little apparent direct utility for national defense. The ONR's first chief scientist, Alan T. Waterman, became the first director of the NSF. National Research Council, *Federal Support of Basic Research in Institutions of Higher Learning* (Washington, D.C.: National Academy of Sciences, 1964), 35–75; David K. Allison, "U.S. Navy Research and Development since World War II," in *Military Enterprise and Technological Change*, ed. Merrit Rae Smith (Cambridge: MIT Press, 1985), 289–328.

13. Corbin Allardia and Edward R. Trapnell, *The Atomic Energy Commission* (New York: Praeger, 1974); George T. Mazuzan and J. Samuel Walker, *Controlling the Atom: The Beginnings of Nuclear Regulation, 1946–1962* (Berkeley: University of California Press, 1985); Richard G. Hewlett and Jack M. Holl, *Atoms for Peace and War, 1953–1960* (Berkeley: University of California Press, 1989); Brian Balogh, *Chain Reaction: Expert Debate and Public Participation in American Commercial Nuclear Power, 1945–1977* (New York: Cambridge University Press, 1991).

14. See Donald C. Swain, "The Rise of a Research Empire: NIH, 1930–1950," *Science* 138 (1962): 1233–37; Stephen P. Strickland, *Politics, Science, and Dread Disease: A Short History of United States Medical Research Policy* (Cambridge: Harvard University Press, 1972).

15. Executive Order 10521, 17 Mar. 1954, reprinted in National Science Foundation, *Fourth Annual Report, for the Fiscal Year Ending June 30, 1954* (Washington, D.C.: U.S. Government Printing Office, 1954), 118–19; National Academy of Sciences, *Federal Support of Basic Research in Institutions of Higher Learning* (Washington, D.C.: National Research Council, 1964), 35–52.

16. Smith, *American Science Policy*, 36–72; Morin, *Science Policy and Politics*, 28–41.

17. Roger L. Geiger, *Research and Relevant Knowledge: American Research Universities since World War II* (New York: Oxford University Press, 1993), 30–61.

18. Ibid., 166–73, quotation on 168.

19. The so-called Seaborg Report was published as President's Science Advisory Committee, *Scientific Progress, the Universities, and the Federal Government* (Washington, D.C.: U.S. Government Printing Office, 1960).

20. James R. Killian, *Sputnik, Scientists, and Eisenhower* (Cambridge: MIT Press, 1977); Bruce L. R. Smith, *The Advisors: Scientists in the Policy Process* (Washington, D.C.: Brookings Institution, 1992). For a contemporary critical view, see Daniel S. Greenberg, *The Politics of Pure Science* (New York: New American Library, 1967).

21. President's Science Advisory Committee, *Scientific Progress, the Universities, and the Federal Government*, 10–11.

22. National Science Foundation, *National Patterns of Science and Technology Resources: 1987*, NSF-88-305 (Washington, D.C.: National Science Foundation, 1987), table B-5.

23. Geiger, *Research and Relevant Knowledge*, 198–203. The three studies of federal-university relationships are Charles V. Kidd, *American Universities and Federal Research* (Cambridge: Harvard University Press, 1959); Harold Orlans, *The Effects of Federal Programs on Higher Education* (Washington, D.C.: Brookings Institution, 1962); and Carnegie Foundation for the Advancement of Teaching, *Annual Report* (1962–63), 9–70.

24. Roger Geiger, looking at the top ten research universities, emphasizes the steady postwar decline of concentration. In 1952 the top ten institutions received 43.4 percent of all federal obligations for university R&D; in 1958 their share was 37 percent, and in 1968, 27.7 percent. See Roger L. Geiger, "The American University and Research" (paper presented at symposium sponsored by National Academy of Sciences, Washington, D.C., 23 Mar. 1989), 22.

25. Clark Kerr, *The Uses of the University* (Cambridge: Harvard University Press, 1963), 50.

26. *First Annual Report of the National Science Foundation, 1950–1951* (Washington, D.C.: U.S. Government Printing Office, 1951), vii.

27. Kerr, *Uses of the University*, 55. Kerr was including in his calculations funds for approximately thirty federal contract centers, such as the Lawrence Radiation Laboratory at Berkeley, which were operated by universities under federal contract. Because funding for contract research centers was negotiated outside the normal peer-review process, federal agencies by the mid-1960s excluded funding for contract research centers from the federal R&D obligations they reported for universities and colleges. Had Kerr referred to project research alone, in 1963 the share won by the top six universities (Berkeley among them) would have been 28 percent, and the share won by the top twenty institutions, 54 percent.

28. National Science Foundation, *Federal Support for Academic Science and Other Educational Activities in Universities and Colleges, Fiscal Year 1965*, NSF 66-30 (Washington, D.C.: U.S. Government Printing Office, 1966).

29. Kerr, *Uses of the University*, 50.

30. Robert K. Merton, "The Matthew Effect in Science," *Science* 159 (1968): 56–63.

31. Harriet Zuckerman, *Scientific Elites* (New York: Free Press, 1977), 250. Zuckerman based her 1965 dissertation on interviews with forty-one of the fifty-six American Nobel science laureates living in the United States in 1963. In *Scientific Elites* she expanded the study to include seventy-seven science laureates living in the United States in 1976.

32. Ibid., table 3–8, 90.

33. The 6-percent allocation for nonscience expenditures included Office of Education funds for undergraduate facilities and equipment and for fellowships and training in fields other than science and engineering.

34. Raymond M. Hughes, *A Study of the Graduate Schools of America* (Oxford, Ohio: Miami University Press, 1925). In 1934 Hughes conducted a similar study with similar findings for the American Council on Education.

35. David S. Webster, "America's Highest Ranked Graduate Schools, 1925–1982," *Change* 15 (May–June 1983): 14–24, aggregated departmental scores in the major studies of graduate programs and ranked institutions according to their department-level performance.

36. Hayward Keniston, *Graduate Study and Research in the Arts and Sciences at the University of Pennsylvania* (Philadelphia: University of Pennsylvania Press, 1959).

37. The early NSF reports often aggregated federal funding for multicampus public university systems, such as Alabama, Illinois, Maryland, and Tennessee, even though the state university's medical school, and the arts-and-sciences or "flagship" campus, were located in different cities.

38. Allan M. Cartter, *An Assessment of Quality in Graduate Education* (Washington, D.C.: American Council on Education, 1966).

39. Kenneth D. Roose and Charles J. Andersen, *A Rating of Graduate Programs* (Washington, D.C.: American Council on Education, 1970).

40. See David S. Webster, *Academic Quality Rankings of American Colleges and Universities* (Springfield, Ill.: Thomas, 1986).

41. Smith, *American Science Policy*, 40–52.

42. President's Science Advisory Committee, *Scientific Progress, the Universities, and the Federal Government* (Washington, D.C.: U.S. Government Printing Office, 15 Nov. 1960), 14.

43. House Committee on Science and Astronautics, Subcommittee on Science, Research, and Development, *Geographic Distribution of Federal Research and Development Funds,* Government and Science Report no. 4, 88th Cong., 2d sess., 1965. In the process of assisting the House investigation, the NSF produced the first detailed report on federal R&D funding by agency and recipient organization, concentrating on fiscal year 1963.

44. Ken Hechler, *Toward the Endless Frontier: History of the Commit-*

tee on Science and Technology, 1959–79 (Washington, D.C.: U.S. Government Printing Office, 1980).

45. House Committee, *Geographic Distribution*, 48.

46. Ibid., 27–29, 31–34.

47. Ibid., 54–55.

48. Lyndon B. Johnson, "Strengthening Academic Capabilities for Science throughout the Country," memorandum to heads of departments and agencies, 14 Sept. 1965, *Public Papers of the Presidents of the United States: Lyndon B. Johnson, 1965* (Washington, D.C.: U.S. Government Printing Office, 1966), 995–98.

49. Stuart Bruchey, *Enterprise: The Dynamic Economy of a Free People* (Cambridge: Harvard University Press, 1990), 491–94.

50. Laure M. Sharp, Barton Sensenig, and Lenore Reid, *Study of NDEA Title IV Fellowship Program* (Washington, D.C.: Bureau of Social Science Research, 1968).

51. National Science Foundation, *Federal Support for Academic Science and Other Education Activities in Universities and Colleges, Fiscal Years 1963–1966* (Washington, D.C.: U.S. Government Printing Office, 1967), vii.

52. Lawrence E. Gladieux and Thomas R. Wolanin, *Congress and the Colleges: The National Politics of Higher Education* (Lexington, Mass.: Lexington Books, 1975), 15–32.

53. Geiger, *Research and Relevant Knowledge*, 94–116, 184. The major foundations channeled much of their support through the Social Science Research Council, and the chief beneficiaries were private universities. In 1967 the National Institute of Mental Health, the chief funding source for academic psychology, became an independent institute within the Public Health Service.

54. James L. Penick Jr., *Politics of American Science*, rev. ed. (Cambridge: MIT Press, 1972), 333–36; W. Henry Lambright, *Presidential Management of Science and Technology: The Johnson Presidency* (Austin: University of Texas Press, 1985), 68–71, 80–84.

55. England, *Patron for Pure Science*, 266–73.

56. National Science Foundation, *Resources for Scientific Activities at Universities and Colleges, 1969* (Washington, D.C.: U.S. Government Printing Office, 1970), 1–10.

57. The 1968 amendments required the NSF, which previously had reported to Congress only through the appropriations subcommittees, to participate in annual hearings before the science authorization committees in both houses. Further, Congress in 1968 increased its oversight and control by shifting the foundation's five top officials from "career" to "political" status in the civil service schedules, and by requiring presidential appointment and hence Senate confirmation for the NSF's deputy director and four assistant directors. Stine, *History of Science Policy*, 50–55; Wilson, *Academic Science*, 30–34.

58. For three years following Johnson's executive order of September

1965, the Committee on Academic Science and Engineering (CASE) of the Federal Council for Science and Technology collected data on federal support for universities and colleges from eight federal agencies, and the NSF had published the data in annual reports. By 1968, the CASE data-collection system had expanded to include twelve federal agencies, and this provided the base for the NSF's first annual report to the president and Congress.

59. Roger L. Geiger, "The Dynamics of University Research in the United States, 1945–90," in *Research and Higher Education: The United Kingdom and the United States,* ed. Thomas G. Whiston and Roger L. Geiger (Buckingham, U.K.: Society for Research into Higher Education and Open University Press, 1991), 9.

60. Government-University-Industry Research Roundtable, *Science and Technology in the Academic Enterprise* (Washington, D.C.: National Academy Press, 1989), p. 1-6.

61. In 1968 AAU membership was held by forty-five institutions. Leadership was provided by roughly twenty-five to thirty universities whose names commonly appeared on the "top twenty" or "top twenty-five" lists in the periodic reputational rankings. Like an exclusive club, the AAU has had a history of bitter disputes over membership. Representation was weakest in the South, the High Plains, and the Rocky Mountain states. Two public universities in Canada, McGill and Toronto, were admitted in 1926. Clark University, a founding member of the group of fourteen doctorate-granting institutions that formed the AAU in 1900, never achieved the growth and status in graduate education and research which had originally been anticipated. See Hugh Hawkins, *Banding Together: The Rise of National Associations in American Higher Education, 1887–1950* (Baltimore: Johns Hopkins University Press, 1992), 13–15, 73–77, 84–88.

62. The HEW budget for university R&D in 1963 was $333 million. R&D obligations at the NIH ($298 million) accounted for 90 percent of the HEW total, and 94 percent of the R&D budget of the Public Health Service, which contained the NIH.

63. Research and development funding for universities at the Department of Defense during 1963–68 grew from $218 million to $243 million, a 2-percent decrease when controlled for inflation. During the same period the number of university-administered federal contract centers increased from twenty-three to thirty-six, but the federal budget for the centers grew only slightly, from $814 million to $945 million, a 2-percent increase when controlled for inflation.

64. Created in 1953, HEW was an institutional triad with weak functional relationships between its programs for health, welfare, and education. The welfare component was dominated by the Social Security Administration and had little connection with universities outside of their schools of social welfare. The Office of Education, a tiny and politically insignificant office engaged since the Civil War in gathering educational sta-

tistics, became through the Higher Education Facilities Act of 1963 a significant funding agency for construction loans and grants. USOE was transformed into a powerful policy-making agency by the Civil Rights Act of 1964 and the Elementary and Secondary Education Act of 1965. In 1978 Congress split HEW into the Department of Education (DE) and the Department of Health and Human Services (HHS).

65. Among the institutions refusing federal contracts and grants was Grove City College, a liberal arts college of Presbyterian affiliation in Pennsylvania whose rejection of institutional assistance and its accompanying regulation from Washington led to a major conflict between the U.S. Supreme Court and Congress during the Reagan administration.

66. In the public sector, state support for research fell as federal support grew. In 1968 state and local governments provided only 11.7 percent of the sponsored research budgets at doctorate-granting institutions, the contribution of foundations and voluntary health associations had declined to 6 percent, and support from private industry had fallen to 2.5 percent. On average, federal dollars in 1968 provided more than half of the sponsored research support at most doctorate-granting institutions, and 62 percent of the sponsored research expenditures at the twenty top-ranked recipients in federal R&D. National Science Foundation, *Resources for Scientific Activities at Universities and Colleges, 1969* (Washington, D.C.: U.S. Government Printing Office, 1970), table B-21.

Chapter 3: Comparing Universities in the Golden Decade of the 1960s

1. Some data—for example, institutional totals for full-time faculty and publications in scientific journals—were reported with less precision in the 1960s than in the 1980s (see the Note on Methods and Sources). This limits the authority of generalizations about individual universities in the earlier period.

2. Allan M. Cartter, *An Assessment of Quality in Graduate Education* (Washington, D.C.: American Council on Education, 1966); Kenneth D. Roose and Charles J. Andersen, *A Rating of Graduate Programs* (Washington, D.C.: American Council on Education, 1970).

3. Janet K. Lawrence and Kenneth C. Green, *A Question of Quality: The Higher Education Ratings Game,* ERIC/Higher Education Research Report No. 5 (Washington, D.C.: American Association for Higher Education, 1980); David S. Webster, *Academic Quality Rankings of American Colleges and Universities* (Springfield, Ill.: Thomas, 1986).

4. In addition to the comparative studies and rankings, and more useful in policy analysis during the post-*Sputnik* decade, were several studies of federal government–university relations and federal science policy. These include A. Hunter Dupree, *Science in the Federal Government* (Cambridge: Harvard University Press, 1959); Dael Wolfle, *Science and*

261

Public Policy (Lincoln: University of Nebraska Press, 1959); James L. Mc-Cary, *Science and Public Administration* (Tuscaloosa: University of Alabama Press, 1960); Alice Rivlin, *The Role of the Federal Government in Financing Higher Education* (Washington, D.C.: Brookings Institution, 1961); Harold Orlans, *The Effect of Federal Programs on Higher Education* (Washington, D.C.: Brookings Institution, 1962); Robert Gilpin and Christopher Wright, eds., *Scientists and National Policy Making* (New York: Columbia University Press, 1964); Don K. Price, *The Scientific Estate* (Cambridge: Harvard University Press, 1965); and James L. Penick Jr. et al., *The Politics of American Science, 1939 to the Present* (Chicago: Rand-McNally, 1965).

5. Ellen Condliffe Lagemann, *Private Power for the Public Good: A History of the Carnegie Foundation for the Advancement of Teaching* (Middletown, Conn.: Wesleyan University Press, 1983), 66–74; idem, *The Politics of Knowledge: The Carnegie Corporation, Philanthropy, and Public Policy* (Middletown, Conn.: Wesleyan University Press, 1989), 136–43, 220–29.

6. Carnegie Commission on Higher Education, *New Students and New Places: Policies for the Future Growth and Development of American Higher Education* (New York: McGraw-Hill, 1971), 5.

7. According to the Carnegie taxonomy, Research I universities awarded at least fifty Ph.D.'s (including M.D.'s) annually and ranked among the top fifty recipients of federal financial support for academic science. Research II universities awarded at least fifty Ph.D.'s and ranked among the top hundred in federal support. Doctoral I universities awarded at least forty Ph.D.'s annually *or* received at least $3 million in total federal assistance; Doctoral II universities annually awarded at least ten Ph.D.'s. For details on classifying criteria, see Carnegie Commission on Higher Education, *A Classification of Institutions of Higher Education* (Berkeley, Calif.: Carnegie Commission on Higher Education, 1973), 1–5.

8. For 1960s AAUP data, see, e.g., William J. Baumol and Peggy Heim, "The Annual Report on the Economic Status of the Profession, 1967–1968," *AAUP Bulletin* 54 (summer 1968): 181–241.

9. The early NSF reports often listed single, systemwide totals in the various federal support categories for multicampus systems, such as the universities of California and Illinois.

10. Most frequently cited among the postwar comparative studies, in addition to the Cartter and Roose-Andersen reports, are Heyward Keniston, *Graduate Study and Research in the Arts and Sciences at the University of Pennsylvania* (Philadelphia: University of Pennsylvania Press, 1959); and Lyle V. Jones, Gardner Lindzey, and Porter E. Coggeshall, eds., *An Assessment of Research-Doctoral Programs in the United States* (Washington, D.C.: National Academy Press, 1982). For institutional rankings compiled from the departmental-level data in these reports, see David S. Webster, "America's Highest Ranked Graduate Schools, 1925–1982," *Change* 15 (May–June 1983): 14–24.

11. Daryl E. Chubin and Edward J. Hackett, *Peerless Science: Peer*

Review and U.S. Science Policy (Albany: State University of New York Press, 1990), 165–90.

12. "Chicago-Kent Law Review Faculty Scholarship Survey," *Chicago-Kent Law Review* 65 (1989): 195, 208.

13. Eugene E. Garfield, *Citation Indexing: Its Theory and Application in Science, Technology, and Humanities*, 3 vols. (New York: Wiley Interscience, 1979).

14. James S. Fairweather, *Entrepreneurship and Higher Education* (Washington, D.C.: Association for the Study of Higher Education, 1988); David Osborne, *The Laboratories of Democracy* (Cambridge, Mass.: Harvard Business School Press, 1988); Thomas J. Chmura, *The Higher Education–Economic Development Connection: Emerging Roles for Public Colleges and Universities in a Changing Economy* (Washington, D.C.: American Association of State Colleges and Universities, 1987).

15. Clark Kerr, *The Uses of the University* (Cambridge: Harvard University Press, 1963), 65–67.

16. Martin J. Finkelstein, *The American Academic Profession: A Synthesis of Social Scientific Inquiry since World War II* (Columbus: Ohio State University Press, 1984), 96–105.

17. Baumol and Hein, "Economic Status of the Profession, 1967–1968." Because the AAUP's annual salary surveys requested that institutions exclude the faculty in medical schools, these data had to be added by the authors. Thus the AAUP total of 1,982 full-time faculty for Michigan State in 1967–68 was increased to 2,049 when medical school faculty were added. Caltech, for example, without a medical school, required no additions to the 241 full-time faculty listed by the AAUP. For further discussion see the Note on Method and Sources.

18. Scores aggregated from the Roose-Andersen data produced a rank of twentieth for Caltech, and for Michigan State a tie for twenty-fourth with North Carolina. See Webster, "America's Highest Ranked Graduate Schools," 23.

19. Like most scientific and technological institutions, Caltech was organized by division rather than by college or school. The Caltech divisions were biology; chemistry; engineering; geology; humanities and social science; and physics, mathematics, and astronomy. Michigan State, a land-grant institution, was organized into colleges of arts and letters, natural science, social science, agriculture and natural resources, business, communications, education, engineering, home economics, medicine, and veterinary science.

20. James S. Fairweather, "Reputational Quality of Academic Programs: The Institutional Halo," *Research in Higher Education* 28 (1988): 345–55. The volumes of data periodically published by the American Council on Education in the *American Universities and Colleges* series provide valuable information in a common format for most institutions, although variations exist in the form and content of the information that institutions have been willing to supply.

21. The data for the 1960s and 1970s provide reliable guidance, on the other hand, for generalizations about the performance of groups of institutions. This includes comparisons of public and private institutions, and comparisons by Carnegie class, by output variables (R&D dollars, publications, fellowships), by region, and by change over time.

22. The share of total academic R&D expenditures devoted to research outside the sciences (provided by federal agencies, foundations, and the academic institutions themselves) rose from 7 percent in the late 1950s to peak at 14 percent in the late 1960s, and then fell back below 10 percent in the 1980s. See Government-University-Industry Research Roundtable, *Science and Technology in the Academic Enterprise: Status, Trends, Issues* (Washington, D.C.: National Academy Press, 1989), p. 2–23.

23. Large R&D projects such as the major national laboratories and accelerators (e.g., the Jet Propulsion Laboratory operated by Caltech in Pasadena under federal contract), are separately funded through the federal funded R&D centers (FFRDCs) and thus are not included in the institutional totals for federal R&D funding.

24. American Council of Learned Societies, *Scholarly Communication: The Report of National Enquiry* (New York: ACLS, 1978); William D. Garvey, *The Essence of Science* (Oxford: Pergamon Press, 1979); Duncan Lindsey, *The Scientific Publication System in the Social Sciences* (San Francisco: Jossey-Bass, 1978); Douglas N. Jackson and Philippe Rushton, eds., *Scientific Excellence: Origins and Assessment* (Newbury Park, Calif.: Sage, 1987); Marcel C. Lafollette, *Stealing into Print: Fraud, Plagiarism, and Misconduct in Scientific Publishing* (Berkeley: University of California Press, 1992).

25. From these sources the ISI identified more than 3.6 million citations to authored items, crediting them to the first-named author and to that person's institutional affiliation. *Science Citation Index, 1968,* vol. 1 (Philadelphia: Institute for Scientific Information, 1969). Science publication information was available on a computer database in the mid-1970s. Thus, for 1968 articles were counted by hand.

26. In the Research I class, for example, the product-moment correlation between institutional rankings on R&D and publications in 1968 was + .76 for public institutions and + .59 for private institutions.

27. Theodore R. Vallance, "Classified Research and Related Issues in Science Communication," *American Association of University Professors Bulletin* 55 (autumn 1969): 360–65; Sheila Slaughter, *The Higher Learning and High Technology* (Albany: State University of New York Press, 1990), 41–50.

28. The publications index excludes books because of practical limitations. Book records such as Bowker's *Books in Print,* although available in machine-readable form, identify books by author, title, subject, and publisher, but not by the institutional affiliation of their authors.

29. For example, during 1965–74 faculty at Yale received 161 fellowships. During this period the 959 full-time faculty at Yale produced an

A&H index of .1679. This ratio was multiplied by 10 and rounded to 1.68 to reduce decimal-point clutter in the tables. The A&H index for the 1960s includes NEH but not NEA fellowships—see the Note on Method and Sources. This index was also replicated for the 1980s. See chapter 5, below.

30. Edward Shils, "The American Private University," *Minerva* 11 (1973): 6–27.

31. Roger L. Geiger, *Private Sectors in Higher Education* (Ann Arbor: University of Michigan Press, 1986), 176.

32. Hugh Hawkins, *Between Harvard and America* (New York: Oxford University Press, 1973); Brooks Mather Kelley, *Yale: A History* (New Haven: Yale University Press, 1974); Richard J. Storr, *Harper's University: The Beginnings* (Chicago: University of Chicago Press, 1966); Paul K. Conkin, *Gone with the Ivy: A Biography of Vanderbilt University* (Knoxville: University of Tennessee Press, 1985); Thomas H. English, *Emory University, 1915–1965* (Atlanta: Emory University, 1966).

33. John E. Burchard, *Q.E.D.: MIT in World War II* (New York: Wiley, 1948), 128.

34. Rashi Fein and Gerald I. Weber, *Financing Medical Education* (New York: McGraw-Hill, 1971), 11–76.

35. As schools of medicine were brought under the umbrella of academic health centers, deans of medicine increasingly reported to the center's chief academic officer, typically a provost or vice chancellor for the health professions. These organizational trends reflected the budgetary strength and independence of health science schools and reinforced a dualism in university structures. See Organization and Governance Project, *The Organization and Governance of Academic Health Centers: Report for the Organization and Governance Project of the Association of Academic Health Centers* (Washington, D.C.: Association of Academic Health Centers, 1980), 3–52.

36. Separate health science campuses, such as the University of California, San Francisco, and the University of Maryland, Baltimore, usually included schools of medicine, nursing, dentistry, and pharmacy.

37. According to David Webster's aggregation of the Roose-Andersen 1970 data on graduate programs, the twenty top-rated institutions were, in rank order: Berkeley, Harvard, Stanford, Michigan, Yale, Wisconsin, Chicago, Princeton, Illinois, UCLA, Cornell, Columbia, Washington, Pennsylvania, MIT, Minnesota, Texas, Indiana, Hopkins, Caltech. Webster, "America's Highest Ranked Graduate Schools," 23.

38. For the data used to determine institutional structures discussed in this section, see *American Universities and Colleges* (Washington, D.C.: American Council on Education, 1964, 1968, 1973).

39. Schools of education, however, were typically of intermediate size, and schools of agriculture were often large. The thirteen schools of education in the Roose-Andersen top-eighteen group averaged 112 faculty each. The schools of agriculture at five large Midwestern land-grant uni-

265

versities (Illinois, Michigan State, Ohio State, and Purdue) averaged 266 faculty each. Programs in agriculture and education enjoyed targeted funding from federal mission agencies, but their R&D funding and especially their publications fell considerably below the levels found in medicine, engineering, and science programs.

40. In fiscal 1968, federal research funding was $403,123 for the school of nursing at Yale and $153,300 for the school of forestry. By comparison, Yale's school of medicine received $16.7 million in federal R&D funds in fiscal 1968 and the college of arts and science (Yale College) received $14.8 million. Yale University, Summary of Grants and Contracts, 1968–69, Office of Institutional Research, supplied to the authors by Yale University.

41. Peter M. Blau and Rebecca Margulies, "The Reputations of American Professional Schools," *Change* 6 (1974–75): 42.

42. Four institutions are excluded from the list: two single-school, scientific institutions, Caltech and MIT; Princeton, which resembled Caltech and MIT in its patterns of research funding and its lack of a medical school; and Cornell, owing to its dual location (Ithaca and New York City) and its mixed private and public control. A private university of "endowed" colleges (of arts and sciences, engineering, law, and hotel administration), Cornell also included four public "statutory" colleges (of agriculture, home economics, veterinary medicine, and industrial and labor relations). The discussion of faculty staffing is drawn from data in the 1968 edition of *American Universities and Colleges.*

43. The rough trifurcation of the arts-and-sciences faculty into science, social science, and arts-and-humanities clusters was equally characteristic of public and private universities. At Stanford in 1968, for example, the division of full-time faculty by area in the School of Humanities and Sciences was as follows: arts and humanities, 179 (36.9%); social science (including history), 149 (30.8%); and science, 156 (32.2%). A comparison at four private campuses (Duke, Harvard, Stanford, and Yale) and four public campuses (Michigan, North Carolina, Texas, and UCLA) produced similar distributions in the 30–38 percentile range. The chief exceptions were science at Yale (24%) and North Carolina (25%), and social science at Michigan (40%).

The size of departments in the arts and sciences, however, varied widely. While departments with heavy teaching commitments, such as English and history, tended to be large on all campuses, those departments with leading national reputations were often exceptionally large. At Yale, for example, English held 67 full-time faculty in 1968, economics 53, and history 63; at Michigan, the psychology department had a faculty of 128, and mathematics had 84.

44. For the seven private universities in the sample, the averages were 39 percent of the full-time campus faculty in medicine and the health science schools and 13 percent in the scientific disciplines in the college of arts and sciences.

45. The public universities held an advantage in engineering, both because schools of engineering were more commonly found on public campuses, and because such schools were typically larger than those at private universities.

46. Typical in this regard is *American Higher Education: A History* (New York: St. Martin's, 1994), by Christopher J. Lucas. In this otherwise comprehensive and well-documented survey, there is no mention of Abraham Flexner and no discussion at all of American medical education.

47. Several major state universities without medical schools often included other health science schools on campus — for example, Berkeley (with schools of optometry and public health), Indiana (dentistry, nursing), Nebraska (dentistry, pharmacy). Schools of pharmacy were located, for example, at Georgia, Oklahoma, Purdue, and Texas. Approximately half of the sixty-one schools of nursing on college and university campuses in 1968 were at institutions (especially land-grant institutions) lacking schools of medicine.

48. Paul Starr, *The Social Transformation of American Medicine* (New York: Basic Books, 1982), 112–22.

49. William G. Rothstein, *American Medical Schools and the Practice of Medicine* (New York: Oxford University Press, 1987), 224–28.

50. The economically vulnerable medical schools in the 1960s included several Jesuit schools associated with urban universities — Creighton, Georgetown, Loyola Stritch, Marquette, and Saint Louis — as well as several private schools not affiliated with universities — Chicago Medical School, Hahnemann, Jefferson, Meharry, and Women's Medical College. During the 1960s, four financially troubled private medical schools shifted to public control: University of Buffalo School of Medicine (shifted to SUNY-Buffalo), California College of Medicine (shifted to UC Irvine), the University of Pittsburgh (shifted to public control without name change), and Seton Hall College of Medicine and Dentistry (shifted to the New Jersey College of Medicine and Dentistry). See Fein and Weber, *Financing Medical Education,* 39–76.

51. Because adjunct teaching affiliation with a medical school provided practicing physicians and surgeons with hospital privileges, patient referrals, and professional prestige, the part-time medical faculty often outnumbered the full-time regular faculty. Columbia's College of Physicians and Surgeons in 1968, for example, listed 412 full-time and 687 part-time faculty. In Baltimore, the Johns Hopkins School of Medicine listed 403 full-time and 571 part-time faculty.

52. In American medical schools, M.D. students are called "undergraduates" even though baccalaureate degrees are required for admission. Basic science departments typically included anatomy, cell biology, biochemistry, microbiology and immunology, pathology, pharmacology, physiology, and toxicology. Rothstein, in *American Medical Schools,* 250–51, argues that medical education suffered from overemphasis on research in glamorous fields such as molecular biology.

53. Between 1958 and 1972 the number of Ph.D.'s awarded by American universities grew from 8,773 to 33,041, an increase of 277 percent; during the same period the number of M.D. awards grew from 7,011 to 10,105, an increase of 44 percent. William G. Bowen and Neil L. Rudenstine, *In Pursuit of the Ph.D.* (Princeton: Princeton University Press, 1992), table G.2-1, 378; Anne E. Crowley, Sylvia I. Etzel, and Edward S. Petersen, "Undergraduate Medical Education," *Journal of the American Medical Association* 254 (1985): 1568.

54. Clinical departments typically included anesthesiology, medicine, neurology, obstetrics-gynecology, opthalmology, orthopedics, pediatrics, preventive medicine–public health, psychiatry, radiology, and surgery.

55. Rachel Carson, *Silent Spring* (Boston: Houghton Mifflin, 1962); Gino J. Marco, Robert H. Hollingworth, and William Durham, *Silent Spring Revisited* (Washington, D.C.: American Chemical Society, 1987).

56. Alvan R. Feinstein, Neal Koss, and John H. Austin, "The Changing Emphasis in Clinical Research," *Annals of Internal Medicine* 66 (1967): 396–408; Alvan R. Feinstein and Neal Koss, "The Changing Emphasis in Clinical Research," *Archives of Internal Medicine* 125 (1970): 885–91.

57. Marjorie Price Wilson and Curtis P. McLaughlin, *Leadership and Management in Academic Medicine* (San Francisco: Jossey-Bass, 1984), 224–64.

58. Irving J. Lewis and Cecil G. Sheps, *The Sick Citadel: The American Academic Medical Center and the Public Interest* (Cambridge, Mass.: Oelgeschlager, Gunn, and Hain, 1983), 165–73.

59. Ray E. Brown, "Financing Medical Education," in *The Future of Medical Education,* ed. William G. Anlyan et al. (Durham, N.C.: Duke University Press, 1973), 173–92.

60. Roger L. Geiger, "Organized Research Units — Their Role in the Development of University Research," *Journal of Higher Education* 61 (Jan.–Feb. 1990): 1–19.

61. In 1968 there were twenty-three schools of public health in the United States accredited by the Association of Schools of Public Health. All were associated with universities — sixteen public and seven private. By far the largest, and generally considered the world's finest, was the one at Johns Hopkins. Other top-ranked schools of public health included Harvard, Columbia, and Yale, among private institutions; and in the public sector, Michigan, North Carolina, Washington, and Berkeley.

62. Chubin and Hackett, *Peerless Science,* 125–53.

63. Note, however, that in table 3.8, among public institutions, the nonmedical campuses show higher average A&H scores than their counterparts at campuses with medical schools. Medical schools elevate R&D and publications index scores but, by increasing the number of faculty while not increasing arts and humanities fellowships, they lower A&H scores. The superior A&H index scores shown by the private universities

with medical schools, produced despite the inclusion of medical faculty, reflect elite traditions of nourishing the arts and humanities.

64. Hugh Davis Graham, "Structure and Governance in American Higher Education: Historical and Comparative Analysis in State Policy," *Journal of Policy History* 1 (winter 1989): 80–107.

65. Examples of this type among Research-class institutions in 1968 included the state universities of Arizona, Florida, Hawaii, Kentucky, Minnesota, Missouri, West Virginia, and Wisconsin, and Ohio State. Land-grant designation refers to the Morrill Act of 1862. In 1890 the "Second Morrill Act" provided for the designation of historically black land-grant institutions. In 1968, however, none of these was classified as doctorate-granting. See Ralph D. Christy and Lionel Williamson, eds., *A Century of Service: Land-Grant Colleges and Universities, 1890–1990* (New Brunswick, N.J.: Transaction, 1992).

66. States with such pairings in 1968 included Iowa, North Carolina, Utah, Virginia, and Washington. Prior to the 1960s, the land-grant universities in Michigan (Michigan State) and Texas (Texas A&M) also fit this pattern.

67. Several of the Research-class institutions with medical schools (table 3.9) established new medical schools or upgraded limited medical programs during the nationwide expansion of higher education during the 1960s. Arizona, UC Davis, Hawaii, and Michigan State were among the public universities that did so. Among private universities, Brown established a full medical program during these years, and Louisville and Pittsburgh, two private universities with medical schools, became public institutions (Pittsburgh in 1966 and Louisville in 1970). Among Doctoral I institutions, public sector medical schools existed at New Mexico, and new medical programs were established at UC Irvine and SUNY–Stony Brook. Full medical degree programs were being planned at South Carolina and South Dakota, and Ohio University included an osteopathic medical school. Private Doctoral I universities with medical schools included Dartmouth, Georgetown, Howard, Louisville (private until 1970), and Saint Louis. There were no medical schools among institutions in the Doctoral II category.

68. Government-University-Industry Research Roundtable, *Science and Technology in the Academic Enterprise: Status, Trends, Issues* (Washington, D.C.: National Academy Press, 1989), pp. 1-5, 1-6.

Chapter 4: The Stagnant Decade Revisited

1. See, e.g., Clark Kerr, "What We Might Learn from the Climacteric," *Daedalus* 2 (winter 1975): 1–7; Bruce L. R. Smith and Joseph J. Karlesky, eds., *The State of Academic Science: The Universities in the Nation's Research Effort*, 2 vols. (New York: Change Magazine Press, 1978); Roger L. Geiger, "The Dynamics of University Research in the United States, 1945–90," in *Research and Higher Education: The United Kingdom and*

the United States, ed. Thomas G. Whiston and Roger L. Geiger (Buckingham, U.K.: Society for Research into Higher Education and Open University, 1991), 3–17.

2. Others who emphasize university adaptations include Eric Ashby, *Adapting Universities to a Technological Society* (San Francisco: Jossey-Bass, 1974); Verne A. Stadtman, *Academic Adaptations: Higher Education Prepares for the 1980s and 1990s* (San Francisco: Jossey-Bass, 1980); Richard M. Freeland, *Academia's Golden Age: Universities in Massachusetts, 1945–1970* (New York: Oxford University Press, 1992).

3. American Association of Universities, *The Federal Financing of Higher Education* (Washington, D.C.: Association of American Universities, 1968), 6; Carnegie Commission on Higher Education, *Quality and Equality: New Levels of Federal Responsibility for Higher Education* (Berkeley: Carnegie Commission, 1968).

4. Earl Cheit, *The New Depression in Higher Education* (New York: McGraw-Hill, 1970).

5. President's Task Force on Higher Education, *Priorities in Higher Education* (Washington, D.C.: U.S. Government Printing Office, 1970). See also U.S. House of Representatives, *Higher Education Amendments of 1971: Hearings before the House Education and Labor Committee,* 92d Cong., 1st sess., 1971. For the Senate proposal, see Carnegie Commission on Higher Education, *Institutional Aid: Federal Support to Colleges and Universities* (New York: McGraw-Hill, 1972), app. K, 251.

6. American Association of University Professors, "At the Brink: Report on the Economic Status of the Profession, 1970–71," *AAUP Bulletin* 57 (summer 1971): 223.

7. *The Gallup Poll Index,* report no. 61 (July 1970), 3.

8. Major discussions of the financial problems facing higher education during the late 1960s and early 1970s include William G. Bowen, "Economic Pressures on the Major Private Universities," *The Economics and Financing of Higher Education in the United States* (Washington, D.C.: U.S. Government Printing Office, 1969), 399–439; William W. Jellema, *The Red and the Black: Special Preliminary Report on the Financial Status, Past and Present, of Private Institutions of Higher Education* (Washington, D.C.: Association of American Colleges, 1971); Cheit, *New Depression in Higher Education;* Cheit, *The New Depression in Higher Education—Two Years Later* (New York: McGraw-Hill, 1972); Lyle H. Lanier and Charles J. Andersen, *A Study of the Financial Conditions of Colleges and Universities, 1972–1975* (Washington, D.C.: American Council on Education, 1975); and Smith and Karlesky, *State of Academic Science;* Roger L. Geiger, *Research and Relevant Knowledge: American Research Universities since World War II* (New York: Oxford University Press, 1993), chaps. 8 and 9, summarized the financial constraints of the 1970s.

9. On coordinating and governing boards see Robert O. Berdahl, *Statewide Coordination of Higher Education* (Washington, D.C.: American Council on Education, 1971); for multicampus systems, see Eugene C. Lee

and Frank M. Bowen, *The Multicampus University: A Study of Academic Governance* (New York: McGraw-Hill, 1971); and James A. Perkins, *Higher Education—From Autonomy to System* (New York: International Council for Educational Development, 1972). The process of delocalization was named by Walter P. Metzger, "Academic Freedom in Delocalized Academic Institutions," in *Dimensions of Academic Freedom,* ed. Metzger et al. (Urbana: University of Illinois Press, 1969), 1–33.

10. Carnegie Commission on Higher Education, *New Students and New Places: Policies for the Future Growth and Development of American Higher Education* (New York: McGraw-Hill, 1971), 1–2.

11. Stadtman, *Academic Adaptations,* 7; National Center for Education Statistics, *The Condition of Education, 1978 Edition* (Washington, D.C.: U.S. Government Printing Office, 1978).

12. American Council on Education, *A Fact Book on Higher Education* (Washington, D.C.: American Council on Education, 1975), tables 75.65, 75.87.

13. Ivan Berg, *Education and Jobs: The Great Training Robbery* (New York: Praeger, 1970); Caroline Bird, *The Case against College* (New York: McKay, 1975).

14. Government-University-Industry Research Roundtable, *Science and Technology in the Academic Enterprise: Status, Trends, and Issues* (Washington, D.C.: National Academy Press, 1989), p. 1-7; William G. Bowen and Neil L. Rudenstine, *In Pursuit of the Ph.D.* (Princeton: Princeton University Press, 1992).

15. National Center for Education Statistics, *Digest of Educational Statistics, 1977–78* (Washington, D.C.: U.S. Government Printing Office, 1978), 104.

16. Allan M. Cartter, *Ph.D.'s and the Academic Labor Market* (New York: McGraw-Hill, 1976).

17. The data is from the Carnegie Council Surveys of 1978, cited in Stadtman, *Academic Adaptations,* 50. Seventy-nine percent of Research I and 67 percent of Research II officials polled expressed this view.

18. Alan C. Bayer, *Teaching Faculty in Academe, 1972–73,* ACE Research Reports, vol. 8, no. 2 (Washington, D.C.: American Council on Education, 1973), 17. A major report on tenure known as the Keast Report was sponsored by the American Association of University Professors and the Association of American Colleges (AAC); see Commission on Academic Tenure in Higher Education (William R. Keast, chairman), *Academic Tenure: Report of the Commission* (San Francisco: Jossey-Bass, 1973). On staff planning and related issues see W. Todd Furniss, *Steady-State Staffing in Tenure-Granting Institutions, and Related Papers* (Washington, D.C.: American Council on Education, 1973).

19. For discussions of nonfaculty research personnel during the late 1960s and early 1970s, see Carlos E. Kruytbosch and Sheldon L. Messinger, "Unequal Peers: The Situation of Researchers at Berkeley," *American Behavioral Scientist* 11 (May-June 1968): 33–43; Carlos E.

Kruytbosch, *The Organization of Research in the University: The Case of Research Personnel* (Ph.D. diss., University of California, Berkeley, 1970); and Smith and Karlesky, *State of Academic Science* 1:237. Albert H. Teich, *Trends in the Organization of Academic Research: The Role of ORUs and Full-time Researchers* (Washington, D.C.: George Washington University Graduate Program in Science, Technology and Public Policy, June 1978), discusses the two-tiered employment system.

20. National Research Council, *Nonfaculty Doctoral Research Staff in Science and Engineering* (Washington, D.C.: National Research Council, 1978).

21. Walter Hobbs, ed., *Government Regulation of Higher Education* (Cambridge, Mass.: Ballinger, 1978), 16–18. Collective bargaining in the private sector was dealt a severe blow when the U.S. Supreme Court decided in early 1980 that faculty members at Yeshiva University were, in effect, the managers of the institution and that their professional interests could not be separated from that of the institution. *NLRB v. Yeshiva University*, 48 U.S.L.W. at 4179. Trustees of other private universities and colleges that refused to bargain with faculty unions were upheld by the courts on the basis of the Yeshiva decision. See Clark Kerr and Marian Gade, "Current and Emerging Issues Facing American Higher Education," in *Higher Education in American Society*, ed. Philip G. Altbach and Robert O. Berdahl (Buffalo: Prometheus Books, 1981), 145–46.

22. Joseph A. Garbarino, *Faculty Bargaining: Change and Conflict* (New York: McGraw-Hill, 1975), 30. See also Seymour Martin Lipset and Everett Carll Ladd, *Professors, Unions, and American Higher Education* (Berkeley: Carnegie Commission on Higher Education, 1973); E. D. Duryea and Robert Fisk, *Faculty Unions and Collective Bargaining* (San Francisco: Jossey-Bass, 1973); and Robert K. Carr and Daniel Van Eyck, *Collective Bargaining Comes to Campus* (Washington, D.C.: American Council on Education, 1973).

23. Dael Wolfle, "Forces Affecting the Research Role of Universities," in Smith and Karlesky, *State of Academic Science* 2:22; National Science Board, *Science and Engineering Indicators, 1989* (Washington, D.C.: U.S. Government Printing Office, 1989), app. table 5-2.

24. Wolfle, "Forces Affecting the Research Role of Universities," 27. Don I. Phillips confirms this trend, noting that funding (in constant dollars) per science and engineering investigator, which had grown at a rate of 4 percent in the prior period, declined slightly between 1972 and 1979. See "Introduction: The Future of Academic Research," in *Research in the Age of the Steady-State University*, ed. Don I. Phillips and Benjamin S. P. Shen (Washington, D.C.: American Association for the Advancement of Science, 1982), 1–19.

25. Geiger, "Dynamics of University Research," 12.

26. Patricia J. Gumport, "The Federal Role in American Graduate Education," in *Higher Education: Handbook of Theory and Research*, ed. John C. Smart, vol. 7 (New York: Agathon Press, 1991), 114.

27. Patricia J. Gumport, "Graduate Education and Organized Research in the United States," in *The Research Foundations of Graduate Education: Germany, Britain, France, United States, Japan*, ed. Burton R. Clark (Berkeley: University of California Press, 1993), 262.

28. Richard M. Nixon, "Special Message to Congress on Higher Education," 19 Mar. 1970, in Chester E. Finn Jr., *Education and the Presidency* (Lexington, Mass.: Heath, 1977), app. B.

29. Carnegie Commission on Higher Education, *Institutional Aid: Federal Support to Colleges and Universities* (New York: McGraw-Hill, 1972), 2.

30. For a historical summary of the federal role in student aid, see Chester Finn Jr., *Scholars, Dollars, and Bureaucrats* (Washington, D.C.: Brookings Institution, 1978), 59–80. For the political history of the 1965 Higher Education Act and its amendments, see James C. Hearn, "The Paradox of Growth in Federal Aid for College Students, 1965–1990," in *Higher Education: Handbook of Theory and Research*, ed. John C. Smart, vol. 9 (New York: Agathon Press, 1993), 94–153.

31. Clark Kerr, "Prologue," *The Great Transformation in Higher Education, 1960–1980* (Albany: State University of New York Press, 1991), xviii. Kerr noted that such institutional support would have become very vulnerable during the Reagan years, as compared to student aid, which was seen as more politically secure.

32. For discussions of the Higher Education Amendments of 1972 and the policy debate that surrounded their passage, see Lawrence E. Gladieux and Thomas R. Wolanin, *Congress and the Colleges* (Lexington, Mass.: Heath, 1976); and Finn, *Education and the Presidency*. Chester E. Finn, "Federal Patronage of Universities: A Rose by Many Other Names?" in *The University and the State: What Role for Government in Higher Education?* ed. Sidney Hook, Paul Kurtz, and Miro Todorovich (Buffalo: Prometheus Books, 1978), table 2, 330–32, summarizes federal obligations for fiscal year 1974 by type of activity.

33. Finn, *Scholars, Dollars, and Bureaucrats*, 37.

34. Later in the decade, the Education Amendments of 1976 reauthorized all of the existing student aid programs, and in 1978 the Middle-Income Student Assistance Act expanded eligibility requirements for most existing student aid programs.

35. Finn, *Scholars, Dollars, and Bureaucrats*, 66.

36. Geiger, *Research and Relevant Knowledge*, 250.

37. Ken Hechler, *Toward the Endless Frontier: History of the Committee on Science and Technology, 1959–1979* (Washington, D.C.: U.S. Government Printing Office, 1980), 612.

38. Assembly on University Goals and Governance, "Theses," *Daedalus* (winter 1975): 323, 336; similar opinions were expressed in Frank Newman et al., *Report on Higher Education* (Washington, D.C.: U.S. Government Printing Office, 1971), 33.

39. Thane Gustafson, "The Controversy over Peer Review," *Science*

190 (1975): 1061. On the NSF study see Stephen Cole, L. Rubin, and Jonathan R. Cole, "Peer Review and the Support of Science," *Scientific American* 237 (1977): 34–41.

40. Wolfle, "Forces Affecting the Research Role of Universities," 19. The total from all sources was 13 percent greater in 1976, with most of the increases provided by university funds. See also Dael Wolfle, *The Home of Science: The Role of the University* (New York: McGraw-Hill, 1972); Roger L. Geiger, "The Home of Scientists: A Perspective on University Research," in *The University Research System*, ed. Björn Wittrock and Aant Elzinga (Stockholm: Almquist and Wittsell, 1985), 53–75.

41. Government-University-Industry Research Roundtable, *Science and Technology in the Academic Enterprise*, p. 1-6.

42. For a discussion of the long-term effects of the Mansfield Amendment, see House Committee on Science and Technology, *Science Support of the Department of Defense*, 97th Congress, 2d sess., 1986, 41. Roger L. Geiger, "Science, Universities, and National Defense, 1945–1970," *OSIRIS*, 2d ser., 7 (1992): 26–48, discusses the changing tone of relations between the defense establishment and the nation's universities and the decline in research support from the DOD.

43. Walter S. Baer, "The Changing Relationships: Universities and Other R&D Performers," in Smith and Karlesky, *State of Academic Science* 2:72; Geiger, *Research and Relevant Knowledge*, 241.

44. National Science Board, *Science and Engineering Indicators, 1989*, app. table 5-5.

45. John T. Wilson, *Academic Science, Higher Education, and the Federal Government, 1950–1983* (Chicago: University of Chicago Press, 1983), 37.

46. Bruce L. R. Smith, *American Science Policy since World War II* (Washington, D.C.: Brookings Institution, 1990), 173.

47. Smith and Karlesky, *State of Academic Science* 1:103.

48. The favorable position of the NCI continued, and in 1974 the institute awarded more money for its research grant programs than all of the other institutes with the exception of the National Heart and Lung Institute. John T. Kalberer Jr., "Impact of the National Cancer Act on Grant Support," *Cancer Research* 35 (Mar. 1975): 473–81. Data from *Federal Support to Universities, Colleges, and Other Non-Profit Institutions, FY 1972* (Washington, D.C.: National Science Foundation, 1973), 4.

49. Bruce L. R. Smith and Joseph Karlesky, "The Future Role of American Universities," in Smith and Karlesky, *State of Academic Science* 2:24.

50. National Science Board, *Science and Engineering Indicators, 1989*, app. table 5.5.

51. Ibid. During the Ford administration, ERDA was also given the responsibility for a federal program of assistance to support commercially promising energy technologies. See Harvey A. Averch, *A Strategic Analysis of Academic Science and Technology Policy* (Baltimore: Johns Hopkins University Press, 1985), 61.

52. Harvey Brooks, "Lessons of History: Successive Challenges to Science Policy," in *The Research System in Transition*, ed. Susan E. Cozzens, Peter Healey, Arie Rip, and John Ziman (Dordrecht: Kluwer Academic, 1986), 11–22.

53. See Carl M. York, "Targeted Research: An American Tradition," in Smith and Karlesky, *State of Academic Science* 2:105–11, for a historical review of federal support of targeted research from precolonial times to 1958. York defines "targeted research" activities as those which cut across the spectrum of "basic research," "applied research," and "development," terms used by the NSF to classify federal obligations and expenditures. Targeted research is similar to mission-oriented research in that the funding agency specifies the type of work to be done and solicits proposals on topics of limited scope.

54. For a recent analysis see Daniel J. Kevles, "Cold War and Hot Physics: Science, Security, and the American State, 1945–56," *Historical Studies in Physics and the Biological Sciences* 20 (1990): 239–64.

55. Wolfle, *Home of Science*, 83.

56. The first quotation is from Kenneth R. Crispell, "The Origin of Chaos: Social and Political Forces Affecting the Organization of Academic Health Centers," in Organization and Governance Project, *The Organization and Governance of Academic Health Centers: Report for the Organization and Governance Project of the Association of Academic Health Centers*, vol. 3 (Washington, D.C.: Association of Academic Health Centers, 1980), 8; the second is from William G. Rothstein, *American Medical Schools and the Practice of Medicine: A History* (New York: Oxford University Press, 1987), 254.

57. National Science Board, *Science and Engineering Indicators, 1989*, app. table 5-1; 1976 data from *Research Universities and the National Interest: A Report from Fifteen University Presidents* (New York: Ford Foundation, Feb. 1978), 15.

58. Barbara J. Culliton, "Kennedy Hearings: Year-Long Probe of Biomedical Research Begins," *Science* 193 (1976): 33.

59. National Science Board, *Science and Engineering Indicators, 1989*, app. table 5-2.

60. In 1980 the federal contribution for R&D activities comprised 62 percent of the total at public institutions and 74 percent at private institutions. National Science Board, *Science and Engineering Indicators, 1989*, app. table 5-3.

61. Marilyn McCoy, Jack Krakower, and David Makowki, "Financing at the Leading One Hundred Research Universities: A Study of Financial Dependency, Concentration, and Related Institutional Characteristics," *Research in Higher Education* 15 (1981): 336.

62. Martin Trow, "The Public and Private Lives of Higher Education," *Daedalus* 104 (winter 1975): 113–27.

63. Robert S. Hatfield, "Introduction," in *Bureaucrats and Brainpower: Government Regulation of the Universities*, ed. Paul Seabury (San Fran-

cisco: Institute for Contemporary Studies, 1979), 2. Between 1965 and 1977 the number of pages in the *Federal Register* devoted to the regulation of higher education increased tenfold, from ninety-two to one thousand.

64. Chester E. Finn, "Exploring the Regulatory Swamp," in Finn, *Scholars, Dollars, and Bureaucrats*, 139–74, provides an overview of the increased regulations affecting universities during the 1970s. For civil rights and affirmative action legislation affecting higher education see Caspar W. Weinberger, "Regulating the Universities," in Seabury, *Bureaucrats and Brainpower*, 47–70. Dallin H. Oaks, "A Private University Looks at Government Regulation," *Journal of College and University Law* 1 (1976): 1–12, discusses Internal Revenue Service rulings. According to some, the higher level of accountability to Washington threatened institutional autonomy and academic freedom. See William J. McGill, "Government Regulation and Academic Freedom," in Hook, Kurtz, and Todorovich, *University and the State*, 139–54; and Allan Bloom, "A Response to President McGill," in ibid., 155–204.

65. David Z. Robinson, "Government Contracting for Academic Research: Accountability in the American Experience," in *The Dilemma of Accountability in Modern Government*, ed. Bruce L. R. Smith and D. C. Hague (New York: St. Martin's, 1971), 114. See also Senate Subcommittee on Education of the Committee on Labor and Public Welfare, *Higher Education Oversight, 1974: Hearings on the Financial Plight, the Stability, and Conditions of Higher Education Institutions*, 93d Cong., 2d sess., 27 Nov. 1974, 140; Edward L. Whalen, "Federal Regulations as Negative Grants," in *Subsidies to Higher Education: The Issues*, ed. Howard P. Tuckman and Edward Whalen (New York: Praeger, 1980), 142–54.

66. Derek Bok, *President's Report, 1974–75* (Cambridge, Mass.: Harvard University Press, 1974–75). These costs included the costs of complying with new regulations such as the Buckley Amendment (which by opening previously confidential files to students complicated the keeping of records) and of administering government programs in equal opportunity, occupational health and safety, environmental protection, and pension reform. For the perspectives of other presidents see Oaks, "Private University Looks at Government Regulation," 8–9; Robben W. Fleming, "Who Will Be Regulated and Why?" in *Government Regulation of Higher Education*, ed. Walter C. Hobbs (Cambridge, Mass.: Ballinger, 1978), 11–24; and Richard R. Lyman, "Federal Regulation and Institutional Autonomy: A University President's View," in Seabury, *Bureaucrats and Brainpower*, 27–46.

67. Louis W. Bender, *Federal Regulation and Higher Education* (Washington, D.C.: American Association for Higher Education, 1977), 1–4, 74–79, summarizes the major studies. For contemporary discussions see George Bonham, "Will Patronage Kill the Universities?" *Change* (winter 1975–76): 11–12; Robert A. Scott, "More than Greenbacks and Red Tape: The Hidden Costs of Government Regulation," *Change* (Apr. 1978):

16–23; H. S. Gutowsky, "Federal Funding of Basic University Research in the Red Tape Mill," *Science* 212 (1981): 636–41.

68. Carolyn Van Alstyne and Sharon L. Coldren, *The Costs of Implementing Federally Mandated Social Programs at Colleges and Universities* (Washington, D.C.: American Council on Education, 1976), 14–15.

69. Howard R. Bowen, *The Costs of Higher Education: How Much Do Colleges and Universities Spend per Student and How Much Should They Spend?* (New York: McGraw Hill, 1980). Bowen's estimate of "7 or 8 percent" included costs resulting from employee fringe benefits, women's athletics, demands for statistical reports, and the Buckley Amendment.

70. "Analyzing Campus Costs of Federal Programs," *Chronicle of Higher Education*, 3 Nov. 1975, 12.

71. Irene K. Spero, *Government and Higher Education: A Summary of Twenty-one Institutional Self-Studies* (Washington, D.C.: Sloan Commission on Government and Higher Education, Jan. 1978).

72. National Commission on Research, *Accountability: Restoring the Quality of the Partnership* (Washington, D.C.: National Commission on Research, Mar. 1980). The commission's recommendations are summarized by Linda S. Wilson, "Accountability in Federally-Supported University Research," in *The Research System in the 1980s: Public Policy Issues*, ed. John M. Longsdon (Philadelphia: Franklin Institute Press, 1982), 53–54.

73. OMB Circular A-21 established the rules and criteria used in determining allowable costs and the share of indirect costs that can be allocated to the university. See "Office of Management and Budget Circular A-21: Principles for Determining Costs Applicable to Grants, Contracts and Other Agreements," *Federal Register* 44:12368–80.

74. Indirect costs from the perspective of the 1970s are discussed in Sanford A. Lakoff, "Accountability and the Research University," in Smith and Karlesky, *State of Academic Science* 2:175–180; Raymond J. Woodrow, *Indirect Costs in Universities* (Washington, D.C.: American Council on Education, Mar. 1976). See also Robert L. Sproull, "Regulation and the Natural Sciences," in Seabury, *Bureaucrats and Brainpower*, 71–94; Emanuel Donchin and Linda Wilson, "Negotiating the Indirect Cost of Research," *American Psychologist* 40 (July 1985): 836–48; and Kenneth T. Brown, "Indirect Costs of Federally Supported Research," *Science* 212 (1981): 411–18.

75. "Executive Summary," in Organization and Governance Project, *Organization and Governance of Academic Health Centers* 1:1–3.

76. The Health Manpower Assistance Amendments of 1976 also sought to change the distribution of physicians by specialty through outright control of the number of residencies in each area. For an account of the origins and background of this legislation, see Antonin Scalia, "Guadalajara! A Case Study in Regulation by Munificence," *Regulation* 2 (Mar.–Apr. 1978): 23–29.

77. The medical schools that would not comply were Baylor, the five University of California medical schools (at Davis, Irvine, UCLA, San

Diego, and San Francisco), Chicago, Duke, Illinois, Johns Hopkins, Northwestern, Stanford, and Yale.

78. Trow, "Public and Private Lives of Higher Education," 120.

79. Geiger, *Research and Relevant Knowledge*, 259.

80. Smith and Karlesky, *State of Academic Science*, vol. 1; G. J. Nozika, *Federally Funded Research and Development at Universities and Colleges: A Distributional Analysis* (Washington, D.C.: Moshman Associates, 1978), 153, observed only a slight trickle-down of funding from the leading institutions, occurring only in those years when federal funding increased significantly.

81. *Research Universities and the National Interest*, 5.

82. Rudy Abramson, "Patron on the Potomac: The National Science Foundation," *Change* (May-June 1971): 38.

83. The dispersion of federal research funding and of academic research during the 1970s is discussed by Wolfle, "Forces Affecting the Research Role of Universities"; and Jennifer Krohn, "Advancing Research Universities: A Study of Institutional Development, 1974–1986" (Ph.D. diss., Pennsylvania State University, 1992). The increased university contribution during the 1980s is documented by Roger L. Geiger and Irwin Feller, "The Dispersion of Academic Research in the 1980s," *Journal of Higher Education* 66 (May-June 1995): 336–60. Roger L. Geiger, "Historical Patterns of Change in Academic Research," in *Science and Technology Policy Yearbook, 1994*, ed. Albert H. Teich, Stephen D. Nelson, and Celia McEnaney (Washington, D.C.: American Association for the Advancement of Science, 1994), 403–18, offers three views of the expansion of academic research.

84. Smith and Karlesky, *State of Academic Science* 2:12.

85. Wolfle, "Forces Affecting the Research Role of Universities," 17–53.

86. Krohn, "Advancing Research Universities"; Geiger and Feller, "Dispersion of Academic Research," 337.

87. Wolfle, "Forces Affecting the Research Role of Universities," 42. Wolfle (48–49) identifies first-tier universities as those receiving $30 million or more of federal research funds in 1963–65 and second-tier universities as those receiving from $10 million to $30 million of federal research funds during 1963–65.

88. Rothstein, *American Medical Schools*, 247. See also American Medical Association, *Money and the Medical Schools* (Chicago: American Medical Association, 1963), 44; Grace M. Carter et al., *Federal Manpower Legislation and Academic Health Centers* (Santa Monica, Calif.: Rand, 1974), 73.

89. David Perry, David R. Challoner, and Robert J. Oberst, "Research Advances and Research Constraints," *New England Journal of Medicine* 305 (1981): 320–23.

90. National Science Board, *Science and Engineering Indicators, 1993* (Washington, D.C.: National Academy of Sciences, 1993), app. table 5-10.

91. Martin J. Finkelstein, *The American Academic Profession: A Synthesis of Social Scientific Inquiry since World War II* (Columbus: Ohio State University Press, 1984), 53.

92. Bayer, *Teaching Faculty in Academe, 1972–73*, 17.

93. Martin Trow, *Aspects of American Higher Education, 1969–1975* (Berkeley: Carnegie Council on Policy Studies in Higher Education, 1977), 9.

94. National Science Foundation, *Young and Senior Science and Engineering Faculty, 1974: Support, Research Participation, and Tenure*, NSF 75-302 (Washington, D.C.: National Science Foundation, 1975); Frank J. Atelsek and Irene Gomberg, *Faculty Research: Level of Activity and Choice of Area*, Higher Education Panel Report no. 29 (Washington, D.C.: American Council on Education, 1976).

95. Finkelstein, *American Academic Profession*, 34.

96. John A. Muffo and John R. Robinson, "Early Science Career Patterns of Recent Graduates from Leading Research Universities," *Review of Higher Education* 5 (fall 1981): 1–13, found a dramatic increase in lower-ranked public universities' hiring of faculty trained in the top ten institutions. Similar results were found for graduates of the twenty-five top-ranked institutions.

97. Richard Bentley and Robert Blackburn, "Changes in Academic Research Performance over Time: A Study of Institutional Accumulative Advantage," *Research in Higher Education* 31 (1990): 327–53.

98. Such declines in market share are discussed by Wolfle, "Forces Affecting the Research Role of Universities"; Krohn, "Advancing Research Universities"; and Geiger and Feller, "Dispersion of Academic Research."

99. For the 1970s, faculty data was published in "Hard Times: Report on the Economic Status of the Profession," *AAUP Bulletin* (summer 1974):171–243. The number of medical faculty excluded from the AAUP report, obtained from the American Association of Medical Colleges, was added to the AAUP totals.

100. The work of Jonathan R. Cole and Stephen Cole was particularly influential. See, for example, Cole and Cole, "Scientific Output and Recognition: A Study in the Operation of the Reward System in Science, *American Sociological Review* 32 (1967): 377–90; idem, "Measuring the Quality of Sociological Research: Problems in the Use of the Science Citation Index," *American Sociologist* 6 (1971): 23–30; and idem, *Social Stratification in Science* (Chicago: University of Chicago Press, 1974).

101. See John M. Braxton and Alan R. Bayer, "Assessing Faculty Scholarly Performance," in *Managing Faculty Research Performance*, ed. John W. Creswell (San Francisco: Jossey-Bass, 1986), 25–42; and John W. Creswell, *Faculty Research Performance: Lessons from the Sciences and Social Sciences*, ASHE-ERIC Higher Education Report no. 4 (Washington, D.C.: Association for the Study of Higher Education, 1985), for a summary of studies that used publication counts to assess faculty productivity. Howard P. Tuckman, *Publication, Teaching, and the Academic*

Reward Structure (Lexington, Mass.: Heath, 1976), discussed the relationship of faculty publication to the academic reward structure.

102. National Science Board, *Science Indicators, 1976*, table 34-21. The selected fields included astronomy, biology, and chemistry, as well as economics, political science, sociology, and psychology. The increase in journal space was also discussed by Jeffery P. Bieber and Robert T. Blackburn, "Faculty Research Productivity, 1972–1988: Development and Application of Constant Units of Measure," *Research in Higher Education* 34 (1993): 551–67.

103. David T. Durack, "The Weight of Medical Knowledge," *New England Journal of Medicine* 298 (1978): 774.

104. Richard Bentley and Robert Blackburn, "Changes in Academic Research Performance over Time: A Study of Institutional Accumulative Advantage," *Research in Higher Education* 31, no. 4 (1990): 327–45, support this assertion. Analyzing faculty surveys from 1969 and 1975, Bentley and Blackburn found that according to self-reported surveys from 1969 and 1975, the mean number of publications rose at Carnegie-classified Research I and II, Doctoral I and II, and Comprehensive campuses.

105. In 1968 ISI collected information about publications in the natural and physical sciences only, and published these in printed volumes. Thus, any comparisons between articles published in 1968 and those published in 1974 must necessarily be confined to science disciplines. To determine the number of science publications produced by a campus faculty, a hand count of the 1968 SCI corporate address file was conducted.

106. In all Carnegie categories, the higher number of publications was produced by an increased number of faculty members. See table 4.3. Readers interested in faculty per capita scores during the 1960s and 1970s should contact the authors.

107. A number of studies have emphasized the significant differences in productivity across disciplines. These include Anthony Biglan, "Relationships between Subject Matter Characteristics and the Structure of Output in University Departments," *Journal of Applied Psychology* 57, no. 3 (1973): 204–13; Yoram Neumann, "Standards of Research Publication: Differences between the Physical and Natural Sciences," *Research in Higher Education* 7 (1977): 355–67; Richard A. Wanner, Lionel S. Lewis, and David I. Gregorio, "Research Productivity in Academia: A Comparative Study of the Sciences, Social Sciences, and Humanities," *Sociology of Education* 54 (Oct. 1981): 238–52; and Leonard L. Baird, "Publication Productivity in Doctoral Research Departments: Interdisciplinary and Intradisciplinary Factors," *Research in Higher Education* 32, no. 3 (1991): 303–18. See also Richard C. Anderson, Francis Narin, and Paul McAllister, "Publication Ratings versus Peer Ratings of Universities," *Journal of the American Society for Information Science* (Mar. 1978): 91–103.

108. A number of other studies used per capita publication output to document faculty research achievement during the 1970s. These included David L. Morgan, Richard C. Kierney, and James L. Regens, "As-

sessing Quality among Graduate Institutions of Higher Education in the United States," *Social Science Quarterly* 57 (1976): 670–79; William R. Petrowski, Evan L. Brown, and John A. Duffy, "National Universities and the ACE Ratings," *Journal of Higher Education* 44 (Oct. 1973): 495–513; W. Miles Cox and Virginia Catt, "Productivity Ratings of Graduate Programs in Psychology in the Journals of the American Psychological Association," *American Psychologist* 32 (Oct. 1977): 793–813.

109. See Eugene E. Garfield, *Citation Indexing: Its Theory and Application in Science and Technology and the Humanities* (New York: Wiley, 1979); and David E. Drew, *Science Development: An Evaluation Study* (Washington, D.C.: National Academy of Sciences, 1975).

110. For technical reasons, top journal indexes covering such a large field of institutions could not be constructed earlier than 1974, when the ISI data files for the *Social Science Citation Index* (established in 1972) and the *Science Citation Index* (established in 1974) were both available in machine-readable form.

111. It must be noted that faculty at Harvard, with 840 publications in top-science journals, led all other campuses in the number of publications in top-science journals, but not in the campus's per capita score. Berkeley, with 799 total publications, and MIT, with 780 publications, were second and third.

112. The arts and humanities indexes developed for this study are among the very few documentations of arts and humanities awards for multiyear periods. Lyle V. Jones, G. Lindsey, and Porter Coggeshall, *Assessment of Research and Doctorate Programs* (Washington, D.C.: National Academy Press, 1982), for example, did not include humanities publication data in their assessment. The recent 1995 National Research Council study did include some objective humanities as part of their largely reputational assessment. The dearth of funding for the humanities was discussed by Irene L. Gomberg and Frank J. Atelsek, *Financial Support for the Humanities: A Special Methodological Report,* Higher Education Panel Report no. 56 (Washington, D.C.: American Council on Education, 1983), 2.

113. Both Carnegie Mellon and Vanderbilt would be reclassified as Research I institutions in the Carnegie typology of 1987. The Claremont Graduate School would be classified as Doctoral I under the new schema.

Chapter 5: The Golden Age Redux

1. National Science Board, *Science and Engineering Indicators, 1996* (Washington, D.C.: U.S. Government Printing Office, 1996), app. table 5-8.

2. During the Carter administration and continuing in the 1980s, the White House science advisor and the OSTP faced competing sources of policy advice from within the federal government. Advice came from advisory bodies located elsewhere in the office of the president (e.g., the national security advisor, the NSC staff, the CIA), as well as from mission

agencies (e.g., the director of defense research and engineering, the Office of Energy Research), and increasingly from an assertive Congress (e.g., the Office of Technology Assessment, the Congressional Research Service, and the General Accounting Office). See Gregg Herken, *Cardinal Choices: Presidential Science Advising from the Atomic Bomb to SDI* (New York: Oxford University Press, 1992), 184–98.

3. National Science Foundation Advisory Council, *Continued Viability of Universities as Centers for Basic Research*, Report of Task Group No. 1 (Washington, D.C., 1978).

4. Jimmy Carter, "Science and Technology, Message to Congress," 27 Mar. 1979, in *Public Papers of the Presidents: Jimmy Carter, 1979* (Washington, D.C.: U.S. Government Printing Office, 1980), 528–46; Frank Press, "Science and Technology in the White House, 1977 to 1980," *Science* 211 (1981): 139–45. For the Commerce report see U.S. Commerce Department, Office of the Assistant Secretary for Science and Technology, *Domestic Policy Review of Industrial Innovation* (Springfield, Va.: National Technical Information Service, 1979).

5. Claude E. Barfield, *Science Policy from Ford to Reagan* (Washington, D.C.: American Enterprise Institute, 1982), 10–17.

6. Herken, *Cardinal Choices*, 200–216. Keyworth, head of physics at Los Alamos and protégé of Edward Teller, had not been recruited from the established circle of scientific leaders. Academic scientists criticized Keyworth for acting as a salesman for administration policies, such as the controversial SDI, rather than representing the views of the scientific community to the president.

7. "The Knives Are Out for OSTP," *Science* 226 (1984): 1399–1400; Harvey A. Averch, *A Strategic Analysis of Science and Technology Policy* (Baltimore: Johns Hopkins University Press, 1985), 28–31.

8. "House Science Panel Throws Down the Gauntlet," *Science* 210 (1981): 144–95; Barfield, *Science Policy*, 45–46.

9. *Science and Engineering Indicators, 1991*, app. table 5-8.

10. Liz McMillen, "Foundations and Corporations Concentrate Giving at Top Universities, Study Finds," *Chronicle of Higher Education*, 5 June 1991, A1, A21; Bernard D. Reams Jr., *University-Industry Research Partnerships* (Westport, Conn.: Quorum Books, 1986).

11. David Osborne, *Economic Competitiveness: The States Take the Lead* (Washington, D.C.: Economic Policy Institute, 1987); idem, *The Laboratories of Democracy* (Cambridge: Harvard Business School Press, 1988); Thomas J. Chmura, *The Higher Education–Economic Development Connection* (Washington, D.C.: American Association of State Colleges and Universities, 1987); Peter K. Eisinger, *The Rise of the Entrepreneurial State* (Madison: University of Wisconsin Press, 1988), 266–89; Hugh Davis Graham, "Structure and Governance in Higher Education: Historical and Comparative Analysis in State Policy," *Journal of Policy History* 1 (winter 1989): 80–107.

12. Universities doubled their own research investment partly be-

cause the growth of federal R&D in the 1980s was accompanied by a decline in federal support for the buildings and equipment necessary to sustain research capacity. Between 1980 and 1990, federal support for R&D plant fell from $1,836 million to $1,809 million. *Science and Engineering Indicators, 1991*, app. tables 4-8, 5-11.

13. Ibid., app. tables 4-2, 4-22; Rick Boucher, "A Science Policy for the Twenty-first Century," *Chronicle of Higher Education*, 1 Sept. 1993, B1–B2.

14. See generally Martin Anderson, *Impostors in the Temple: American Intellectuals Are Destroying Our Universities and Cheating Our Students* (New York: Simon and Schuster, 1992); Allan Bloom, *The Closing of the American Mind* (New York: Simon and Schuster, 1987); Paul von Blum, *Stillborn Education: A Critique of the American Research University* (Lanham, Md.: University Press of America, 1986); David Bromwich, *Politics by Other Means: Higher Education and Group Thinking* (New Haven: Yale University Press, 1992); Dinesh D'Souza, *Liberal Education: The Politics of Race and Sex on Campus* (New York: Free Press, 1991); Russell Jacoby, *The Last Intellectuals* (New York: Doubleday, 1987); and idem, *Dogmatic Wisdom: How the Culture Wars Divert Education and Distract America* (New York: Doubleday, 1994); Roger Kimball, *Tenured Radicals: How Politics Has Corrupted Our Higher Education* (New York: Harper and Row, 1989); Charles J. Sykes, *Profscam: Professors and the Demise of Higher Education* (Washington, D.C.: Regnery-Gateway, 1985); Bruce Wilshire, *The Moral Collapse of the University* (Albany: State University of New York Press, 1990).

15. Jim Henderson, "When Scientists Fake It," *American Way*, 1 Mar. 1990; Anthony DePalma, "Foreigners Flood U.S. Graduate Schools," *New York Times*, 29 Nov. 1990; Judy Sarasohn, *Science on Trial: The Whistle-Blower, the Accused, and the Nobel Laureate* (New York: St. Martin's Press, 1993); Julie L. Nicklin, "University Deals with Drug Companies Raises Concerns over Autonomy, Secrecy," *Chronicle of Higher Education*, 24 Mar. 1993, A25–A26; Gary Taubes, *Bad Science: The Short Life and Weird Times of Cold Fusion* (New York: Random House, 1993); Robert L. Park, "A Growing Rebellion against Science," *New York Times*, 16 July 1995.

16. *Science and Engineering Indicators, 1991*, app. table 5-8.

17. Ibid., app. table 5-25.

18. Judith M. Feder, *Medicare: The Politics of Federal Hospital Insurance* (Lexington, Mass.: Lexington Books, 1977).

19. Anne M. Stoline and Jonathan P. Weiner, *The New Medical Marketplace* (Baltimore: Johns Hopkins University Press, 1993), 22–30.

20. Paul Starr, *The Social Transformation of American Medicine* (New York: Basic Books, 1982), 383–88; William G. Rothstein, *American Medical Schools and the Practice of Medicine* (New York: Oxford University Press, 1987), 250–55.

21. When the *Chronicle of Higher Education* in the early 1990s began publishing academic salaries compiled from the Form 990 filed by each

private institution under federal law, attention focused on the half-million-dollar pay and benefits received by several university presidents— for example, John R. Silber of Boston University and Peter Daimandopoulos of Adelphi. But in the *Chronicle* surveys of 1992–93 and 1993–94, all of the ten best-paid employees of private universities were clinical professors in university medical schools. In the 1993–94 survey, for example, nine professors of clinical medicine earned more than $1 million each in pay and benefits, and the top earner, a professor of cardiac surgery at Cornell, earned $1,785,066. Douglas Lederman, "Private Colleges' Pay: A 'Chronicle' Survey," *Chronicle of Higher Education*, 29 Sept. 1995, A23, A41.

22. John V. Lombardi, quoted in William C. Richardson, "The Appropriate Scale of Health Sciences Enterprises," *Daedalus* 122 (fall 1993): 188–89.

23. Ibid., 179–97.

24. "Clinical Practice Medical Service Plan: Collections 1973–1992" (Baltimore: Johns Hopkins University Medical School, 1993).

25. Richardson, "Appropriate Scale," 186.

26. Institutional rankings in seven major reputational studies of graduate schools between 1925 and 1982 are compared in David S. Webster, "America's Highest Ranked Graduate Schools, 1925–1982," *Change* 15 (May–June 1983): 23. Two private medical schools, Cornell and Harvard, were excluded from our sample. Cornell was excluded because its medical school was located in New York City, not on the university's arts-and-sciences Ithaca campus. Harvard was excluded because its faculty size was unusually large. Harvard's full-time clinical faculty in 1988, listed as 2,835 by the Association of American Medical Colleges, reflected Harvard's tradition of including, as part of its medical faculty, clinical faculty in Boston's major teaching hospitals, such as Massachusetts General and Brigham and Women's.

27. At the Vanderbilt School of Medicine in fiscal 1993, for example, 66 percent of the 192 full-time preclinical faculty in the basic science departments were supported by federal research grants, which totaled $20.6 million in direct costs. In the clinical departments, 31 percent of the 674 full-time clinical faculty were supported by federal research grants, which totaled $24.8 million in direct costs. Thus the basic science faculty accounted for 22 percent of the full-time medical faculty and generated 45 percent of the research support from federal agencies. Associate Dean John H. Hash to Hugh D. Graham, personal communication, 15 Dec. 1993. Vanderbilt, ranked nineteenth among 124 medical schools in NIH research funding in fiscal 1990, appeared to be generally representative in its research profile of the top quartile of university-based medical schools.

28. *Science and Engineering Indicators, 1991*, app. table 5-26. The source did not define the fields of clinical medicine or biomedical research.

29. Stephen Strickland, *Politics, Science, and Dread Disease: A Short History of U.S. Medical Research Policy* (Cambridge: Harvard University Press, 1972).

30. Starr, *Social Transformation*, 338–51; Rothstein, *American Medical Schools*, 236–49.

31. Excluded from table 5.3 are medical schools located on university health science campuses, such as the University of Maryland at Baltimore. The only such institution in Class I is UC San Francisco, with per capita NIH funding in fiscal 1990 of $122,980. Because UC San Francisco was the nation's top-ranked medical school in per capita R&D funding from the NIH, we included it in table 5.3. There are three such Class II medical schools: South Carolina–Charleston ($67,770), Massachusetts-Worcester ($64,810), and Texas-Dallas ($61,900). Class III medical schools on separate health science campuses include Baylor (Houston; $56,980), Oregon-Portland ($56,760), Maryland-Baltimore ($51,310), Texas–San Antonio ($46,240), Penn State–Hershey ($45,660), Colorado-Denver ($43,960), CUNY-Sinai ($41,660), and Texas-Houston ($40,600).

32. The Carnegie classification of 1994 moved two universities with medical schools, one private and one public, from the Comprehensive I category (now Masters I) to the Doctoral II category. The private institution is Wake Forest, where the Bowman Gray School of Medicine, were it included in this study, would be a Class III medical school ranking twenty-eighth (between Dartmouth and UC Davis), with $45,800 in per capita funding. The public institution is Wright State, where the medical school's per capita funding ($11,570) places it in Class V. Four universities that have Class V medical schools but are below the Carnegie Research and Doctoral classifications and are thus not included in this study are Creighton ($9,870), which is private, and three public institutions: East Carolina ($9,050), East Tennessee ($5,790), and Marshall ($4,930). For the 1994 Carnegie Classification see *A Classification of Institutions of Higher Education* (Princeton, N.J.: Carnegie Foundation for the Advancement of Teaching, 1994).

33. The published data do not show how many of Harvard's 3,231 full-time faculty funded their research grants through area hospitals. This problem of research accounting, though most severe at Harvard, is found at many metropolitan campuses. It testifies to the uniqueness of medical schools as components of American universities, and especially to the multiple roles, affiliations, and loyalties available to medical faculty.

34. In fiscal 1990 the NIH awarded Harvard University $99.5 million in research funds, roughly half going to the medical school. In the same year, NIH research awards to Boston-area hospitals and medical research institutions associated with Harvard included the following: $63.7 million to Massachusetts General Hospital, $62.7 million to Brigham and Women's Hospital, $39.5 million to Dana-Farber Cancer Institute, $26.3 million to Children's Hospital, and $13.1 million to Beth Israel Hospital.

35. Rothstein, *American Medical Schools*, 224–28; Organization and

Governance Project, *The Organization and Governance of Academic Health Centers* (Washington, D.C.: Association of Academic Health Centers, 1980); Marjorie P. Wilson and Charles P. McLaughlin, *Leadership and Management in Academic Medicine* (San Francisco: Jossey-Bass, 1984).

36. According to the National Science Board, in 1989 academic institutions employed the following numbers of doctorate-holding social scientists: 10,497 economists; 9,278 political scientists; 6,949 sociologists; 2,763 anthropologists; 1,430 linguists; and 1,077 historians of science. *Science and Engineering Indicators, 1991*, app. table 5-20.

37. Of the 70,000 doctorate-holding social scientists, almost half were teaching (33,300), and fewer than 1 percent worked in professional services. Psychology led all fields in the number of doctorates held by women. Between 1977 and 1989 the percentage of women doctoral degree-holders in psychology increased from 23 percent to 36 percent; equivalent increases in other fields were from 13 percent to 21 percent in the social sciences, from 5 percent to 20 percent in the sciences, and from .6 percent to 3 percent in engineering. *Science and Engineering Indicators, 1991*, app. tables 3-12, 3-14; National Science Foundation, *Profiles — Psychology: Human Resources and Funding*, NSF 88-325 (Washington, D.C.: National Science Foundation, 1988).

38. With regard to federal support for graduate students, however, psychologists during the 1980s dined at the lean table of the social scientists. Between 1980 and 1990 the percentage of full-time graduate students supported by federal funds remained relatively steady in science and engineering, at around one-fifth. In psychology, however, the proportion of federally supported graduate students declined from 13 percent to 8 percent, and in the social sciences it declined from 9 percent to 6 percent. *Science and Engineering Indicators, 1991*, app. table 2-20.

39. Definitions of disciplines and hence their R&D totals vary in NSF reports. Most data for the social sciences, for example, show economics leading sociology in federal R&D funding.

40. Economic research was also funded by the Department of Housing and Urban Development, the Treasury, HHS, and the International Trade Commission. See National Science Foundation, *Profiles — Economics: Human Resources and Funding*, NSF 88-333 (Washington, D.C.: National Science Foundation, 1988).

41. Sociological research sponsored by HHS was concentrated in the Agency for Health Care Policy Research and ADAMHA.

42. In 1989 social scientists accounted for 70,000 (19%) of the nation's 373,900 doctorate-holding scientists, and 13,200 (11%) of the 123,300 engaged in research. Nonfederal support for the social sciences was generally fragmented among private foundations (Ford, Rockefeller, MacArthur, Field) supporting targeted, problem-solving and policy-oriented research in such areas as minority health and welfare, antipoverty programs, juvenile justice, child abuse, and domestic violence.

43. Susan H. Russell et al., *Faculty in Higher Education Institutions*,

1988, NCES Survey Report (Washington, D.C.: U.S. Department of Education, Office of Research and Improvement, 1990). The number of full-time faculty for all institutions was 489,164, listed by Carnegie category as follows: public research, 96,228; private research, 39,136; public doctoral, 53,871; private doctoral, 22,107; public comprehensive, 93,144; private comprehensive, 35,160; liberal arts, 39,086; public two-year, 91,559; and other, 14,778.

44. Ibid., 5–17. The NCES survey of 1987 listed 378,732 full-time faculty in four-year institutions, ranked by field, as follows: health sciences, 78,927; natural sciences, 60,347; humanities, 47,426; social sciences, 40,369; fine arts, 24,789; education, 24,464; business, 24,329; engineering, 24,464; agriculture and home economics, 10,912; other, 48,488.

45. For succinct institutional histories of the two agencies see Donald R. Whitnah, ed., *Government Agencies* (Westport, Conn.: Greenwood Press, 1983), 327–32 (on the NEA) and 332–38 (on the NEH).

46. Stephen Miller, *Excellence and Equity: The National Endowment for the Humanities* (Lexington: University Press of Kentucky, 1984).

47. There is considerably more literature on the NEA than on the NEH. This is not surprising, given the greater arena of controversy surrounding the arts, and the tensions inherent in spending tax dollars to subsidize constitutionally protected expression by artists whose work may offend large segments of public opinion. See generally Barry Schwartz, "Politics and Art: A Case of Cultural Confusion," *Arts in Society* 10 (fall–winter 1973): 22–47; C. Richard Swain, "The NEA, 1965–1980," in *Public Policy and the Arts*, ed. Kevin V. Mulcahy and C. Richard Swain (Boulder, Colo.: Westview Press, 1982), 169–94; Milton Cummings, *The Patron State: Government and the Arts in Europe, North America, and Japan* (New York: Oxford University Press, 1987); Stephen Benedict, ed., *Public Policy and the Muse: Essays on Government Funding for the Arts* (New York: Norton, 1991).

48. Stephen Burd, "Endowments Survival in Doubt," *Chronicle of Higher Education*, 7 July 1995, A20.

49. Roger L. Geiger, *Research and Relevant Knowledge: American Research Universities since World War II* (New York: Oxford University Press, 1993), 310–12.

50. Roger L. Geiger and Irwin Feller, *The Dispersion of Academic Research during the 1980s*, Report to the Andrew W. Mellon Foundation (University Park, Pa.: Institute for Policy Research and Evaluation, Pennsylvania State University, May 1993).

51. Geiger, *Research and Relevant Knowledge*, 204.

52. Office of Technology Assessment, *Federally Funded Research: Decision for a Decade* (Washington, D.C.: U.S. Government Printing Office, 1991).

53. U.S. House of Representatives, House Committee on Science, Space, and Technology, *Report of the Task Force on the Health of Research* (Washington, D.C.: U.S. Government Printing Office, 1992), 6.

54. Government-University-Industry Research Roundtable, *Fateful Choices: The Future of the U.S. Academic Research Enterprise* (Washington, D.C.: National Academy Press, 1992); President's Council of Advisors on Science and Technology, *Renewing the Promise: Research-Intensive Universities and the Nation* (Washington, D.C., 1992), 12.

55. Roger L. Geiger and Irwin Feller, "The Dispersion of Academic Research in the 1980s," *Journal of Higher Education* 66 (May–June 1995): 338.

56. H. De Groot, W. McMahon, and J. Volkwein, "The Cost Structure of American Research Universities," *Review of Economics and Statistics* 73 (1991): 424–31.

57. Derek Bok, *President's Report, 1989–1990* (Cambridge: Harvard University, 1990).

Chapter 6: The Public Research Universities

1. Carnegie Foundation for the Advancement of Teaching, *A Classification of Institutions of Higher Education* (Princeton, N.J.: Carnegie Foundation for the Advancement of Teaching, 1987), 7. The Carnegie classification of 1994 retained these stipulations for all four of the doctorate-granting categories. See Jean Evangelauf, "A New 'Carnegie Classification,' " *Chronicle of Higher Education*, 6 Apr. 1994, A17, A26.

2. UC San Francisco (UCSF), with only 367 full-time instructional faculty but with a full-time staff of 1,547, won $167 million in federal R&D in 1990 and was credited with more than four thousand scientific articles. When evaluated in per capita terms, this extraordinary level of activity won UCSF faculty top rank among all public universities in the United States in both the R&D index ($428,937) and the publications index (11.92). In this performance UCSF exceeded the achievement of its nearest competitor in the public sector, UC San Diego, by roughly a factor of 2. UCSF, with its glittering array of Nobel laureates, remains one of the world's premier academic health centers. But unlike the other eight UC campuses, UCSF is not an arts-and-sciences campus.

3. International College, though listed as a Doctoral I private institution in California in the Carnegie classification of 1987, was not listed in American Council on Education, *American Universities and Colleges* (New York: de Gruyter, 1987), and received no federal obligations in 1987–90 according to the NSF annual reports on federal obligations to universities and colleges. Union, as its name denotes, is a consortium devoted to experimental approaches to education; it relies for instruction primarily on a dispersed network of part-time adjunct faculty. Nova University, located in Fort Lauderdale, has relied primarily on a national network of part-time faculty to offer graduate degrees through a system of correspondence and mentoring arrangements. Higher education associations and coordinating boards in several states have attempted to prohibit Nova from offering degrees in their jurisdictions because Nova lacked minimal

quality requirements in graduate faculty, research library, program curriculum, and quality control.

4. For public institutions in the Carnegie Research I category, the Pearson product-moment coefficient of correlation between the R&D index (1988–90) and the publications index (1986–88) is .93. Similarly, the correlation between the R&D and the top-science index is .87; the correlation between the publications and the top-science indexes is .88.

5. As a general pattern, the social science and the A&H indexes in this study show strong and positive statistical correlations with each other but not with the other three indicators. For example, for public Carnegie Research I institutions, the 1986–90 data show a correlation of .26 between the R&D and social science indexes and a correlation of .02 between R&D and the A&H indexes, but the correlation between the social science and the A&H index is .73. This pattern reflects in part a tendency among land-grant and technical institutions to emphasize applied fields, which often depresses their per capita performance in the social sciences and humanities.

6. The Research 1 class includes not only universities that have been traditionally ranked high in national reputational studies, such as Iowa and Ohio State, but also flagship universities such as Arizona, Colorado, Maryland–College Park, Utah, and Virginia, which have more recent claims to national recognition.

7. The AAU universities in the public sector which are not classified in this study's Research 1 category are Florida, Iowa State, Kansas, Michigan State, Missouri-Columbia, Nebraska, Oregon, and Rutgers–New Brunswick.

8. Verne Stadtman, *Origin and Development of the University of California* (New York: McGraw-Hill, 1970), 225–34.

9. John A. Douglass, "Politics and Policy in California Higher Education, 1850 to 1960" (Ph.D. diss., University of California, Santa Barbara, 1992).

10. Robert L. Kelley, *Transformation: University of California, Santa Barbara, 1909–1979* (Santa Barbara: Associated Students, UCSB, 1981).

11. Neil J. Smelser and Gabriel Almond, *Public Higher Education in California* (Berkeley: University of California Press, 1974).

12. SUNY-Buffalo became a member of the AAU in 1989.

13. Robert R. Kracke and William G. Kracke, "The University of Alabama Medical Center: The Past, the Present, the Future," *Alabama Lawyer* 28 (1967): 78–88; Christopher Scribner, "Federal Funding, Urban Renewal, and Race Relations: Birmingham in Transition, 1945–1955," *Alabama Review* 47 (Oct. 1995): 269–95.

14. James B. Sellers, *History of the University of Alabama* (Tuscaloosa: University of Alabama Press, 1953); James Holmes, *A History of the University of Alabama Hospitals* (Birmingham: University Hospitals Auxiliary, 1974); James E. Ferguson III, *The University of Alabama in Huntsville* (Huntsville: University of Alabama in Huntsville, 1975).

15. Another merger, less dramatic but effective in rapidly building a substantial state research university in a major American city, was the creation of Virginia Commonwealth University in Richmond in 1968 by combining the Medical College of Virginia and the Richmond Professional Institute.

16. By 1990 the average number of full-time faculty at medical schools on public university campuses exceeded 600. At some public universities, the full-time medical faculty exceeded 1,000—for example, 1,287 at UCLA, and 1,241 at Washington (Seattle). Even the relatively young medical school at Alabama-Birmingham had 938 faculty members. Compare this with the size of the medical faculties in 1990 at Hawaii-Manoa (129), Missouri-Columbia (292), Michigan State (321), and New Mexico (323). Of the ten Research 2 universities with medical schools, only Cincinnati and Virginia Commonwealth had large faculties (791 and 705, respectively).

17. See table 5.4, above; National Institutes of Health, "FY 1990 NIH Extramural Awards to Medical Schools" (Washington, D.C.: U.S. Public Health Service, 1992).

18. See Joseph M. Stetar, "In Search of a Direction: Southern Higher Education after the Civil War," *History of Education Quarterly* 25 (fall 1985): 341–57; Allan M. Cartter, "Qualitative Aspects of Southern University Education," *Southern Economic Journal* 32 (July 1965): 39–69.

19. Michigan State's medical school, established in the 1960s, had a full-time faculty in 1990 of 321. Texas A&M was one of five institutions able to convert Veterans Administration hospitals into medical schools under the VA Medical School Assistance and Health Manpower Training Act of 1972 (the others were East Tennessee State; Marshall University, in West Virginia; South Carolina–Charleston; and Wright State, in Ohio). In each case, powerful members of congressional committees favored universities in their home districts, although the AMA and most other medical authorities opposed the establishment of new M.D. programs. The benefactor of Texas A&M was Congressman Olin E. Teague, chairman of the House Veterans Affairs Committee. See *Congress and the Nation, 1969–1972* (Washington, D.C.: Congressional Quarterly, 1973), 545–46; William G. Rothstein, *American Medical Schools* (New York: Oxford University Press, 1987), 277–80; Benjamin J. Lewis, *VA Medical Programs in Relation to Medical Schools* (Washington, D.C.: U.S. Government Printing Office, 1970).

20. The seven nonflagship land-grant universities in the Research 2 group are Colorado State, Iowa State, Michigan State, Oregon State, Texas A&M, Virginia Tech, and Washington State. The four Research 2 flagship campuses that have land-grant status but lack medical schools are Delaware, Georgia, Louisiana State, and Rutgers. The four land-grant flagships that include medical schools are Florida, Hawaii-Manoa, Kentucky, and Missouri-Columbia.

21. Land-grant universities winning low percentages of USDA re-

search funding in fiscal 1990 from competitive programs include Wyoming, with 20 percent; Tennessee-Knoxville, with 24 percent; and Delaware, with 28 percent. See "Distribution of Federal Payments for Research and Education at State Agricultural Experiment Stations and Other State Institutions—FY 1990" (Washington, D.C.: Cooperative State Research Service, United States Department of Agriculture, 1991).

22. In the process of removing Department of Defense military development funds from the institutional R&D averages for 1988–90, $11 million was subtracted from the New Mexico State total. Other large deductions of defense development funds were made in the case of Johns Hopkins ($223 million), Penn State ($37.6 million), Utah State ($29.6 million), Georgia Tech ($27.8 million), Texas-Austin ($19.3 million), and Carnegie Mellon and Pittsburgh ($7.5 million each).

23. The full-time medical faculty in 1990 numbered 432 at Temple, 326 at West Virginia, and only 169 at South Carolina–Columbia. The medical school at Temple is ranked in Class III and those at South Carolina and West Virginia are ranked in Class V. (See table 5.4, above).

24. The University of Maryland already had a presence in Baltimore—the University of Maryland at Baltimore (UMAB), a campus of professional schools (of dentistry, law, medicine, nursing, pharmacy, and social work) that traced its institutional roots to the founding of the College of Medicine of Maryland in 1807. UMBC, located beyond the city limits at the intersection of the Baltimore beltway and Interstate 95 to Washington, was thus named after Baltimore County. See also Hugh Davis Graham and Nancy Diamond, *Economic Competitiveness and Research Productivity: Comparing the Campuses in Maryland and the Nation* (Baltimore: Maryland Institute for Policy Analysis and Research, 1989).

25. Another group of urban campuses in state university systems, such as Colorado-Denver and Indiana-Purdue at Indianapolis, were not classified by Carnegie as doctorate-granting institutions in 1987 and are not included in this study. Urban institutions of this type, categorized by Carnegie in 1987 as Comprehensive I, were institutions having student enrollments of at least ten thousand. These included Arkansas–Little Rock, Colorado-Denver, Indiana-Purdue at Indianapolis, Massachusetts-Boston, Minnesota-Duluth, Nebraska-Omaha, Nevada-Las Vegas, Texas–El Paso, Texas–San Antonio, and campuses in large state university systems in California and New York. The revised Carnegie classifications of 1994 shifted three of these institutions—San Diego State University, Colorado-Denver, and Indiana-Purdue at Indianapolis—to the Doctoral II category.

26. In Florida's statewide system for governing and coordinating higher education, regional universities such as South Florida have not been governed by the same board as the University of Florida in Gainesville. For a critical view of the politics of higher education in Florida, see Robert B. Mautz, *The Power Game: Governance of Higher Education in Florida* (Tallahassee, 1982).

291

27. A major exception is found in California, where the twenty-campus California State University and College (CSUC) system has been unsuccessful in its periodic campaigns to break the monopoly on doctoral programs awarded by the 1960 Master Plan to the University of California. Although several of the larger CSUC institutions, such as San Diego State (the informal "flagship" of the system) have developed joint doctoral programs with UC campuses, the lack of stand-alone doctoral authority has remained a major source of frustration for the CSUC system. Prior to 1994 all CSUC campuses with university designation were classified by the Carnegie Commission as Comprehensive rather than as doctorate-granting institutions. In the revised Carnegie classification of 1994 the "Comprehensive" designation for such regional state universities was replaced by the designation Masters (I and II). San Diego State, alone among the CSUC campuses, was designated a doctorate-granting institution (Doctoral II). The largest CSUC campus in student enrollment and faculty size, San Diego State included a school of public health, at which research funded by the NIH helped boost federal R&D to an average of $12.3 million during 1988–90. In 1990 this was the top R&D total in the nation for institutions not (then) included in the Carnegie Doctoral classes. This success in federal research funding would produce at San Diego State, with a full-time faculty of 1,168 in 1987, an R&D index of $10,500, large enough to qualify for this study's Research 3 class.

In the other four indicators, however, San Diego State, as well as the other four large campuses in the CSUC system, generally fell below the mean for the Research 4 class (see table N.1). Faculty at the nation's state colleges and regional universities, which developed as nondoctoral teaching institutions, were generally not competitive on a per capita basis with faculty at doctoral-research institutions.

28. Although two of the new urban campuses, Missouri–Kansas City and South Florida, established small medical schools, their faculty research productivity, as assessed in per capita terms, does not appear to have grown significantly faster than that of their nonmedical peers in the Research 4 class.

29. See, for example, reports in the *Chronicle of Higher Education* on federal court litigation over state policy in desegregating higher education in Louisiana (5 Jan. 1994), Alabama (9 Mar. 1994), and Mississippi (18 May 1994).

30. John D. Millett, *Conflict in Higher Education: State Government Coordination versus Institutional Independence* (San Francisco: Jossey-Bass, 1984); Hugh Davis Graham, "Structure and Governance in American Higher Education: Historical and Comparative Analysis in State Policy," *Journal of Policy History* 1 (1989): 80–107; N. Marshall, "Coordination: Anglo-American Systems," in *The International Encyclopedia of Higher Education*, ed. Burton R. Clark and Guy R. Neave (Oxford: Pergamon Press, 1992), 1338–47; Joye Mercer, "Fighting over Autonomy," *Chronicle of Higher Education*, 1 June 1994, A26–A27.

Table N.1
Per Capita Indicators of Research Productivity for the Five Largest Campuses in the California State University and College System, 1986–1990

CSUC campus	R&D Index	Publications Index	Top-Science Index	Top–Social Science Index	A&H Index
San Diego	$10,500	.80	.04	.03	.133
San Jose	6,060	.50	.01	.03	.012
Los Angeles	3,770	.52	.02	.03	.046
San Francisco	2,820	.46	.02	.01	.334
Long Beach	2,540	.50	.01	.03	.046
Research 4 public mean	6,648	.79	.04	.03	.015
UC system mean	81,460	4.38	5.09	1.15	.569

Source: Data in all tables in the notes derive from the authors' calculations. See Note on Method and Sources.

Chapter 7: The Private Research Universities and Rising Institutions

1. In 1968 the average per capita R&D index of private institutions was 97 percent higher than that of their public counterparts in Research II, 43 percent higher in Doctoral I, and 41 percent higher in Doctoral II. The publications index shows private institutions with a smaller but still substantial lead: 66 percent higher than the public average in Research I, 63 percent in Research II, 22 percent in Doctoral I, and 14 percent in Doctoral II.

2. The public institutions joining the AAU during 1957–77 were Iowa State, Penn State, and Purdue (all in 1958), Michigan State (1964), Colorado (1966), Maryland–College Park and Oregon (1969), and UCLA and Pittsburgh (1974). The private institutions were Tulane (1958), Syracuse (1966), and Case Western Reserve and Southern California (1969).

3. See, for example, Carnegie Council on Policy Studies in Higher Education, *The States and Private Higher Education: Problems and Policies in a New Era* (San Francisco: Jossey-Bass, 1977); Task Force on State Policy and Independent Higher Education, *Final Report and Recommendations* (Denver: Education Commission of the States, 1977); and idem, *The Preservation of Excellence in American Higher Education: The Essential Role of Private Colleges and Universities* (Denver: Education Commission of the States, 1990).

4. Edward Gross and Paul V. Grambsch, *Changes in University Organization, 1964–1971* (New York: McGraw-Hill, 1974), 198–99.

5. Derek Bok, *Universities and the Future of America* (Durham, N.C.: Duke University Press, 1990); Patrick M. Callan, "Government and Higher Education," in *Higher Learning in America, 1980–2000*, ed. Arthur Levine (Baltimore: Johns Hopkins University Press, 1993); Education Commission of the States, *Assessment and Accountability in Higher Education* (Denver: Education Commission of the States, 1990); Hugh D. Graham, "Structure and Governance in Higher Education," *Journal of Policy History* 1 (1989): 88–107.

6. Between 1968 and 1988 the private advantage in federal R&D funding diminished in the Research I and Doctoral II categories but increased in the Research II and Doctoral I categories. In the publications index, the private advantage was reduced in all four categories, but the index includes only science and engineering journals in 1968, whereas in the late 1980s it includes journals in all academic areas.

7. See table N.2.

8. See table N.3.

9. For example, the mean top-science score for public institutions in the 1987 Carnegie taxonomy was .27 for Research I campuses and .06 for Doctoral II, a ratio of 1 to 4.4. For private institutions, the mean top-science score was .54 for Research I campuses and .07 for Doctoral II, a ratio of 1 to 7.6.

10. For private universities in the late 1980s, the product-moment correlations between the R&D index and the publications and top-science indexes were positive and strong—.67 for R&D and publications, and .87 for R&D and the top-science indicator.

11. The 1995 "almanac issue" of the *Chronicle of Higher Education,* 1 Sept. 1995, lists the private institutions that had endowments exceeding $1 billion in value as of 30 June 1994 as follows (in millions):

Harvard	$6,201 million
Yale	3,529
Princeton	3,447
Stanford	2,751
Columbia	1,918
MIT	1,778
Washington	1,738
Emory	1,691
Pennsylvania	1,464
Rice	1,279
Northwestern	1,275
Cornell	1,249
Chicago	1,224

The public institutions included in the billion-dollar-endowment club were the University of Texas system (ranked second, with $4.6 billion), the Texas A&M system (ranked sixth, with $2.1 billion), and the University of California (ranked ninth, with $1.8 billion).

12. Clayton R. Koppes, *JPL and the American Space Program: A History of the Jet Propulsion Laboratory* (New Haven: Yale University Press, 1982); Roger L. Geiger, *Research and Relevant Knowledge* (New York: Oxford University Press, 1993), 56–57. Funding for federal research labs such as the JPL at Caltech, Lawrence Livermore at Berkeley, and the Stanford Linear Accelerator is excluded from the R&D totals in this study, but many journal publications authored by on-campus researchers em-

TABLE N.2

Mean Per Capita Indexes of Research Productivity for Institutions in the 1987 Carnegie Doctoral I and II Categories, 1980–1990

Carnegie Category	Research Index	Public Institutions	Private Institutions	Public as % of Private
Doctoral I	R&D	$7,440	$15,400	48
	Publications	1.11	1.35	82
	Top-science	.082	.106	77
	Top–social science	.040	.046	87
	A&H	.019	.029	68
Doctoral II	R&D	$14,120	$12,670	111
	Publications	.94	1.07	88
	Top-science	.061	.072	85
	Top–social science	.162	.023	70
	A&H	.016	.017	94

TABLE N.3

Mean Per Capita Indexes of Research Productivity for Institutions in the 1987 Carnegie Research I and II Categories, 1980–1990

Carnegie Category	Research Index	Public Institutions	Private Institutions	Public as % of Private
Research I	R&D	$50,780	$110,370	46
	Publications	2.76	4.59	60
	Top-Science	.270	.544	50
	Top–social science	.077	.131	59
	A&H	.031	.068	46
Research II	R&D	$20,500	$46,630	44
	Publications	1.64	2.68	61
	Top-science	.132	.181	74
	Top–social science	.050	.068	67
	A&H	.022	.048	46

ployed by such federal research labs are credited by the ISI to the host campus.

13. Brown, Emory, and Tufts were reclassified as Research I universities in the Carnegie revision of 1994.

14. National Commission for Education Statistics, *National Study of Postsecondary Faculty, 1987* (Washington, D.C.: National Commission for Education Statistics, 1988)

15. Rayford W. Logan, *Howard University: The First Hundred Years, 1867–1967* (Washington, D.C.: Howard University Press, 1969).

16. One curious attribute of the Carnegie classification system has been its use of total federal support, not federal R&D support, as a criterion to define its Research I and II categories. Because Howard, like Gallaudet (a college for the deaf), is a private institution in the District of Co-

lumbia which receives substantial federal support for its operating budget, the Carnegie definition has placed Howard in the Research I category.

17. See Ernest L. Wilkinson, *BYU—The First One Hundred Years* (Provo, Utah: Brigham Young University Press, 1975).

18. Claus-Dieter Krohn, *Intellectuals in Exile: Refugee Scholars and the New School for Social Research* (Amherst: University of Massachusetts Press, 1993). The New School lacks a science curriculum but includes degree programs in business management, health professions, fine arts, and theology, as well as the social and behavioral sciences.

19. As of 1994, the Research 4 institutions ranked among the largest one hundred in endowment value were Boston College (ranked thirty-third, with $447 million), Texas Christian (thirty-eighth, with $404 million), Tulsa (forty-eighth, with $363 million), Baylor (fifty-seventh, with $319 million), and Northeastern (ninetieth, with $213 million).

20. The faculty and academic programs at Yeshiva have been dominated by graduate and professional programs in medicine and biomedical science, psychology, law, and Hebrew and Jewish studies. See Gilbert Klapperman, *The Story of Yeshiva University* (London: Macmillan, 1969).

21. See Alexander Leitch, *A Princeton Companion* (Princeton: Princeton University Press, 1976).

22. See Morris Bishop, *A History of Cornell* (Ithaca: Cornell University Press, 1962).

23. See Abram L. Sachar, *A Host at Last* (Boston: Little, Brown, 1976); Richard M. Freeland, *Academia's Golden Age* (New York: Oxford University Press, 1992), chap. 4.

24. This distinction was originally anticipated for the Catholic University of America, which was established as a graduate institution in 1887 and in 1900 became a charter member of the AAU. As was the case with Clark University, another charter member of the AAU, Catholic University's development as a modern research university, modeled after Johns Hopkins, fell short of its own ambitions and the AAU's expectations.

25. In discussing public universities in the previous chapter we noted, on the one hand, the generally high intercorrelation between the indexes for R&D, publications, and top-science journals; and, on the other hand, the low correlations between all three of these indicators and the social science index. Among Research 1 public universities, for example, the social science index produced a coefficient of correlation of .07 with the R&D index, .32 with the publications index, and .16 with the top-science index.

26. Freeland, *Academia's Golden Age*, 144–45; Geiger, *Research and Relevant Knowledge*, 63–66.

27. Edward D. Eddy Jr., *Colleges for Our Land and Time: The Land-Grant Idea in American Education* (New York: Harper and Brothers, 1956); Ralph D. Christy and Lionel Williamson, eds., *A Century of Service: Land-*

Grant Colleges and Universities, 1890–1990 (New Brunswick, N.J.: Transaction, 1992). Selected private institutions have historically played a small role in the land-grant system. Since the nineteenth century Cornell has been the land-grant institution for New York, MIT has shared land-grant roles with the University of Massachusetts, and Yale with the University of Connecticut, and Tuskegee Institute has been funded by the U.S. Department of Agriculture under the 1890 land-grant program for historically black institutions.

28. Among Research 1 and 2 universities in the public sector, strength in the arts and humanities tends to be closely associated with strength in the social sciences. In the Research 2 group, for example, Rutgers (25-4-3) and Missouri-Columbia (20-7-7) demonstrate patterns of strength in the social sciences and humanities but weakness in the sciences. Demonstrating the opposite pattern are Iowa State (2-24-20) and Georgia Tech (3-22-25).

29. Among private institutions, MIT was ranked fourth and Caltech was ranked tenth according to the 1982 National Research Council data. In David Webster's grand ranking based on the 1995 National Research Council data, MIT was ranked first and Caltech was tied for fourth with Princeton. Webster, correspondence with authors.

30. In 1988–89 the average number of basic science faculty holding full-time appointments at six leading private medical schools (see table 5.2) was 130. At Harvard the full-time basic science faculty numbered 396. We counted only the 396 basic science faculty members, not Harvard's full legion of 3,231 full-time medical faculty. Nonetheless, for purposes of per capita comparisons the size of the medical faculty at Harvard increased the full-time faculty total by approximately 27 percent, compared with an average, medical-school-based increase of 13 percent for the six comparable private universities (Chicago, Columbia, Northwestern, Pennsylvania, Stanford, and Yale).

31. In our classification of medical schools by NIH research funding in 1990 (see table 5.4), the medical school at Boston University was ranked in Class II (per capita funding between $60,000 and $100,000). The medical schools at Dartmouth, Miami, and NYU were in Class III ($35,000–$60,000), and the schools at Georgetown and George Washington were in Class IV ($18,000–$35,000).

32. In the 1990s NYU won attention for a major fund-raising campaign designed less to build endowment than to invest in faculty recruitment, program development, and physical plant. Such recent changes would not be reflected in data drawn from the period 1980–90. *New York Times*, 17 Feb. 1995.

33. Even in California, where private institutions tend to have been more recently founded than their counterparts in states east of the Rocky Mountains, the founding of most private universities predates World War II. Prior to 1966, U.S. International University was called California Western, and prior to 1952 it was Balboa University. Pepperdine was estab-

lished in 1937. Biola University was founded as the Bible Institute of Los Angeles in 1908.

34. Faculty at institutions in the Research 4 category retaining their Protestant denominational affiliations and mission were less successful in terms of per capita research performance. Note that Mississippi College (Baptist), Biola (whose Talbot School of Theology is Protestant interdenominational), Pepperdine (Church of Christ), Andrews (Seventh-Day Adventist), and Baylor (Baptist) are ranked toward the bottom.

35. Faculty at institutions ranked 1–33 (table 7.13) achieved scores lower than 100 in the combined rankings. The institutions ranked 34–40 are Penn State, Delaware, Houston, Ohio State, Oregon State, Missouri, and Hawaii.

36. The University of Pittsburgh fits neither the flagship nor the new-institution category. A private university prior to 1966, Pittsburgh became a member of the AAU in 1974.

37. The Santa Barbara campus became part of the University of California in 1944 by an act of the state legislature and against the wishes of UC administrators. In 1995 Clark Kerr, speaking on the occasion of UC Santa Barbara's fiftieth anniversary as a UC campus, recalled that "Santa Barbara was an unwanted child at a mandated adoption."

> A universitywide faculty committee chaired by Gordon Watkins, long-time dean of the Graduate division at UCLA, recommended that Santa Barbara be accepted into the University of California but only as a "regional college" with its own separate salary scale and with the condition that its faculty not be permitted within the Academic Senate.

Clark Kerr, "Don't Forget Santa Barbara," Golden Anniversary Celebration, University of California, Santa Barbara, 9 Oct. 1995.

38. In New York State, the Albany campus was founded in 1944 and was designated a research center in the SUNY system after World War II. SUNY-Buffalo was admitted to the AAU in 1989. The UC campuses at Davis, Riverside, and Santa Barbara were founded in the first decade of the twentieth century and became general UC campuses after World War II. In 1982 the University of Illinois Medical Center in Chicago was consolidated with the University of Illinois at Chicago Circle, originally established in 1946 as a two-year division located at the Navy Pier.

39. The Keniston study of 1959 ranked the University of Washington 20th. According to the Cartter data (1966), Washington (Seattle) was ranked 16th, Purdue 24th, and Brown 25th. According to the Roose-Andersen data (1970), Washington was 13th, Purdue 21st, Duke 22d, and Brown 23d.

40. Washington University (St. Louis) was ranked twenty-fourth in the Hughes study of 1934, sponsored by the American Council on Education. Rochester was ranked nineteenth in the Ladd-Lipset survey of 1979.

41. The reputational rankings published in the National Research Council's (NRC's) study *Research-Doctorate Programs in the United States* (Washington, D.C.: National Academy Press, 1995), as aggregated by Webster and Skinner in *Change* (May–June 1996), included among the top twenty-five only one private university designated as rising: Carnegie Mellon. Webster ranked Carnegie Mellon as 20.5 (in a four-way tie for 20.5) on the basis of NRC's reputational ranking of faculty quality. Among public institutions, none of the universities we designate as "rising universities" was included in the top twenty-five, but three appeared for the first time among the top thirty: UC Irvine (27th), Virginia (28th), and Arizona (30th). Webster and Skinner's ranking (with ties indicated by decimal-point rankings) produced the following top thirty:

1.	MIT	16.	Texas-Austin
2.	UC Berkeley	17.	Washington (Seattle)
3.	Harvard	18.	Northwestern
4.5.	Caltech	20.5.	Carnegie Mellon
4.5.	Princeton	20.5.	Duke
6.	Stanford	20.5.	Illinois-Urbana
7.	Chicago	20.5.	Johns Hopkins
8.	Yale	23.	Minnesota
9.	Cornell	24.	North Carolina–Chapel Hill
10.	UC San Diego	25.	Brown
11.	Columbia	26.	New York University
12.5.	UCLA	27.	UC Irvine
12.5.	Michigan	28.	Virginia
14.	Pennsylvania	29.	Purdue
15.	Wisconsin-Madison	30.	Arizona

Conclusion

1. On the historiographic debate over American exceptionalism see Byron E. Shafer, ed., *Is America Different? A New Look at American Exceptionalism* (Oxford: Clarendon Press, 1991).

2. See George Keller, *Academic Strategy: The Management Revolution in American Higher Education* (Baltimore: Johns Hopkins University Press, 1983).

3. See generally E. C. Bowen and E. C. Lee, *The Multicampus University: A Study of Academic Governance* (New York: McGraw-Hill, 1971); Burton R. Clark, *The Higher Education System: Academic Organization in Cross-National Perspective* (Berkeley: University of California Press, 1983); Aims C. McGuinness Jr., *State Coordinating and Governing Boards* (Denver: Education Commission of the States, 1988); Clark Kerr and M. L. Gade, *The Guardians: Boards of Trustees of American Colleges and Universities* (Washington, D.C.: Association of Governing Boards of Universities and Colleges, 1989); Hugh Davis Graham, "Structure and Gover-

nance in American Higher Education: Historical and Comparative Analysis in State Policy," *Journal of Policy History* 1 (1989): 80–107; J. Fredericks Volkwein, "Changes in Quality among Public Universities," *Journal of Higher Education* 60 (Mar.–Apr. 1989): 136–50.

4. The ten institutions are drawn in order from the grand ranking that David Webster constructed from the data contained in the National Research Council study of 1982. See David S. Webster, "America's Highest Ranked Graduate Schools, 1925–1982," *Change* 15 (May–June 1983): 23. The medical school requirement (on campus) eliminates Berkeley, MIT, Princeton, Cornell, Illinois, and Texas. Harvard is excluded because its large medical faculty is disproportionately drawn from local teaching hospitals.

5. From the list of eight top-ranked private institutions we omitted Cornell, tied with Columbia for eleventh place in Webster's aggregation of the 1982 NRC data, owing to Cornell's unique public-private configuration.

6. Institutions lacking programs in the discipline or academic area in question (for example, Chicago and Indiana lack engineering programs) were omitted from the averages.

7. The NRC study omitted a count of journal articles for the arts and humanities disciplines because publications in these fields customarily take the form of books; and book publishing by faculty members cannot effectively be measured in studies such as the NRC project (or indeed in this one), in which so many institutions and disciplines are involved.

8. National Research Council, *Research-Doctorate Programs in the United States* (Washington, D.C.: National Academy Press, 1995).

9. Both NRC studies relied on ISI data showing source items attributed to program faculty. For the 1982 assessment the ISI data covered the period 1978–79; for the 1995 study the ISI data covered 1988–90. Like the 1982 comparisons, the 1995 comparisons are based on total ISI source items and thus lack the qualitative weight of top-journal indicators.

10. Edward Shils, "The American Private University," *Minerva* 11 (1973): 6–27.

11. On the distinctive role of private institutions in the postwar era, see generally Elaine El-Khawas, *Public and Private Higher Education: Differences in Role, Character, and Clientele* (Washington, D.C.: American Council on Education, 1976); Carnegie Commission on Higher Education, *The States and Private Higher Education* (San Francisco: Jossey-Bass, 1977); Roger L. Geiger, *Private Sectors in Higher Education: Structure, Function, and Change in Eight Countries* (Ann Arbor: University of Michigan Press, 1986); Daniel C. Levy, ed., *Private Education: Studies in Choice and Public Policy* (New York: Oxford University Press, 1986); Walter W. Powell, ed., *The Nonprofit Sector: A Research Handbook* (New Haven: Yale University Press, 1987).

12. The question of the superiority of private institutions is under-

standably a sensitive one in American higher education. In the internal politics of the AAU, tensions between the public and private sectors have historically been eased by pursuing a rough public-private balance in membership (when possible the AAU has admitted new members in public-private pairs, as in the 1995 admission of UC Santa Barbara and Emory) and by emphasizing solidarity among elite research universities in policy lobbying.

13. It is arguable that as knowledge becomes increasingly specialized, the large size of faculty units in public universities gives them an advantage over private universities and compensates in part for qualitative disadvantages.

14. On American medical education see generally S. W. Bloom, "The Medical School as a Social Organization: The Sources of Resistance to Change," *Medical Education* 23 (1989): 228–41; Kenneth M. Ludmerer, *Learning to Heal: The Development of American Medical Education* (New York: Basic Books, 1985); Ronald L. Numbers, ed., *The Education of American Physicians: Historical Essays* (Berkeley: University of California Press, 1980); William G. Rothstein, *American Medical Schools and the Practice of Medicine* (New York: Oxford University Press, 1987); Paul M. Starr, *The Transformation of American Medicine* (New York: Basic Books, 1982).

15. See, e.g., William C. Richardson, "The Appropriate Scale of the Health Sciences Enterprise," *Daedalus* 122 (fall 1993): 179–95, esp. 192–94.

16. There was one exception: in a comparison of graduate education sponsored by the American Council on Education, the Hughes study of 1934 ranked Iowa State nineteenth. See Raymond M. Hughes, *Report of the Committee on Graduate Instruction* (Washington, D.C.: American Council on Education, 1934).

17. In 1990 a majority of Americans lived in only nine states—California, New York, Texas, Florida, Pennsylvania, Illinois, Ohio, Michigan, and New Jersey (ranked by population size). Most states lacked the combination of population density and underserved cities that led to second-flagship challenges. In many states with strong agricultural traditions, especially in the South, the High Plains, and the western mountains (for example, Mississippi, South Carolina, Kansas, Oklahoma, the Dakotas, and Montana), the combined opposition of flagship and land-grant campuses, which normally competed with each other, effectively preempted the entry of new urban challengers. In many rural states where the flagship campus also carried the land-grant designation (e.g., Arkansas, Nebraska, Idaho, New Hampshire, and West Virginia), the cities were not large enough to mount effective political challenges to flagship dominance. Arguably, in such states, where the flagships rarely contended for national ranking, the economic base was insufficient to justify building new urban research campuses.

18. The University of California's San Francisco campus, established

as a medical center in 1873, functioned independently as a medical flagship, much like the similar health science campuses of state universities in cities such as Baltimore, Chicago, Dallas, and Portland. In 1990, UCSF ranked first nationally among such medical campuses in per capita research funding from the NIH.

19. Verne A. Stadtman, *The University of California, 1868-1968* (New York: McGraw-Hill, 1970); Neil J. Smelser and Gabriel Almond, *Public Higher Education in California* (Berkeley: University of California Press, 1974); Organisation for Economic Cooperation and Development, *Higher Education in California* (Paris: OECD, 1990).

20. In other urban, industrial states where the tripartite model was widely adopted in the 1960s, the middle tier of state colleges and universities was generally able to dismantle the barriers. In states such as Illinois, Indiana, Maryland, New Jersey, Ohio, and Texas, the proliferation of new doctoral programs and the blurring of mission distinctions led political leaders to create statewide coordinating boards. The economic decline of the 1970s prompted legislators to strengthen the boards' authority, empowering them not only to approve new academic proposals but also to review and terminate existing programs and even to transfer programs from one institution to another. See John D. Millett, *Conflict in Higher Education: State Government Coordination versus Institutional Independence* (San Francisco: Jossey-Bass, 1984); McGuinness, *State Coordinating and Governing Boards*.

21. The SUNY model of consolidating most public campuses under a statewide governing board or "superboard" was followed by several other large states, but for different reasons and with different results. In North Carolina, the flagship campus at Chapel Hill and the land-grant campus at Raleigh combined in a preemptive alliance in 1971 to dominate the research-doctoral mission in a consolidated sixteen-campus system of four-year institutions. In Wisconsin in 1973, political leaders displeased by the radical turmoil at Madison and the squabbling among state campuses combined the four-campus University of Wisconsin system based at Madison, the eleven-campus Wisconsin State University system, and eleven two-year campuses. In Massachusetts in 1980, legislators similarly irritated by program duplication and interinstitutional bickering abolished all existing governing boards and replaced them with a single governing board for all twenty-eight public institutions in the commonwealth. See Graham, "Structure and Governance in American Higher Education," esp. 89–93.

22. Harvey Brooks, "Current Criticisms of Research Universities," in *The Research University in a Time of Discontent*, ed. Jonathan R. Cole, Elinor G. Barber, and Stephen R. Graubard (Baltimore: Johns Hopkins University Press, 1994), 231–52; Jon Wiener, "Dealing with Deadwood," *Lingua Franca* 2 (Dec. 1990): 14–17, 29. A perceptive review essay is John Searle, "The Storm over the University," *New York Review of Books*, 6 Dec. 1990, 34–42.

23. John Burgess, "Bombs into Bulldozers," *Washington Post,* 23 Aug. 1992; William J. Broad, "Big Science Squeezes Small-Scale Researchers," *New York Times,* 29 Dec. 1992; Scott Jaschik, "Defense Budget Approved by House Would Halve President's Request for University Research," *Chronicle of Higher Education,* 6 July 1994, A31.

24. Katherine S. Mangan, "Tearing Down a Dream," *Chronicle of Higher Education,* 3 Nov. 1993, A40.

25. Academic job prospects for new holders of Ph.D.'s in the sciences, on the other hand, were threatened by growing campus reliance on part-time and foreign-born instructors. Anthony de Palma, "Foreigners Flood U.S. Graduate Schools," *New York Times,* 29 Nov. 1990; Malcolm W. Browne, "Cold War's End Clouds Research as Openings in Science Dwindle," *New York Times,* 20 Feb. 1994.

26. Burton R. Clark, *Places of Inquiry: Research and Advanced Education in Modern Universities* (Berkeley: University of California Press, 1995), 189–202.

27. John K. Iglehart, "Rapid Changes for Academic Medicine," *New England Journal of Medicine* 331 (17 Nov. 1994): 1391–95; Goldie Blumenstyk, "Reform at Medical Centers," *Chronicle of Higher Education,* 13 July 1994, A25; Scott Jaschik, "Supreme Court Rejects Millions in Medicare Claims Sought by Universities with Teaching Hospitals," *Chronicle of Higher Education,* 6 July 1994, A34. Reflecting divided opinion on health care reform within the nation's health care community, the Association of American Medical Colleges in 1994 endorsed universal health care coverage; to many medical school deans, universal insurance offered relief from the flood of uninsured patients in the teaching hospitals.

28. Martha Frase-Blunt, "Preparing for a 'New Medical Order,' " *AAMC Reporter* 3 (Jan. 1994): 1–6.

29. "The Assault on Teaching Hospitals," *New York Times,* 15 May 1995; Elisabeth Rosenthal, "Columbia-Presbyterian Seeks a Merger," ibid., 8 July 1995; David R. Olmos, "UCLA, Santa Monica Hospitals to Merge," *Los Angeles Times,* 21 July 1995; Joye Mercer, "Medical Centers in Trouble," *Chronicle of Higher Education,* 11 Aug. 1995, A29.

30. Colleen Cordes and Stephen Burd, "Science Budget Alarm," *Chronicle of Higher Education,* 17 July 1995, A19.

31. Colleen Cordes, "Lower Overhead Costs," *Chronicle of Higher Education,* 8 Dec. 1993. At Stanford, for example, with a 70-percent overhead rate in 1991 and $265.7 million in federal R&D obligations, the indirect cost recovery was a handsome $186 million.

32. Robert M. Rosenzweig, "The Debate over Indirect Costs Raises Fundamental Policy Issues," *Chronicle of Higher Education,* 6 Mar. 1991, A40.

33. Seth Rolbein, "Mr. Pork," *Boston Magazine* 86 (Jan. 1994): 54–57; "R&D Pork Barrel Heading for a Big Year in Congress," *Science and Government Report* 23 (1 Dec. 1993): 1–3; "Curbing Earmarks," *Chronicle of Higher Education,* 3 Nov. 1993, A25; "With Money Tight, Scientific Pork Barrel Faces More Scrutiny," *Los Angeles Times,* 22 June 1993, A5.

34. Testimony of Joe B. Wyatt, chancellor of Vanderbilt University, before House Committee on Science, Space, and Technology, 16 June 1993; National Research Council, *Investing in Research* (Washington, D.C.: National Academy Press, 1989).

35. *Congressional Earmarks in the FY 1993 Appropriations,* Office of Science and Technology Policy (Jan. 1993); George E. Brown Jr., *Academic Earmarks: An Interim Report by the Chairman of the Committee on Science, Space, and Technology* (Washington, D.C.: U.S. Government Printing Office, 9 Aug. 1993); Colleen Cordes, "Campuses Offer a Variety of Reasons Why the Earmarks They Received from Congress Were Justified," *Chronicle of Higher Education,* 11 Aug. 1993, A25. The institutions benefiting from earmarks were disproportionately located in districts or states represented by strategically located members of Congress, including, in addition to the Massachusetts officials, Representative John P. Murtha (D.-Pa.), chairman of the House Appropriations Committee, and Senator Robert C. Byrd (D.-W.Va.), chairman of the Senate Appropriations Committee.

36. David L. Wheeler, "U. of Md. Conference That Critics Charge Might Foster Racism Loses NIH Support," *Chronicle of Higher Education,* 2 Sept. 1992, A6–A7.

37. Scott Jaschik, "Senate Will Punish Campuses That Ban Military Recruiters," *Chronicle of Higher Education,* 6 July 1994, A23.

38. In 1992 the U.S. Supreme Court, in an 8-to-1 ruling in *United States v. Fordice* (originally the "Ayers" case), overturned the findings of lower federal courts that Mississippi had met the constitutional requirement for desegregating the state's eight public four-year campuses (five of them historically white and three historically black). When state authorities then proposed merging some white and black campuses to concentrate scarce resources, black leaders demanded a policy protecting the racial identity of the three historically black institutions. *New York Times,* 27 June 1992.

39. In Texas, charges were sustained in lower state courts that failure to locate prestigious campuses and programs in southwest Texas constituted discrimination against Mexican Americans. In a unanimous ruling in 1993 the state supreme court reversed that decision, holding that access to higher education was not a "fundamental right" under the Texas constitution and that state officials had not intentionally discriminated against Mexican Americans living in South Texas. Katherine S. Mangan, "Top Texas Court Sees No Evidence State Was Biased," *Chronicle of Higher Education,* 13 Oct. 1993, A25.

40. Sam Verhovek, "250 at City U. Sue New York on Bias," *New York Times,* 27 Feb. 1992.

41. "University's Leaders Are Torn by Affirmative-Action Ban," *New York Times,* 29 Jan. 1996.

42. Peter Applebone, "Ruling Threatens College Policies on Racial En-

tries," *New York Times*, 21 Mar. 1996; Jeffrey Rosen, "The Day the Quotas Died," *New Republic*, 22 Apr. 1996, 21–27.

43. See, for example, Russell Jacoby, *The Last Intellectuals: American Culture in the Age of Academe* (New York: Basic Books, 1987); idem, *Dogmatic Wisdom: How the Culture Wars Divert Education and Distract America* (New York: Doubleday, 1994); Page Smith, *Killing the Spirit: Higher Education in America* (New York: Viking, 1990). More concerned with teaching and learning than culture and politics are Ernest L. Boyer, *Campus Life: In Search of Community* (Princeton, N.J.: Carnegie Foundation for the Advancement of Teaching, 1990); and Thomas Toch, *In the Name of Excellence* (New York: Oxford University Press, 1991).

44. Gary S. Becker, *Human Capital* (Chicago: University of Chicago Press, 1964); Howard R. Bowen, *Investment in Learning: The Individual and Social Value of American Higher Education* (San Francisco: Jossey-Bass, 1977); George Psacharopoulos, ed., *The Economics of Education: Research and Studies* (Oxford: Pergamon Press, 1987). On credentialism see Ronald P. Dore, *The Diploma Disease: Education, Qualification, and Development* (Berkeley: University of California Press, 1976).

45. Derek C. Bok, *The Cost of Talent* (New York: Free Press, 1993), 160.

46. Michael D. Cohen and James G. March, *Leadership and Ambiguity: The American College President* (New York: McGraw-Hill, 1974); Gary L. Riley and J. Victor Baldridge, *Governing Academic Organizations* (Berkeley, Calif.: McCutchan, 1977); Robert Birnbaum, *How Colleges Work: The Cybernetics of Academic Organization and Leadership* (San Francisco: Jossey-Bass, 1988); Clark, *Higher Education System.*

47. Walter E. Massey, "Can the Research University Adapt to a Changing Future?" in Cole, Barber, and Graubard, *The Research University in a Time of Discontent*, 191–202; Francis X. Sutton, "The Distinction and Durability of American Research Universities," in ibid., 309–32.

48. David Ransel, "The Present and Future of Historical Journals," *Perspective* 33 (Oct. 1995): 5–6.

Note on Method and Sources

1. National Research Council, *Research-Doctorate Programs in the United States: Continuity and Change* (Washington, D.C.: National Academy Press, 1995).

2. Janet K. Lawrence and Kenneth C. Green, *A Question of Quality: The Higher Education Ratings Game*, AAHE-ERIC Higher Education Research Report no. 5 (Washington, D.C.: American Association for Higher Education, 1980); D. L. Tan, "The Assessment of Quality in Higher Education: A Critical Review of the Literature," *Research in Higher Education* 24 (1986): 223–65; Robert Merton, "The Self-Fulfilling Prophecy," in *Social Theory and Social Structure* (New York: Free Press, 1968); Jonathan

R. Cole and Stephen Cole, *Social Stratification in Science* (Chicago: University of Chicago Press, 1973); Jonathan R. Cole and James A. Lipton, "The Reputation of American Medical Schools," *Social Forces* 55 (1977): 662–84.

3. Hugh Davis Graham and Nancy Diamond, *Economic Competitiveness and Research Productivity: Comparing Campuses across the Nation* (Baltimore: Maryland Institute for Policy Analysis and Research, June 1989).

4. Peter G. Blau, among others, has argued that when the measurement of scholarly work is in question, the size of the faculty is an appropriate measure of institutional size. Blau, *The Organization of Academic Work* (New York: John Wiley, 1973).

5. National Science Foundation, *Federal Support to Universities, Colleges, and Selected Non-Profit Institutions, Fiscal Year 1968* (Washington, D.C.: National Science Foundation, 1968). The NSF's *Federal Support Series* for fiscal 1988, fiscal 1989, and fiscal 1990 were used to identify R&D funds obligated to campuses during those years.

6. For ten state university systems and one mixed institution (Cornell), annual NSF reports on federal R&D obligations listed lump-sum totals under the flagship campus that included funding for medical and health science schools located in distant cities. For these eleven institutions—Colorado, Connecticut, Cornell, Indiana, Kansas, Louisiana State, Massachusetts, Mississippi, Oklahoma, Penn State, and Tennessee—federal R&D for the health science campuses was separately identified and deducted from flagship campus totals.

7. In 1991 the NSF, for the first time since beginning its annual report to Congress on federal obligations to academic institutions in 1968, separately listed (for fiscal 1990) the research and the development obligations from the Department of Defense.

8. Because the 1991 NSF report identified DOD development funding by campus for fiscal 1990 but not for fiscal 1988 or 1989, R&D averages for the 38 institutions were reduced by only 90 percent of their development contract totals.

9. There are four main formula USDA grant programs: the Hatch Act formula, the 1890 land-grant program for sixteen historically black institutions, and two other small formula programs, one for forestry research and one for animal health and disease research.

10. Institute for Scientific Information, *Science Citation Index* (Philadelphia, Pa.: ISI, various years); idem, *Social Science Citation Index* (Philadelphia, Pa.: ISI, various years); idem, *Arts and Humanities Citation Index* (Philadelphia, Pa.: ISI, various years). The ISI databases also provide information about the citation of faculty scholarship, listed according to the name of each author who is cited. While citation counts provide a qualitative indication of faculty productivity, the difficulty of assessing, in this way, faculty scholarship at more than two hundred institutions over three decades prohibited an evaluation in terms of citations.

11. Richard A. Wanner, Lionel S. Lewis, and David I. Gregorio, "Research Productivity in Academia: A Comparative Study of the Sciences, Social Sciences, and Humanities," *Sociology of Education* 54 (Oct. 1981): 238-53, noted that receipt of a grant apparently results in greater article productivity for natural scientists than for social scientists. They further commented that the greater article productivity of scientists was a function of the greater availability of journal pages and the higher acceptance rate of journals in the sciences (251). Oliver Fulton and Martin Trow, "Research Activity in American Higher Education," *Sociology of Education* 47 (winter 1974): 29-73, also offer evidence that there is a broad rank ordering of research by field, with the biological sciences showing consistently the highest rates of publication of any subject group. See also Yoram Neumann, "Standards of Research Publication: Differences between the Physical Sciences and the Social Sciences," *Research in Higher Education* 7 (1977): 335-67.

12. See Eugene E. Garfield, *Citation Indexing: Its Theory and Application in Science, Technology and the Humanities* (New York: Wiley, 1979); Institute for Scientific Information, "Journals Ranked by Times Cited in 1988," *SCI Journal Citation Reports* 1988 Annual, vol. 19, 41-80.

13. For examples of reputational studies of social scientists that used books, articles, and chapters in edited collections, see Diane E. Davis and Helen S. Astin, "Reputational Standing in Academe," *Journal of Higher Education* 58 (May–June 1987): 262-75; and Wanner, Lewis, and Gregorio, "Research Productivity in Academia," 238-53. Researchers for both projects noted that there were no safeguards for checking the accuracy of self-reported information.

14. National Center for Education Statistics, *Salaries of Full-Time Instructional Faculty, 1987–88* (Washington, D.C.: Department of Education, 1988).

15. Data on medical school faculty were supplied through the courtesy of Brooke E. Whiting, Director, Faculty Roster System, Association of American Medical Colleges, Washington, D.C.

16. William J. Baumol and Peggy Heim, "The Annual Report on the Economic Status of the Profession," *AAUP Bulletin* 54 (summer 1968): 182-241; idem, "Hard Times: Report on the Economic Status of the Profession, 1973-74," ibid., summer 1974, 171-243.

17. Robert Birnbaum, "Leadership and Productivity" (1990).

18. John M. Braxton and William Toombs, "Faculty Uses of Doctoral Training: Consideration of a Technique for the Differentiation of Scholarly Effort from Research Activity," *Research in Higher Education* 16 (1982): 265-82. The authors validated seventy-one scholarly activities that included processes as well as products. See also Ernest L. Boyer, *Scholarship Reconsidered: Priorities of the Professoriate* (Princeton: Princeton University Press, 1990).

19. Glenn R. Pellino, Robert T. Blackburn, and Alice Boberg, "The Dimensions of Faculty Scholarship: Faculty and Administrator Views," *Re-*

search in Higher Education 20 (1984): 103–15; Donna L. Sundre, "The Specification of the Content Domain of Faculty Scholarship," ibid., 33 (1992): 297–315, generated an inventory of 249 activities considered scholarly.

20. P. Wilner, "The Main Drift of Sociology between 1936 and 1982," *History of Sociology* 2 (1985): 1–20.

21. Robert W. Fogel and Stanley L. Engerman, *Which Road to the Past: Two Views of History* (New Haven: Yale University Press, 1983).

22. Jeffrey P. Bieber and Robert T. Blackburn, "Faculty Research Productivity, 1972–1980: Development and Application of Constant Units of Measure" (unpublished).

23. See Richard J. Bentley, Robert T. Blackburn, and Jeffrey P. Bieber, "Research Note: Some Corrections and Suggestions for Working with the National Faculty Survey Databases," *Research in Higher Education* 31 (1990): 587–604, on the difficulty of working with the national faculty databases.

24. Cornell's six private, endowed colleges are Arts and Sciences, Architecture, Engineering, Hotel Administration, Law, and Medicine. The four public colleges under New York Statutes are Agriculture and Life Sciences, Human Ecology, Industrial and Labor Relations, and Veterinary Medicine.

25. Lowell L. Hargens, Barbara F. Reskin, and Paul D. Allison, "Problems in Estimating Measurement Error from Panel Data: An Example Involving the Measurement of Scientific Productivity," *Sociological Methods and Research* 4 (1976): 439–58.

INDEX

■

enrollments, growth of, effects on American universities, 86
equal educational opportunity, 53, 89, 96, 219

faculty: basic science and clinical medicine, 76; as basis for classifying institutions, 146; changes in, 87; comparing, 4; and departmental organization, 22; growth of, 101–3; in health sciences, 73–74; nationalization of market for, 22; professionalization of, 22–23; publication rates of, 106–8; research of, 61, 103–14; salaries of, 140; staffing ratios of, 73–74; "unfaculty," 59, 78, 87, 178
Federal Nonnuclear Energy Research and Development Act, 94
federal research policy: shifts in, 133; and threats to academic research, 215–20
federal responsibility for research, and Seaborg Report, 33–34
federal science policy, 215; benchmarks of, 4; continuity of (1980s), 117; effects on higher education, 11; levels of, 118; pluralist nature of, 30–33; postwar debates over, 26–50; and Sputnik, 33; and World War II, 25
Feller, Irwin, and research in 1980s, 140, 142
fellowships, as indicator of faculty achievement, 61
flagship schools, compared to land grant schools, 156–58. See also public universities
Flexner, Abraham, and 1910 report, 76
Ford, Gerald, 98
Friedman, Milton, and National Science Foundation, 120
funding, federal: of academic R&D, 133–35, 136; of academic research, 88; of applied research and basic research, 34, 94–95; of

arts and humanities, 133, 138–40; assumptions about, 84; of biomedical research (1980s), 122; changes in, 85–86, 88–92, 103–5; concentration of, 38, 41–42, 48–49; dispersion of, 100–101, 104; of elite universities, 27; expansion of, 31–32; increase in (1960s), 46–48; as indicator of faculty achievement, 61; and interest group liberalism, 42–43; and journal publication, 66–67; merit as basis for, 29; of nonscientific activities, 27, 43, 46, 48; of R&D, 38, 83, 104–5, 216; of R&D and academic research, 91–92; regional distribution of, 100; of social science, 27, 31–32, 45, 133, 136–38; sources of, 32, 120; of student aid, 88–90
funding, nonfederal sources of, 95–96

Geiger, Roger: and basic research, 33; and federal role in research, 27; and history of twentieth-century American universities, 5; and private universities, 68; and research in 1980s, 140, 142; and university economies of scale, 24
General Accounting Office, 90
Georgia Institute of Technology (Georgia Tech), and Pentagon funding, 67
government-university collaboration, during World War II, 28
graduate and professional schools, as part of Standard Model university, 69
graduate programs, 19, 72, 86–87
graduate students, as "unfaculty," 59
Great Society: and equal opportunity, 89; and redistribution of federal funds, 42
Guggenheim (John Simon) Foundation, 67, 112

Office of. *See other part of name*

Ohio State University: low reputational ranking, 56; per capita comparisons, 64

Oregon, University of, as "flagship," 155–56, 212

Oregon State University, and land grant status, 155–56

organized research units (ORUs), 178

peer review competition: as basis for grants, 26–27; continued under Reagan, 120; criticism of, 91; threatened, 217–18

Pell, Claiborne (D-R.I.), and criticism of NEH, 139

Pennsylvania State University (Penn State), and Pentagon funding, 67

Pentagon, and publications productivity, 66

per capita comparison, 5, 201; and "horsepower" rankings, 64; of institutions (1960s), 51–83; and medical schools, 79; reclassification of institutions based on, 144–47; usefulness of, 56–63

philanthropic foundations, and research funding, 28

Pittsburgh, University of, low reputational ranking, 56

pluralism: of American higher education, 14–18; of federal science policy, 30–33; and role of private institutions, 11

practitioner programs, and land grant universities, 154–55

President's Science Advisory Committee (PSAC), 33, 118

President's Task Force on Higher Education, 84

Press, Frank (MIT), and Carter science policy, 118

Princeton University: low total R&D funding, 56; and Nobel laureates, 37; performance despite lack of medical school, 75, 109, 178,

182–83; and private universities' research performance (1970s), 109, 110, 111, 112

private universities: advantages of, 7, 63–64, 67–75, 203–8; and American educational standards, 16; and balanced budget, 206–7; Carnegie classification of, 51–55; and federal funding, 38; and journal publication, 65–66; per capita research performance, 110–14, 182–84; and pluralism, 11; ranking of, 186–92; reclassification of, 176–82; Research I, 176–78, 187–89; Research II, 178–79,189; Research III, 179–80; Research IV, 180–82; resistant to change, 3; rising, 196–98; without medical schools, 82. *See also* universities, American

professional schools, 19

Proxmire, William, and perceived waste of federal funds, 91

psychology, 135–36

publication: and faculty research achievement, 61, 105–12; scientific, patterns of, 127

Public Health Service, and psychological research, 136

public universities: advantages and disadvantages of, 163–65; and arts and humanities, 113–14; Carnegie classification of, 51–55; diversification of, 79–80; "flagship" campuses, 212; imbalance of, 187; and importance of size, 158–59; models of, 81–82; obligations of, 70; and patterns of institution building, 202–3; and per capita research performance, 71–74, 110–14; ranking of, 168–73; reclassification of, 146–61; Research I, 147–52; Research II, 152–59; Research III and Research IV, 159–61; resistant to change, 3; rising, 193–96; "second flagship," 149, 151–52,

Silicon Valley, 59
Smith, Bruce, and federal research support (1970s), 99
social science, federal funding of, 27, 31–32, 45, 133, 136–38
specialized institutions, 53, 55, 71
Sputnik, 27, 33, 34, 40, 43
Standard Model university, 17, 69, 72, 128
Stanford University: loss of defense laboratory funding, 92; medical school funding, 129; per capita comparisons, 58; and private universities' research performance (1970s), 109, 110, 111, 112, 113
state university system, and protection of public universities, 7
Stockman, David (OMB), and Reagan science policy, 119, 120
student-faculty ratio, 63

technical institutions, 53
technology, and higher education, 222
Texas, University of, at Austin: balanced research performance of, 166; low total R&D funding, 56; and Pentagon funding, 67; and public universities' research performance (1970s), 110–11, 112; and southern public universities, 212
Texas, University of, at Dallas, 170
Texas A&M University, 65
Thomas Jefferson University, excluded from reclassification, 145
Trow, Martin, and European model of higher education, 14, 23, 96
Tufts University: balanced research performance of, 114; and private universities' research performance (1970s), 110, 111, 113; and small universities' performance, 178
Tulane University, per capita publications index, 107
Twenty-Sixth Amendment, 89
two-year institutions, 55

undergraduate education, 19–20
"unfaculty," 59, 78, 87, 178
Union for Experimenting Colleges and Universities, excluded from reclassification, 146
unionizing, of faculty, 87–88
universities, American: administration of, 23; characteristics of, 2; competition among, 1–2, 83; criticism of, 121, 214–15; faculty market of, 22–23; international reputation of, 10; problems of (1970s), 84–86; public and private, comparison of, 22, 71–74, 174, 182–86, 203–6; —, difference as strength, 201; —, student-faculty ratios of, 63; rise of (dual meaning), 1–2; sources of funding, 23, 32, 47, 95–96, 120; Standard Model of, 17, 69, 128; value to policymakers of, 59. *See also* higher education, American; private universities; public universities
University of. *See other part of name*
urban renewal, 151
U.S. Congress, 215: and "academic earmarking," 217–18; and arts and humanities, 139; and clinical research, 127–28; and distrust of universities, 91; and increased research funding, 115; House Committee on Science, hearings, 41; and proposal for national university, 15; research priorities of, 120, 133; Senate, 85, 95
U.S. Constitution, 15, 17
U.S. Department of. *See other part of name*
U.S. Office of. *See other part of name*
U.S. Supreme Court, and *Dartmouth College* case, 17
Utah State University, and Pentagon funding, 67

Vanderbilt University: balanced research performance of, 114; per capita publications index, 107;

Library of Congress Cataloging-in-Publication Data

Graham, Hugh Davis.
  The rise of American research universities : elites and
challengers in the postwar era / Hugh Davis Graham and Nancy
Diamond.
      p.   cm.
  Includes bibliographical references (p.   ) and index.
  ISBN 0-8018-5425-3 (alk. paper)
  1. Universities and colleges—United States—History—20th
century.   2. Research—United States—History—20th century.
3. Federal aid to higher education—United States—History—20th
century.   4. Federal aid to research—United States—History—20th
century.   5. Science and state—United States—History—20th
century.   I. Diamond, Nancy A.   II. Title.
LA227.4.G73   1997
378.73'09'045—DC20   96-30432
                                                          CIP